Composite Construction
Design for Buildings

Composite Construction Design for Buildings

Ivan M. Viest Editor-in-Chief
President, IMV Consulting

Joseph P. Colaco Editor
President, CBM Engineers, Inc.

Richard W. Furlong Editor
E. C. H. Bantel Professor of Engineering Practice
University of Texas, Austin

Lawrence G. Griffis Editor
Senior Vice President, Walter P. Moore & Associates, Inc.

Roberto T. Leon Editor
Professor of Civil and Environmental Engineering
Georgia Institute of Technology

Loring A. Wyllie, Jr. Editor
Chairman, Degenkolb Engineers

Co-published by the
American Society of Civil Engineers
345 East 47th Street
New York, New York 10017-2398

McGraw-Hill

New York San Francisco Washington, D.C. Auckland Bogotá
Caracas Lisbon London Madrid Mexico City Milan
Montreal New Delhi San Juan Singapore
Sydney Tokyo Toronto

Library of Congress Cataloging-in-Publication Data

Composite construction design for buildings / Ivan M. Viest, editor
... [et al.].
     p.   cm.
   Includes index.
   ISBN 0-07-067457-4 (acid-free paper)
   1. Composite construction. 2. Structural design. 3. Buildings.
4. Load factor design. 5. Elastoplasticity. I. Viest, Ivan M.
(Ivan Miroslav), date.
TA664.C6367   1997
693—dc20   96-28309
                                                 CIP

McGraw-Hill

*A Division of The **McGraw·Hill** Companies*

ISBN 0-07-067457-4

The sponsoring editor for this book was Larry S. Hager, the editing supervisor was Stephen M. Smith, and the production supervisor was Pamela A. Pelton. It was set in Century Schoolbook by Victoria Khavkina of McGraw-Hill's Professional Book Group composition unit.

Printed and bound by R. R. Donnelley & Sons Company.

Contents

Contributors

The following persons participated in the preparation of this book by contributing materials to the identified chapters in the form of a complete or partial first draft of one or more sections or by reviewing parts of the manuscript.

Horatio Allison, Consultant, Dagsboro, Del.: contributor to Chapter 3

Abolhassan Astaneh-Asl, Professor of Structural Engineering, University of California at Berkeley: contributor to Chapter 6

Atorod Azizinamini, Associate Professor of Civil Engineering, University of Nebraska: contributor to Chapter 6

Reidar Bjorhovde, Professor and Chairman of Civil and Environmental Engineering, University of Pittsburgh: contributor to Chapter 3; served as the first editor of Chapter 3

H. Richard Corry, Vice President, Turner Construction Co., Houston: contributor to Chapter 2

David Darwin, Dean E. Ackers Professor of Civil Engineering, University of Kansas: contributor to Chapter 3

Gregory G. Deierlein, Associate Professor, Cornell University: contributor to Chapters 2 and 6; reviewer of Chapters 4 and 5

W. Samuel Easterling, Associate Professor of Civil Engineering, Virginia Polytechnic Institute and State University: contributor to Chapter 3

Ali A. K. Haris, President, Haris Engineering, Inc., Kansas City: contributor to Chapter 4

Hal Iyengar, Skidmore, Owings & Merrill, LLP, Chicago: contributor to Chapters 2 and 3

D. J. L. Kennedy, Professor Emeritus of Civil Engineering, University of Alberta: contributor to Chapter 3

Stanley D. Lindsey, President, Stanley D. Lindsey & Assoc., Atlanta: contributor to Chapter 3

James O. Malley, Principal, Degenkolb Engineers, San Francisco: contributor to Chapter 5

James M. Ricles, Associate Professor of Civil Engineering, Lehigh University: contributor to Chapter 4

John L. Ruddy, Vice President, Fletcher Thompson, Bridgeport: contributor to Chapter 3

Bahram M. Shahrooz, Associate Professor of Civil Engineering, University of Cincinnati: contributor to Chapter 6

Robert Sinn, Skidmore, Owings & Merrill, LLP, Chicago: contributor to Chapters 2 and 3

Kurt D. Swensson, Associate, Stanley D. Lindsey & Assoc., Atlanta: contributor to Chapter 3

Preface

Since the 1958 publication of the book *Composite Construction in Steel and Concrete for Bridges and Buildings*,[D15]* I was asked several times to update it. I declined primarily because by the mid-1960s composite design of beams and floors, based on working loads and stresses, was well established and known by the design community in the United States. The situation regarding composite design changed drastically during the 1970s and 1980s with the introduction of three major innovations into the structural building design practice: composite columns and walls, load and resistance factor design (LRFD), and elastoplastic analyses. None of these tools is used universally as yet, even though it is clear that all of them will become basic tools in the arsenal of the structural engineer in the foreseeable future. None of the existing books on composite construciton for buildings encompassed all three of these innovations. Now, this book provides structural engineers with a unique guide toward an early adoption of the innovative technology that will enable them to furnish their clients with better, more economical structures.

At least 11 English-language books were published over the years on the subject of composite construction. Of these, four appeared in the United States,[C57,D15,M7,M8] five in Great Britain,[D85,M6,M11,M15,153] one in Canada,[D47] and one in India.[M4] Additionally, there have been issued numerous proceedings of conferences dealing mainly with research and with descriptions of completed structures, as discussed in Sec. 1.1.4. Of the 11 books, all but three were concerned primarily with questions of design. Two exceptions were American; one dealt with construction[C57] and the other was a state-of-the-art survey.[M7] A third American book,[M8] published in 1979, covered composite structures of steel, reinforced concrete, prestressed concrete, masonry, wood, and timber. Books published abroad were based on other countries' codes, which differed to varying degress from American practices. In view of this and of the emerging new technologies, it appeared that there was a need for an up-to-date book on American practice for the design of composite construction for buildings.

---

*Superscript D15 refers to Ref. D15 in Chap. 7, Literature.

At the Apr. 28, 1991, meeting of the Committee on Composite Construction of the American Society of Civil Engineers (ASCE) it was reported that the subcommittee on education was planning to initiate work on a textbook on composite design. The book was to cover the design of basic composite elements, with emphasis on the needs of the design engineer and stressing design simplicity and economy. During the following year, an outline was developed and over onescore experts were found to draft manuscripts in the areas of their specialties. Six of them undertook the job of organizing the effort and bringing the book to the profession. Chapter 2 was the responsibility of J. P. Colaco; Chapter 3, R. T. Leon; Chapter 4, R. W. Furlong; Chapter 5, L. A. Wyllie, Jr.; and Chapter 6, L. G. Griffis. Chapter 1 and all other contents of the book, as well as the overall coordination of the work, were the responsibility of the editor-in-chief. The six editors collated the expert contributions and produced the manuscripts of individual chapters, selected the publisher, and helped to bring the project to a successful conclusion. The names of all other participants and their affiliations are given in the list of contributors.

This book is a comprehensive presentation of current knowledge. It covers the structural aspects of framing for all types of buildings in which the steel framing is combined with concrete elements, such as slabs, walls, and encasement, to provide an efficient, economical structural system. This book is intended for the design engineer who conceives, designs, and is responsible for construction of structural framing for buildings; and for students, both formal and informal, of structural engineering.

The text's chapters are as follows: Introduction, Composite Systems, Composite Beams, Composite Columns, Lateral Resisting Systems, Design of Joints, and Literature. The four chapters covering the design of composite elements, i.e., beams, columns, bracing, and joints, are illustrated with numerous examples that designers can follow step by step in their own work. These chapters are based on the latest LRFD design procedures. Methods of analysis are described in the chapter on composite systems, providing guidance to nonlinear as well as linear analyses. The chapter includes discussion of materials and loading, and brief descriptions of various floor and building systems. Construction considerations are discussed in the same chapter.

The text is illustrated with close to 200 figures and supported by more than 450 references. The references are listed in Chapter 7. Those dealing specifically with composite construction are divided according to their principal characteristics: research, design, and construction. A historical review of composite construction, starting in 1877, and 18 building case histories are included in the introductory chapter. Although the case histories cover only tall buildings, this book is applicable to buildings of all heights. Detail analyses for composite beams and columns are presented in Appendixes A and B, respectively. This book concludes with a comprehensive index.

Numerous figures, some of the tabular materials, and a few quotations came from prior publications. All such items are identified in the text by superscripts referring to references listed in Chapter 7. Grateful acknowledgment is made to many organizations for permission to reprint previously published materials, including American Institute of Steel Construction; American Society of Civil Engineers; Bethlehem Steel Corporation, Sales Engineering Division; Canadian Institute of Steel Construction; Chapman & Hall's *Constructional Steel Design: An International Guide*; *Concrete Construction* magazine; *Engineering News Record*; Japanese Society of Steel Construction; McGraw-Hill; Paul Weidlinger & Associates; and Skilling Ward Magnusson Barkshire Inc.

The basic strength of this book lies in the fact that it presents the essence of the knowledge of numerous experts on various aspects of composite construction. For this I am most grateful to all contributors and the editors. They have given generously of their time to the project. My thanks in particular go to Dr. Joseph P. Colaco, chairman of the ASCE Committee on Composite Construction when the project was launched, for his continued interest, encouragement, and advice; and to his secretary Mrs. Elaine (Dolly) Wertz for her sympathetic, efficient, and prompt handling of numerous problems as they arose from time to time. Finally, I want to express my deep appreciation to my wife Barbara for her many-faceted support, including her tolerance of my frequent absences in spirit during the course of the work.

Ivan M. Viest
Editor-in-Chief

Notation

The meaning of each symbol and abbreviation used in this book is generally explained when it first appears in the text. For convenient reference, the symbols and abbreviations are listed below except for those used in App. A. The latter symbols are listed in Sec. A.2.

Symbols

A	Cross-sectional area; or a numerical constant; or a design parameter
A_a	Cross-sectional area of a seat angle leg
A_b	Cross-sectional area of a bolt
A_{bc}	Required bottom chord area
A_c	Area of a concrete slab; or cross-sectional area of column concrete; or area per unit width of a concrete slab
A_{ch}	Cross-sectional area of the reinforced core of a column section measured out-to-out of the transverse reinforcement
A_{ct}	Cross-sectional area of reinforcing bars in each layer of column ties spaced at s_h through the beam depth
A_{cv}	One half of the actual area of the encased concrete in a filled composite column
A_d	Total cross-sectional area of dowels
A_e	Effective area of a cross section
A_g	Gross area of a cross section
A_H	Area of H-shaped portion of a base plate in light columns (Fig. 6.2)
A_n	Net area of a cross section
A_o	Product of the effective joint width, taken as $2b_f$, and the column diameter d_c
A_r	Cross-sectional area of total bar reinforcement; or cross-sectional area of one reinforcing bar; or area of longitudinal reinforcement in a column cross section; or area of properly developed reinforcement within effective slab width placed parallel to the steel beam
A_s	Cross-sectional area of a structural steel shape, pipe, or tube
A_{sc}	Cross-sectional area of one stud shear connector
A_{sh}	Cross-sectional area of transverse reinforcement, including cross ties, within spacing s_h and perpendicular to dimension h_c

A_t Required area of a tension diagonal

A_{ti} Total cross-sectional area of column ties, located within vertical distance of $0.4d$ from the beam, measured in a plane perpendicular to the beam

A_w Web area of a steel shape plus any longitudinal bars at the center of column cross section

A_1 Area of the base plate in an encased column

A_2 In a base plate, maximum area of the portion of the supporting surface that is geometrically similar to and concentric with the loaded area

a Depth of a compression stress block; or depth of the neutral axis; or a design parameter defined in Table 8-38 in the AISC LRFD Manual;[G87] or distance from the neutral axis to the extreme fiber in compression (Fig. 6.28)

a_{bw} Distance from bolt line to weld line

a_c Length of a bearing zone; or a design parameter

a_o Length of a web opening

a_u Ratio M_u/V_u

a_w Depth of compression zone in the web; or fillet weld size

B A numerical constant

B_p Side dimension of a base plate

b Total slab width; or cross section width

b_c Column width measured perpendicular to the beam

b_{cp} Cover plate width

b_e Effective slab width; or joist spacing

b_E Effective shear width in an encased composite column

b_f Beam or column flange width

b_i Width of inner panel

b_j Effective width of a joint

b_m Average of beam flange width and column width

b_o Width of outer panel

b_p Width of face bearing plate

b_{pe} Flange width of a steel column; or width of an extended face bearing place

b_s Beam spacing; or flange width of a steel shape

C Compression force; or a coefficient listed in Table 8-18 of the AISC LRFD Manual;[G87] or a design parameter

C_c Vertical bearing force shown in Fig. 6.18c; or concrete compressive force bearing against the beam flange

C_{cn} Nominal bearing strength of concrete

C_d Deflection amplification factor in seismic design

C_f Compression force in concrete for a fully composite section

C_h Creep coefficient accounting for relative humidity

C_{st} Compressive force in concrete compression strut (Fig. 6.28)

C_t Creep coefficient accounting for time under sustained load

C_{tc}	Compressive force in the top chord of a steel joist
C_{ti}	Creep coefficient accounting for the age of concrete at the time of loading
C_v	Force in the vertical reinforcement shown in Fig. 6.18c
C_{vn}	Nominal compression strength of the vertical joint reinforcement attached directly to a steel beam
C_{vs}	Creep coefficient accounting for member size or shape
C_1	Electrode strength coefficient from Table 8-37 of the AISC LRFD Manual[G87]; or a design parameter; or the force shown in Fig. 6.28 and given by Eq. (6.23)
C_2, C_3	Design parameters defined in Sec. 6.5.2
c	1.0 in; or a dimension defined in Fig. 6.2
c_r	Thickness of concrete cover
c_1, c_2, c_3	Numerical coefficients listed in Table 4.1
D	Dead load
D_w	Fillet weld size
D_{16}	Required weld size in sixteenth of an inch[D95]
d	Beam depth; or depth of the tensile reinforcement relative to the extreme concrete compressive fiber; or the distance from the tensile force to the compressive force; or pipe diameter; or diameter of a concrete-filled pipe column; or interior moment arm in a stub girder
d_b	Bolt diameter
d_c	Steel column depth; or column diameter; or steel pipe diameter
d_{cc}	Distance between chord centroids in a truss
d_{cs}	Distance from the tensile force in the bottom chord to the compressive force in the slab
d_f	Center-to-center distance between beam flanges
d_o	0.25 times the beam depth d when a steel column is present or the lesser of $0.25d$ and the height of the extended face bearing plates when these plates are present; or additional effective joint depth provided by attachments to beam flanges (Fig. 6.12)
d_p	Plate height
d_r	Reinforcing bar diameter
d_s	Steel beam depth
d_t	Total depth of a steel joist; or distance between centroids of truss chords
d_w	Steel beam web depth
d_{wc}	Depth of compression yielding in the web
d_1, d_2, d_3	Distances used in Eqs. (3.9) and (3.14)
E	Modulus of elasticity
E_c	Modulus of elasticity of concrete
E_m	Modified modulus of elasticity
E_s	Modulus of elasticity of steel
E_{st}	Modulus of elasticity of concrete at time of loading
E_t	Tangent modulus of elasticity

e	Eccentricity
e_b	Eccentricity of a reaction from a bolt line
$e_{\min}$	Minimum eccentricity of axial force in a column
e_w	Eccentricity of a reaction from a weld line
e_x	Horizontal component of eccentricity e as defined in Table 8-18 of the AISC LRFD Manual[G87]
F	Force
F_{cD}	Factored construction dead load
F_{cL}	Factored construction live load
F_{cr}	Critical column stress
F_{cT}	Factored construction loads
F_D	Factored dead load
F_{EXX}	Yield strength of a weld[D95]
F_f	Force in the flange
F_L	Factored live load
F_{my}	Modified yield stress
F_t	Force carried by concrete slab attached to steel beams
F_u	Specified minimum tensile strength of steel
F_{up}	Specified minimum tensile strength of bearing plate steel
F_{uv}	Specified minimum shear strength of bolt steel
F_w	Force in the web; or strength of a weld
F_y	Specified minimum yield stress of steel
F_{ya}	Yield stress of a seat angle
F_{yd}	Yield stress of dowel bars
F_{yf}	Beam flange yield stress
F_{yh}	Specified yield strength of transverse reinforcement
F_{yp}	Yield stress of a steel panel
F_{yr}	Specified yield strength of slab reinforcement
F_{yt}	Yield stress of a steel pipe
F_{yw}	Beam web yield stress
F_1	Compression force in a steel diagonal brace (Fig. 6.46)
F_2	Tension force in a steel diagonal brace (Fig. 6.46)
f_b	Bearing strength
f_c	Compressive stress in concrete
f_t	Tensile strength of concrete
f_{tc}	Compressive stress in steel pipe or tube
f_{tt}	Tensile stress in steel pipe or tube
f'_c	Specified compressive strength of concrete
f'_{cc}	Compressive strength of confined concrete
f'_{ct}	Compressive strength of concrete at time t_d

f'_{c28}	Compressive strength of concrete at 28 days
g	$\frac{1}{16}$ in
H	Horizontal shear force; or total shear applied to a composite column
H_a	Horizontal force applied to a seat angle
H_r	Annual average ambient relative humidity
H_s	Length of shear stud connector after welding
h	Depth of a steel section; or overall depth of a composite or a reinforced concrete column; or column width in the plane of bending
h_c	Clear distance between flanges less the fillet or corner radius for rolled shapes; or for built-up sections, the distance between adjacent lines of fasteners or the clear distance between flanges when welds are used; or cross-sectional dimension of the column core measured center-to-center of confining reinforcement
h_r	Nominal rib height
h_s	Web height of a steel shape
h_{vr}	Distance between longitudinal bars
h_1	Concrete width perpendicular to the plane of bending; or depth of a steel tube
h_2	Concrete thickness in the plane of bending; or width of a steel tube
I	Moment of inertia
I_c	Moment of inertia of a composite section
I_e	Effective moment of inertia of a partially composite section
I_g	Moment of inertia of a gross section
I_{LB}	Lower-bound moment of inertia[D95]
I_{Ln}	Lower-bound moment of inertia for negative bending
I_{Lp}	Lower-bound moment of inertia for positive bending
I_s	Moment of inertia of a steel section
I_t	Moment of inertia of a composite truss
I_{tr}	Moment of inertia of a composite section transformed into equivalent steel
I_x	Moment of inertia about x axis
I'_s	$I_s/1.10$
I'_t	$I_t/1.10$
jh	Effective beam depth; or effective joint length
K	Effective column length factor
K_h	Relative humidity influence factor for shrinkage
K_p	A design parameter
K_{vs}	Size effect factor for shrinkage
K_t	Time-dependent shrinkage factor based on age of concrete
k	Flange thickness plus the depth of the steel fillet between the flange and the web of a hot-rolled steel section; or a coefficient in Tables 8-38 through 8-45 of the AISC LRFD Manual[G87]
k_s	Shear stiffness of a shear connector
k_t	Axial stiffness of a shear connector

L	Live load
L_r	Roof load
l	Length
l_a	Width of an angle
l_b	Beam length
l_d	Development length
l_e	Embedment length
l_h	Horizontal edge distance of bolts
l_p	Length of a plate
l_t	Length of a tee
l_u	Length of a U weld
l_v	Vertical edge distance of bolts
l_w	Weld length
l_1	Ratio of ultimate beam moment to ultimate beam shear
l_2	Ratio of ultimate column moment to ultimate column shear
M	Bending moment; or primary bending moment at the centerline of a web opening
M_a	Moment at point A
M_b	Bending moment along a bolt line; or ultimate beam moment
M_{bh}	Secondary bending moment below a web opening at the high-moment end
M_{bl}	Secondary bending moment below a web opening at the low-moment end
M_{bu}	Ultimate beam moment
M_{b1}	Beam moment to the left of a joint
M_{b2}	Beam moment to the right of a joint
M_c	Ultimate column moment; or limit flexural strength of the reinforced concrete portion
M_{cf}	Design moment due to factored construction loads
M_{c1}	Column moment above a joint
M_{c2}	Column moment below a joint
M_D	Design dead-load moment
M_f	Fixed-end moment
M_{fc}	Flexural strength of a fully composite beam
M_{ff}	Fixed-end moment at factored load
M_{fl}	Factored live-load moment
M_{fo}	Moment at the face of an opening
M_{fs}	Fixed-end moment at service load
M_{max}	Maximum moment
M_{min}	Minimum moment
M_n	Nominal moment
M_{nx}	Nominal bending strength for bending in the plane of the x axis

M_{ny}	Nominal bending strength for bending in the plane of the y axis
M_{n1}	Total moment on a column cross section about middepth when the plastic neutral axis is at the distance z below middepth
M_{n2}	Total moment on a column cross section about middepth when the plastic neutral axis is a at middepth
M_p	Plastic moment capacity
M_{pc}	Plastic moment capacity of a composite section
M_{pp}	Plastic moment capacity of a plate
M_{pw}	Plastic moment capacity of a weld throat section
M_s	Moment capacity at service load; or service design moment
M_{sl}	Service live-load moment
M_{so}	Limit flexural strength of steel portion subjected to bending alone
M_{ss}	Limit flexural strength of steel portion
M_{th}	Secondary bending moment above a web opening at the high-moment end
M_{tl}	Secondary bending moment above a web opening at the low-moment end
M_u	Ultimate moment; or factored moment
M_{uc}	Factored moment at the beam center
M_{ue}	Factored live-load moment at the supports; or bending moment at the end of a panel
M_{um}	Bending moment at midspan
M_{us}	Ultimate simply supported factored moment
M_{ux}	Required moment capacity for bending component in the plane of the x axis
M_{uy}	Required moment capacity for bending component in the plane of the y axis
M_{u1}	The smaller required moment applied at one end of a column
M_{u2}	The larger required moment applied at the end of a column opposite to M_{u1}
M_w	Bending moment along a weld line
M_y	Moment at first yielding
$M(\theta)$	Moment expressed as a function of end rotation θ
$M_{2.5}$	Moment corresponding to end rotation of 2.5 milliradians
M_{10}	Moment corresponding to end rotation of 10 milliradians
m	Design parameter for base plates
N	Number of stud shear connectors
N_d	Actual number of stud connectors used in design
N_{est}	Number of shear connectors required for partial interaction
N_p	Side dimension of a base plate
N_r	Number of studs in one rib at a beam intersection
n	Modular ratio E_s/E_c; or a design parameter defined in Sec. 6.2.2
n_b	Number of bolts
P	Concentrated load; or the total force transferred from a steel to a concrete column (Fig. 6.46); or vertical load; or compressive force
P_b	Bearing load on a foundation; or a tensile force below a web opening

P_{b1}	Axial load in a beam to the left of a joint
P_c	Euler buckling index for a column (see also P_E)
P_{cc}	Limit compressive strength of reinforced concrete portions subjected to compression alone
P_{cf}	Factored construction point load on girder
P_{co}	Limit compressive strength of reinforced concrete portion subjected to compression alone
P_{ct}	Limit tensile strength of reinforced concrete portion subjected to tension alone, taken negative
P_{c1}	Column axial load above a joint; or force in the concrete fill of a filled tube column; or force on concrete above the distance $+z$ from middepth
P_{c2}	Column axial load below a joint; or force on concrete from the distance $\pm z$ to middepth
P_D	Point load due to service dead load
P_{Df}	Factored point load due to service dead load
P_E	Euler column buckling strength
P_{eq}	Resultant of vertical forces acting on an inner panel
P_f	Factored point load
P_i	Capacity for biaxially eccentric axial force
P_L	Point load due to service live load
P_{Lf}	Factored point load due to service live load
P_n	Nominal strength of a column
P_{nc}	Limit compressive strength of reinforced concrete portion
P_{no}	Nominal squash load of a composite column section
P_{nx}	Nominal column strength about the x axis
P_{ny}	Nominal column strength about the y axis
P_{n1}	Total axial force on a column cross section when the plastic neutral axis is at the distance z below the middepth
P_{n2}	Total axial force on a column cross section when the plastic neutral axis is at middepth
P_o	Theoretical squash load of a composite column section; or factored load corresponding to the area enclosed by a structural shape
P_{r1}	Force on reinforcement at the top or bottom of a section
P_{r2}	Force on reinforcement at middepth
P_s	Portion of factored axial load resisted by a steel shape
P_{st}	Limit compressive strength of the steel portion
P_{s1}, P_{s2}, P_{s3}	Forces defined in App. B
P_t	Compressive force above a web opening
P_u	Strength in compression; or factored transfer force; or factored axial load; or axial compression
P_w	Wind load
P_x	Axial-force capacity for eccentricity e_x in the plane of the x axis

P_y Tensile yield strength of a steel section; or axial force capacity for eccentricity e_y in the plane of the y axis

P_{yc} Compressive strength of a steel section, $A_s F_y$

P_{yf} Compressive yield force in the top flange

P_{yp} Tensile yield force in a cover plate

P_{yr} Tensile yield force in a rolled shape

P_{yw} Compressive yield force in the web

Q Load resisted by one shear connector; or the reduction coefficient Q_s

Q_n Nominal strength of a stud shear connector

Q_s Reduction coefficient

Q_u Ultimate strength of a shear connector

R External force; or reaction; or the numerical factor in Eq. (6.30); or the resultant horizontal forces (Fig. 6.46); or the response modification coefficient in seismic design

R_b Required lateral bracing force

R_{br} Design strength in bearing

R_m Response modification coefficient in seismic design

R_n Nominal strength of bolts, welds, and connected elements

R_{ne} Capacity of the effective net area

R_{ns} Shear capacity of a net section

R_o Yield or vertical shear capacity of a gross section of a plate

R_{pa} Strength-reduction factor for studs in a formed steel deck with the ribs oriented parallel to the supporting beams

R_{pe} Strength-reduction factor for studs in a formed steel deck with the ribs oriented perpendicular to the supporting beams

R_u Required strength of bolts, welds, and connected elements; or factored shear

r Radius of gyration; or design strength of a bolt group

r_m Modified radius of gyration

r_s Radius of gyration of a steel pipe or tube

r_v Design shear strength of one bolt

r_x Radius of gyration about x axis

r_z Radius of gyration about z axis

S Internal force; or surface area of concrete

S_b Section modulus for the bottom flange

S_{cD} Construction dead load

S_{cL} Construction live load

S_D Service dead load

S_e Effective section modulus of a partially composite section

S_L Service live load

S_s Section modulus of a structural steel section

S_t Section modulus for the top flange

S_{tr}	Section modulus of a transformed composite section
S_x	Section modulus about x axis
s	Slip
s_{max}	Maximum slip; or maximum tie spacing
s_h	Spacing of column ties
s_t	Spacing of transverse reinforcement measured along the longitudinal axis of a structural member
T	Tensile force
T_a, T_d	Chord forces at A and D, respectively
T_{fo}	Tensile force at the face of an opening
T_g	Tensile yield force on a gross section
T_{max}	Maximum chord force
T_n	Tensile ultimate force on a net section
T_{rg}	Factored tensile yield force on the gross area of the bottom chord of a truss
T_{rn}	Factored fracture load on the net section of the bottom chord of a truss
T_s	Required force
T_u	Factored axial tension
T_v	Force in the vertical reinforcement shown in Fig. 6.18c
T_{vn}	Nominal strength in tension of vertical joint reinforcement directly attached to a steel beam
T_1	Force shown in Fig. 6.28 and given by Eq. (6.24)
t	Thickness
t_a	Angle thickness
t_{cp}	Cover plate thickness
t_d	Time in days after casting
t_f	Flange thickness
t_{fc}	Thickness of column flange
t_i	Age of concrete at time of loading
t_p	Plate thickness
t_s	Slab thickness
t_{sp}	Steel panel thickness
t_{st}	Thickness of the stem of a tee
t_t	Thickness of a steel pipe
t_{tc}	Top chord thickness
t_w	Web thickness; or width of a wall
V	Shear; or volume of concrete; or shear at the centerline of a web opening
V_b	Required shear strength of a bolt at service load; or ultimate beam shear; or average of beam shears applied to a joint; or shear below a web opening
V_{b1}	Beam shear to the left of a joint
V_{b2}	Beam shear to the right of a joint

V_c	Volume of concrete; or average of column shears applied to a joint; or nominal shear resistance of a concrete column; or shear assigned to concrete
V_{cj}	Column shear acting on a joint
V_{cn}	Nominal shear resistance of the inner concrete compression strut
V_{cu}	Ultimate column shear
V_{c1}	Column shear above a joint (Fig. 6.14)
V_{c2}	Column shear below a joint (Fig. 6.14)
V_{es}	Total shear force in an exterior stub
V_{fn}	Nominal shear resistance of an outer concrete compression field (Fig. 6.19); or compression field strength
V_{is}	Total shear force in an interior stub
V_{max}	Maximum shear
V_n	Nominal shear resistance
V_p	Vertical shear capacity of a composite plate
V_s	Shear strength of steel; or shear assigned to a steel shape
V_{sn}	Nominal shear resistance of a steel panel (Fig. 6.19)
V_t	Shear strength of ties; or shear assigned to ties; or shear above a web opening
V_u	Ultimate shear; or shear capacity; or shear force; or shear stress
V_w	Shear force in the beam web at ultimate
V_{wy}	Shear yield capacity of the beam web
V_{yp}	Shear yield strength of a plate
V_{yw}	Shear yield strength of a weld
V_c'	Strength provided by concrete given by Eq. (6.10)
V_s'	Strength provided by horizontal ties given by Eq. (6.11)
v_c	Shear strength of concrete
v_u	Ultimate shear stress
W	Wind load; or weight
w	Unit weight of concrete
w_c	Construction load per foot of a joist
w_d	Load per linear foot
w_r	Average width of a rib in slab cast on a formed steel deck
w_s	Service load per foot of a joist
w_u	Factored design floor load
x	h when extended face bearing plates are present; or $h/2 + d_c/2$ when only the steel column is present
Y_2	Distance from the top of the steel beam to the centerline of the concrete slab[D95]
y	A coordinate; or the greater of steel column and extended face bearing plate width
y_{bc}	Distance from elastic neutral axis to the outside surface of bottom angles
y_p	Depth of plastic neutral axis for double angles

y_{tc}	Distance from elastic neutral axis to the outside surface of top angles
Z	Plastic section modulus
Z_s	Plastic section modulus of a steel beam
Z_x	Plastic section modulus of a steel section with respect to x axis
z	Distance between points about which secondary moments are calculated at a web opening; or a distance from the midheight of a cross section to the neutral axis
Δ	Lateral deflection
Δ_s	Shortening of a steel column
ΔF_{vb}	Change in force in vertical bars through a joint region
ΔV_b	Applied force; or net vertical beam shear transferred into a column
ΔV_c	Net horizontal column shear transferred into a beam
ΣM_b	Sum of beam moments applied to a joint
ΣM_c	Sum of column moments applied to a joint
ΣQ_n	Sum of nominal strengths of shear connectors between the point of maximum positive or negative moment and the point of zero moment to either side
α	A number between 1 and 2 for defining the shape of the biaxial moment contour; or ratio of column shear V_c to beam shear V_b
α_1	A coefficient defined by Eq. (4.7a)
β	Coefficient of friction
β_d	Ratio of required permanent axial load to required total axial load usually taken as $1.4P_D/P_u$
β_1	Coefficient defined by Eqs. (4.7b) and (6.41)
γ	A numerical coefficient reflecting the portion of the steel pipe effective in carrying tensile stress
δ	Moment magnifier
δ_d	Dead-load deflection
δ_l	Live-load deflection
ϵ	Strain; estimated shortening strain including creep under sustained load
ϵ_c	Maximum strain in concrete
ϵ_i	Initial elastic strain
ϵ_s	Linear shortening strain due to shrinkage of a composite column
ϵ_t	Steel pipe tensile strain
θ	arctan (d/d_c)
θ_{rf}	Rotation at an intersection of a beam line at factored loads
θ_{rs}	Rotation at an intersection of a beam line at service loads
θ_s	End rotation in a simply supported beam
θ_{sf}	End rotation in a simply supported beam at factored loads
θ_{ss}	End rotation in a simply supported beam at service loads
λ_c	Column slenderness parameter
λ_r	Stem slenderness

μ Displacement ductility

ξ A numerical coefficient that determines the stress level which a steel pipe filled with concrete is allowed to approach at ultimate load

ρ_s A_s/A_g

σ Stress

σ_D Dead-load stress

σ_L Live-load stress

σ_{max} Maximum stress

σ_x Stress in the slab

ϕ Resistance factor

ϕ_b Resistance factor for flexure

ϕ_c Resistance factor for compression

ϕ_t Resistance factor for tension

ϕ_v Resistance factor for shear

ϕ_w Resistance factor for welds

Abbreviations

AASHO	American Association of State Highway Officials
AASHTO	American Association of State Highway and Transportation Officials
ACI	American Concrete Institute
AISC	American Institute of Steel Construction
AISI	American Iron and Steel Institute
ASCE	American Society of Civil Engineers
ASTM	American Society for Testing and Materials
AWS	American Welding Society
BSSC	Building Seismic Safety Council
CEB	Comité Euro-Internationale du Béton
HRB	Highway Research Board
HSS	Hollow structural sections
IABSE	International Association for Bridge and Structural Engineering
ICE	Institution of Civil Engineers (Great Britain)
ISO	International Organization for Standardization
L	Structural angles
LRFD	Load and resistance factor design
NEHRP	National Earthquake Hazard Reduction Program
SSM	Superposed strength method
WSE	Western Society of Engineers
WT	Structural tees cut from a W shape
2L	Structural double angles

Composite Construction
Design for Buildings

1

Introduction

1.1 Milestones

On August 8, 1988, the Bank of China was topped out in Hong Kong. This, one of the most spectacular buildings of combined structural steel and concrete, was a fitting tribute to a century of progress in the field of composite construction. When topped out, Bank of China was the tallest building outside the United States. The structural engineers made perfect use of the principal virtues of the component materials: the tensile strength of steel and the compressive strength of concrete.

1.1.1 Concrete-encased steel

The combined structural use of steel and concrete was first encountered almost as soon as the two materials became available to structural engineers.

Early construction. According to Hogan,[G21]* the first blast furnace and iron works in America were built at Saugus, Mass., in about 1645, but in those days and for the next two centuries steel was far too valuable a commodity for general structural use. The cement industry traces its beginnings in America to 1818, when a source of natural hydraulic cement was discovered near Sullivan, N.Y.[G16] The noted canal engineer Canvass White patented this "water lime" in 1819 and used it for stone masonry walls and aqueducts of the Erie Canal. A half-century later, in 1871, David Saylor applied for a U.S.

---

*Superscript G21 refers to Ref. G21 in Chap. 7, Literature.

patent on a "new and improved cement" he claimed to be "in every respect equal to the portland cement made in England." Saylor built a mill at Copley, Pa., and produced the first portland cement in the United States.[G11] By 1889, rotary kilns were built in Lehigh Valley, marking the beginning of the mass production of cement.[G2]

Meanwhile, the steel producers were also making progress. Bessemer converters, introduced in the 1860s, made it possible to supply steel in quantity. From that time, output grew rapidly.[G21] In 1869, Captain James Eads obtained cast alloy steel tubes[G8] for his bridge across the Mississippi River at St. Louis, the first important use of steel for bridgework in the United States.[G7] The Glasgow Bridge was the first large, all-steel crossing.[G5-G7] Started in 1878, it spanned the Missouri River at Glasgow, Mo. The five river spans, 314 ft (95.7 m) each, were deck and through Whipple trusses. Soon after, William LeBaron Jenny used steel in the skeleton of the Home Insurance Building in Chicago. Its construction commenced in 1884 with wrought-iron beams for the first six floors but was completed with bessemer steel beams.[G13] Thus, by about 1890, the prerequisites for composite construction were on hand.[C11,C13]

The first well-documented structural use in America of rolled beams embedded in concrete was in the Ward House, a private residence completed in Port Chester, N.Y., in 1877.[C1,C2] It was more than another decade before the new combination began to find wider applications. In buildings, concrete began replacing wood and masonry in floor construction during the late 1880s and the 1890s.[C3,C5,C7-C9,C13,C17,C21,C25,G1] The Methodist Building, built in 1894 in Pittsburgh, was among the early ones that used concrete-encased steel floor beams.[C25] In 1897, a fire started in a nearby building, leaped across an alley, and consumed the contents of the Methodist Building, but the basic structure remained relatively unaffected.[C21,C25] In 1896, several companies submitted their floor constructions to fire tests in response to a request from Stevenson Constable, New York City Superintendent of Buildings.[C25] In his 1905 inaugural address as president of the American Society of Civil Engineers (ASCE), C. C. Schneider stated that reinforced concrete proved satisfactory for fireproofing steel in buildings and as a protection to the steelwork over railroad tracks.[G3]

In 1894, Josef Melan, an engineer from Vienna, Austria, obtained an American patent for highway bridge construction[G13] consisting of several steel I beams, bent to the curvature of an arch, completely embedded in concrete.[C32] Melan claimed that the steel and concrete acted together; he submitted deflection calculations to prove his point.[C10,C32] One of the first bridges of this type was built near Rock Rapids, Iowa, in the same year,[C32,G13] and construction of many other Melan bridges was reported in the following years.[C14,C15,C16,C18,C23,C24,C26,C28] Replacement of the curved beams with straight as-rolled or riveted girders was the next step.[C22,C29] By the turn of the century, steel beam encasement in concrete was a regular practice in both buildings and bridges, primarily to protect steel against fire and other elements.

The Druecker warehouses, built in Chicago in 1898, were among the first to use steel columns fully encased in concrete.[C19,C25] This scheme was reversed in the new Government Printing Office in Washington in 1901, where pipe columns were filled with concrete to increase the capacity of a crane runway.[C27]

Early research and specifications. The first systematic tests of composite columns were conducted at Columbia University's Civil Engineering Laboratory in 1908 by W. H. Burr.[1] In 1912, A. N. Talbot and A. R. Lord reported on tests of 31 columns made at the University of Illinois including 21 composite and 10 bare steel columns.[2] The tests indicated that the strength of composite columns may be predicted best by adding the separate strengths of the steel and concrete parts of the column. Rules for the design of composite columns were included in the earliest nationwide recommendations for reinforced concrete design.[D2,D4,D5] These rules tended to permit very low stresses for concrete and reflected considerable caution regarding column instability. The early rules had no provisions for bending.

In 1922, the Dominion Bridge Company of Canada conducted tests of two floor panels, each consisting of a concrete slab and two steel I beams encased in concrete. In reporting on the results of these tests, H. M. MacKay, P. Gillespie, and C. Leluau[3] wrote:

> While such tests have hitherto been designed on the assumption that the entire load ... is carried by the steel, it was thought that the steel and concrete might really act together so as to form a composite beam. ...

At about the same time, tests of composite beams were carried out also in the United States[4] and in England.[6] All of them indicated good interaction between the two materials. Thus a starting point was provided for a chain of studies of composite beams which have continued to this day. In 1924, H. M. MacKay of McGill University in Montreal, who was involved in the Dominion Bridge program, conducted a new series of tests[7] to obtain additional bond and horizontal shear data. As an innovation and departure from the traditional full encasement, several specimens had only their top flanges embedded in the slab, a case of partial encasement.

In 1928, R. R. Zipprodt,[D7] structural engineer of the Portland Cement Association, reported that American and Canadian building codes made little or no allowance for the strengthening effect of concrete encasement. Later that same year, Chicago structural engineer F. A. Randall suggested testing a full-size floor section. He was named chairman of a Western Society of Engineers committee organized to conduct the tests.[8] The six-panel floor, 40 by 64 ft (12 by 20 m), contained steel beams fully encased in concrete made with gravel aggregates in four panels and cinder in the other two.[9] The tests demonstrated the strengthening effect of concrete. The committee recommended higher allowable steel stresses for encased steel beams.[10] Within 2 years, the strengthening effect was recognized by an amendment to the New York City Building Code permitting steel stress of 20 kips per square inch (ksi) (138 MPa) for encased beams as compared to 18 ksi (124 MPa) for unencased beams.[D8] The Empire State Building, built in New York City between 1929 and 1931, had its steel frame encased in cinder concrete,[M2,G20,C33] but the strengthening effect of the encasement was not accounted for in stress design calculations for either the gravity or the wind loads. On the other hand, in drift calculations the stiffening effect of the encasement was included by doubling the stiffnesses of individual frame members from those based on the properties of their steel sections alone.

In 1936, the American Institute of Steel Construction (AISC) adopted a revised version of its 1923 Standard Specification under the title Specification for the Design, Fabrication and Erection of Structural Steel for Buildings.[D11] The document included a new Section 8 Composite Beams specifying general requirements for the use of steel beams encased in concrete. The same provisions were included in the 1946 revision and thus remained in force without change until 1961.

From 1922 to 1925, a cooperative study of bridge impact loading was conducted by the Engineering Experiment Station of Iowa State College, Iowa State Highway Commission, and the U.S. Bureau of Public Roads.[5] The first experiments were made near Ames, Iowa, on the Skunk River Bridge, a through-truss structure whose stringers were partially encased beams. The tests indicated that most of the stringers exhibited complete bond between concrete and structural steel. Before replacement of the bridge in 1948, additional tests were made to check the remaining composite action.[24] The west approach span had full composite action, but the bond was lost in the west panel of the bridge and was deteriorating in other bridge stringers. This finding pointed out a major weakness of composite action obtained through partial encasement: in time, long after construction and for many often unpredictable reasons, adhesive bond between steel and concrete may be lost.[23]

1.1.2 Shear connectors

The solution to the loss of bond was indicated in two U.S. patents issued in 1903[D1] and 1926.[D6.]

First mechanical connectors. The first patent, applied for in 1903, was issued to Julius Khan of Detroit and the second, applied for in 1921, to Julius Khan of Youngstown. Both proposed to connect the steel beam to the concrete slab by mechanical means. These may have been the first proposals for mechanical connectors, an important contribution to the evolution of composite construction. Beams of this type were evaluated in the early twenties at the Massachusetts Institute of Technology, Purdue University, Truscon Steel Company, and the University of Nebraska.[4] Six out of eight specimens tested failed in flexural compression in the slab after yielding of the steel beam, one failed in bond, and one test was discontinued before failure. Good interaction at working loads and high overload capacities were observed.[39] Tests of another six composite beams were reported by R. A. Caughey[M1] in 1929. On the basis of these tests and a historical review of tests reported in the literature prior to 1929, Caughey concluded that composite beams may be designed safely on the basis of "elementary principles of design" and recommended allowable bond stress of 60 psi (413 kPa) for 2 ksi (14 MPa) concrete. For the case of higher bond stresses, Caughey suggested the use of angles riveted to the top flange of the steel beam.[M2]

Other forms of mechanical connectors were used on the approaches to two major New York area bridges to increase the stiffness of their floors.[C34,C35] Anchor bolts, hooked at the upper end to prevent uplift, were attached by double nuts at the Bayonne Bridge built in 1928 and bulb angles connected with rivets on the New York approach to the 1930 vintage George Washington Bridge. The corresponding beams were designed as steel members without composite action.

Composite action of concrete and structural steel attracted early attention not only in North America but also in Europe. In 1887, an article in *Engineering News* reported on Lindsay's flooring in England: rolled steel sections riveted into sheet piling–like configurations filled with concrete were proposed for bridge and building floors and for columns.[C4] A comprehensive paper presented before the Institution of Civil Engineers in 1891 described several fireproof systems, considering separately the fire-resisting properties of various materials and their combinations.[C6] In a paper read on Apr. 4, 1894, before the ASCE, the well-known Austrian engineer Fritz von Emperger reported on three "concrete-iron" systems used in Europe for highway bridges.[C12] Two of these used rolled shapes in combination with concrete; one was introduced by R. Wünsch of Hungary in 1884 and the other was called "System Melan" after its Austrian inventor. By the time of von Emperger's presentation, several bridges of both types were in service in central Europe. Tables and design methods for composite beams were published in England between 1910 and 1920,[D3] and the National Physical Laboratory tested slab specimens reinforced with rolled beams in 1922–23.[6] Widespread interest in continental Europe was evident from the large number of papers published on the subject. But even by 1932 the published reports were concerned only with encased construction relying on natural bond; and a thorough report on tests of fully and partially encased rolled steel beams, a few of them with flexible angle shear connectors, was published as late as 1939.[14] However, the decade of the thirties contributed a landmark: Otto Schaub received a Swiss patent for spiral shear connectors on July 30, 1932. The following year Schaub applied in the United States. He was granted a U.S. patent under the name "spiral shear connectors" on Oct. 8, 1935.[D10]

Second-generation connectors. The first systematic studies of composite beams with mechanical shear connectors were made in Switzerland in connection with the development of the so-called alpha system. The system appears to have had its origin in Belgium and some early applications in France. In this method of construction, the transfer of horizontal shear from the concrete slab to the steel beam was assured by round bars formed into a helix. The helix, called a spiral shear connector, was welded to the top flange of the steel section at the points of contact along the length of the beam. Tests of spiral shear connectors, carried out by Voellmy, Brunner, and Roš at the Swiss Federal Institute for Testing Materials in Zürich, were completed in 1936.[11,12,19,20] The system was then introduced commercially in the United States, where additional tests were conducted at Columbia[13] and Lehigh[16,17] universities and more than a decade later at the University of Illinois.[30] Porete Company of New Jersey published a design manual,[D13] and practical applications spread rapidly in the field of highway bridges, principally in New York and other northeastern states. The first American application, the Van Dam Street Bridge was designed in 1939 as a part of the approach viaduct to the Queens-Midtown Tunnel in New York.[D13,D12] Another early bridge with spiral shear connectors was the Coney Island Avenue Bridge on the Belt Parkway in Brooklyn, N.Y., built in 1940.[D13] Two years later, spiral connectors were used on the approach spans of the Lackawanna Avenue Bridge in Scranton, Pa.[C36] The first building with spiral shear connectors was a New York apartment house on the Grand Concourse at 175th Street built in 1946.[D13]

After the early studies of spiral connectors, the European research community turned its attention to two new types: (1) connectors made from reinforcing bars in the form of hooks or loops, and (2) stiff connectors made from rectangular steel bars or from rolled shapes welded to the steel beam in such a manner as to offer most resistance to bending. The two types were often combined, with the stiff connector assigned the function of preventing slip while the hook or loop was to resist uplift. Tests conducted in Switzerland[18] and Germany[C37,15,21,22,25] were followed by general acceptance in practical applications to highway bridges. A few tests of stiff connectors were carried out in the United States.[17,27–29] Their practical use was limited mostly to angles welded along the cut end. Wisconsin and Iowa state highway departments were their principal users.

While European practices turned to stiff connectors combined with hooks, American engineers showed preference for flexible connectors requiring less fabrication. The experimental investigations carried out before the emergence of stud connectors included flexible connectors made from rolled shapes, mostly channels. The channel connectors had one flange welded to the beam; the other flange furnished resistance to uplift. The tests were made at Lehigh University[16] and at the University of Illinois.[27,28] The tests at Illinois were extensive, involving 152 quarter-scale and 47 full-size specimens, of which 92 were T beams and 107 push-out specimens. Both static and fatigue tests were included. A part of a cooperative investigation between the university, the Illinois Division of Highways, and the U.S. Bureau of Public Roads, they were led by N. M. Newmark and C. P. Siess. The flexible channel shear connector found practical applications in many highway bridges. The bridges on the initial construction of the New Jersey Turnpike were the first major application.[C38] The Ohio Turnpike was another major user. But in less than a decade after the completion of the Illinois studies, the flexible channel shear connectors were supplanted by stud connectors.

Stud shear connectors.   Perhaps the most important innovation in the field of mechanical shear connectors was the entry of end-welded studs. The studs not only provided a more economical shear connector but also made practical the application of composite construction to building floors. Studies of stud connectors began at the University of Illinois in 1954[32] as commercial tests for Nelson Stud Welding of Lorain, Ohio. Aimed principally at the bridge market, they included four series of push-out tests[33] and fatigue tests of bare studs.[31] Additional tests at Illinois were concerned with plate reinforced concrete.[34] The Illinois tests were followed shortly by tests of 1 full-size double T beam[36] and 10 push-out specimens at Lehigh University[37] for KSM Products, Inc., of New Jersey. In the late 1950s, more extensive tests, aimed at the building market, were started at Lehigh University[45] under the sponsorship of the AISC. The first structures with stud shear connectors were erected in 1956: a continuous plate girder bridge at Ft. Pierre, S.D.,[C40,D15] composite framing for IBM's Engineering Laboratory at Poughkeepsie, N.Y.,[C39] and storage tank platforms of the American Sugar Refining Company in Philadelphia.[C45] Within a few years, major buildings were built with composite floors. The seven-story court house and the four-story federal office building in Brooklyn were designed and the contract for their construction awarded in 1960.[C43] Two-way composite floor made its debut at Detroit's Cobo Hall.[C44] Completed in 1961, the steel framing for Hall C was designed for continuity in both directions and for composite action in positive-moment zones.

Outside North America, the stud connectors were introduced through experimental investigations started in the second half of the 1950s at Imperial College in London.[42,62] By 1960, their tests included 28 full-scale and 66 small-scale beams and push-out specimens with stud shear connectors.[38] The British studies were soon followed by studies on the continent,[M3] in Australia,[54] and in Japan.[71] An innovative application took place in France on the Tancarville suspension bridge over River Seine near Le Havre in the form of a deck comprised of steel plates connected to a concrete overlay with studs.[C41,C42] Today, the stud connector is used throughout the world with the exception of those countries where semiautomatic stud welding is uneconomical.

In spite of the obvious practical and economic advantages of stud connectors, new ideas for connecting the concrete slab to the supporting steel beams are being encountered. Two recent proposals can be used to eliminate specific drawbacks of studs: (1) large power requirements for welding and (2) construction hazards presented by shop-welded studs. Both were developed in Europe, one in Liechtenstein[101] aimed at the building market and the other in Germany[D62] proposed for bridge applications. The first is cold-formed from sheet steel in the form of an angle and fastened to the steel beam using a powder-actuated tool. The second, called Perfobond rib, is a $\frac{1}{2} \times 2\frac{3}{8}$-in (13 × 60-mm) perforated steel bar welded continuously along the top flange of the bridge girder.

In 1956, the Committee on Bridges and Structures of the American Association of State Highway Officials (AASHO) adopted for the first time an expanded set of provisions for the design of composite beams. The major innovation was a set of detail rules for the design of shear connectors forcing the concrete slab and the supporting steel beams to respond to loading as a unit. Three types of connectors were included: the older spiral and channel connectors, and the then new stud connectors. The new provisions became a part of the 1957 edition of the specification.[D14] A rapid spread of the use of composite bridge construction followed. The stud connector soon gained a wide acceptance and, thanks to its economy as well as other practical advantages, replaced the older spiral and channel connectors within a few years.

Gypsum plaster and mineral wool sprayed-on coatings, introduced in the early 1950s, and other new methods of fire protection made concrete encasement obsolete. Thus composite action obtained by encasement was no longer available to the structural engineer, creating incentive for the development and use of mechanical shear connectors. One of the first steps toward acceptance of composite construction without encasement in buildings was the formation of a committee to develop design recommendations. Organized in 1957 under the auspices of ASCE and the American Concrete Institute, the Joint ASCE-ACI Committee on Composite Construction had 18 members. It has been active to this day; about 100 persons have served on it under 12 different chairs thus far. In December 1960, the committee issued Tentative Recommendations for the Design and Construction of Composite Beams and Girders for Buildings.[D16] They were the basis for the 1961[D17] and 1963[D18] AISC specification provisions for composite beams with one exception: The procedure for the design of shear connectors was based on research then being completed at Lehigh University under the sponsorship of AISC.[45] The ready availability of authoritative, well-founded design rules combined with commercial incentive on the part of stud suppliers led to a rapid adoption of the technical and economic advantages of composite floors throughout the building industry in North America.

1.1.3 Steel decks and flooring

Two other related developments had lasting effect on composite floor construction: formed (corrugated) steel decks and cellular steel flooring.

Formed steel decks.   Formed steel decks were designed to support freshly cast concrete and carry construction loads. However, it was soon observed that the decks bonded to the concrete and contributed to the structural response of the finished slabs.[M5] The steel deck form served as one-way slab reinforcement. When loaded to failure, large slips occurred between the decking and concrete before the ultimate load was reached. The final failure was usually by a combination of shear and bond.[75] Based on proprietary tests, the deck manufacturers published load tables and installation guidelines for their products.[M5] Since no general specification for the design of composite slabs was available, the American Iron and Steel Institute (AISI) initiated in 1966 an extensive theoretical and experimental investigation of steel form-reinforced slabs at Iowa State University.[75] After the original investigation was completed in 1974, studies have continued to this day under the sponsorship of the

National Science Foundation and several industrial sources. In 1984, the ASCE issued the Specification for the Design and Construction of Composite Slabs[D50,D87] based on the results of research at Iowa State. Today, deck-reinforced slabs are used universally in steel-framed buildings.

For composite floor construction, the permanent steel forms resulted in a complete elimination of bond between the concrete slab and the steel section unless the forms spanned only between the flanges of the supporting beams. This last form of construction was adopted for bridges and has been used to this day. On the other hand, in building construction the economy favored continuous coverage over the supporting beams. Thus, to obtain composite action between the concrete slab and the supporting steel framing, it was necessary to weld the shear connectors through the deck. Granco Steel Products Company of St. Louis developed a special connector made of steel sheet that fitted into the corrugations and was welded manually through the deck to the supporting beams. For early applications of stud connectors, holes were punched in the steel deck, but by the middle sixties the stud manufacturers developed methods for semiautomatic welding through not only black but also lightly galvanized deck. Further development included hot-dipped decks as well.[D25] Since the early 1970s, welding of studs through galvanized decks has been a standard practice.

Cellular steel flooring.   On the basis of several interviews with design engineers in New York City and other involved personnel, an article published in *Civil Engineering* in 1971[D25] traced the development of cellular steel floors. Even as far back as 1925, some engineers were concerned about the heavy weight of concrete floor slabs. Could not a lightweight floor be designed that could be mass-produced, cheaply shipped to the site, and rapidly laid in place, making possible big savings in the steel frame and foundations? Indeed it could. The answer proved to be a cellular steel floor made by H. H. Robertson Company of Pittsburgh, until then a manufacturer of metal roof decks. During the thirties, this steel deck began to be used for floor systems, mostly in two- and three-story industrial buildings. By 1938, engineers started to use its floor cells for electrification to run a building's power, telephone, and signal wires. The first cellular floor was laid in the early 1930s at a Baltimore & Ohio Railroad Company warehouse in Pittsburgh. Following World War II, cellular steel floors started their climb in high-rise structures. Among the several forces that brought steel-deck floors to the fore, the two major factors were sharply rising labor costs, making the installation and removal of wood forms less attractive, and the dwindling supply of cinder, forcing engineers to go to more expensive lightweight aggregates.

In the early metal floors, the steel decking was the only structural element. Concrete fill was added on the top of the deck to obtain the needed fire rating and provide a level surface. But the growth of this early system was limited because it had to be combined with a fireproof ceiling system, invariably an expensive item. The birth of spray-on fireproofing set off a rapid growth of cellular steel floors. Sprayed on beams and the underside of steel decking, the new fire protection eliminated the need for costly fireproof ceilings. Another question arose in the minds of engineers: Since there is concrete on the top of steel decking, why not make it carry part of the load? About 1950, Granco Steel Products Company became the first to market a steel deck with wires welded to its top surface perpendicular to the corrugations. Thus the concrete and the deck were linked together, forming a composite slab. In the early 1960s, Inland-Ryerson Company of Chicago came out with a cellular steel flooring with embossed sidewalls. The embossments augmented the natural bond between the steel deck and the concrete. Now the engineer could get a slab system as strong as or stronger than before using a thinner-gage steel for the deck or get longer spans with the same thickness.

A major obstacle to the use of composite design with steel decking was caused by the holes created over the beams when the steel deck corrugations run perpendicular to the beams. After consulting engineer A. H. Atkinson of Hamilton, Ontario, suggested the use of composite floor construction for slabs cast on uninterrupted steel forms with deep corrugations, a pilot test of a full-size T beam was conducted at McMaster University.[60] The beam was composed of a rolled steel section, a 3-in-deep (76-mm) steel deck with corrugations running perpendicular to the steel beam, stud shear connectors welded in the deck troughs, and a concrete slab cast on the steel deck. The test demonstrated the feasibility of designing composite beams with deep decks. During the following decade, many tests were made of composite construction with proprietary products, often for specific applications. The results of a more detailed investigation at McMaster University were reported in 1967.[53] It was observed that the proportions of the deck ribs influenced the mode of failure. If a deep rib is too narrow, then a horizontal force applied to the slab would tend to crack the concrete along the top of the deck. After initial horizontal cracking, the anchorage of the stud in the solid portion of the slab above the deck corrugations made a significant contribution to the ability of the composite beam to maintain the load.

In 1970, researchers at Lehigh University analyzed the results of many commercial tests made during the preceding years and published tentative design recommendations for composite beams with steel decks 3 in (76 mm) or less in depth.[D24] For decks up to 1.5 in (38 mm) deep, they found no significant reduction in ultimate load; the beam can be designed as if the slab were solid. They followed up the study with a systematic experimental investigation of the effects of known variables using rolled beams and break-formed decks made specifically for the investigation. Additional beams were tested at the University of Texas. The final report of the Lehigh investigation,[77] including the tests at the University of Texas and earlier commercial tests in addition to those made at Lehigh, contained design guidelines based on a total of 75 full-size beam tests. These guidelines were adopted by AISC in 1978 as a part of their specification for buildings.[D39] The method, utilizing a reduction formula applied to the strength of shear connectors embedded in a solid slab, has been used to this day. It is applicable to both normal-weight and light-weight concrete.

During the past 20 years, the use of steel decks became widespread throughout the world, and problems arising from their use have been studied intensively abroad, particularly in Australia,[111] Canada,[106] Germany,[D46] and Switzerland.[103] It can be expected that such studies and the subsequent exchange of ideas will lead to a much better understanding of the structural behavior that will eventually be reflected in better, more rational design methods.

1.1.4 Developments after 1960

Continuing research resulted eventually in the transition from the allowable stress design to design based on the strength of members and connections.

Bridges. To take advantage in bridge design of the latest research on the ultimate static strength of shear connectors, researchers on both sides of the Atlantic examined their fatigue strength. Initial fatigue tests at Lehigh University[37] carried out principally on push-out specimens were followed by a series of 12 beam tests. Seven full-size beams were tested at the University of Texas.[46] The American studies were completed with a systematic series of push-out tests at Lehigh University[48] that resulted in a fatigue design procedure which was adopted by the AASHO Committee on Bridges and Structures in 1967.[D21] The procedure was noteworthy for its simplicity. It based fatigue design on the concept of shear stress range, i.e., the difference between the maximum and minimum shear stresses. The stress-range concept simplified design and permitted uniform spacing of connectors, a feature particularly desirable from the standpoint of fabrication. While the research in the United States was limited to stud connectors, British fatigue studies involved stud, channel, and bar connectors.[52]

In 1965, an advisory committee was formed by AISI to review bridge design practices and to develop design recommendations for a more consistent and efficient use of steel in highway bridges.[D26] The committee initiated a study that resulted in the Tentative Criteria for Load Factor Design of Steel Highway Bridges.[D26] The criteria were presented to the AASHO Committee on Bridges and Structures in 1968 and published in the 1971 AASHO Interim Specifications as an alternate design method.[D27]

Still other investigations included composite plate and box girders commonly used in bridges but not in buildings.[D29,59] Limited research was completed on composite beams with inverted steel T sections that were used in the construction of a two-span continuous bridge in Kansas.[D19]

Buildings. Research on the application of lightweight concrete to composite beams was started by J. Chin at the University of Colorado who reported the results of push-out tests in 1965.[44] Other investigations of proprietary aggregates followed. The results of systematic push-out tests at Lehigh University[64] and beam tests at the University of Missouri[43A] were published, and included in the 1978 AISC specification.[D39] The studies revealed that the strength of a composite beam with a lightweight concrete slab is the same as that of a beam with a normal-weight concrete of the same compressive strength. However, deflections are larger with lightweight concrete and the strength of connectors is reduced. These and follow-up studies at Lehigh University[77] led to a revised formula for the ultimate strength of a stud connector applicable to both normal-weight and lightweight concrete.

Among other significant developments in composite construction, research at Lehigh University showed that uniform spacing of shear connectors is satisfactory for beams subjected to uniformly distributed load.[45] In 1964, tests at Imperial College in London demonstrated that heavy concentrated loads on composite beams with uniformly spaced stud connectors could inhibit the redistribution of shear forces among the connectors and cause a premature failure of the composite beam.[43] To guard against this condition, the 1969 AISC specification[D23] added a requirement for a minimum number of connectors that must be placed between a concentrated load and the nearest point of zero moment. The effect of beam flange thickness on the strength of stud connectors was investigated at Case Institute of Technology in 1968.[58] Based on these tests, the 1969 AISC specification[D23] called for a minimum flange thickness for stud shear connectors that are located away from the beam web. Theoretical and experimental investigations of the negative moment regions of continuous composite beams were carried out in England[51] and the United States[49] during the 1960s. All of them reached the conclusion that beams with adequately anchored longitudinal reinforcement for slabs in the negative-moment regions can be analyzed by simple plastic theory. In 1970, work at the University of Warwick resulted in a method for determining the minimum amount of transverse reinforcement required in simple and continuous beams to prevent longitudinal splitting of the slab along the shear connectors.[61] Further studies of the effects of vertical shear and the effects of local buckling of the steel compression flange were completed in 1972.[70]

The 1969 AISC specification[D23] included another innovation: rules for composite beams having fewer connectors than the number required for full composite action. Research at Lehigh University[45] has shown that for a given steel beam and concrete slab the increase in bending strength intermediate between no composite action and full composite action is proportional to the shear resistance developed between the steel and concrete, i.e., to the number of shear connectors provided between these limits. Since at times it may not be feasible or it may be unnecessary to provide full composite action, the specification recognized for the first time two conditions: full and incomplete composite action.

A design method for composite castellated beams was proposed in 1966.[47] Several investigations of composite open-web joists with various types of mechanical connectors were carried out at Washington University in St. Louis between 1965 and 1970.[63] Such joists were used in parking decks. Composite trusses with steel decks appear economical for spans between 40 and 80 ft (12 and 24 m). Floor systems of this type have been tested and used for the World Trade Center towers in New York,[C47] the Sears Building in

Chicago,[D25] and several other tall buildings. A floor system falling between trusses and full-web girders was introduced in 1972, the so-called stub-girder system.[C52] Short stub beams were welded to the top flange of the girder and connected to the slab with shear connectors. The spaces between the stub beams accommodated continuous floor beams and allowed for the passage of ducts and pipes. The stub-girder floor system was used in several buildings in the United States, Canada, and Mexico.

Work on a major improvement of the design of composite beams was started in the early 1970s as a part of the development of a new design method for steel buildings that eventually became known as load and resistance factor design (LRFD).[G31] Based on fully plastic strength of composite sections, the method resulted in better utilization of materials and substantial simplification of design.[D37] It became a part of the LRFD Specification for Structural Steel Buildings adopted by AISC in 1986[D55] and revised in 1993.[D91] The same document included another major innovation: rules for the design of composite columns. Prior to 1986, the design of composite columns was covered only by Building Code Requirements for Reinforced Concrete, published by the ACI.[D80] The ACI rules for composite columns are based on the same principles as the design of reinforced concrete; the strength approaches that of reinforced concrete columns as the percentage of the steel section decreases. On the other hand, the AISC rules are akin to steel column design and require that the cross-sectional area of the steel shape, pipe, or tubing comprises at least 4 percent of the total composite cross section; the strength of composite columns approaches that of steel columns as the percentage of steel section increases.

Composite columns were used frequently in buildings during the first half of this century. While the primary function of the concrete encasement was fire protection, it was assigned a portion of the total load resisted by the column even in some of the very early applications.[C30] However, the introduction of lightweight fireproofing after World War II resulted in an almost complete elimination of composite columns from new buildings. They returned only in the early 1970s, as will be described later. The work on the AISC rules for composite columns started as an activity of the Structural Specification Liaison Committee organized by George Winter in the 1970s with the support of the ACI, AISC, and AISI. The rules were first developed in terms of working stresses,[D40] later adjusted to the ultimate-strength level[D42] and adopted by AISC.[D55] Extensive studies of composite columns have been reported in recent years from abroad.[C70,M10,100,109,114] Experimental studies of composite columns with high-strength concrete were carried out at the University of California.[131]

The area of perhaps the least progress is that of composite structural joints. As an illustration, a well-documented state-of-the-art report prepared for the Structural Specification Liaison Committee in 1977[M7] contained a 10-page section consisting mostly of drawings but no references on this subject. To this day, most of the joints for composite members are designed as for steel structures without any regard for concrete. Some early experiments were carried out on beam-to-column joints at Lehigh University.[67] More recently work was completed on connections between composite beams and concrete columns.[120] Work at the University of Minnesota on beam-to-column connections[108] and at Virginia Tech on beam-to-girder connections[149] promises to result in significant economies in floor construction.[108] Over the years, considerable work was reported from abroad.[68,69,72] Studies of connections were particularly numerous in Japan and were concerned principally with the resistance of joints to earthquake forces.[115]

The elements of a composite structure are well tied together. This major characteristic of composite construction is particularly beneficial in areas subject to frequent strong earthquakes. It is this characteristic that made composite design particularly popular in Japan. The acceptance of composite construction in California was much slower than in the rest of the United States. At first, shear connectors were relied on only to connect the horizontal diaphragms to the steel framing, but the beams were designed as noncomposite. However, during recent years composite floors became standard practice. Even so, little research effort was directed toward problems of seismic resistance of composite structures. Studies of floor beams at the University of California at Berkeley,[119] columns at the University of California at San Diego,[140] and frames and subassemblies at Lehigh[118] and Stanford[G59] universities are a part of a United States–Japan cooperative research effort.

Extensive studies of the design of composite buildings have been under way in Europe since about 1980[D85] in connection with their development of structural design codes with multinational applicability, the so-called Eurocodes. Provisions for composite construction comprise Eurocode 4, the first part of which is concerned primarily with buildings.

Conferences.   To evaluate progress in composite construction, to study current design practices, and to identify areas for future research, a joint United States–Japan seminar was held in Tokyo in 1978. It was attended by 22 invited attendees, mostly from academia. In addition to the participants from Japan and the United States, one representative attended from each of Canada, England, and Germany. The papers presented at the seminar were published in 1980.[M12] The second United States–Japan seminar was held in Seattle in 1984.[M14] It included attendees from five countries other than the United States and Japan. In 1987, the United States–Japan seminars were followed up by the first Engineering Foundation conference on composite construction held at Henniker, N.H.[M18] Attended by 96 professionals from 17 countries, it provided a truly worldwide survey of the status of composite construction. Also in 1987, an international symposium on composite steel concrete structures was held in Bratislava, Czechoslovakia.[M17] A symposium on mixed structures including new materials was held by the International Association for Bridge and Structural Engineering (IABSE) in Brussels in 1990.[M19] Fukuoka, Japan, was the site of the International Conference on Steel-Concrete Composite Structures in 1991.[M20] A second Engineering Foundation conference on composite construction, held in 1992 at Potosi,

Mo.,[M23] had attendance similar to the one at Henniker. More than a quarter of the participants at Potosi also attended the first Engineering Foundation conference. A United States–Japan workshop on composite and hybrid structures was held in Berkeley, Calif., in September 1992.[M22] An international meeting on composite bridges convened in Barcelona at the end of November 1992. The second United States–Japan workshop, called the Second Joint Technical Coordinating Committee Meeting, convened in Honolulu in June 1995, and the third Engineering Foundation Conference on Composite Construction was held at Irsee, Germany, in June 1996.

1.1.5 Recent building construction

Almost without exception, skyscrapers built during the past three decades have composite floors and frequently also a composite exterior shell or a few principal composite columns. In 1968, construction was completed on the 100-story John Hancock Center in Chicago[C63] that was designed with exterior walls as the principal wind-resisting elements. The structure was framed in steel with shear stiffness of exterior walls provided by massive diagonal X braces extending the full width of the building and over the depth of many floors. The John Hancock building is about 10 percent shorter than the then still tallest Empire State Building in New York. The 110-story World Trade Center twin towers in New York City,[C47] completed in 1972 and for a short time the tallest buildings in the world, are essentially vertical tubes consisting of closely spaced welded steel exterior columns and deep spandrels, and an interior service core also framed in steel. The space between the outside walls and the core is bridged with composite trusses erected as subassemblies of two trusses each and brought to the construction site by barges.

Currently the tallest building in the world is the 1450-ft-high (442-m) Sears Tower of 1974 vintage located in Chicago.[C51,C64] It, as well as the John Hancock Building, was conceived and designed by Fazlur R. Khan, a brilliant structural engineer and innovator, and his team at the Chicago office of Skidmore, Owens and Merrill. It was made possible by Khan's recognition that in very tall buildings the wind forces must be assigned to the exterior walls rather than to the core in the interior as was done in the past, and that the available technology made such a solution economically feasible. The exterior wind-resisting wall framed in steel, such as those in the Sears and John Hancock buildings, required heavy sections and expensive fabrication. Khan reasoned that significant economies could be achieved if all steel columns, both interior and exterior, were designed for vertical loads only and the wind forces taken care of by embedding the exterior columns in concrete. Thus the system utilizing exterior steel columns for erection, reusable temporary wind bracing, and exterior composite columns and walls came into being. During the past decade such a system has been used extensively in the 50- to 75-story range. Its first application was the 20-story Control Data Corporation building in Houston,[C48,C50] completed in 1970. With this initial step successfully completed, the system was soon adopted on a broad scale.

The 75-story Texas Commerce Tower, completed in 1982 in Houston,[C61] was at that time the tallest building with an exterior composite shell. The steel erection was allowed to proceed 12 floors ahead of concrete. The building was designed by CBM Engineers of Houston. Three First National Plaza Building in the Chicago[C77] loop, completed in 1982, was designed by Skidmore, Owings & Merrill using composite floors and exterior walls. It has 57 stories and is 757 ft (231 m) high. A variation on the tube concept was developed by LeMessurier Associates/SCI for the 73-story Dallas Main Center,[C73] completed in 1985. To satisfy the request for offices with uninterrupted view, the weight of the entire building was placed on 16 composite columns located up to 20 ft (6 m) inside the outside envelope of the building. For the 60-story Momentum Place completed in Dallas[C78] in 1988, slip forms were used to build concrete walls at the four corners of the building. Structural engineers, the Datum/Moore Partnership, designed these walls to work integrally with the perimeter composite frame in resisting lateral forces. The Office of Irwin G. Cantor of New York designed a composite system that joins steel and concrete throughout the building in the 54-story $200 million Mellon Bank Center completed in Philadelphia in 1990.[C82]

In 1972, A. G. Tarics proposed the use of concrete-filled steel columns to decrease the cost of multistory buildings.[D30] Six of the recently completed tall buildings in Seattle are supported on huge pipe columns filled with concrete.[C81] Two Union Square Building is the most advanced application of this composite system developed by Skilling Ward Magnusson Barkshire Inc. The 58-story building includes a core that carries 40 percent of the gravity loads, resists the lateral loads, and supports one end of the floors extending column-free to the perimeter columns. The core is supported on four 10-ft-diameter (3-m) pipe columns filled with 19-ksi (130-MPa) concrete.

The skyscrapers built during the past 30 years are office buildings in which column-free rentable space is an economic necessity. This often led to bridging the space between the service core and the exterior structure with composite trusses that not only satisfied the architectural requirement but also helped stiffen the structure in its resistance to horizontal loads. It should be noted, however, that composite construction is used universally in low-rise as well as in high-rise buildings. Virtually all steel-framed buildings built with concrete floor slabs capitalize on the advantages of composite construction. As the tonnage of steel used in low-rise buildings greatly exceeds that for high-rise construction, the importance of the former in the application of composite design is readily apparent.

1.1.6 Recent bridge construction

Most of the steel bridges on the 41,000-mi (66,000-km) interstate network of limited-access highways are of composite construction.[C60] Built principally during the 1960s and 1970s, the system included a huge number of short crossings and overpasses as well as many medium-span bridges, the latter generally constructed with trusses as the main load-carrying elements. With few exceptions, the overpasses and short crossings were of composite I-beam construction whenever built in structural steel. The medium-span bridges of truss construction frequently included composite floors. A typical example of a medium-span truss bridge with composite flooring is the main structure that carries Interstate Highway 80 over the Clarion River valley in western Pennsylvania. Two three-span continuous deck trusses, with the main span of 612 ft (187 m), support a floor of composite stringers and a concrete slab.

An interesting system for construction of composite bridges was developed in Switzerland in the early 1970s.[C53,D70] The method, called slip-decking, utilized casting of the bridge deck in segments, after the erection of the steel superstructure, on stationary forms located near one end or in the middle of the bridge. All deck segments, usually 80 to 130 ft (24 to 40 m) long, were cast and cured in the same forms. After each curing period, the whole slab was jacked, i.e., moved ahead atop the steel girders, to make room for the next segment. The sliding was aided by steel shoes placed intermittently between the concrete deck and the steel girders. After the whole deck was cast and moved in place, stud shear connectors were welded through preformed openings in the deck, and the openings around the studs and the gap between the slab and the steel girders were grouted.

A significant development in the construction of composite bridges is currently in progress in Europe. Europe's railroads have been declining since 1945, but improvements of the late 1980s and of the 1990s in France, Germany, and other countries may reverse that trend. The German Federal Railways are spending about $1.1 billion annually on a new 1250-mi (2000-km) network for trains traveling at speeds up to 155 mph (250 km/h).[G70] On the link between Hannover and Würzburg, designed for speeds exceeding 200 mph (320 km/h), the horizontal and vertical alignment required curves with minimum radius of 23,000 (7000) and 17,000 ft (5200 m), respectively, and very stiff bridges with a limiting deflection equal to 1/2000 of the span length.[C79] Composite deck box girders and composite trusses provided the required stiffness. The trusses are of the Warren type. The resulting structures are noteworthy for their excellent riding quality and their aesthetically outstanding appearance.

1.2 Purpose, Scope, and Approach

LRFD provisions[D91] for composite design include beams and columns. For beams, they result in economy and simplification of design. For columns, they are the preferred method when the percentage of steel is large. Because of these characteristics and because of the rather limited current use of both LRFD and composite columns, it was considered timely to prepare a text that can serve as a design guide.

Dimensioning based on LRFD is carried out at the maximum strength level. As inelastic deformations take place in the structure before the failure loads are reached, the internal forces can be assessed accurately only with elastoplastic analyses. Such analyses have been developed and used in occasional applications. An elastoplastic analysis was adopted for this book where applicable.

Composite columns, LRFD, and elastoplastic analyses are relatively new tools that have not yet enjoyed universal acceptance. It is the purpose of this book to present them to the profession as applied to the design of composite structures in steel and concrete, and to provide guidance for their use. The book covers the design of composite beams, columns, bracing, and joints that are combined into floor and frame building systems. The design procedures are presented in a form aimed at ready use by the designer. For this reason, explanations of assumptions and derivations of equations are given only when not readily found in generally available literature. The reader who is interested in a more scholarly study of the subject is referred to the references in Chap. 7.

The approach to the design of composite steel-concrete buildings selected for this book is based on the most recent information on the behavior of such structures under various types of loading. The internal forces are found by an analysis appropriate for the loading conditions under consideration. Generally, an elastic analysis is appropriate under service loads and a plastic or elastoplastic analysis is needed for loads at maximum strength. The resistance of the cross section is determined by LRFD.

The book is divided into seven chapters. Chapter 1 features an extensive history of composite construction and case histories for 17 composite buildings completed during the period 1968 through 1992. Both elastic and inelastic analyses are covered in Chap. 2, concerned with the design and construction of composite systems. Design of composite beams and columns is covered in Chaps. 3 and 4, respectively. Instruction on the design for lateral loads is presented in Chap. 5, which includes also a brief discussion of retrofitting of existing buildings. The design of various types of joints is covered comprehensively in Chap. 6. The four chapters covering the design of composite elements, i.e., beams, columns, bracing, and joints, are illustrated with 27 examples that designers can follow in their work. An extensive list of references classified into five categories is included in Chap. 7.

Composite construction as used in this book may be defined as the joint use of structural steel and structural concrete in individual elements, such as beams and columns, and in different parts of a structure. The term "composite construction" is used throughout the book for all combinations of structural steel and structural concrete. During the 1970s, the term "mixed structures" was introduced to distinguish between those elements and structures in which concrete and steel are forced to act together as a unit and structures in which concrete and steel elements act independently. The latter type of structure is rarely mentioned in this book. Furthermore, it is often difficult to distinguish between the two types.

The overwhelming reason for using composite construction is economy. Steel is particularly good in resisting tension and concrete is strong in compression. Thus, with proper design, their combined use is structurally efficient. Furthermore, in steel-framed buildings, floors and often also exterior walls are built of reinforced concrete. In such structures the additional efficiency gained through composite interaction between the concrete and structural steel can be obtained at a usually very small cost of interconnecting the two elements.

1.3   Building Case Histories

The application of composite construction is illustrated in this section by descriptions of 18 tall buildings completed in 1931 and from 1968 through 1992. Since 1930, the New York City building code permitted higher allowable stresses for steel beams encased in concrete. Connecting steel beams to concrete floor slabs with shear connectors became a common practice during the 1960s. The beginning of frequent use of composite columns in tall buildings dates to about 1980. The case histories are based mostly on information contained in the references cited with individual buildings. However, frequent use was also made of other sources such as personal information from structural engineers of record, and various publications and files of the Council on Tall Buildings and Urban Habitat.

1.3.1   Prior to 1980

The Empire State Building[M2,G20,C33,C56] in New York City was the tallest building in the world for more than 40 years, from the day of its completion in 1931 until 1972 when the twin towers of New York's World Trade Center exceeded its 1250-ft (381-m) height by almost 120 ft (37 m). It was conceived by the designers as an 85-story building but was upgraded to 102 floors by public relations interests. The structural steel frame with riveted joints, while encased in cinder concrete, was designed to carry 100 percent of the gravity and 100 percent of the wind loads imposed on the building. The encasement, although neglected in strength analyses, stiffened the frame, particularly against wind loads. Working with frequency of vibration measured on the completed building, the actual stiffness was estimated at 4.8 times the stiffness of the bare steel frame. The speed of the design and construction was truly remarkable; it took only 18 months from the architect's first sketches to the completion of the building. The erection of 57,000 tons [52,000 tonnes (t)] of steel took only 6 months with a 5 day work week. Except for its height, the building was typical of the construction of its era. The structure was designed by H. G. Balcom of New York.

The 100-story John Hancock Center[C63] (Fig. 1.1) in Chicago is a multiuse building involving commercial, parking, office, and apartment-type space in one building. The ground-floor plan measures 154 by 262 ft (47 by 80 m), and the clear span from the central core is approximately 60 ft (18 m). The building is tapered to the top to a dimension of 100 (30) by 160 ft (49 m), and the clear span reduces to 30 ft (9 m). The floor height is 12 ft 6 in (3.8 m) in the office sector and 9 ft 4 in (2.8 m) in the apartment sector. The structural system consists of diagonally braced exterior frames which act together as a

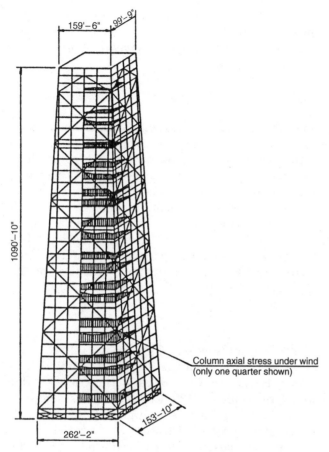

159'−6"

99'−9"

1090'−10"

Column axial stress under wind
(only one quarter shown)

153'−10"

262'−2"

Figure 1.1 John Hancock Center schematics.[C63]

tube. The distribution of axial forces when the tower is subjected to wind on
the broad face is shown in Fig. 1.1. The almost uniform distribution on the
flange face and the approximately linear decrease across the web indicate the
predominant cantilever mode of deformation and very little shear lag effect in
the tower's response. The floors have 5-in-thick (127-mm) slabs of lightweight
concrete of medium unit weight placed directly on the supporting steel beams
and connected to them with stud shear connectors. The columns, diagonals,
and ties are I sections fabricated from three plates with maximum thickness
of 6 in (150 mm) and the maximum column dimension of 36 in (920 mm).
Floor framing, fabricated from rolled beams with simple connections, was
designed for gravity loading only. The interior columns were designed for
gravity loads using rolled and built-up sections. Almost all steel was
American Society for Testing and Materials (ASTM) grade A36. Connections
were shop-welded and field-bolted except that field welding was used in spandrels, main ties, and column splices. The building, designed by the Chicago

office of Skidmore, Owings & Merrill, was completed in 1968 reaching 1127 ft (344 m) toward the skies.

The pair of World Trade Center towers[C47,C56] in New York City is noteworthy in its magnitude and complexity and in its pioneering advances of high-rise building technology. At 1368 ft (417 m) above the street level, the towers accommodate 110 floors, each 207 ft 2 in (63 m) square. With almost 1 full acre (about 0.4 ha) per level, each tower contains 4.8 million gross ft^2 (446,000 m^2) of floor area. Over 200,000 tons (182,000 t) of structural steel were required for the project. The resistance to the wind loads was assigned to the exterior walls made up of 240 tubular columns spaced at 3-ft 4-in (1.0-m) and 52-in-deep (1.3-m) steel plate spandrels to form a Vierendeel truss. The vertical loads are transferred from the 4-in-thick (100-mm) concrete floor slabs to the exterior and core columns by trusses spanning 60 to 35 ft (18 to 11 m). The 6-ft 8-in (2.0-m) space between two adjacent trusses is spanned with corrugated steel decking that tied the two trusses into an erection unit and served also as forms for concrete. The web members of the trusses extend 3 in (76 mm) above the top chords into the slabs to provide composite floor action. An architectural first introduced in the construction of the World Trade Center was the fire-rated "Shaftwall" made of steel studs and gypsum wallboard which has since completely replaced block masonry in high-rise office buildings. To avoid objectionable accelerations during high winds, viscoelastic dampers were installed between the exterior columns and the ends of the bottom chords of the floor trusses. The directions, velocities, and other characteristics of wind gusts were obtained from several sources and checked by wind-tunnel tests. Acceptable levels of horizontal acceleration were determined by comprehensive human-sensitivity tests. Skilling, Helle, Christiansen, Robertson were the structural engineers. The first tenants moved into the north tower in December 1970, and the construction was completed in 1973.

Sears Tower[C51,C64] is currently the world's tallest building, reaching to a height of 1450 ft (442 m) above the street. It contains 109 floors and encloses 3.9 million gross ft^2 (362,000 m^2) of office space. The owner—Sears, Roebuck & Co.—required large floor areas for their own operations but smaller areas for rental purposes. Thus a modular approach illustrated in Fig. 1.2 was adopted. The basic shape is composed of nine areas 75 ft (22.9 m) square, for an overall floor dimension 225 ft (68.6 m) square. Two of the nine constituent tubes are terminated at the 50th floor, two more at the 66th, and three at the 90th, creating a variety of floor shapes ranging from 41,000 to 12,000 ft^2 (3800 to 1100 m^2) in gross area. The structure acts as a vertical cantilever fixed at the ground in resisting wind loads. The walls of the nine tubes bundled together are composed of columns 15 ft (4.6 m) on centers and deep beams at each floor. Every two adjacent tubes share one set of columns and beams. All beam-column connections are welded. Trussed levels with diagonals between columns are provided at three intermediate mechanical levels, two of them immediately below the setbacks at the 66th and 90th floors. The beams are 42- and columns 39-in-deep (1.1- and 0.99-m) built-up I sections, with the flange width and thickness decreasing with increasing height. A total of 76,000 tons (69,000 t)

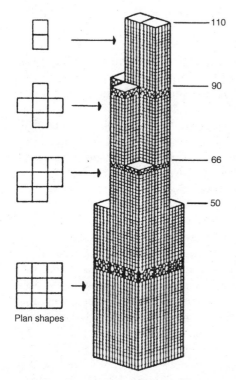

110

90

66

50

Plan shapes

Figure 1.2 Sears Tower schematics.[C64]

of A36, A572, and A588 steel was used in the project. Except for column splices, all field connections were bolted. The floors are supported on one-way 40-in-deep (1.0 m) trusses spanning 75 ft (23 m) and spaced at 15 ft (4.6 m). Each truss frames directly into a column. The span direction is alternated every six floors to equalize the gravity loads on columns. The floor slabs of 2.5-in (63-mm) lightweight concrete cast on a 3-in (76-mm) steel deck span the 15 ft (4.6 m) between the trusses. Composite action between the concrete and the steel deck relies on bond augmented by embossments in the steel deck, and that between the slab and the supporting trusses is assured by stud connectors welded through the deck. The design of the studs was based on extensive tests involving push-off specimens, simple and multiple-span slabs, and a full-scale slab-deck-truss assembly. The building, designed by the Chicago office of Skidmore, Owings & Merrill, was completed in 1974.

The 22-story Control Data Building[C48,M21] in Houston, designed by F. R. Khan and his staff at the Chicago office of Skidmore, Owings & Merrill, was the first building constructed with composite exterior framing. Built in 1969, it is an office building 180 × 90 ft (55 × 27 m) in plan. The frame has exterior composite columns spaced 10 ft (3 m) on centers containing rolled-steel sections W8 × 35 that served as erection columns. The steel frame was erected 8 stories ahead of concrete. The normal-weight 4-ksi (28-MPa) concrete included precast exterior cladding and cast-in-place fill for spandrels and exterior

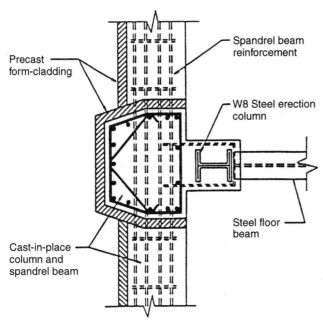

Figure 1.3 Control Data Building—typical exterior column.[M21]

columns. Typical exterior columns, shown in Fig. 1.3, measure 31 × 22 in (0.8 × 0.5 m) outside the erection column. The encasement of the erection column is 12 × 11 in (0.3 × 0.3 m). Temporary bracing was provided to stabilize the erection frame. The exterior composite frame carries the entire wind load in both orthogonal directions. A typical spandrel beam is 21 in (0.5 m) wide and 5 ft (1.5 m) deep. The floor beams, located at each exterior column, are W18 × 50 rolled sections of A36 steel spanning 35 ft (11 m) between the exterior wall and an interior core. Three-inch lightweight concrete slab is supported on 20-gage metal deck $1\frac{7}{8}$ in deep (48 mm). The interior core columns vary from W12 × 40 at the roof to W14 × 246 at the ground floor and are of 50-ksi (345-MPa) steel. The building is 303 ft (92 m) high and is supported on a 4-ft 6-in–thick (1.4-m) mat.

The 772-ft-high (235-m) 57-story IDS Center[C49] in Minneapolis completed in 1972 was another early user of exterior composite columns. Its octagonal plan with serrated edges along the four diagonal sides (Fig. 1.4) resulted in 32 corner offices per floor. The structural system, designed by New York City consulting engineers Severud-Perrone-Sturm-Conlin-Bandel, consists of perimeter columns, concrete core, column-free steel framing spanning between the core and the perimeter columns, and two-story outrigger trusses located at three widely separated levels along the height of the building. The columns are W14 sections embedded in 5-ksi (34-MPa) concrete. The core is a vertical concrete box with two 12-in-thick (0.3-m) flanges and five 18-in-thick (0.46-m) webs. The flanges are penetrated by doorways to the elevators so

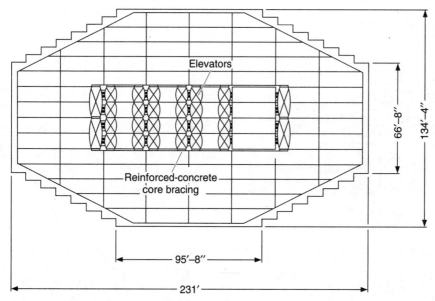

Figure 1.4   IDS Center floor plan.[C49]

that in plan the core resembles five wide-flange sections 38 ft (12 m) deep with 17-ft-long (5-m) flanges (Fig. 1.4). Steel channels 12 and 18 in (0.3 and 0.46 m) deep are embedded in the walls of the core. The steel framing includes 3-ft-deep (0.9-m) trusses spaced 29 ft (8.8 m) on centers and filler beams that support composite flooring. The outrigger trusses are located at the 9th and 10th floors, the 27th and 28th floors, and the top two floors. The diagonals are 3-ft-deep (0.9-m) 1-ft-wide (0.3-m) plate girders. During construction, a 10-story lead was maintained by the steel crews over the concrete crews. The steel workers braced the core channels with $10 \times {}^3\!/_8$-in (254 × 10-mm) diagonals for stability prior to placement of concrete.

1.3.2   The decade of the 1980s

Rising to a height of 1000 ft (305 m) the 75-story Texas Commerce Tower[C61,C62] in Houston was, when completed in 1982, the tallest composite building in the world and the tallest building outside Chicago and New York. The structure, designed by CBM Engineers, Inc., of Houston, is 160 ft (49 m) square with one corner chamfered at 45° to create an 85-ft (26-m) column-free fifth side of steel girders and dual-pane glass (Fig. 1.5). The exterior structure of the building is a composite system made of cast-in-place spandrels 4 ft (1.2 m) deep and columns spaced 10 ft (3 m) on center on all sides except the front face of 85 ft. The exterior columns were constructed with steel erection columns embedded in cast-in-place concrete. The missing 85-ft (26-m) fifth side of the exterior tube was replaced with an interior concrete shear wall connected to the exteri-

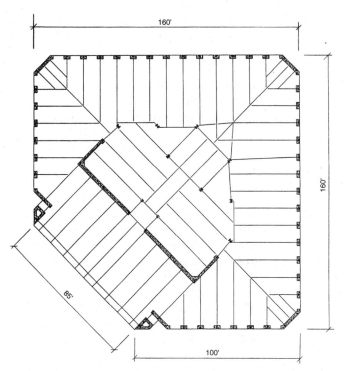

Figure 1.5 Texas Commerce Plaza—typical floor framing plan.

or tube with very stiff link beams embedded in the floors. The exterior rup-tured tube and the interior shear wall were assigned to resist the wind loads. The steel girders on the 85-ft side respond to wind loading as secondary stiff-ness elements above the 60th floor. The interior columns and floor framing are of structural steel. They support composite concrete slabs placed on 2-in-deep (5-cm) metal decks. The tower is supported on a 216-ft (66-m) square 10-ft-thick (3-m) foundation mat chamfered in the same manner as the plan of the building. The mat rests on stiff clay 63 ft (19 m) below the street level. The perimeter composite framing was constructed with custom-built jump forms and concrete pumped to record heights. The contractor maintained a 3-day cycle per floor. The bare steel frame was allowed to proceed 12 floors ahead of the embedment in concrete. It was stabilized by temporary steel bracing that was moved upward with the steel frame.

The first three floors of the 52-story Gulf Tower[C65,M21] in Houston are framed in steel since they have atypical layout to accommodate a lobby, an auditorium, and other service spaces. But from the fourth level up, the perimeter columns are steel wide-flange sections encased in concrete with the remainder of the framing in steel. According to the structural engineers Walter P. Moore and Associates of Houston, the extra material cost of the steel base was less than the added time and forming cost would have been had the composite columns started at the ground level. The exterior composite columns are spaced 10 ft on centers while the spacing of the steel columns at the base is 20 ft. A steel box girder 5 ft (1.5 m) deep and 20 in (510 mm) wide transfers the loads from the composite columns to the steel base. The 725-ft (221-m) structure was topped out in 1982 just 15 months after the ground-breaking ceremonies. Concrete placement kept up with steel erection following it by 8 to 10 stories. Because of setbacks at the upper levels, steel erection was slowed down so that concrete was only a couple of floors behind by the time the steel frame was topped out. The tower's basically square plan was modified to provide 10 corner offices per floor (Fig. 1.6). The building, completed in 1983, is clad with 3200 white granite panels 1.25 in (30 mm) thick, imported from Italy, alternating with bands of reflective glass.

The 72-story 921-ft-tall (281-m) InterFirst Plaza Tower[C62,C66,C68,C71,C73,C90,M21] at Dallas Main Center, with gleaming glass exterior uninterrupted by perimeter columns or X bracing, has a plan which maximizes the number of corner offices. The building is supported on 16 composite columns, spaced at 30 ft (9.1 m) in two orthogonal directions, with centers located 20 ft (6.1 m) inside the glass line (Fig. 1.7). This 20-ft distance between the columns and the perimeter glass allowed for a continuous band of offices with uninterrupted views. To compensate for the loss of bending rigidity, all loads are transferred to the ground through the 16 composite columns interconnected with a seven-story two-way grid of Vierendeel trusses spanning 120 and 150 ft (36.6 and 45.7 m). The composite columns, made with 10-ksi (69-MPa) concrete,

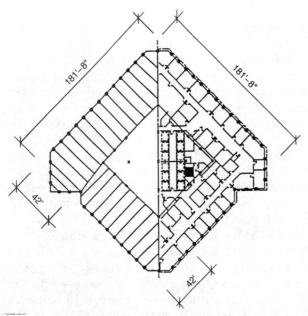

Figure 1.6 Gulf Tower—structural and architectural floor plan.[M21]

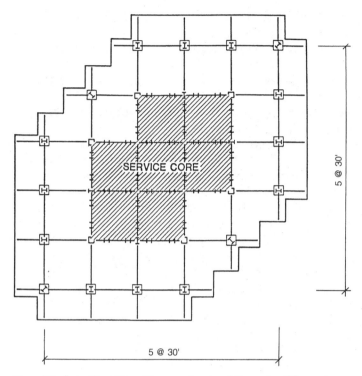

Figure 1.7 InterFirst Plaza Tower—structural floor plan.[C68]

vary in size from 5 to 7 ft (1.5 to 2.1 m) square and are reinforced with 75-ksi (517-MPa) reinforcing bars and 50-ksi (345-MPa) W36 shapes. The concrete encasement of the wide-flange shapes ends at the 62nd floor level. The seven-story truss system begins at the fifth level, supporting the core verticals and the elevators. One of the unusual features of the tower is its slenderness: The ratio of the height to structural width of the InterFirst Plaza Tower is 7:1. The steel frame was topped out in July 1984 and the construction completed in 1985. The structural engineers were LeMessurier Assoc./SCI of Cambridge, Mass., in a joint venture with Brockette & Associates of Dallas, Tex.

The Singapore Treasury Building[C62,C72] is a cylindrical 52-story office tower at the center of Singapore. Rising to a height of 751 ft (229 m) above grade, it was for a time the tallest building in Asia. The tower's concrete core is used to its limit as the only element carrying vertical gravity loads and lateral wind loads. Elevators, stairs, and sanitary facilities are contained within a cylindrical concrete core 82 ft (25 m) in outside diameter with a wall 39.4 in (1.0 m) thick. With only four openings per floor, the core wall has close to ideal shear rigidity. Floors cantilever 38.5 ft (11.7 m) to a cylindrical exterior glass and aluminum wall. The floor is supported on sixteen 4-ft-deep (1.2-m) radial cantilever plate girders welded at their inner ends to steel columns which were subsequently embedded in the concrete core wall. During steel erection, the plate girders were provided with temporary exterior supports. Because there are no exterior columns, all gravity loads are carried on the concrete core wall, thus increasing its overturning resistance to make the 52-story height feasible. The steel advanced eight stories above the concrete core wall, which was cast in forms designed to be jumped vertically through temporary openings in the steel floor. This sequence was chosen to provide the fastest erection with the most foolproof connections of steel to the core. The structural design was by LeMessurier Assoc./SCI of Cambridge and Ove Arup & Partners of Singapore. The building was completed in 1986.

A monumental granite-clad arch entry and a flamboyant rooftop are the hallmarks of the Momentum Place[C74,C75,C78,M21] completed in Dallas in 1988. The 60-story office tower has an atrium banking hall in its six-story podium, a semicircular arch roof at the 26th floor, and quarter-circle vaulted skylights at the 50th, where the shape of the plan changes from rectangular to cruciform. On top is a cross-vaulted arch clad in copper. The structural engineer for the project, the Datum/Moore Partnership of Dallas, carried out a detailed analysis of six floor and four wind framing systems. The final scheme has punched concrete shear walls at the four corners of the rectangular floor plan (Fig. 1.8), steel spandrels and four composite columns between the shear walls on each side of the building, and composite steel and concrete beams for the floor fram-

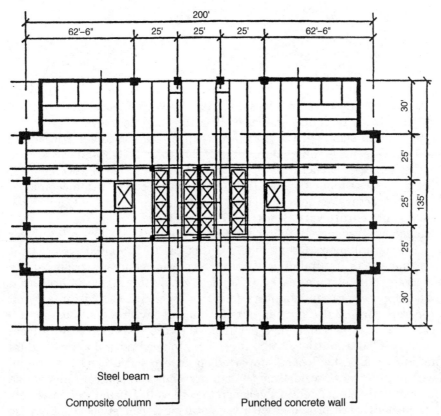

Figure 1.8 Momentum Place—typical floor plan for levels 30 to 50.[M21]

ing. The core is framed in steel. Above the 50th level all framing is in steel. The shear walls are 18 in (0.46 m) thick and are reinforced with no. 18 bars at the base and no. 7 bars at the top. The concrete strength in the walls varies from 7.5 ksi at the base to 5 ksi at the top (52 to 35 MPa). Window openings in the walls allow for 18-in-square (0.46-m) columns 5 ft (1.5 m) on centers and 4-ft 6-in-deep (1.4-m) spandrel beams. The exterior composite columns are 32 in (0.81 m) square including a W14 × 61 erection column and have the same concrete strength as the shear walls. The interior columns at the base of the core are built-up 28-in-square (0.71-m) box sections of A572 grade 42 steel. W14 rolled shapes replace the box sections above the 32d level. The shear walls were designed to work integrally with the perimeter composite steel frame to resist lateral forces. The building rises to a height of 787 ft (240 m) above the street.

For the 1209-ft (369-m) Bank of China[C80,C90,M21] in Hong Kong, of structural design by Leslie E. Robertson Associates of New York, the design floor and wind loads were twice those required by the New York City building code and the design seismic loads four times those required in Los Angeles. The building, unique by its geometry (Fig. 1.9), was topped out on Aug. 8, 1988. Its

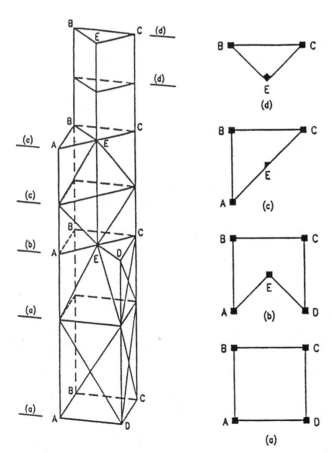

Figure 1.9   Bank of China schematics.[M21]

160-ft-square (49-m) floor at the base is divided by diagonals into four quad-rant triangles. Moving up the building, one quadrant tapers off at the 25th, another at the 38th, and the third at the 51st story. The structure is support-ed on four huge composite corner columns and a fifth column starting at the 25th floor. The exterior walls are giant vertical planar trusses consisting of the five columns and composite diagonals extending over 12 floors. The resulting structure is a vertical 73-story space truss that provides the needed resistance to horizontal loads. Almost the entire gravity load is transmitted through the diagonals to the four corner columns. The concrete of the compos-ite corner columns provides a simple connection between the vertical planar trusses eliminating any need for complex out-of-plane connections. The composite columns were made with 8-ksi (55-MPa) concrete and bundled 2-in (50-mm) reinforcing bars. The diagonals are box members, from 15×39 in (0.4×1.0 m) to 16×59 in (0.4×1.5 m), fabricated from four steel plates and filled with concrete to increase their stiffness. The structure is supported on 30-ft-diameter (9-m) hand-dug caissons located under the corner columns.

1.3.3   Early 1990s

Two Union Square[C76,C81] in Seattle combines two innovating features: 10-ft-diameter (3-m) composite pipe columns and 19-ksi (131-MPa) concrete. The 58-story 140×190-ft office building of irregular floor plan (Fig. 1.10), designed by Seattle-based structural engineer Skilling Ward Magnusson Barkshire Inc., has four of these huge columns at the corners of its core. Fourteen more composite pipe columns of smaller diameter are placed along the periphery of the building to support gravity loads. The steel pipes provid-ed erection steel and replaced forms as well as vertical bars and horizontal ties for the high-strength concrete. There are no reinforcing bars in the pipe columns. The pipes are connected to the concrete with studs welded to the pipes' interior surfaces. The core carries about 40 percent of the gravity loads of the building and provides resistance to sway and to lateral loads. The space between the core and the widely spaced perimeter columns is column-free. The construction of Two Union Square was completed in 1990. Other structural systems combining large-diameter composite pipes with column-free space between the core and the exterior shell were used in several build-ings in Seattle. The 44-story 110×170-ft Pacific First Center[C81] includes eight 7.5-ft-diameter (2.3-m) pipe columns at the building's core and perime-ter columns a maximum of 2.5 ft (0.76 m) in diameter, both filled with 19-ksi concrete (Fig. 1.11). Yet another example is the 62-story 90×160-ft Gateway Tower[C81] (Fig. 1.12) in which 9-ft (2.7-m) pipe columns exposed at the four corners of the inner square of the hexagon are tied together with 10-story-high X braces. The larger cross section of the widely spaced columns permit-ted the use of 11-ksi concrete.

For the 794-ft-high (242-m) Mellon Bank Center[C82,C85] in Philadelphia the decision to use a composite structural system was made about halfway through the design process. Wind-tunnel tests on an early steel design showed

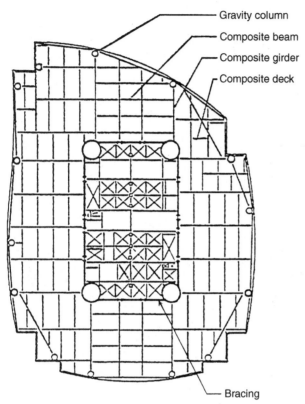

Gravity column
Composite beam
Composite girder
Composite deck
Bracing

Figure 1.10 Two Union Square floor plan.[C81] (*© 1986, Skilling Ward Magnusson Barkshire Inc., all rights reserved; used with permission.*)

that the cross-wind structural response was 50 percent higher than allowed by the code. Consequently, stiffening of the building structure was required. The alternative selected added concrete to the perimeter columns and combined concrete and steel in the core. Because of the building's proximity to the historic City Hall, the building has a 10-story granite-clad base. An aluminum-and-glass tower with corner cutouts starts above the base and continues to the roof. The tower is topped with a protruding cornice and a steel-framed pyramid hat that conceals the cooling towers. Total wind and gravity forces of the building are carried by the core between the sixth floor and the building's base four levels below grade. A massive vertical supertruss transfers the loads to the four corners of the core. In the tower above the base the lateral system is formed by composite perimeter columns spaced 9-ft 8-in (2.95 m) on centers, forming a perimeter tube. The steel section in the perimeter columns ranged from W14 × 398 at the base to W24 × 76 near the top. The Office of Irwin G. Cantor of New York City was the structural engineer on the project. Mellon Bank Center, completed in 1991, was the first tall building in the northeast designed to take full advantage of composite columns.

To accommodate efficiently the complicated geometry (Fig. 1.13) of

Composite girder

Composite deck

Gravity columns

Composite beam

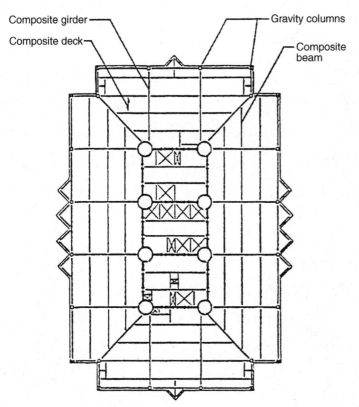

Figure 1.11 Pacific First Center floor plan.[C81]

Minneapolis' 775-ft (236-m) tower called First Bank Place,[C86] CBM Engineers, Inc., of Houston decided to use a cruciform spine including four massive steel-and-concrete composite supercolumns which rise uninterrupted through the tower's 53 stories (Fig. 1.14). The supercolumns, located in the middle of each face of the tower, are 75 ft^2 (7 m^2) in plan at the base and 50 ft^2 (4.6 m^2) near the top. To impart to the tower the necessary torsional rigidity, perimeter bracing was needed. Two complementary systems were provided: vertical trusses with six-story diagonals on the east and west faces of the building, and three horizontal Vierendeel bandages on the other two faces where the presence of diagonals was considered objectionable. The Vierendeels, three stories high, were placed where the building profile changed. Building these three floors required an unusual construction procedure using temporary steel columns to support the bandages, adjacent floor framing, and floor decking during erection. The temporary columns were removed before concrete was poured for the floor slab immediately above. The tower's finishing touch is a 45-ft-tall (13.7-m) cantilevered crown constructed of steel frame with glass infill. The purpose of the crown is to conceal antennas. The building was completed in 1992.

Composite beam ─
Composite deck ─
Gravity columns
Composite girder

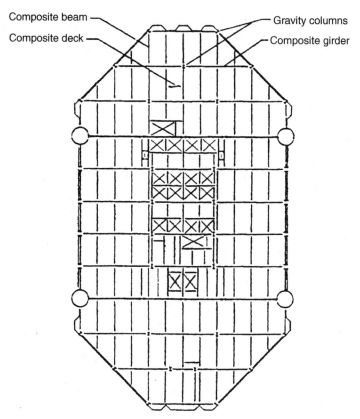

Figure 1.12 Gateway Tower floor plan.[C81]

The NationsBank Tower in Atlanta[C84,C87,C88] opened for occupancy early in 1992. A composite structure topped with an open steel frame cone that supports a 90-ft (27-m) spire of steel and fiberglass provides 57 stories above the ground for office space and five basements for parking and assembly occupancy. The corners of the building have been serrated (Fig. 1.15) to create more corner office space. The tower, including the spire, rises 1000 ft (300 m) above the surrounding terrain. A structural system composed of twelve composite supercolumns, one at each corner of a rectangular core and two on each side of the building, linked by moment-connected girders and diagonal bracing, provides a completely column-free rentable space above ground. The supercolumns include W14 × 808 rolled sections, the heaviest rolled in the United States. The concrete strength in the supercolumns varies from 10 ksi (69 MPa) at the lower levels to 7 ksi (48 MPa) at the upper levels. Typical floor framing consists of W18 composite beams spanning from the core to the perimeter. A 5¼-in-thick (133-mm) slab, including 2-in (51-mm) metal deck, spans the distance between the floor beams. The core and the perimeter supercolumns are tied together with eight trusses between the 56th and 59th

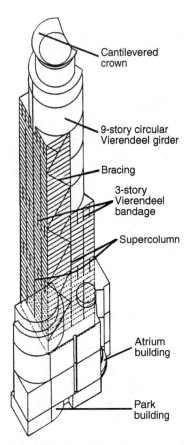

Cantilevered crown

9-story circular Vierendeel girder

Bracing

3-story Vierendeel bandage

Supercolumn

Atrium building

Park building

Figure 1.13 First Bank Place schematics.[C86]

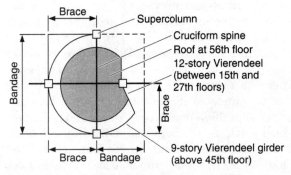

Brace

Supercolumn

Cruciform spine

Roof at 56th floor

12-story Vierendeel (between 15th and 27th floors)

Bandage

Brace

Brace   Bandage

9-story Vierendeel girder (above 45th floor)

Figure 1.14 First Bank Place Tower floor plan.[C86]

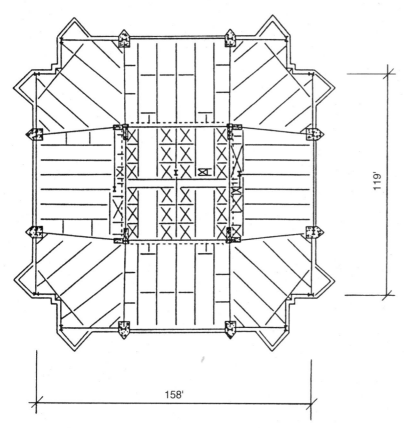

119'

158'

Figure 1.15 NationsBank Plaza—typical floor plan.[C88]

floors. The basement levels are of flat-slab concrete construction. The structure was designed by CBM Engineers, Inc., of Houston.

1.4 SI Equivalents

The conventional system of units was adopted for this book because it is expected to remain for several years by far the most commonly used system in the design of buildings in the United States. However, in view of the metric conversion that has been mandated for all federal procurement, grants, and business-related activities by the Executive Order of July 25, 1991, and in view of the progress of metrication in many U.S. industries, SI equivalents are listed in parentheses throughout the text except in design examples. To retain clarity, each design example is solely in conventional units, with the SI equivalents listed only in the statement of the problem. SI equivalents[G31A,G83A,G90] for conventional units used in this book are listed in Table 1.1 on page 1.36.

TABLE 1.1   Metric Conversion Factors*

Quantity	C	F[†]	M
Area	in²	**645.16**	mm²
	ft²	**0.092 903 04**	m²
	acre	4046.856	m²
Bending moment	in-kip	0.112 985	kN · m
	ft-kip	1.355 82	kN · m
Density	lb/ft³	16.018 5	kg/m³
Force	lb	4.448 22	N
	kip	4.448 22	kN
Length	in	**25.4**	mm
	ft	**0.3048**	m
	mile	**1.609 344**	km
Mass	lb	0.453 592	kg
	kip	0.453 592	t
	ton	0.907 184	t
Mass per unit area	lb/ft²	4.882 43	kg/m²
Mass per unit length	lb/ft	1.488 16	kg/m
Moment of inertia	in⁴	416,231	mm⁴
Pressure	lb/ft²	0.047 880 3	kPa
Stress, modulus of elasticity	lb/in²	6.894 76	kPa
	kip/in²	6.894 76	MPa
Velocity	m/h	**1.609 344**	km/h
Volume	in³	**16.387 064**	cm³
	yd³	0.764 555	m³
Work	yd³/h	0.764 555	m³/h

*To convert from conventional (C) to metric (M) units, multiply the number in conventional units by conversion factor F.

†Exact numbers are shown bold.

2

Composite Systems

2.1 Materials

Composite construction is characterized by interactive behavior between structural steel and concrete components designed to use the best load-resisting characteristics of each material. The components may be discrete isolated elements which form a portion of a structural system. They may also be structural steel and/or concrete subsystems which together resist the entire set of loads imposed on the structure. The resulting elements and composite systems generally represent a high order of efficiency in resisting the applied loads and consequently are cost-effective.

The most important characteristics of *structural steel* are high strength, high modulus of elasticity, and high ductility, which result in small size members, long clear spans, and adaptability in fabrication and use. Other major advantages relate to steel's low weight per square foot of a building, dimensional stability, ease of modification, and high speed of erection, the last resulting from the prefabrication of members and connections. The role of structural steel in composite construction is therefore oriented toward the following:

Floor framing where the ability to span long column-free areas and the potential for future modification of structural elements is required.

Gravity columns to reduce the cross-sectional area requirements for columns, allowing more column-free rentable floor space, and as erection elements to speed construction.

Areas of high seismic activity where high ductility and low building mass are distinct advantages.

Structural steel sections used in composite construction include the entire catalog of rolled shapes, structural pipe, square and rectangular tubing, built-up girders, fabricated trusses, and prefabricated joists. The most frequently used rolled shapes are wide-flange sections, channels, angles, and tees. ASTM grades A36 and A572 with yield stress of 36 and 50 ksi (248 and 345 MPa), respectively, and other higher-strength steels are in common use. A shift is in progress toward 50-ksi (345-MPa) strength as the primary steel for composite building construction.

Structural concrete has excellent fire-resistive properties, high inherent mass, and relatively low material cost. It can be molded into any shape to produce complex structural and architectural forms, including precasting into efficient structural shapes. The use of concrete in composite construction is therefore advantageous in the following applications:

Floor slabs where the insulating properties of concrete provide the required fire and acoustical separation between habitable spaces; a concrete floor slab forms a rigid horizontal diaphragm, lending stability to the building system while distributing wind and seismic shears to the lateral load resisting elements.

Columns where concrete compressive strength is most effectively utilized and material costs are minimized.

Exterior framed tube and rigid moment-resisting frame systems where properly reinforced beam-column joints can be utilized to efficiently resist imposed lateral loads. Exterior concrete frame systems may be exposed without any additional protection to completely define the architectural character of the building.

Vertical core wall lateral and gravity load-resisting systems utilizing the versatility of concrete to be shaped into any required form.

The choice of concrete for composite building construction is based primarily on compressive strength, modulus of elasticity, and unit weight. Lightweight concrete with a unit weight of 110 lb/ft^3 (1.76 t/m^3) is often used in floor slab construction to keep down the overall weight of the structure and to reduce or eliminate shoring requirements. It is a better insulator than normal-weight concrete, which weighs 145 lb/ft^3 (2.32 t/m^3) and can therefore provide the required fire separation between floors with thinner slabs. Heavily loaded multistory building columns, shear walls, and other lateral load-resisting elements designed with concrete compressive strength from 4 up to 10 ksi (30 up to 70 MPa) are common. Concrete-filled composite steel pipe columns with concrete compressive strengths up to 19 ksi (130 MPa) have been used recently.

The connection between the two structural materials, namely, steel and concrete, in composite construction of individual members is crucial. Many types of connectors including steel studs, channels, angles, bars, spirals, high-strength bolts, and hooked bars transferring the shear along steel-concrete interfaces have been used in the past for this purpose. The headed steel stud is by far the most common type of shear connector today. Shear studs are easily welded through the steel deck or directly to the surface of any steel member by the use of a stud welding gun.

Formed steel deck or profiled steel sheeting supporting fresh concrete is an integral component in many composite systems and is used nearly exclusively in one form or another in steel-framed composite floor systems in the United States. Steel deck can be used as permanent formwork for a conventionally reinforced concrete slab or may itself act compositely with the concrete slab as the positive bending tension reinforcement. In the latter case, the shear connection between the deck and the concrete is provided through lugs, ridges, corrugations, or embossments formed in the profile of the steel sheet to augment the natural bond between the two materials (Fig. 2.1). Composite steel deck slabs are effective in reducing the overall structural depth, increasing floor load capacity, and improving horizontal diaphragm action. Typically, the steel deck is of trapezoidal profile with relatively wide flutes suitable for through-deck

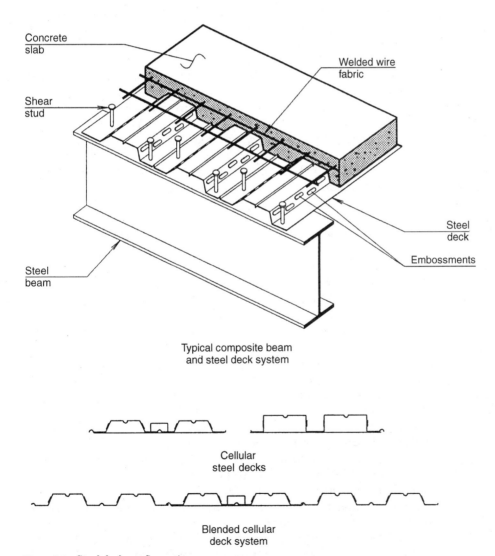

Typical composite beam
and steel deck system

Cellular
steel decks

Blended cellular
deck system

Figure 2.1 Steel deck configurations.

welding of shear studs to the steel beams. Steel decking may also include closed cells which accommodate floor electrification lines, communications and computer conduits, and power distribution. Cellular deck panels may be blended with noncellular panels as part of the total floor system design.

2.2 Loading

The design of a composite member must take into account the joint behavior of steel and concrete materials which is characterized by time-dependent interaction including the effects of resistance to temporary construction loads, load sharing, and deformation compatibility.[D51] Further changes in load sharing are caused by creep and shrinkage of concrete. Similarly, the behavior of entire systems composed of composite members, such as a concrete-encased composite steel moment-resisting frame or framed tube lateral load-resisting systems, is also sensitive to the history of load application.

Dead loads include the weight of all permanent elements including steel framing, concrete walls and columns, concrete encasement, floor slabs, steel deck, etc. Composite beam and truss design may involve precambering for all or a portion of the calculated dead-load deflection to ensure construction of reasonably level floors. The trend toward frequent application of higher-strength steels in composite construction based on little or no material cost premium over lower-grade steels has produced lighter, more flexible members that made cambering a more common requirement.

Live loads encompass all loads that are expected to change after application to the completed structure. Live loads include some architectural finishes, furniture, equipment and services of other trades, partitions, and occupancy loadings.

The presence or absence of shoring during construction has a direct relationship to the dead- and live-load sharing between composite materials. In the past, composite floor framing systems were often designed as shored to prevent high dead-load bending stresses in the steel member due to the weight of steel and fresh concrete. Such high stresses are typical of unshored construction. However, experiments on composite beams demonstrated that significant stress redistribution takes place in the composite section as the ultimate limit state is approached. The ultimate strength of the composite cross section is independent of the presence or absence of shoring during construction. As a result, currently the entire load is assumed to act on the full composite section even in allowable stress design. On the other hand, dead-load deflection estimates for unshored construction must be based on the stiffness $E_s I_s$ of the steel section alone. The strength design criteria require consideration of one additional limit state for composite beams: safety of the steel beam alone subjected to construction loading. It should also be noted that composite beam and truss systems for buildings are today primarily of unshored design, thus further enhancing the economy of these floor systems.

The use of load factors specified in ASCE 7-93[G88] is recommended. Load factors required by AISC Load and Resistance Factor Design[D91] are essentially the same. Also essentially the same are alternative load factors included in the new Appendix C of the Building Code Requirements for Reinforced Concrete.[D97, 100] The new Appendix C was developed "to facilitate the proportioning of building structures that include members made of materials other than concrete."

2.3 Composite Floor Systems

Composite floor systems[C54,D28,D47,D64,M7,M8] typically involve simply supported structural steel beams, joists, girders, or trusses linked by shear connectors with a concrete floor slab to form an effective T beam resisting primarily gravity loads by bending. The versatility of the system results from the inherent strength of the concrete floor component in compression and the ability of the steel member to span long distances. Composite floor systems are advantageous in reducing material cost, on-site labor, and construction time. They also result in simple and repetitive connection details, reduced structural depth and consequent efficient use of interstitial ceiling space, and lower building mass, which is important in zones of high seismicity. When a composite floor framing member is combined with a composite steel deck and concrete floor slab, an extremely efficient system is the result. The composite action of the beam or truss element is effected by direct welding of shear studs through the steel deck while the composite action of the steel deck as flexural reinforcement for the concrete slab itself results from side embossments incorporated into the steel-sheet profile. The slab-and-beam arrangement typical in composite floor systems produces a rigid horizontal diaphragm that provides stability to the overall building system while distributing wind and seismic shears to the lateral load-resisting elements.

2.3.1 Floor slabs

The slab elements of a composite floor system may take the form of a flat soffit reinforced concrete slab, precast-concrete planks or floor panels with a cast-in-place topping, or profiled steel deck with cast-in-place concrete (Fig. 2.2).

Early composite floor systems involved concrete-encased steel beams supporting a formed reinforced concrete slab spanning between the supporting beams. The concrete encasement of the steel beam was eliminated with the development of economical lightweight sprayed-on fireproofing. The reinforcement for the slab in the direction perpendicular to the beam span is determined through conventional continuous reinforced concrete design for the calculated gravity-load moments. Light slab reinforcement is placed parallel to the beam span to control shrinkage and thermal cracking.

To eliminate the cost and additional construction time involved in temporary formwork for the slab, precast-concrete planks or steel deck may be used effectively as permanent formwork which provides an effective working platform for the construction trades. Precast, prestressed hollow-core concrete planks spanning between the steel floor beams are well suited for jobs where a repetitive organization of beam spacings allows for effective prefabrication

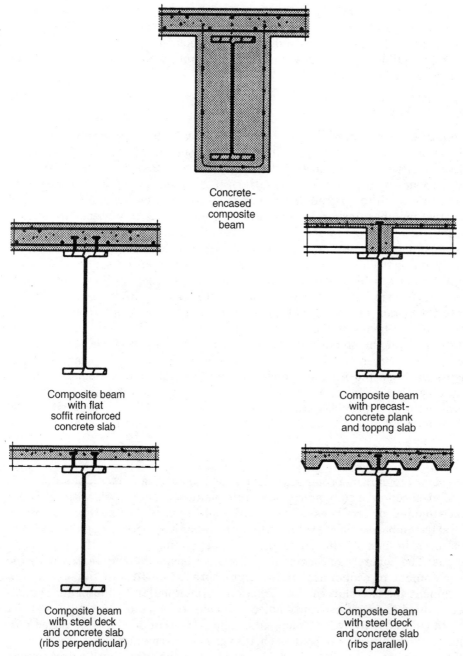

Figure 2.2   Composite-beam systems.

of the planks. Two to three inches (51 to 76 mm) of concrete is cast atop the planks to provide an effective diaphragm as well as a level, continuous floor surface. The concrete topping must be reinforced, usually with welded-wire fabric, to control cracking. Composite design of the steel floor beams requires that the topping extends down to the surface of the steel beams and the shear studs extend up into the topping above the hollow concrete planks.

Today, the most common arrangement found in composite floor systems is a rolled or built-up steel beam connected to a formed steel deck and a concrete slab. The steel deck corrugations may be oriented parallel or perpendicular to the composite beam span and either the slab may be composite with the steel deck or the steel deck may serve only as the formwork for the slab. For light office use and residential floors, welded-wire fabric reinforcement is used to control cracking of the concrete slab. The steel deck provides tension reinforcement for the slab, usually based on the assumption that the deck consists of a series of simply supported spans. For heavily loaded storage or mechanical area, i.e., floors with greater than 200 lb/ft^2 (10 kN/m^2) live-load allowance, bar reinforcement may be placed in the deck flutes as well as near the top of the slab. The design of such a slab follows conventional reinforced concrete design. The steel deck is chosen such that no temporary shoring is required. Strength and deflections are calculated ignoring the contribution from the deck itself.

The following are some considerations in designing and specifying steel decking for floor slabs:

1. Steel deck slabs preferably are designed as unshored. Two- and three-inch-deep (51- and 76-mm) deck profiles are available in a variety of deck gages. For 16-gage and thicker decks, through-deck stud welding may not be possible, requiring prepunched holes in the deck. The resulting premiums for fabricating and erecting the deck are usually prohibitive. In addition, grout loss through the holes can result in voids surrounding the shear studs and consequent loss of composite action. Twenty-two-gage and thinner decks are difficult to attach reliably to steel framing so that the diaphragm stiffness is reduced.

2. The concrete thickness above the top of the steel deck is normally controlled by fire separation and acoustical requirements. The choice of either lightweight or normal-weight concrete to satisfy these requirements depends upon economic considerations which vary regionally and nationally. Adequate concrete above the top of the metal deck is necessary to encase and fully develop the capacity of the shear studs. AISC requires that shear connectors extend not less than $1\frac{1}{2}$ in (38 mm) above the top of the steel deck, and not less than 2 in (51 mm) of concrete cover above the top of the deck is allowed for composite construction.

2.3.2 Beams and girders

Steel and concrete composite beams may be formed by either completely encasing a steel member in concrete, with the composite action depending upon the natural bond between the steel and concrete, or by connecting the

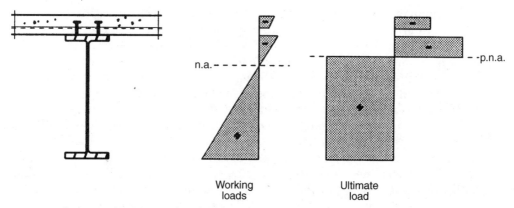

Figure 2.3 Composite-beam stress distributions.

concrete floor to the top flange of the steel framing member by shear connectors (Fig. 2.2). The stress distributions on a composite section at working and ultimate loads are shown in Fig. 2.3. As the top flange of the steel section is normally near the neutral axis and consequently lightly stressed, a number of built-up or hybrid composite beam schemes have been proposed in an attempt to use the structural steel more efficiently (Fig. 2.4). Hybrid beams fabricated from 36 ksi yield (248 MPa) top flange steel and 50 ksi (345 MPa) yield bottom flange steel are possible. Also, built-up composite-beam or tapered-flange-beam schemes more fully utilize the structural steel material. In all of these cases, however, significant fabrication costs tend to offset the relative material efficiency. In addition, a relatively wide and reasonably thick top flange must be provided for proper and effective shear stud installation.

A prismatic composite steel beam has two basic disadvantages over other types of composite floor framing types. One, the member must be designed for the maximum bending moment near midspan and thus is understressed at all other sections along the span and, two, building services ductwork and piping must pass beneath the beam or the beam must be provided with web penetrations (usually reinforced with plates or angles leading to high fabrication costs) to allow access for this equipment. For this reason, a number of composite girder forms allowing the free passage of mechanical ducts and related services through the depth of the girder have been developed. They include tapered and dapped girders, castellated beams, and stub-girder systems[D28] (Fig. 2.5). As the tapered girders are completely fabricated from plate elements or cut from rolled shapes, these composite members are frequently hybrid, with the top flange designed in lower-strength steel. Applications of tapered composite girders to office building construction are limited, as the main mechanical duct loop normally runs through the center of the lease span rather than at each end. The castellated composite beam is formed from a single rolled wide-flange steel beam cut and then reassembled by welding with the resulting increased depth and hexagonal openings. These

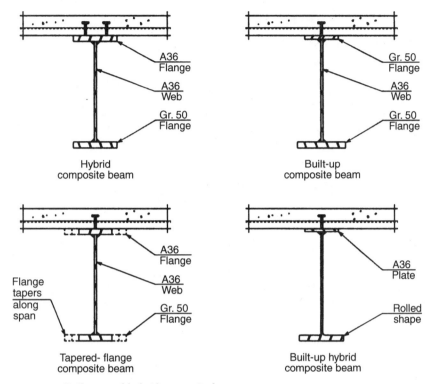

Figure 2.4 Built-up and hybrid composite beams.

members are standard shapes available by serial size and are quite common in the United Kingdom and the rest of Europe. Use in the United States is limited because of increased fabrication cost and the fact that standard castellated openings are not large enough to accommodate the large mechanical ductwork common in modern building construction. The stub-girder system involves the use of short sections of beam welded to the top flange of a continuous, heavier bottom girder member. Continuous transverse secondary beams and ducts pass through the openings formed by the beam stubs. This system has been used in many building projects but requires shored construction, which offsets some of the cost savings.

Successful composite-beam design requires consideration of various serviceability issues such as long-term (creep) deflections and floor vibrations. Of particular concern is the issue of perceptibility of occupant-induced floor vibrations. The relatively high flexural stiffness of most composite floor framing systems results in relatively low vibration amplitudes from transitory heel-drop excitations and therefore is effective in reducing perceptibility. Recent studies have shown that for short spans of less than about 25 ft (8 m) and very long spans of more than about 45 ft (14 m) composite floor framing systems perform quite well and are rarely found to transmit annoying vibra-

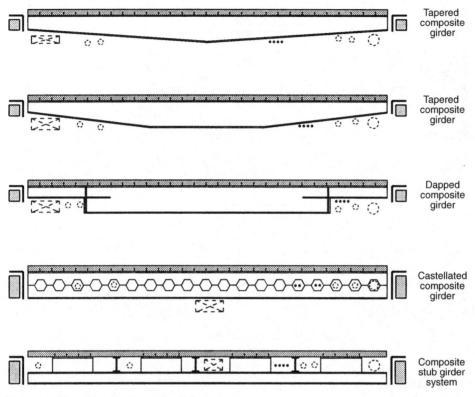

Figure 2.5 Nonprismatic composite girders.

tions to the occupants. Particular care for spans in the 30- to 35-ft (9- to 11-m) range is recommended. Anticipated damping provided by partitions, services, ceiling construction, and the structure itself should be considered in conjunction with state-of-the-art prediction models to evaluate the potential for perceptible floor vibrations.[D82,G66]

It has been suggested that serviceability characteristics may be significantly improved through the use of semirigid composite connections. A typical disposition of such a joint is shown in Fig. 2.6. The capacity of the connection to provide partial end restraint is mobilized through the addition of a bottom flange plate or angle cleat and heavier reinforcement within the concrete slab in a band centered on the steel column. For unshored construction, the initial dead-load deflection is hardly altered, but live-load deflections, and perhaps also floor vibrations, are significantly reduced through the partial end restraint. Reduced in-span positive moment results in a saving in steel tonnage. The partial end restraint may be used to shorten the effective unbraced length of the column as well. Full benefit of the system is obtained through shored construction where all loads are resisted by the semirigid composite connection. Experimental data are limited to beam-to-column flange connec-

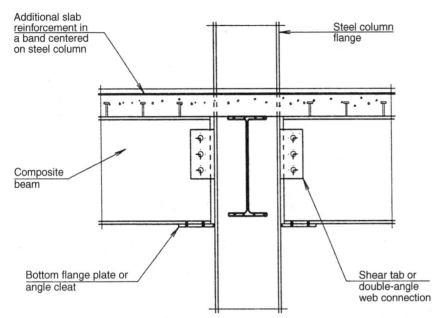

Additional slab reinforcement in a band centered on steel column

Steel column flange

Composite beam

Bottom flange plate or angle cleat

Shear tab or double-angle web connection

Figure 2.6 Semirigid composite-beam connection.[D96]

tions, although similar beam-to-column web and beam-to-girder connections are possible.[G33] Application of the system has been limited owing to the difficulty in accurately determining the moment-rotation characteristics of the joint. In addition, a continuous multispan column arrangement is required, as the connection is not recommended for unbalanced exterior and simple-span conditions.[125]

Continuous composite-beam systems over multiple supports have the advantages of reduced steel quantity and improved stiffness over simply supported composite beams. Additional slab reinforcement is placed in areas of negative moment. At the ultimate-limit state, the stress distribution in the positive-moment regions is as indicated in Fig. 2.3, with the plastic neutral axis located either in the slab, the beam top flange, or the beam web. The ultimate positive plastic moment capacity is much higher than the moment capacity over the support (Fig. 2.7). The concrete slab compressive strength is utilized in the former, but only the slab reinforcement can be counted on over the support. Consequently, with the onset of cracking in the negative-moment region, a portion of the support moment is redistributed to the midspan. The redistribution occurs at a higher rate than in continuous reinforced concrete beams as the midspan section of the continuous composite steel beam remains uncracked. Significant redistribution can be realized as long as local failure in the support region due to flange or web instability in compression is precluded. British Standard BS 5950 allows up to 40 percent redistribution of support moments depending on the section compactness and the method of

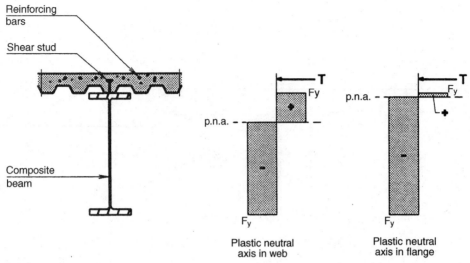

Figure 2.7 Plastic stress distribution for negative moment.

analysis used. Elastic analysis including alternate-span loading is normally employed with cracked section properties used over the end 15 percent of the span roughly corresponding to the length of the continuous beam to the inflection point. The detailed design of floor framing members is given in Chap. 3.

2.3.3 Joists and trusses

Preengineered, proprietary open-web floor joists, joist girders, and fabricated floor trusses when combined with a concrete floor slab are viable composite members. The advantages of an open-web floor framing system include increased span length and stiffness due to the greater structural depth, and ease in accommodating electrical conduits, plumbing and heating, and air-conditioning ductwork. Composite open-web joists have been used with flat soffit concrete slabs and steel deck slabs supporting concrete fill with and without shear connectors. The design for these systems is based primarily on test data. The maximum tensile force in an open-web steel joist is equal to its value at first yielding. Furthermore, the increase in the moment arm from a noncomposite to a composite joist (Fig. 2.8) is small. Thus the potential for increased efficiency due to composite action is considerably less than for other floor systems. However, the advantage of composite over noncomposite design for open-web joist floors based on increased stiffness and ductility has been demonstrated.[55,D47]

Built-up fabricated composite floor trusses[C54] combine material efficiency in relatively long-span applications with maximum flexibility for incorporating building services ductwork and piping into the ceiling cavity. The triangular

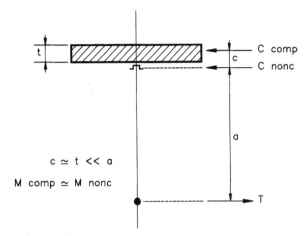

Figure 2.8 Moment resistance of open-web joists.

openings formed by web members of the truss allow the passage of large mechanical air ducts as well as other piping and electrical lines. The increased depth of the composite truss system over a standard rolled shape composite-beam system, with building services ductwork and piping passing below the beam, results in maximum material efficiency and high flexural stiffness. Generally, composite floor trusses are considered economical for floor spans in excess of 30 ft (9 m). A further requirement for floor truss systems is that the framing layout must be uniform and repetitive, resulting in relatively few types of trusses, which can be readily built in the fabrication shop using a jig. Otherwise the high level of fabrication inherent in the floor truss assemblage tends to offset the relative material efficiency. For this reason, composite floor truss systems are particularly attractive in high-rise office building applications where large column-free areas are required and floor configurations are generally repetitive over the height of the building. Figure 2.9 shows an example of a project utilizing composite floor trusses as part of an overall composite steel and concrete building frame.

Any triangulated open-web form can be used to define the geometry of the fabricated floor truss; however, the Warren truss with or without web verticals is used most often (Fig. 2.10). The Warren truss without verticals provides the maximum open-web area to accommodate ductwork and piping. Vertical web members may be added to the Warren truss when the unbraced length of the compression chord is critical. A Vierendeel panel in the low-shear zone near the center of the span is often incorporated into the truss to accommodate the main air-handling mechanical duct. The spacing of the web members should be chosen such that the free passage of ductwork and piping is not inhibited while maintaining a reasonable unbraced length of the compression top chord during construction. On the other hand, the angle of the web diagonals should be made relatively shallow to reduce the number of

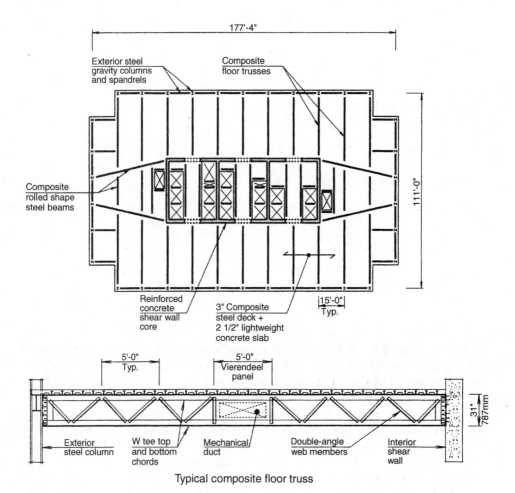

Typical composite floor truss

Figure 2.9 One North Franklin, Chicago, Ill.

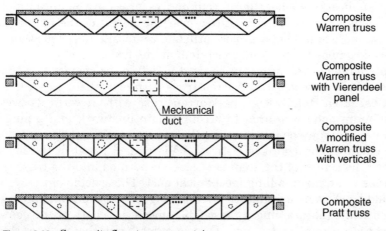

Composite
Warren truss

Composite
Warren truss
with Vierendeel
panel

Mechanical
duct

Composite
modified
Warren truss
with verticals

Composite
Pratt truss

Figure 2.10 Composite floor truss geometries.

members and associated joint welding. This must be balanced by the fact that shallower web members result in longer unbraced lengths and higher member axial forces, often requiring connection gusset plates, thereby increasing fabrication costs and decreasing the clear area for ductwork and piping. A panel spacing roughly two to three times the truss depth is a good rule of thumb. The floor truss configuration should be detailed such that any significant point loads are applied at truss panel points. A vertical web member may be introduced into the truss girder geometry to transfer these imposed shear loads into the truss system.

A variety of chord and web member cross sections may be used (Fig. 2.11). Chord members may be wide-flange tee or single-angle sections to allow easy, direct connection of web members without gusset plates. Double-angle sections and tubes are less common for chord members as they require gusset-plated connections. Web members are most often tees, single-angle or double-angle sections welded directly to the chord tee or angle stem, although tube sections have been used. The composite floor trusses are connected to the concrete floor slab by shear connectors welded to the top chord of the truss. The floor trusses are normally spaced such that the metal deck can span between the trusses without shoring.

The steel truss component of the composite floor truss system has high flexural stiffness and is most efficiently designed unshored for all concrete-floor

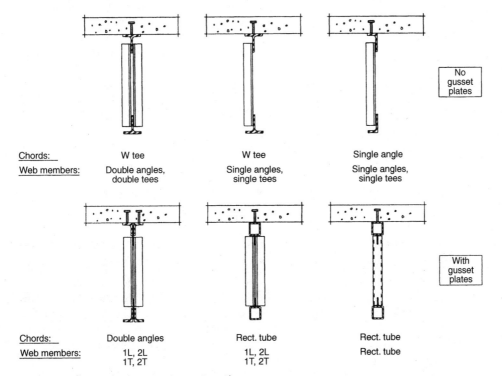

Chords:	W tee	W tee	Single angle
Web members:	Double angles, double tees	Single angles, single tees	Single angles, single tees

No gusset plates

Chords:	Double angles	Rect. tube	Rect. tube
Web members:	1L, 2L 1T, 2T	1L, 2L 1T, 2T	Rect. tube

With gusset plates

Figure 2.11 Composite truss component sections.

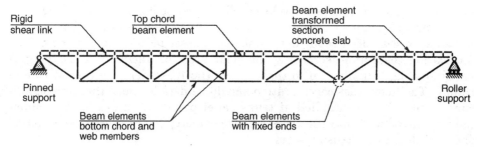

Figure 2.12 Composite truss modeling.

dead loads. Camber is usually not required. Preliminary sizes for web members may be obtained by manual calculation assuming the full design shear forces. The minimum top chord size is obtained from the dead load alone. The use of computer analysis greatly facilitates the composite floor truss design. Figure 2.12 indicates one of many methods which can be used for modeling the composite floor truss system. The plane frame model includes beam elements for all chord and web members oriented along centroidal axes. The intersecting joints are completely fixed, although web member end moments are usually insignificant. To simplify the fabrication required for the web member ends at the chord connections, the diagonals may be moved slightly away from the node points to allow for uninterrupted welding and right-angle member cuts. The resulting eccentricities should be specifically modeled with an additional short chord beam element. The steel truss alone is analyzed for concrete slab dead load and construction live load assuming unshored construction. For the composite condition supporting all superimposed dead and live loads, the concrete slab is modeled with appropriate transformed section properties based on an equivalent slab width determined by the standard AISC provisions for composite construction. Rigid vertical shear link truss elements model the slab-to-top chord connection.

Some additional items to be considered in designing efficient composite floor trusses include:

Vierendeel panel.   Unbalanced live load should be considered in designing the Vierendeel panel. Member eccentricities due to chord reinforcing must be accounted for in the analysis.

Single-angle web and chord members.   Out-of-plane eccentricity between member centroids must be included in the analysis and design of the truss.

Retrofitting composite floor truss systems.   Upgrading the truss chord load-carrying capacity is accomplished by cover-plating. On the other hand, cover-plating the web diagonal members is difficult and expensive. For this reason, the web member design may include provision for a somewhat higher than specified live-load allowance to avoid costly modifications for special tenant requirements.

2.3.4 Value engineering

Many options are available to frame a floor in a steel building. The study of the options is generally referred to as value engineering. An example of such studies is a 46-story building in New York completed in 1982. One type of framing included in the study is shown in Fig. 2.13. The parameters studied were:

Depth of deck	$1\frac{5}{16}$, 2, and 3 in (33, 51, and 76 mm)
Type of concrete	Lightweight and normal weight
Strength of steel	A36 and A572-50
Slab-to-steel connection	Composite and noncomposite
Type of construction	Shored and unshored
Type of design	Allowable stress and plastic composite
Type of framing	Various directions of beams and girders

A total of 66 alternates were considered. The results for the framing type of Fig. 2.13 are listed in Table 2.1. There were many possible alternates, and each

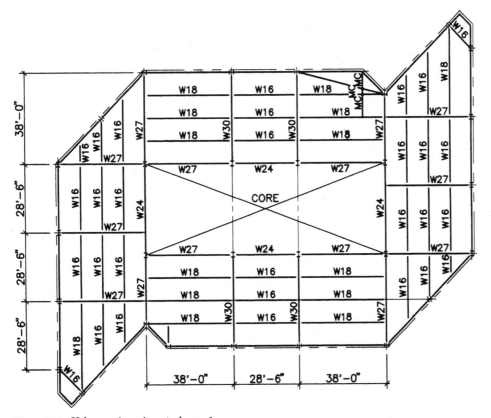

Figure 2.13   Value engineering study no. 1.

TABLE 2.1 Value Engineering for Building Shown in Fig. 2.13

Scheme	Beams	Composite	Concrete	Deck	Steel lb/ft^2	Cost/ft^2
2A	A36	No	$3\frac{1}{4}$-in lightweight	3 in 16 gage	11.2	$12.32
2B	A572-50	No	$3\frac{1}{4}$-in lightweight	3 in 16 gage	11.2	$12.02
2C	A36	Yes	$3\frac{1}{4}$-in lightweight	3 in 16 gage	9.8	$11.64
2D	A572-50	Yes	$3\frac{1}{4}$-in lightweight	3 in 16 gage	9.0	$11.43
2E	A36	No	$4\frac{3}{16}$-in lightweight	$1\frac{5}{16}$ in 20 gage shored	11.2	$12.17
2F	A572-50	No	$4\frac{3}{16}$-in lightweight	$1\frac{5}{16}$ in 20 gage shored	10.2	$11.88
2G	A36	Yes	$4\frac{3}{16}$-in lightweight	$1\frac{5}{16}$ in 20 gage shored	9.8	$11.49
2H	A572-50	Yes	$4\frac{3}{16}$-in lightweight	$1\frac{5}{16}$ in 20 gage shored	9.0	$11.28
2I	A36	No	$2\frac{1}{2}$-in stone	2 in 16 gage	11.2	$11.71
2J	A572-50	No	$2\frac{1}{2}$-in stone	2 in 16 gage	10.2	$11.42

of them had its own structural cost. In addition, the impact of the structural depth on mechanical and architectural requirements was evaluated separately.

Another example is a 45-story office building shown in Fig. 2.14. Alternate designs were made of composite framing members for the typical 45-ft (14-m) span using beams, trusses, or stub girders (Fig. 2.15). The objective was to compare material quantities, floor heights, and deflection characteristics of the three systems. Two-hour fire separation between floors was required. The designs were based on the AISC LRFD specification.[D91] The results are listed in Table 2.2.

The composite floor truss alternate represents the least-steel-weight design. The floor truss and stub-girder systems reduce the floor height cavity by 5 to 6

TABLE 2.2 Value Engineering for Building Shown in Fig. 2.14

	Principal steel element		
	W21 × 44	Truss	Stub beam
Unit steel quantity, lb/ft^2	6.18	4.67	4.76
Deck gage no.	20	18	18
Number of studs	30	44	50
Dead-load deflection, in	2.02	1.06	0.84
Camber, in	1.5	0.75	None
Superimposed dead-load deflection, in	0.34	0.10	0.30
Live-load deflection, in	0.68	0.38	0.78

NOTE: W21 × 44, 50 percent composite design.

Truss:	Top chord	WT6 × 15
	Bottom chord	WT6 × 17.5
	Web members	Double angles 3 × 3, 2.5 × 2.5, and 2 × 2
Stub girder:	Bottom chord	W16 × 57
	Stubs 5 ft long	W16 × 26
	Continuous purlins	W16 and W12

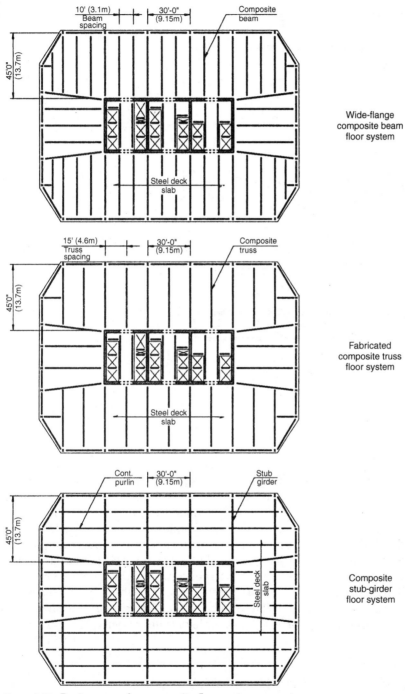

Figure 2.14 Design example—composite floor systems.

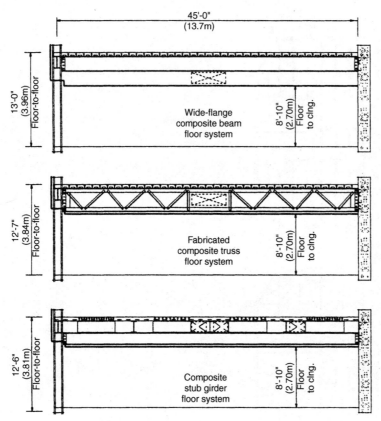

Figure 2.15 Value engineering study no. 2.

in (127 to 153 mm), which can translate into significant cost savings in exterior cladding costs over the height of a multistory building. The stub-girder system allows for maximum flexibility in accommodating building services ductwork, but it should be noted that this system includes an added cost associated with the required temporary shoring of the girders. The low material quantity indicated for the floor truss option must be balanced against increased fabrication cost as well as some premium for fireproofing of the many component pieces. While the simple composite prismatic beam appears to be the least efficient option, this scheme is often found to be cost-effective overall based on the ease of fabrication and erection and the simple detailing involved.

2.4 Composite Building Systems

The success of combining steel and concrete into composite floor systems gave rise to the impetus to develop composite building systems. Since 1967, there has been a growing realization that important economic and functional benefits can be obtained by combining steel and concrete in the *vertical building system*.

Economic studies in the United States have consistently shown that to develop a given strength and stiffness, a concrete or composite column is more economical than a pure steel column. The inherent advantages of steel, i.e., strength, speed of construction, and light weight, can be combined with the advantages of concrete, i.e., stiffness, fireproofing, and economics.

Engineers and constructors have used these ideas to develop a variety of composite building systems which can be broadly categorized as:

1. Exterior composite frame

2. Interior composite frame

3. Supercolumn framing

Each of them is described in the following paragraphs.

2.4.1 Exterior composite frame

Composite columns with concrete or steel girders, and concrete columns with steel girders or trusses have been used as discussed below.

Proposed by Khan[G18] in 1967, composite columns with concrete spandrels were first used on the 20-story Control Data building in Houston. The concept of the design and construction was clever and elegant.

A basic steel frame was erected (Fig. 2.16) using very small (W8) exterior columns at 10 ft (3 m) on centers. The exterior columns were designed to carry up to 14 floors of the steel framing with 6 floors of concrete slabs in place. Temporary diagonal bracing in the vertical plane using angles or cables was provided for stability. At this stage of construction the exterior steel columns were encased in cast-in-place concrete using the exterior architectural precast panels (Fig. 1.3) as the major part of the formwork. The exterior frame system was completed with cast-in-place concrete spandrel beams once again using the precast panels as the major part of the formwork. The spandrels were cast at the same time as the columns.

This system has been used on several subsequent buildings such as the 50-story One Shell Square, New Orleans,[G18] 50-story United Bank Center, Denver, 53-story Southeast Financial Center, Miami,[M13] 55-story First Interstate Bank, Houston, and 75-story Texas Commerce Plaza, Houston.[C67]

The combination of exterior composite columns with steel girders has received a great deal of research effort,[89,90] primarily in Japan, where many structures have been constructed using the so-called SRC system (Fig. 2.17). Most of the underlying research was concerned with the resistance to lateral loads.

More recently, similar investigations were carried out by Sheikh et al.[120] at the University of Texas. Tests were conducted with lateral load reversals to study hysteretic behavior of steel beam to composite column joints. Guidelines for the design of the joints between steel beams and concrete columns were the result.[D92] Another possibility is to use a concrete column with steel girders or trusses as shown in Fig. 2.18. This type of construction has had limited use, generally for low-rise structures. The girders or trusses

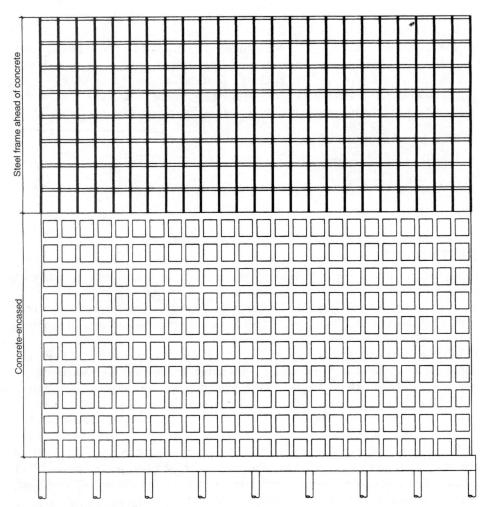

Figure 2.16 Erection sequence.

are provided with base plates. In case of light loads, weld plates can be embedded in the concrete column and the truss chords field-welded to the weld plates as shown in Fig. 2.18. For heavy loads, the connection detail is accomplished by bolting the girders to the columns with through bolts.

2.4.2 Interior composite frame

Shear walls with steel frames or steel link beams and composite columns with welded steel girders with or without diagonal bracing are described in this section.

When a building structure is comprised of shear walls with steel frames, the concrete shear walls are placed in the core of the building and generally slip-

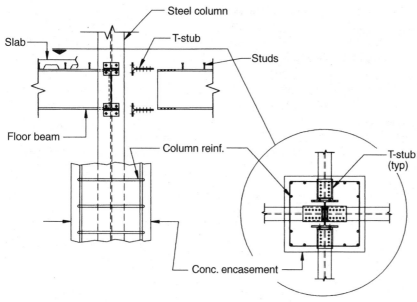

Figure 2.17 Composite columns with steel girders.[89]

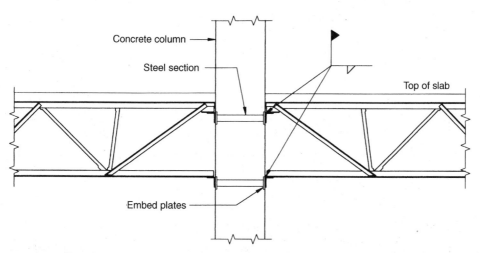

Figure 2.18 Exterior concrete columns with steel trusses.

formed first. A simple steel frame is then attached to the concrete walls to complete the structure. Generally the concrete walls provide the entire lateral stability for the structure. Many examples of tall buildings can be found with conventional steel frames attached to the shear wall core such as the 772-ft (235-m) 57-story IDS Building in Minneapolis[C49] and the 725-ft-tall (221-m) core for the Atlantic Center project in Atlanta. In low-rise structures two or more cores are common; also frequently used in such structures are concrete shear walls between two adjacent steel columns located independently of the core.

The steel frame may consist of conventionally loaded columns. In some cases the steel frame has been hung from the top of the concrete shear walls. Examples of this type of structure are the Russian Embassy in Brooklyn, N.Y. (Fig. 2.19), and the 15-story West Coast Transmission Building in Vancouver, Canada. The steel structure for both buildings was hung from their concrete cores.

The design of this type of construction is limited by the strength and lateral and torsional stiffness of the wall for taller heights and large lateral loads. From the construction standpoint, the plumbness of the wall and the result-

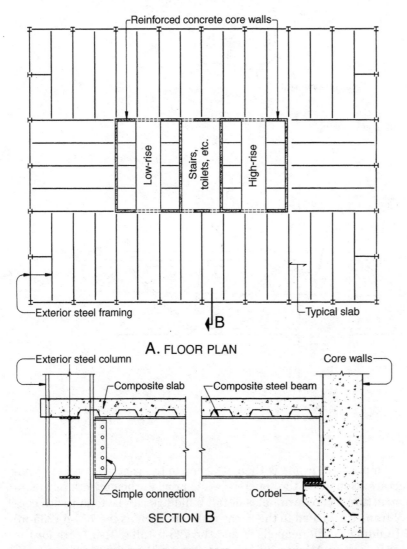

Figure 2.19 Russian Embassy, Brooklyn, N.Y.

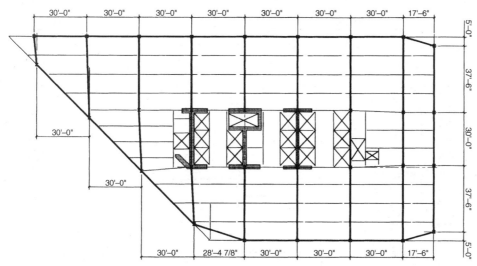

Figure 2.20 Pennzoil Place, Houston.

ing tolerances for the attachment of the steel framing members are the major challenges.

Composite shear walls with simple steel frames are a variation of the construction technique described above. In the case of composite shear walls, the steel frame is erected first. The frame includes steel columns to be encased in the concrete wall, steel floor beams, and concrete floor slabs. The concrete shear wall construction generally lags 8 to 12 floors behind the steel. One of the major projects utilizing this system is the twin 38-story Pennzoil Place Buildings in Houston[C55] shown in Fig. 2.20.

The main advantages claimed for this system are:

The steel erection is done in a conventional manner without the obstruction of a concrete wall.

The tolerances in the wall location are determined by the steel core columns and hence do not depend on the tolerances of a slip-formed wall.

The need for the weld plates when the wall is built ahead of the steel is eliminated.

Particular care is needed in this and other systems described below to make reasonable predictions of the axial shortening of the composite wall due to gravity loads, concrete shrinkage, and creep. These calculations serve as the basis for corrections for differential axial shortening between vertical elements.

The beneficial effects of in-fill masonry inside a steel frame have been observed for many years in nonseismic areas. An analysis of the system using precast-concrete in-fill walls was reported by Weidlinger[D31] in 1972. The essential concept is shown in Fig. 2.21. A type 1 connection is used where the panel forces are transmitted only to the steel columns. Type 2 connections

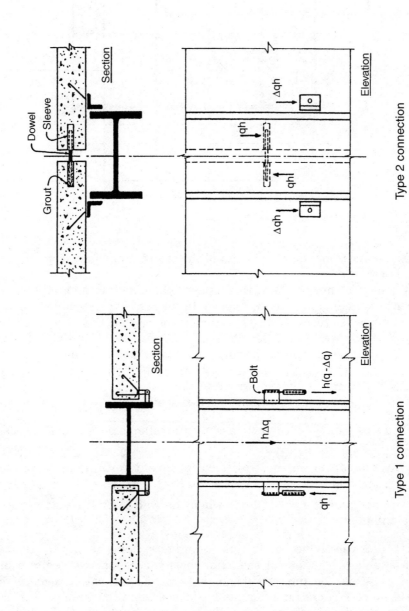

Figure 2.21 Precast concrete shear walls with steel frame as proposed by Weidlinger.[D31]

have a direct panel-to-panel joint, and hence the panel forces are transmitted not only to the steel column but also between panels. The system was used on the 45-story Yasuda Fire and Marine Insurance Building in Tokyo.

Analytical models of concrete shear walls with steel link beams indicate that high shear forces are induced in link beams in coupled shear walls. This can result in brittle shear failures of concrete in conventional link beams unless the reinforcing bars are properly detailed. One possible means for increasing the ductility is to provide for structural steel link beams as shown in Fig. 2.22. Once again the problem is the connection of the steel link beam to the shear wall. Current research[D88] is aimed at the development of design guidelines for this type of structure but needs to progress much further before definitive recommendations can be made.

In taller buildings the core may be inadequate to resist all lateral loads by itself. One of the remedial techniques is to link the core to the exterior columns through steel girders, sometimes called outrigger beams, contained within the ceiling space at each floor (Fig. 2.23). The core is either a composite column system or a composite shear wall. The detail of the critical joint

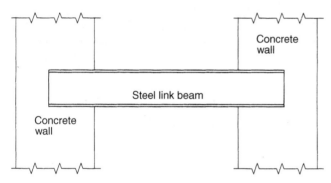

Figure 2.22 Concrete shear walls with steel link beams.

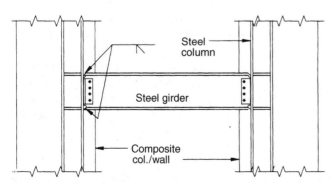

Figure 2.23 Composite column or wall with welded steel girder.

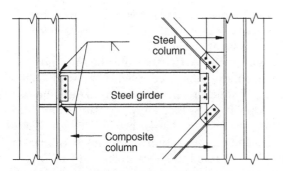

Figure 2.24 Composite column with diagonal bracing.

between the steel girder and the composite column is similar to that described in Refs. 89, 90, C55, D59, and D92. The detail between the steel girder and the composite wall is generally an extension of the principles used in the steel girder to composite column connection.

Diagonal bracing attached to the steel section of a composite column (Fig. 2.24) is often designed to carry the shear due to the lateral loads while the composite columns carry not only the gravity loads but also the axial components of the lateral load overturning moment. The presence of the diagonals complicates the details of the composite column, since it is difficult to provide the necessary lateral ties between the longitudinal reinforcing bars in the composite columns. Long studs are generally welded to the encased steel column, the steel girder, and the steel diagonal. The column ties are lapped with the long studs. This type of construction was used on the 29-story 1000 Town Center Project in Southfield, Mich.

2.4.3 Supercolumn framing

It has long been recognized that the most efficient method to resist lateral loads in tall buildings is to provide only a few large columns, called supercolumns, as far apart as possible and to connect them with diagonals or Vierendeel frames. A whole category of composite buildings characterized by the use of the supercolumns has been developed over the years. They include various concrete-filled steel sections with steel girders, with or without steel diagonal bracing, and composite columns with composite diagonal bracing.

For the system shown in Fig. 2.25, steel girders are welded to the outside surfaces of large-diameter steel pipes, which are filled with concrete of 6 to 19 ksi (40 to 130 MPa) strength. If needed, plate diaphragms are welded inside the pipes to reduce local stresses. This construction method has the following advantages:

The steel pipe provides formwork and confinement for the concrete.

Generally longitudinal reinforcing bars are not used, thereby simplifying construction.

In most cases no diaphragms are used inside the pipe for girder flange continuity: the flange forces are carried directly by the pipe.

Some unanswered questions remain. The heat of hydration of the concrete, the bond between the concrete and the steel pipe under cyclic loading, the potential for local buckling of the pipe, and the postyield behavior of the system need further investigation. There is obviously no potential for visual observation of the concrete after a major seismic event. It may be of interest in this connection, however, that a Japanese research project indicated some benefit of deliberately preventing bond between the steel pipe and the in-fill concrete.[110]

Concrete-filled steel tubes with steel girders were used in Japan and more recently in Taiwan (Fig. 2.26). The system is similar to the round steel pipe system described above except that rectangular or square steel tubes were

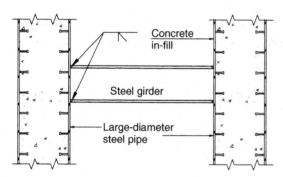

Figure 2.25 Composite steel pipes with welded steel girder.

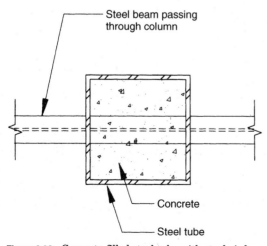

Figure 2.26 Concrete-filled steel tube with steel girders.

used instead. Research by Morita et al.[137] in Japan and by Azizinamini et al.[132] in the United States provided a basic understanding of the behavior of the critical joints in this type of structure.

In the case of large concrete-filled steel pipes or tubes, the area of the structural steel is in the range of 2 to 4 percent of the area of the column cross section, and since these steel elements have to be specially fabricated their costs are high. An alternate is to form the supercolumn as in a conventional reinforced concrete structure and to use a relatively light structural steel section, i.e., less than 1 percent of the cross-sectional area of the column. The structural steel girder is embedded in the cast-in-place concrete. The design of the columns is treated as a reinforced concrete column with an embedded steel column section. The joint detail follows the design criteria discussed in Ref. 98 for regular composite columns with steel girders. A typical joint detail is shown in Fig. 2.27. Some examples of the use of this system are in the 57-story Norwest Bank Building in Minneapolis and the 60-story NationsBank Plaza in Atlanta.[C88] In the former case the supercolumns measure 8 × 8 ft (2.4 × 2.4 m) and are connected by Vierendeel steel girders that span 100 ft (30 m). In the case of the NationsBank the exterior supercolumns are connected by W36 (90-cm) steel girders in two directions. These girders span 60 and 45 ft (18 and 14 m), respectively.

The design of the longitudinal reinforcement in the supercolumns is based on standard reinforced concrete column design. At the joint, additional ties are required based on ASCE recommendations for composite column to steel girder joints.[D92] The continuity of the ties in the region of the girder web is generally achieved by lapping the ties with long deformed studs welded to the web. In some cases, the ties are passed through holes in the web. Since the supercolumns are of relatively large size, the placement of concrete requires special techniques to reduce the effects of the heat of hydration. Longitudinal cracks at the surface have been caused by this phenomenon. Insulated forms have proved to be useful in this regard.

The advantages of this system over the one using steel pipes or tubes are:

The column details can be made to ensure ductile behavior of the column and yielding of the girder in a seismic event.

The system is economical since the formwork is used repetitively.

The concrete is visible and thus can be readily inspected after a seismic event.

The disadvantages are:

It is more time-consuming to place the longitudinal and lateral reinforcing and the formwork.

In the case where the girders terminate at the joint (as opposed to continuous girders) the column size is governed by the length of anchorage required by the girder.

Supercolumns are often connected with diagonal bracing. Figure 1.10 shows a

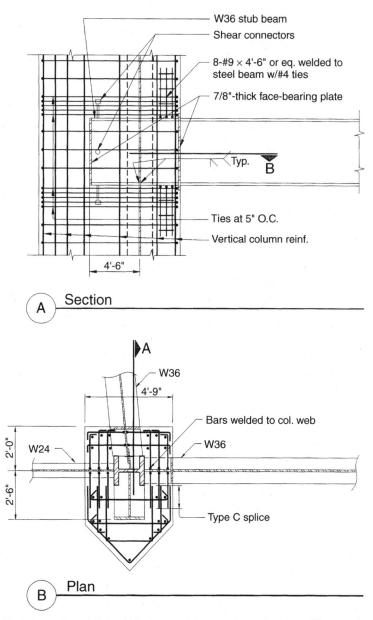

W36 stub beam

Shear connectors

8-#9 × 4'-6" or eq. welded to
steel beam w/#4 ties

7/8"-thick face-bearing plate

Typ. B

Ties at 5" O.C.

Vertical column reinf.

4'-6"

A Section

A

W36

4'-9"

Bars welded to col. web

W36

2'-0"

W24

2'-6"

Type C splice

B Plan

Figure 2.27 Formed composite supercolumns with steel girders.[C88]

floor plan of the 50-story Two Union Square building in Seattle. Each steel
pipe supercolumn in the core is connected by diagonal bracing to the adjacent
steel column. This type of design transfers primarily axial force and shear
into the column and almost eliminates bending moments. This type of design
has also been used in the 62-story Gateway Tower in Seattle and was pro-

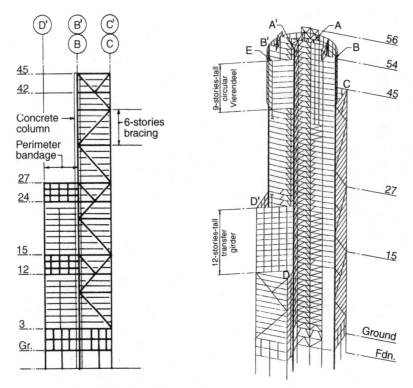

Figure 2.28 First Bank Place, Minneapolis.

posed for tall structures in Asia. In some cases the gusset plate joints need to be stress-relieved owing to high locked-in welding stresses.

The overall concept described above is applicable also when the composite columns are formed in place. A good example of this type of construction is the 57-story First Bank Place project in Minneapolis (Figs. 1.3, 1.4, and 2.28). Additional care is required in detailing the lateral column ties in the vicinity of the diagonals. In the United States, the use of diagonally braced systems in heavy seismic zones is generally frowned upon because of the ductility requirements. In Japan, where a more deterministic philosophy of seismic design is practiced, the use of a diagonally braced system is popular because it reduces the building movements in the case of moderate seismic events and consequently minimizes property damage.

In the 1209-ft-tall (369-m) Bank of China building in Hong Kong, composite diagonals transfer the gravity loads into five composite supercolumns as illustrated in Figs. 1.9 and 2.29. The main advantages of composite diagonals over steel diagonals is that they obviate the need for large steel gusset plate assemblies, which may need to be stress-relieved, and the simplicity of the joint details. The majority of the diagonal forces are transferred directly from concrete to concrete.

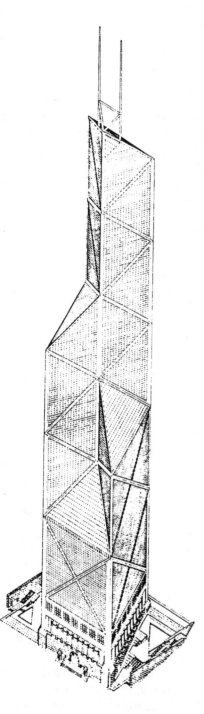

Figure 2.29 Bank of China building, Hong Kong.

2.5 Methods of Analysis

The analysis of composite building systems often presents a greater challenge than for other structures owing to nontypical construction sequences, the variable and time-dependent properties of concrete, and the interaction and load sharing between structural steel and reinforced concrete. Since commercial software which directly handles these and other special aspects of composite construction is not generally available, designers often resort to a combination of analysis models, techniques, and special bookkeeping procedures to calculate member forces and deflections during construction and in the completed structure.

Generally, methods of structural analysis can be categorized by the degree to which they account for nonlinear material and geometric behavior. Also, methods may be distinguished between computer-based matrix (finite-element) approaches which rigorously enforce equilibrium and compatibility, and more approximate methods which may or may not be computerized. Since some aspects of the behavior of composite systems such as the time-dependent constitutive properties of composite elements are difficult to quantify, approximate methods are often as reliable as more sophisticated techniques. The primary concern of the engineer should be to use analysis methods which capture the relevant behavioral effects for the important limit states in a predictable and efficient manner.

2.5.1 General considerations

Behavioral effects that influence the response of composite structures at various limit states are discussed below. These are not all of the behavioral effects which need to be considered,[G74] but they are the ones which are more important for composite structures than for either pure steel or reinforced concrete structures. Recognition of the role these have in the structural response will influence the types and methods of analysis used.

Construction sequence. Depending on the type of composite system and the anticipated construction sequence, the final design loads in certain members and connections may be controlled by conditions during construction. Deformations due to construction loads on the partially completed structure are also an important consideration, since they will influence the final configuration of the structure such as floor levelness and plumb.

Construction sequence effects are most apparent in composite frames where the steel erection elements and floor slabs are constructed prior to placement of the reinforced concrete encasement of columns and walls that provide for stability in the completed structure.[122,M13] An example of a typical construction sequence used in mid- to high-rise composite structures is shown in Fig. 2.16. Of concern during construction is the stability of the partially completed structure consisting of the steel frame above the concrete encasement. In addition, the construction sequence results in a preloading of the steel columns which may cause them to shorten considerably more than would be predicted by an analysis of the completed composite frame.

Material properties.   For analysis purposes, the stress-strain behavior of steel and concrete may be idealized as shown in Fig. 2.30. In addition, the time-dependent properties of concrete need to be considered. Under long-term loads and at loads near the strength-limit condition, the combination of structural steel and reinforced concrete elements results in deflections and member force distributions which can change from those predicted by elastic analyses. For example, of primary concern in tall or long-span structures are the long-term deformations which result from creep and shrinkage in the concrete. Time-dependent column shortening in tall composite buildings poses a unique challenge where steel and concrete elements with different stiffnesses and/or heavily and lightly stressed concrete elements deform differently. The

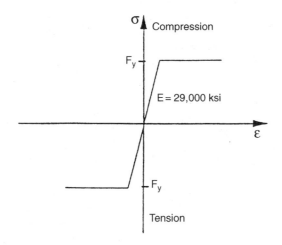

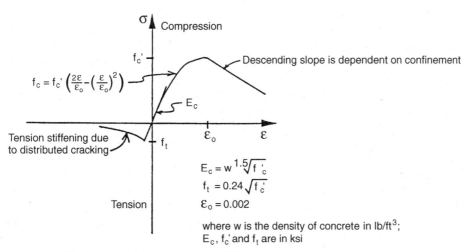

Figure 2.30 Idealized stress-strain properties.[G27]

extent of the potential problem is evidenced by one example study of an 80-story-tall structure where for a composite column, roughly 50 to 80 percent of the total shortening is due to creep and shrinkage effects.[G50]

Composite members and elements. For the analysis of overall systems, composite member stiffnesses are usually formulated assuming that plane sections remain plane and shear deformations can be ignored. Some exceptions to this are made for walls and link beams with low aspect ratios where shear deformations are significant. For elastic analysis under service loads, the stress-strain behavior of concrete in compression is often assumed to be linear, and member properties are adjusted to reflect the loss in stiffness due to cracking. Procedures for modifying composite member stiffnesses are usually based on methods used for reinforced concrete members[D66] and composite beams.[D91] Generally, such procedures range from rough approximations of the effective areas and moments of inertia to more detailed methods based on transformed section calculations. In unencased partially composite beams, the stiffness under service loads should also be modified to account for slip between the structural steel and concrete,[D91] but in other members, the effect of slip is usually considered to be negligible under service loads.

For analysis of the overall structural system, it is generally impractical to use precise formulas to include the effects of concrete cracking and slip on member stiffnesses. Rather, approximate methods are used to calculate the effective axial and flexural stiffness of members EA_e and EI_e, which lie between the transformed stiffnesses of the total uncracked sections, i.e., gross sections, and the fully cracked sections. For example, in columns and walls where axial compressive loads are generally large enough to inhibit cracking, gross transformed properties are generally used. On the other hand, cracking under negative bending can reduce the stiffness of beams considerably.

In determining appropriate member stiffnesses for analysis, it is important to recognize the specific purpose of the analysis and whether the analysis is for service or factored ultimate loads. The degree of cracking under service loads will be less than under factored loads, and the relative member stiffnesses therefore may change. The shear stiffness can be lower by a factor of 10 after cracking as described by Perdikaris and White.[91] An analysis made to calculate service-load deflections may not be appropriate for calculating the member force distributions at the strength-limit state. In particular, stiffnesses based on factored loads should be used for evaluating forces induced by second-order geometric nonlinear behavior. The significance of changes in stiffness from service to factored loads will vary depending on the type and configuration of the structure.

Connections. Careful judgment is required realistically to idealize the connections between different types of members in composite systems. A number of beam-column connections which are common in composite construction are shown in Figs. 2.6 and 2.31. For design purposes, they may be considered as moment-resisting connections. On the other hand, for analysis purposes one should consider finite-size effects and the stiffness of the connections and

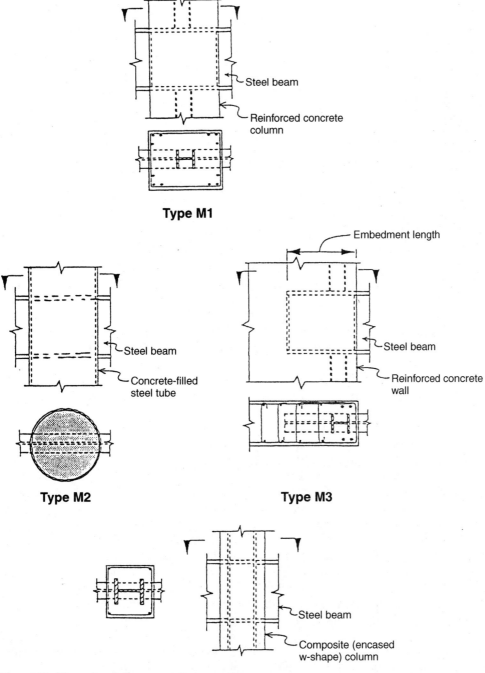

Type M1

Type M2

Type M3

Figure 2.31 Moment-resisting composite connections.

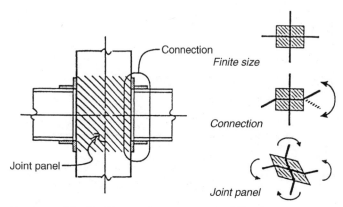

Figure 2.32 Idealized beam-column connection behavior.

joint panels (Fig. 2.32). As is the case for steel or concrete structures, there are no firmly established rules for modeling connection flexibility other than to either (1) model the joint region explicitly in the analysis or (2) use engineering judgment and general rules of thumb to approximate the connection behavior. For example, in steel structures it is common to treat fully welded moment connections as perfectly rigid but to neglect the finite joint size effects by basing the analysis model on centerline dimensions. In this case, the centerline dimensions are intended to reflect the flexibility induced by panel zone distortion in the joint. On the other hand, in reinforced concrete structures moment connections are often modeled using a finite joint region assuming that a portion of the joint is perfectly rigid.

Because of the uncertainties involved, it is impractical to attempt precise stiffness characteristic modeling of the joints since they vary depending on the geometry, detailing, and load level of the joint. For many cases, it is probably reasonable to assume that composite moment connections have a rigidity greater than those of reinforced concrete and less than those of steel and to use similar approximate techniques for modeling joint response. Tests reported by Sheikh et al.[120] indicate that the deformations in connections of type M1 are similar to those in similarly proportioned reinforced concrete joints. Tests on link beam connections of type M4[148] indicate that the beams can be considered as fully fixed at a distance inside the face of the concrete approximately one-third of the dimension of the embedment length of the beam.

Two types of composite bracing connections, A1 and A2, are shown in Fig. 2.33a. In general, modeling these as truss or frame connections is relatively straightforward; however, the analytic idealization sometimes becomes complicated when the intersection of the centerlines of the braces do not coincide with the centerline of the columns. A notable example of this is in the Bank of China building in Hong Kong where, as shown in Fig. 2.33b, braces in three planes have noncoincident working points inside the corner concrete columns. In this case, the working points were positioned in order to simplify

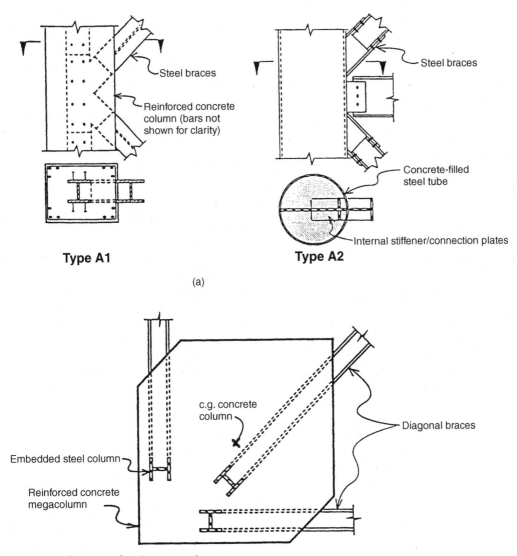

Type A1

Type A2

(a)

Figure 2.33   Composite bracing connections.

the steel detailing by avoiding complicated three-dimensional intersections of the steel braces. Also, the brace locations were dictated in large part by architectural requirements. For analysis purposes, such eccentricities can be modeled using fictitious rigid links or kinematic constraints. It is important, however, that such models account for out-of-plane bracing forces caused by the noncoincident working points.

Loading.   More than for steel or concrete structures, in composite structures it is important to distinguish between short- and long-term loads during and after construction. During construction, the loading and related design checks should be determined based on the anticipated construction sequence and methods. To properly calculate long-term deflections in the structure, one needs the time of load application to the structure and the duration of those loads. A common example is the case of composite beams where the total deflection is the sum of the deflections of the noncomposite steel beam under construction loads and the elastic and long-term deflections of the composite beam under superimposed dead and live loads. Similar reasoning applies for calculating the deflections in composite frames where, during construction, the steel erection members are unencased under some of the load and are later encased under the remainder of the design load.

Uncertainties. The uncertainties in predicting the applied loads, response, and strength of composite systems are similar to those encountered in steel or reinforced concrete structures. However, certain circumstances in composite structures increase the potential adverse impact of deviations from the assumed conditions. For example, uncertainties of the time-dependent material properties of concrete are a major concern for design and analysis. These affect both the deformations and the force distribution between members. As described by Robertson,[G63] rather than trying to analyze such effects, in certain cases it is best to design the structural system so as to mitigate the impact of uncertainties in the material properties on the structural response. Another instance where uncertainties are of concern is in the construction sequence where contractors may not follow the scheme anticipated by the engineer. For example, in composite framed structures it is typically assumed that the steel framing will advance 8 to 12 stories ahead of the concrete encasement, but the designer should anticipate deviations. For analysis purposes, the potential impact of these and other uncertainties must be considered.

2.5.2   Frame analysis

The basic types of nonlinear analyses may be categorized by their ability to model the nonlinear response of structures as represented by the load-deflection plot of the simple frame shown in Fig. 2.34.[G53,G74] In general, all except the first-order elastic analysis require nonlinear solution procedures where loads are applied incrementally to the structure. As described below, the main differences in the analysis methods are how geometric and material nonlinearities are accounted for.

For the past 20 years, linear-elastic matrix structural analysis using line-type beam-column elements has been the mainstay of engineering practice. Linear-elastic methods are fairly good for calculating the response of the structure under service loads. However, for evaluating the strength-limit state of the structure under ultimate loads, the results of elastic analyses need to be combined with member-based design provisions which account for nonlinear and out-of-plane destabilizing effects. For example, the beam-column design equations in the AISC LRFD specification[D91] are a semiempirical way of taking account of second-order inelastic deflections under combined axial and biaxial bending loads. This situation is changing, however, as modern computer technologies are beginning to permit the use of advanced methods of analysis to more realistically model the nonlinear response of structures for large deformations and inelastic effects. Aspects of such nonlinear analyses are outlined below.

One example of the application of inelastic analysis to design is shown in Fig. 2.35.[G76] This example is for a steel-framed structure, but the basic behavior would be similar to that for a composite frame. In this example, the frame

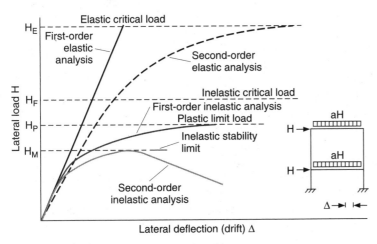

Figure 2.34 Comparison of methods of analysis.

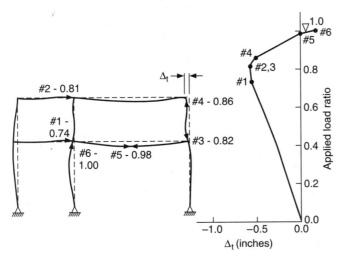

Figure 2.35 Inelastic analysis of low-rise frames.[G76]

is loaded under gravity forces, and the results shown include a plot of the load vs. deformation behavior and the sequence of inelastic hinge formation. The load is reported as a fraction of the total factored dead and live loads. As shown, the first hinge forms at a load equal to 74 percent of the inelastic limit strength. Under continued loading as subsequent hinges form, the behavior of the structure changes dramatically from the initial elastic response. The strength-limit point is reached through a combination of material and geometric nonlinear behavior as the structure fails in sideway to the left. One point to recognize from this example is the obvious inability of elastic analysis to predict the true behavior near the strength-limit state. Nevertheless, if one is willing to limit the design strength of the structure to the elastic region, i.e., in the example this is the region where the load ratio is less than 0.74, elastic analysis provides an effective means of developing a conservative design. Further examples of the inelastic limit state design of composite structures are presented by Schleich.[M16]

Geometric nonlinearity.   By definition, first-order or linear analyses consider only force equilibrium based on the undeformed geometry of the structure. As such, these methods do not capture the destabilizing effects associated with story drift, P-Δ effects, and member buckling, P-δ effects. As shown in Fig. 2.36, Δ refers to deflections at nodes or story levels and δ refers to deflections between the ends of members. Various formulations are available for considering second-order effects, and all generally involve incremental and/or iterative solution techniques where the geometry of the structure is continuously updated.

One type of second-order approach is an updated lagrangian procedure for which the equilibrium equations are formulated based on the current configuration of the structure. In addition to updating the structural geometry, geometric stiffness matrices, which are a function of the current member forces,

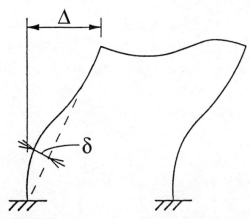

Figure 2.36 Definitions for second-order deformation effects.

are added to the basic elastic stiffness at each load step.[G57] This formulation is characterized by the following incremental stiffness equilibrium equation:

$$(K_e + K_g)(dq) = (dR) + (R - S)_{i-1} \qquad (2.1)$$

where K_e = elastic global stiffness matrix
K_g = geometric stiffness matrix at increment i
dq = global displacement for increment i
dR = incremental force vector for increment i
$R - S$ = unbalance of external R and internal S forces from previous load increment $i - 1$

Second-order analysis techniques are not in themselves material-dependent, and the formulations and procedures are the same for steel, concrete, and composite systems.

Material nonlinearity. Material nonlinear effects can be included in matrix structural analysis techniques in a variety of ways with varying levels of sophistication. At the most basic level, cracking and other inelastic effects in concrete and composite elements may be handled by using adjusted member section properties and/or material modulus values in an otherwise elastic analysis. Given the capabilities of presently available computer software, this is the technique most frequently used in design practice. However, more refined methods are available which are currently used in research and may increasingly find use in engineering practice.

Two general types of advanced inelastic analysis methodologies are concentrated plasticity methods and spread of plasticity methods. In concentrated plasticity methods, sometimes called plastic or inelastic hinge methods, inelastic deformations are concentrated at the ends of the beam-column elements. This is the type of analysis used by Ziemian[G76] in the example shown in Fig. 2.37. Such methods typically employ stress-resultant yield-surface expressions to monitor and control the plastic deformations. Descriptions of formulations for such methods applied to steel structures have been reported by Porter and Powell[G22] and Hsieh et al.[G57] To date, concentrated plasticity methods have not been applied extensively to composite structures, but the same principles and methodologies would apply as for steel structures. The major difference is in the shape of the yield surface used for steel vs. composite sections.

More exact methods of inelastic analysis are termed spread of plasticity (or plastic zone) methods. These generally involve discretization of the member cross section into a collection of "fibers" to allow the calculation of the inelastic member stiffness by numerical integration (Fig. 2.38). These integrations are typically made at the ends of the beam-column elements, and the inelastic section stiffness is assumed to vary linearly between the ends. The change in member stiffness due to the spread of inelasticity along the length of members is modeled by discretizing each member into several elements. Examples of the application of such methods to composite columns have been reported by Schleich,[M16] Roik and Bergmann,[D76] and Mirza and Skrabek.[130] While

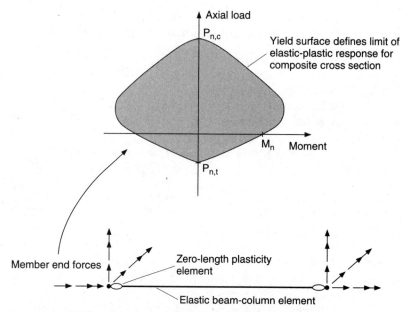

Figure 2.37 Yield-surface representation of inelastic behavior.

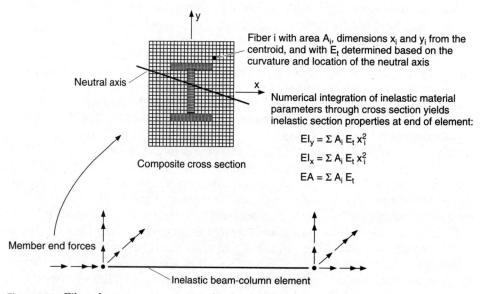

Figure 2.38 Fiber-element representation of inelastic behavior.

spread of plasticity methods are usually more accurate than concentrated plasticity methods, they generally require more computations and for that reason are less suited to the analysis of large structural systems.

2.5.3 Finite-element models

In certain instances it may be appropriate to use two- or three-dimensional finite elements to model structural continua which cannot be represented accurately by line elements. For example, two-dimensional plane stress elements are sometimes used to model irregularly shaped walls for in-plane stresses, and occasionally two-dimensional shell elements may be used to model out-of-plane effects in walls and slabs. For design practice most finite-element analyses are limited to elastic response to calculate the distribution of stresses under service loads. For strength design purposes, the results of elastic analyses should be interpreted carefully since the effects of concrete cracking can have a major influence on the magnitude and distribution of stresses and on the deflections.

On occasion, nonlinear analyses have been applied to composite structures for very specialized studies; however, the cost to perform such analyses is usually not warranted for routine building design, and the necessary budgets to perform the work are rarely available. Moreover, state-of-the-art nonlinear finite-element modeling of composite elements is not yet developed to the point that it is fully reliable, so users must be very knowledgeable about the limits of the analysis. Nevertheless, nonlinear finite-element methods are often used in research, and cases of their use in practice have been reported. One notable example where a three-dimensional nonlinear analysis was used was during the design of the 72-story InterFirst Plaza building in Dallas.[C89] In this case the computer code Adina[G29] was used to analyze the inelastic behavior of large beam-column joints between steel beams and composite columns, similar to joint type M1 shown in Fig. 2.31. It should be noted that all inelastic analyses must be a load-history study, as superposition of other load states is not valid.

2.5.4 Special analysis procedures

Special attention should be given to column shortening, time-dependent force redistribution, and construction sequence.

Calculation of column shortening. Differential column shortening in buildings more than about 20 stories high is one of the more serious effects caused by the combination of steel and concrete elements. If measures are not taken to avoid or compensate for differential shortening, it can lead to unlevel floors and other problems. Several good references are available on the subject.[G17,G50] The methods described in these references are not directly applicable to implementation in a matrix structural analysis, but rather they are applied on a column-by-column basis using loads from a separate analysis. Thus these methods neglect the change in column loads due to the differential shortening. Therefore, when applied on a column-by-column basis, these methods are only appropriate for flexible framed structures where the axial stiffness of the columns is much larger than the stiffness of beams connecting the columns. On the other hand, for rigid braced or Vierendeel systems, it may not be appropriate to neglect the load sharing between columns when calculating inelastic shortening. The methods referenced above include the sequence and duration of loading and other parameters which affect the creep and shrinkage of concrete, e.g., age at loading, size effects, and ambient temperature and humidity. More detailed discussion of the factors affecting concrete creep and shrinkage are described in an ACI committee report.[G65] Further discussion of differential column shortening and of creep and shrinkage effects on composite columns may be found in Chap. 4.

Time-dependent force redistribution.   In redundant structural configurations where concrete and steel elements share loads, creep and shrinkage of the concrete can transfer significant stresses to the steel above those predicted by elastic analyses. In certain instances, such as the design of composite beams, this effect can be safely ignored for purposes of strength calculations. However, in systems where large concrete or composite supercolumns are used in conjunction with smaller steel elements, column shortening can cause overloading and buckling of the steel members. In certain cases this problem can be overcome by designing the system so as to avoid overloading the steel members when the concrete columns shorten. For example, as shown in Fig. 2.39, this technique was used in the 57-story Norwest Center Building in Minneapolis where vertical joints in the steel columns of the Vierendeel frame were installed every five stories.

One approach for conservatively calculating the distribution of member forces between the steel, concrete, and composite members is to bracket the range of load sharing which may occur because of the relative stiffness of the steel and concrete elements. The principal uncertainties involved are the effective modulus of the concrete, which is a function of its elastic instantaneous stiffness, and the effects of long-term creep and shrinkage. When other nonlinear effects are small and superposition is valid, the effect of the change in concrete stiffness can be calculated by performing multiple analyses under long-term loads using upper- and lower-bound values of the estimated concrete modulus. Individual design member forces for long-term loads can then be set equal to the maximum values calculated from the upper- and lower-bound analyses.

Construction sequence.   In principle, analysis techniques which can track the sequence of loading and deflections during construction are no different from standard matrix-based methods. However, such analyses require a specialized implementation which handles the extra bookkeeping involved with adding members, updating the geometry, storing member forces from previous analysis steps, and reformulating the equilibrium equations for the new configura-

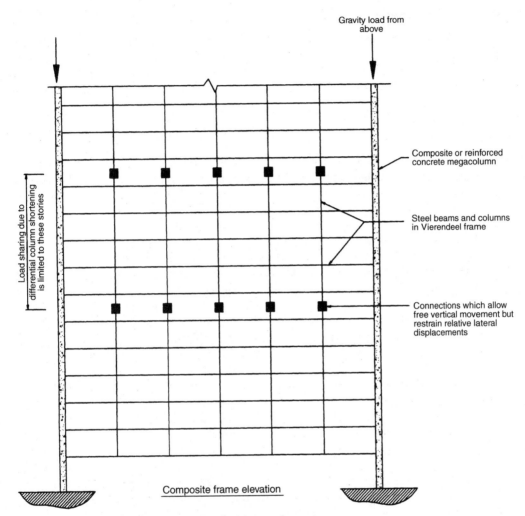

Figure 2.39 Load sharing between steel and concrete columns.

tion, i.e., the stiffness matrix and force and displacement vectors. In the absence of specialized software which can handle this, there are two approaches one can take. One is to simply analyze the structure independently at various stages of construction and check that strength and deflection limits are met at each stage. The shortcoming of this approach is that it may overlook cumulative load or deformation effects which are nonlinear from one construction stage to the next. A second approach is to use multiple independent analyses but to carry forward member load and displacement information from one analysis to the next. This method should always provide accurate answers, but unfortunately, the bookkeeping involved is rather cumbersome and time-consuming. Nevertheless, these measures may be necessary when the construction sequence induces behavior quite different from that in the completed structure.

2.6   Construction Considerations

Selection of the most advantageous composite framing system depends on cost, speed of erection, architectural requirements, marketing considerations, height-to-footprint ratio, and wind and seismic conditions. The following is a generalized discussion of construction considerations for several common systems.

2.6.1   Types of structures

Four types of structures are discussed: a concrete core combined with a steel frame, concrete-filled steel pipe supercolumns combined with a steel frame, a composite system with formed composite supercolumns, and an exterior composite tube.

Concrete core—steel frame.   A composite system using steel members framing into a concrete core provides several construction challenges (Fig. 2.14). Phasing of the concrete and steel erection and efficient utilization of the equipment affect the economics of the project. When the core can be started and substantially completed during the lead time required for structural steel, maximum benefits are achieved. If the site is congested and access to pickup points is limited, logistics become a problem.

Selection of the core-forming system depends on the building configuration, local practice, and need to coordinate with steel erection. Jump forms, self-jacking forms, and slip forms for the core each have their application. During core construction, vertical transportation for personnel can be provided by a man hoist, usually located in an elevator shaft. Material hoisting requirements vary with the selected forming system.

The core rising above the steel limits the swing and location of steel erection cranes, unless a tower crane is used to erect the core and is adequate to erect the steel. The concrete core progressing independently ahead of steel erection permits an efficient concrete operation and early completion. Early completion of the core allows an early start on the permanent elevators and eliminates them from the critical path to occupancy.

When steel erection columns are located within the concrete core walls and the walls follow steel erection (Fig. 2.20) out-of-tolerance problems are eliminated but at the expense of increased concrete cost and loss of time. The forming of the walls should follow placing of the concrete slab. The elevator-shaft side of the walls should be gang-formed and the other face formed with panels sized for convenient handling.

In all forming systems vertical plumbness and control of twisting require careful planning and monitoring. If out-of-plumbness of the walls exceeds required tolerances, adjustments to steel members or chipping of the concrete add cost and time to the erection. Provision for steel connections is customarily provided by weld plates in the core wall to receive clip angles. Weld plates embedded in walls should be oversized to allow for minor discrepancies in location.

Concrete-filled steel pipe supercolumns with steel frame. For tall buildings a composite system comprised of steel framing supported by large-diameter steel pipe core supercolumns and small-diameter steel pipe perimeter columns filled with very high strength concrete can be a fast and efficient system (Fig. 1.10). Low unit weight of steel can be achieved, but a local source of satisfactory aggregates for very high strength concrete is required as well as experience in the batching and handling of the product. Erection rates of a tier in 3 days are obtainable, but concrete placing in columns and slabs must be maintained close to the erection level for structural stability. Erection equipment should not impose loads on the unfilled columns. For maximum efficiency the high-strength concrete should be placed on a night shift and two tiers of columns filled at a time. Concrete is pumped into the bottom of the columns to prevent voids, and no vibration is required. Slumps of 8 or 9 in (20 or 23 cm) at the pump are required. Heat of hydration in the supercolumns is adequate to protect the concrete in cold weather.

Successful handling of very high strength pumpable concrete requires a well-thought-out quality control and quality assurance program and close monitoring and control of the moisture content of the sand and aggregate. The concrete has a truck life of 30 min or less, once it is on-site and plasticized. To complete concreting of all columns in a single shift may require more than one batch plant and one concrete pump as well as a mechanized system to handle hose relocations from column to column.

Shortening of columns during erection, caused by axial loads, requires close monitoring of elevations and adjustments as determined by the design engineer.

Composite systems with formed composite supercolumns. Structural steel framing with formed reinforced concrete composite supercolumns presents construction problems not experienced with circular steel pipe composite supercolumns. Particular difficulty is experienced with interior composite columns (Fig. 2.24) owing to core wind bracing which connects to the steel column within the composite column, thus penetrating the formwork. Furthermore, the placing of reinforcing bars through and around structural members requires holes in the steel or welding of bar anchors to the members. The erection rate of progress may be determined by the installation rate of interior column reinforcing bars.

The difficulty of forming around penetrations and the hoisting of forms in the congested core area makes the use of a stick forming system most economical for interior columns. Custom forms and lifting systems are applicable for use on perimeter columns. Column forms are filled from the bottom up with pumped concrete, which avoids the necessity of either external or internal vibration. The heat of hydration is adequate to protect the concrete in cold weather provided the columns are immediately sealed and wrapped with insulation following stripping.

The preferred erection sequence is for floor slabs to be placed prior to column reinforcing bars, to provide a working platform. Column completion follows 10 to 12 floors behind the erection level, and consideration must be given to imposed construction loads prior to the development of the strength of the supercolumns.

Exterior composite tube.   A composite tube system utilizing closely spaced composite perimeter columns and spandrel beams with structural steel interior columns and beams which frame into the exterior columns and support a composite deck is efficient for very tall buildings with a small footprint. Additional economies result since the exterior concrete framing forms a wall complete with window openings and is a ready support for exterior cladding and the securing of window frames.

Since light steel erection columns and spandrels support the steel framing system prior to concrete placement, the stability of the structure during erection is critical and requires precise sequencing of operations to maintain the required minimum number of floors between steel erection and concrete. Standby provisions for supplemental bracing in the advent of unusually high winds is also mandatory. A highly mechanized concrete forming system is required to ensure that the concreting operation can maintain pace with the steel erection, which generally progresses at the rate of a floor every 3 working days. Figures 2.40 and 2.41 show the forming and lifting system utilized during the construction of the 75-story Texas Commerce Plaza in Houston, Tex. An entire side of the building was formed as a unit with an attached self-lifting system.

The placing of the reinforcing steel in the columns and spandrels is critical to the schedule since the steel erection columns and spandrels eliminate the possibility of prefabrication of reinforcing-bar cages. Each bar, tie, and stirrup must be individually placed but still maintain the same completion rate per floor as the structural steel and concrete. For the perimeter columns and beams, the reinforcing steel can be placed immediately after the concreting of the floor slabs, since the bars are supported by the erection columns. Figure 2.42 shows the sequence of construction used on the Texas Commerce Plaza, which had interior shear walls through the 60th floor to compensate for interrupting the exterior tube at one corner of the building (Fig. 1.5).

Logistically, the material-handling demands can best be met by utilizing a self-jacking forming system, pumping the concrete and hoisting reinforcing bars during off-hours with the steel erection rig. Winter weather requires taking the necessary measures to ensure adequate concrete set in the very limited time allowed by the erection rate. Such measures include the use of insulated forms and the wrapping of concrete with insulation immediately following stripping.

Axial column shortening is a major consideration owing to the differential compression rate between the steel interior columns and the perimeter composite columns. Every two tiers, the elevation of the top of the columns should be surveyed and the results reported to the design engineer for calculation of what adjustments must be made by shimming columns in the next tier. Since the concrete columns are subject to different load conditions and to creep over time, the perimeter columns will be held to an elevation different

Figure 2.40 Formwork system for Texas Commerce Plaza.

from that of the interior columns so that in time and under full-load conditions, the floors will come close to level.

2.6.2 Site factors

Of the many items that must be considered for a particular construction site, at least the following five deserve brief discussion: erection schedules, equipment selection, selection of concrete placing systems, labor and staff requirements, and quality-control program.

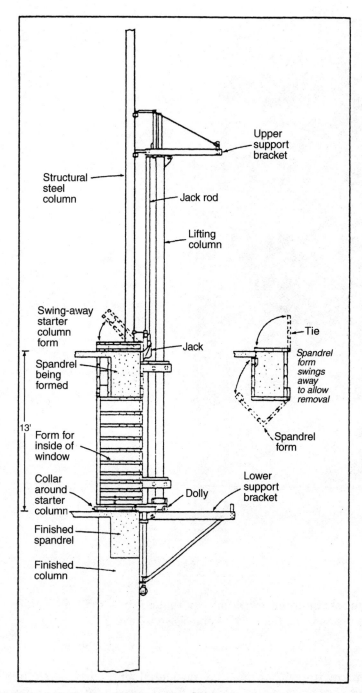

Figure 2.41 Formwork lifting system.[C60A]

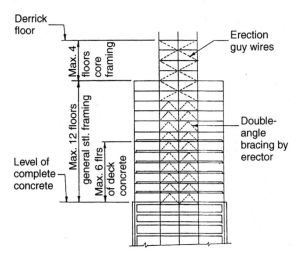

Derrick floor

Erection guy wires

Max. 4 floors core framing

Max. 12 floors general stl. framing

Max. 6 flrs of deck concrete

Level of complete concrete

Double-angle bracing by erector

Figure 2.42 Construction sequence.[C61]

Erection schedules. In all the aforementioned systems the rate of construction depends less on the type of system than on the following factors:

1. Number of crane hooks which can economically be used

2. Number of pieces of steel per floor

3. Local practice and restrictions

4. Experience and skill of the contractor

The systems which require the placing and stripping of forms for vertical concrete can progress at the rate of a floor every 3 days. Slip-formed cores progress at the rate of 1 ft (0.3 m) per hour. The concreting of in-filled steel tubes is paced by the steel erection rate. The steel erection rate with all systems should be a two-floor tier every $2\frac{1}{2}$ to 3 days.

Equipment selection. The crane and derrick selection process is driven by the steel erection requirements and site logistics. When the concrete core precedes steel erection, the same crane might be utilized for both operations; otherwise forming and concreting are independent from steel and require their own equipment.

Selection of concrete placement systems. With the exception of where the concrete core precedes steel erection, concrete placing can be handled most efficiently by pumping. Concrete core construction normally utilizes a crane, and therefore hook time is available for placing concrete by bucket. Since very high strength concrete is susceptible to segregation, it should be placed by pumping.

Pumping rates vary with the activity (slab, columns, and walls) and will decrease with height by as much as 50 percent at the top of a very tall building. Pumping rates of 75 yd³ (58 m³) per hour are achievable on lower-level slab pours.

Labor and staff requirements. Any system requiring significant quantities of concrete will be more labor-intensive than structural steel systems. However, the construction trades involved in concrete work are generally available locally, and concrete labor and material cost should be adequately offset by the reduction in structural steel cost. The contractor's management supervision can be expected to require an additional supervisor to oversee the concrete operation.

Quality-control program. The composite systems requiring other than standard quality-control programs are those using very high strength concrete and those requiring the concrete core to precede steel erection. The design mix for high-strength concrete requires a minimum of 6 months' effort to achieve a satisfactory pumpable mix. A full-time quality-control inspector is recommended during the concrete placing operation. The construction of the concrete core requires constant attention to assure plumbness within the required tolerances and accurate placement of embedments.

2.6.3 Cost factors

Cost comparisons for the various systems fluctuate with location and changing market conditions. Each individual project requires its own cost analysis. An experienced contractor should have no preference because of degree of difficulty between all-concrete, all-steel, and composite construction and be equally adaptable to all three provided the design has been executed by a knowledgeable engineer in adequate detail.

Some composite systems have additional advantages in how they affect nonstructural items. The exterior concrete perimeter reduces waterproofing and insulation requirements and is an in-place support system for attachment of the exterior skin. When the concrete core of a steel frame structure is completed early, it allows an early start of elevators which are frequently on the critical path to completion.

2.6.4 Construction of Texas Commerce Tower

At 75 stories, this Houston, Tex.,[C67] building is currently the tallest structure in the United States with a composite frame and is an appropriate case history for the review of major construction issues. This building, owned and developed by Gerald D. Hines Interests and Texas Commerce Bank, was designed by I. M. Pei & Partners. The structural engineer was CBM Engineers, Inc., and the general contractor was Turner Construction Co.

Figure 1.5 shows a typical floor plan with perimeter composite columns spaced 10 ft (3.1 m) on centers with composite spandrels, an interior structural steel framing system, and interior concrete shear walls. The shear walls rise to the 60th floor to compensate for the interruption of the exterior tube at one face of the building.

During erection the structural steel floor framing was supported temporarily by perimeter lightweight steel columns and spandrel beams until these lightweight members could be encased in reinforced concrete. The steel perimeter columns were designed to support 12 floors of steel framing and floor slabs. Thus concrete encasement was mandatory before erection could proceed to a higher level. Since Houston is in a hurricane-prone area, it was necessary to have a contingency plan to provide additional stability with standby cables and braces in the event of high winds.

The building is supported on a 9-ft 9-in–deep (3-m) concrete mat 63 ft (19 m) below grade and 40 ft (12 m) below the existing water table. The weight of the volume of excavated earth was equal to the weight of the building to minimize settlement. The retention system was composed of a series of drilled reinforced concrete piers extending well below the bottom of the mat and laterally supported by tiebacks drilled through the 1-ft (0.3-m) space between adjacent piers. A temporary well-point system was installed outside the piers and spaced to avoid the tiebacks. The water table was lowered to 4 ft (1.2 m) below the bottom of the mat to prevent uplift of the subgrade prior to placement of the mat. As basement work progressed a permanent well-point system was installed through the foundation walls.

The foundation walls are composed of reinforced concrete piers with 8 in (0.2 m) of reinforced concrete applied to the inner face of the piers. To expedite the schedule the 8 in (0.2 m) of concrete was applied top down by guniting as the excavation progressed so that the walls would be completed by the time structural steel which framed into the walls was started. The 15,500 yd³ (11,900 m³) mat was placed in two approximately equal pours. The construction joint was formed with metal rib lath on a metal frame to eliminate stripping. Utilizing 5 batch plants, 153 trucks, and 12 concrete pumps, the first mat pour was placed in 15 h and the second pour took 12 h. Work was performed on a weekend night to avoid traffic congestion.

Structural steel for the tower was erected to the 4th floor level by mobile cranes operating in the excavation. At the 4th floor level a guy derrick was erected while the mobile cranes completed erection of the surrounding structure to the plaza level. Meanwhile concrete encasement of the tower perimeter columns and spandrels in the basement levels was pushed so that tower steel erection could resume. Since the concrete formwork was nontypical from the mat to the 4th floor level, the formwork was basically hand-set using modular units to the extent that they were practical. With completion of the surrounding steel and steel deck to grade, the portion of the plaza required for the steel delivery trucks servicing the guy derrick was concreted and erection of tower steel resumed.

From almost the start of excavation, work was in progress designing and fabricating the steel prefabricated forming and self-jacking system which was first installed on the typical 4th floor. This sophisticated system formed the columns and spandrels into essentially four units—one for each side of the building. Each unit carried with it a safety net and was jacked in one piece to the next level. The forming system had no loose parts. Cam fasteners locked the hinged form sides together as they folded into place. When stripped and folded open, the entire unit was rolled out and jacked to the next level and rolled back into place. The forms had an adjustment to allow the depth of the columns to be reduced. The width of the columns was constant, since they formed the sides of the window openings.

The contract required that the structure be erected at the rate of a floor every 3 days for the typical floors. The forming and concreting operation achieved this pace but at the lower levels required a large crew working overtime. As work progressed, the crew size was reduced by 75 percent and the work was performed in a standard work day. The 72 levels from the 4th through the roof were accomplished in 11 months using Saturdays as makeup days for inclement weather.

Considerable study also went into planning the reinforcing-steel operation, since it had to be placed around the steel columns and spandrels, which made prefabrication impossible, yet the 3-day cycle had to be met. Perimeter column reinforcing bars were placed in two-story lengths and connected with mechanical compression splices at varying elevations. Spandrel reinforcing bars had to be threaded through stirrups and past the columns using the longest lengths possible to minimize lap splices.

The sequence of operations required concrete to be placed every day starting with the deck pour seven floors below the derrick on day 1. Concrete shear walls at nine floors below the derrick were poured on day 2, and the perimeter columns and spandrels followed on day 3, averaging 275 yd^3 (210 m^3) of concrete per day.

Concrete placement for the entire structure was by pump located at ground level and pumped through a single riser. Placing rates of 75 yd^3/h (57 m^3/h) at the lower levels fell off to 40 yd^3/h (30 m^3/h) at the upper levels. Superplasticizer was used in the columns and spandrels during the winter months, which—thanks to Houston's moderate climate—proved adequate for next-day stripping on most days. Forms were cleaned with a water–compressed-air jet.

In addition to the rigidity the composite tube design provided for this very tall slim structure, it also eliminated the need for a structural support system for the building's granite cladding and also for waterproofing and insulating the exterior walls. The perimeter columns and spandrels formed a complete concrete envelope except for the window openings. The granite and window-washing tracks were bolted directly to the concrete envelope. Preglazed window units were bolted to the columns in the openings formed by the concrete and the granite cladding.

All trades subsequent to the structural work, including tenant finishes, followed closely behind at the same 3 day per floor schedule. By utilizing a temporary portable air-conditioning installation at the ground level outside the building and by zoning all mechanical, electrical, plumbing, and life safety

TABLE 2.3 Adjustment of Column Elevations[C61]

Levels	Zones (Fig. 2.43)							
	A	B	C	D	E	F	G	H
Roof	27.3	25.4	24.8	21.0	25.4	26.7	24.8	26.7
70th	26.7	24.8	24.1	20.3	24.1	25.4	24.1	25.4
60th	24.8	22.2	21.6	19.1	22.2	23.5	21.6	23.5
50th	22.2	19.7	20.3	17.1	21.8	21.6	20.3	21.0
40th	19.4	17.1	17.8	15.2	18.4	19.1	17.8	19.1
30th	16.5	15.2	15.2	14.0	17.1	17.1	15.9	17.1
20th	13.3	12.1	12.7	11.4	14.6	14.6	14.0	14.6
10th	10.2	9.5	9.5	8.9	12.1	12.1	12.1	12.1

NOTE: All adjustments are in inches.

systems, initial occupancy was achieved 3 months after topout of concrete. Substantial completion of the building was accomplished in 32 months.

The structural engineer had calculated the anticipated vertical movement in all the columns from settlement, mat deflection, and axial compression (Table 2.3 and Fig. 2.43). The first tier columns were increased in length to compensate for settlement and mat deflection. As erection proceeded, the elevation of the tops of columns was checked every four floors, and the engineer provided instructions as to the shimming necessary to compensate for differential shortening. Since the concrete perimeter columns and the interior steel columns compressed at different amounts and rates, the floors were actually cast slightly out of level at a uniform thickness to allow for the differences to dissipate as the building became fully loaded. Since the actual compression within a story height was only $\frac{3}{32}$ in (2.4 mm), it was not necessary to maintain the theoretical floor elevation, as this amount could be absorbed in the stone joints, etc. All adjustments were made to achieve level floors over time as the building was loaded. The composite tubular frame performed as anticipated and was without question an excellent solution for economical framing of this building.

2.6.5 Construction of Two Union Square

The design and construction of the composite frame of the Two Union Square[C81] project in Seattle, Wash., makes an interesting comparison to the Texas Commerce Tower. This 56-story office building of 1,766,000 gross ft² (164,000 m²) was built for Unico Properties, Inc., by Turner Construction Company's Seattle office. The architect was the NBBJ Group and the structural design was furnished by Skilling, Ward, Magnusson, Barkshire, Inc.

The height-to-footprint ratio was much less severe on Two Union Square than that of the Texas Commerce Tower, and the curtain wall exterior obvious-

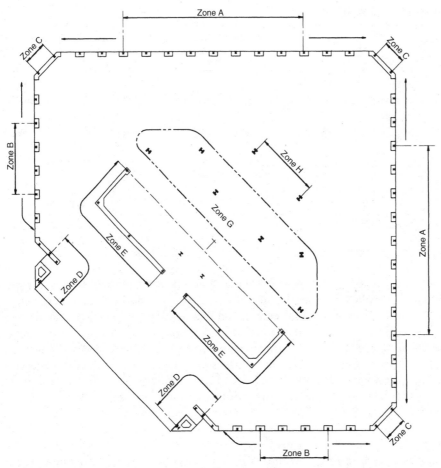

Figure 2.43 Axial shortening compensation.[C61]

ly did not require a stone cladding support system, so the structural design criteria differed significantly. Code requirements for both projects were demanding, since Seattle is in a Seismic Zone 3 and the Texas Commerce Tower is located in a hurricane zone.

As in most projects, the cost per square foot of the frame (consistent with meeting all requirements) was an important consideration in the selection of the structural framing system. In order to best utilize the differing structural advantages of concrete and steel, a design using 10-ft-diameter (3-m) super-columns consisting of a steel tube filled with very high strength concrete was developed. This reduced the structural steel required to 14 lb/ft^2 (68 kg/m^2). The four main load-bearing supercolumns were located in the core while concrete-filled 14-in-diameter (350-mm) columns were used at the building's perimeter. The basic floor plan is shown in Fig. 1.10. Wind loads and seismic forces were resisted by the core supercolumns and bracing.

Initial concrete requirements were for concrete with a strength of 14-ksi (97-MPa) concrete, but successful trial mixes resulted in consistent results of 19 ksi (131 MPa), and the specification was raised to the higher strength. This resulted in a higher modulus of elasticity of the concrete.

Further economies in the frame were available at the time by utilizing steel fabricated in Korea. However, the use of foreign steel, particularly on a project where 12,000 of the 22,000 pieces were unique, required extensive coordination and monitoring of the detailing, fabrication, and shipping processes. A local fabricating plant was used to handle missing and misfabricated pieces.

The excavation of the four basement levels required a tieback soldier pile and lagging system and the underpinning of an adjacent 36-story building. Ramps were used to truck out most of the excavated material, but the last 20 ft (6 m) were removed with mining conveyors. The tower was supported on belled caissons and the buildings in the adjacent parking, retail, and plaza area by spread footings. It took 9 months to complete the foundation required for the start of steel erection.

A strike at the Korean fabricating plant for 50 days extended the time to complete the frame to 8 months, but steel erection rates as high as a tier (two floors) in 3 days were achieved using two tower cranes. Structural requirements called for columns to be concreted within six floors of the erection deck and for floor slabs to be placed within eight floors of the same. The erection pace forced a demanding schedule for concrete placement to avoid discontinuity of work. Since adequate floor space was available at the top of the columns, all concrete was pumped into the base of the columns.

Initial attempts at concreting a partial number of columns in a tier as welding was completed proved inefficient. The concrete operation evolved with close coordination with the steel erection into economical placing of the high-strength concrete in all the columns for two tiers in a single second shift. Two pumps were required to place the 700 yd^3 (535 m^3) of concrete. Standpipes were used and were supplied by a dedicated batch plant with another plant on standby. Mechanical assistance was required to move the hoses efficiently from column to column and to minimize downtime and the resulting loss of slump in the standpipe and possible blockage. Line blockage caused by delays resulting from concrete arriving with the improper slump was an early problem until uniform moisture content of the sand was achieved by using a water spray bar on the conveyor loading the bunker prior to mixing. This addition along with doubling up the moisture content test procedure resulted in uniform pumpable mixes.

The project construction team required only 28 months from start of excavation to initial occupancy in spite of the challenges of an innovative framing system, foreign steel, and very high strength concrete.

3

Composite Beams

3.1 Components and Systems

Composite beams have long been recognized as the most economical elements for floor systems built of a concrete slab and supporting steel sections. Their ease of construction, superior strength and stiffness-to-weight ratios, and favorable fireproofing characteristics make them the preferred system components in applications where the floor is required to carry primarily gravity loads. Three variants on the traditional composite beam have been developed over the years to meet height limitations and the need for complex mechanical, electrical, and communication installations: composite beams with web openings, composite joists and trusses, and stub girders (Fig. 3.1). These systems are intended to provide high span-to-depth ratios while retaining flexibility in relocating building services. The design of traditional composite beams and of these innovative alternatives is presented in this chapter. Before looking at design, however, the fundamentals of composite action are discussed to foster an insight into the limitations and necessary simplifications inherent in the proposed approach.

Each of the three components of a composite floor system—beams, slab, and connectors—has its own material characteristics. The beams are typically made from ASTM A36, A572, or A36/A572 steel. Detailed information regarding these steels may be found in ASTM publications.[G83] From the practical design standpoint, their most important characteristics are (1) the sharply defined yield stress which allows their stress-strain characteristics to be accurately modeled by an elastoplastic curve, and (2) high ductilities that ensure that the plastic capacity of the cross section can be reached.

The concrete used for floors varies considerably, ranging from extreme lightweight to normal weight. The characteristics of structural normal-weight concrete are well known and are not repeated here.[G72,G75] Because of the need to limit the self-weight, lightweight concrete is commonly specified for com-

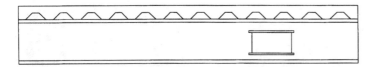

Composite beam showing reinforced-web opening

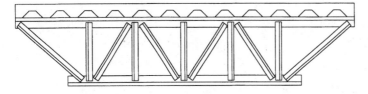

Composite joist or truss with double-angle members

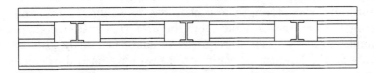

Stub girder system showing perpendicular floor beams

Figure 3.1   Composite floor systems.

posite floors when available. It typically ranges in strength from 3 to 5 ksi and has stress-strain characteristics similar to those of normal-weight concrete.[G48] Although some lightweight concrete has lower shear and bearing capacity, the ultimate flexural capacity of the section is the same as for normal-weight concrete of the same strength. If, however, the ribs are narrow and the slab is thin, longitudinal shear must be checked in the slab, since cracking along the top of the ribs can occur. Narrow ribs and thin slabs are exceptions rather than the rule in U.S. practice.

Serviceability characteristics such as creep and shrinkage vary considerably from normal-weight to lightweight concrete. The latter tends to be made with porous, coarse aggregates that are characterized by high absorption and low modulus of elasticity, both of which can have significant impact on long-term behavior. It is therefore advisable to evaluate carefully the long-term response of lightweight concrete proposed for use in composite floors.

The steel element and the concrete slab are most often mechanically connected using headed steel studs welded to the top flange of the steel beam (Fig. 3.2). Other types of shear connectors include rolled steel channels, bent

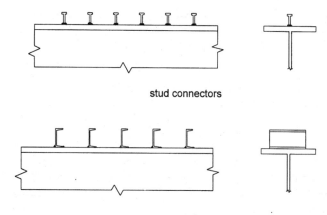

stud connectors

channel connectors

Figure 3.2 Types of shear connectors.

reinforcing bars, and plates and bars welded directly to the top of the steel beam. The stud shear connectors are used in the United States to the almost complete exclusion of other types. The AISC specification[D67,D91] for the design of buildings and the American Association of State Highway and Transportation Officials (AASHTO) specifications[D98] for the design of highway bridges include data for stud and channel shear connectors, and the American Welding Society (AWS) Structural Welding Code[D99] includes a chapter on stud welding that governs materials, welding procedures, and inspection.

Originally most composite floors were built with solid concrete slabs cast on removable forms. During the 1950s it became apparent that a composite slab system, in which a steel sheet is used as the formwork for the concrete and left in place after casting, would have many practical advantages. This led to the development of a great variety of cold-formed steel decks (Fig. 3.3).[D50,D81] The main difference between a solid slab and one cast on a steel deck is the presence of voids immediately above the steel beam. The voids can influence significantly the effectiveness of the shear connection by reducing the strength and stiffness of individual connectors. Empirical rules have been

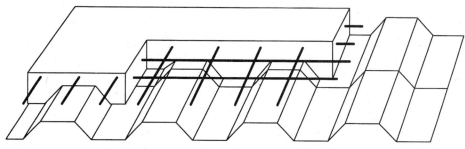

Figure 3.3 Profiled steel deck slab.

derived from test data to ensure that the reduction in shear capacity is accounted for in design.

3.2   Fundamentals of Composite Action

The most common type of composite construction is a composite beam, where a steel wide-flange section is intermittently connected to a concrete slab. In general terms it is assumed that these composite beams are loaded primarily in flexure, and that the steel beam carries all of the tension and the slab part or all of the compression. To transfer the horizontal shear at the interface between the steel beam and the concrete slab several mechanisms can be postulated, including adhesion, friction, and bearing. Except for steel sections fully encased in concrete, adhesion and friction are generally disregarded because of their lack of reliability. It is assumed for most composite beams that the shear connection is provided by steel elements welded to the steel beam and embedded in the concrete. These elements transfer the force between the steel beam and the connector by shear and between the connector and the concrete by bearing.

The degree of connection provided at the steel beam–concrete slab interface gives rise to a broad range of behavior:

1. At one extreme it could be assumed that there is no connection at all. The steel beam and the concrete slab respond to loading independently, and a reliable ultimate strength is given by the plastic capacity of the beam alone (Fig. 3.4) as in many older steel structures where no mechanical connectors were provided between the beam and the slab. In reality most of these structures tend to respond to load as composite at the service level because of frictional forces and adhesion. This type of construction is seldom built today, since the cost of providing mechanical connectors is usually lower than that of providing a larger steel-beam section capable of carrying the loads by itself.

2. At the other extreme one can assume perfect connection. The steel beam and the concrete slab respond as a single unit (Fig. 3.5) because there is no discontinuity of strains at the interface. Perfect connection requires a connector with infinite shear, bending, and axial stiffness. Since no mechanical shear connector is capable of providing this degree of stiffness, perfect connection is

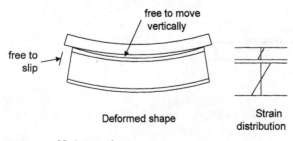

Deformed shape   Strain distribution

Figure 3.4   No interaction.

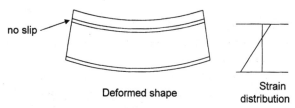

Figure 3.5 Complete interaction.

not practical. However, a small amount of slip at the interface does not reduce significantly the capacity of the section provided that the connectors can transfer the required maximum shear. Assuming that the concrete cannot resist tensile forces at ultimate, the most economical design for this system is the one in which the connectors can transfer as a shear force the smaller of either the tensile capacity of the steel beam $A_s F_y$ or the compressive capacity of the concrete slab $0.85A_c f_c'$. Known as complete interaction or full shear connection, this solution provides the maximum possible cross-sectional strength for a given beam and slab geometry.

3. Between no connection and complete interaction lies a region known as incomplete interaction or partial shear connection (Fig. 3.6). In this case the amount of connection provided is less than the smaller of $A_s F_y$ and $0.85A_c f_c'$. The strength provided by partial interaction can be taken, conservatively, as a linear interpolation between no and complete interaction (Fig. 3.7). As will be

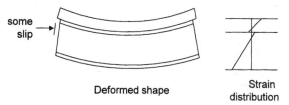

Figure 3.6 Incomplete interaction.

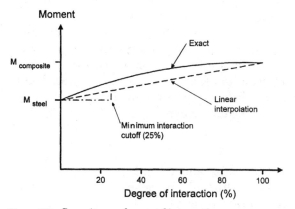

Figure 3.7 Capacity vs. degree of interaction.

discussed in more detail later, the real interaction curve falls somewhere above this straight line. Partial shear connection is popular because in most cases the cross section of the steel beam is larger than the minimum needed for full interaction while the number of shear connectors can be tailored closely to the required minimum. Because some degree of ductility is desirable after a section reaches its design capacity, codes limit the minimum amount of interaction to between 25 and 50 percent of full composite action. Very low percentages of interaction may result in a sudden shear failure of the connection.[76,129]

A rigorous elastic analysis of partial interaction is given in App. A. This type of analysis is valid only for the case of service loads where both the stiffness of the studs and the stress-strain characteristics of the steel and concrete can be assumed to be linear. As the loads increase, the stiffness of the studs begins to decrease, as is discussed in Sec. 3.3. As long as the concrete and steel remain elastic, a linear step-by-step analysis can be carried out to determine the forces, moments, and slips. Once the steel and concrete become nonlinear, however, a full inelastic iterative analysis is required. For design purposes this level of sophistication is not warranted, since a simple plastic analysis, as is discussed in Sec. 3.4, gives excellent results for the ultimate-strength-limit state.

3.3   Shear Connection

3.3.1   Principles of shear connection

Shear connection at the steel-concrete interface is the key element for achieving composite action in structural members. An accurate quantitative description of the shear connector strength is required if one is to precisely calculate the strength of a composite beam. Various means of shear connection have been used in the past,[39,C57] but without question the welded headed shear stud is the most prominent in construction today. The remainder of this section deals exclusively with the headed shear stud.

The fundamental principle by which all shear connectors are designed is that they must resist the horizontal shear force developed at the interface between the steel beam and the concrete slab. This force may range from the full yield strength of the steel section, as in complete interaction design governed by the strength of the steel section, to a relatively small percentage of the steel section yield strength, as in a design with the minimum permitted amount of interaction. Additionally, the stud connector must resist bending and the tendency of the slab and beam to separate vertically as described in App. A. Neither vertical separation nor bending forces in the connectors is a mode of behavior that is typically checked in design.

3.3.2   Behavior and strength of studs

The behavior and strength of welded headed shear studs are most often studied on the basis of push-out test data. Although the push-out test was developed in the 1930s,[39,D33] to this day there is no generally accepted or standard-

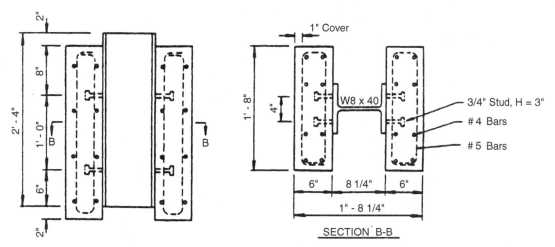

Figure 3.8 Conventional push-out test specimen.[64]

ized procedure for fabricating and testing push-out specimens. Consequently, researchers that have investigated shear stud behavior have often used similar but yet different procedures for conducting the tests. The results typically consist of a load vs. slip relationship for a shear stud, with the test conducted to failure of the specimen to resist load.

Most of the push-out specimens are similar to those tested at Lehigh University by Ollgaard et al.,[64] as shown in Fig. 3.8. A problem associated with this configuration is that the concrete must be cast on two different days, resulting in varying concrete properties for the two sides. Alternatively, formwork for the specimen can be built such that the slabs are cast vertically. This alleviates the problem of different concrete batches but causes the plastic concrete to settle and cure in an atypical position.

Modifications to the typical specimen can alleviate the problems identified in the previous paragraph.[144] One modification consists of forming the specimen in halves. Each half of a push-out specimen is constructed by attaching formwork to a structural tee. After the slabs are cast and cured, two halves are bolted through the stems of the structural tees to form a complete specimen. This manner of casting permits the slabs to be cast horizontally and from the same batch of concrete. This procedure avoids the problems associated with casting the two concrete slabs either at different times or in the vertical position. Overlapping the stems of the tees induces an eccentricity in the built-up steel section, as compared to using a rolled H shape. The effect due to this eccentricity is deemed negligible. Furthermore, the eccentricity can be eliminated by butt welding the two tees[144] or by bolting with two splice plates.

An additional modification has been recently introduced to improve the push-out test procedure.[144] To prevent premature separation between the slab and the steel deck in the direction normal to the slab surface, a yoke device is placed on the specimen. This manner of loading simulates the gravity load placed on a

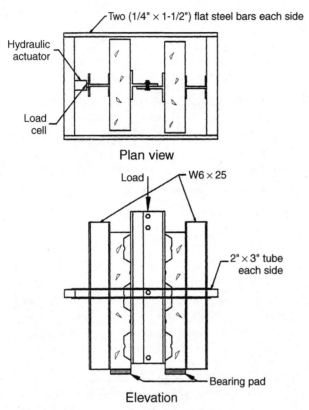

Figure 3.9   Modified push-out test specimen.[144]

slab of a floor. A load cell and hydraulic ram are part of the yoke assembly. The specimen configuration with the yoke in place is shown in Fig. 3.9.

Specimens are placed in a universal testing machine on a bed of plaster of Paris or on an elastomeric bearing pad, which minimizes the effects caused by any unevenness in the bottom of the specimen. Shear load is applied with the testing machine to the steel beam in load increments equal to approximately 10 percent of the expected specimen capacity. Displacement control is used once the load levels reach about 80 percent of the expected capacity. Load normal to the slab surface, applied using the yoke assembly, is monitored with a load cell and controlled with a hydraulic hand pump and ram. The normal load is increased along with the applied shear load. Results similar to those shown in Fig. 3.10 are typically obtained. The test is generally run monotonically, but an unloading curve is shown in Fig. 3.10 to illustrate the unloading behavior after significant slip has occurred as in the case of a major overload event. The unloading characteristics may have significant impact on the system's serviceability.

Generally the basic relationship between strength and slip has an exponential form typically given by

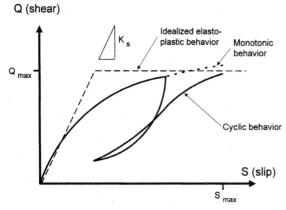

Figure 3.10   Shear-slip curve for headed stud connector.

$$Q = Q_u \, (1 - e^{-As})^B \tag{3.1}$$

where Q_u is the ultimate strength, s is the slip, and A and B are constants derived from curve fitting to test results. Ollgaard et al.[64] give $A = 18$ and $B = 0.4$ for the results of numerous tests conducted at Lehigh University and elsewhere. This type of relationship is useful if the behavior of a composite beam section needs to be tracked through the nonlinear range.

Tests of push-out specimens such as those shown in Fig. 3.8 were used to determine the ultimate strength of studs as reported by Ollgaard et al.[64] The nominal stud strength Q_n, which has been incorporated in the AISC LRFD specification,[D91] is given by

$$Q_n = 0.5 \, A_{sc} \sqrt{E_c f'_c} \leq A_{sc} F_u \tag{3.2}$$

where A_{sc} = cross-sectional area of a stud shear connector
f'_c = specified compressive strength of concrete
E_c = modulus of elasticity of concrete
F_u = minimum specified tensile strength of stud steel

The modulus of elasticity of concrete E_c in Eq. (3.2) may be computed from the empirical expression[D95]

$$E_c = w^{1.5} \sqrt{f'_c} \tag{3.2a}$$

where the units of E_c and f'_c are ksi and that of the unit weight of concrete w is lb/ft^3.

Two distinct limit states are indicated in Eq. (3.2), one governed by concrete and the other by the steel shear stud. The shear connector strength increases with increasing concrete compressive strength up to a maximum value equal to the tensile strength of the shear stud. The relationship given in Eq. (3.2) appears to indicate that failures in push-out tests would be controlled by concrete failure (e.g., pullout, splitting) for relatively low values of

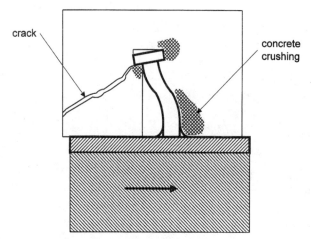

crack

concrete
crushing

Figure 3.11 Stud deformation in concrete.

concrete compressive strength, and steel failure for relatively high values of concrete strength. However, Ollgaard et al.[64] reported that virtually all tests exhibited a combination of concrete and steel failures. Early results of a research program underway at Virginia Polytechnic Institute and State University[144] at the time of this writing have indicated similar behavior. That is, tests with calculated strengths governed by concrete strength have exhibited a combination of concrete and steel failures. The experimental strengths are in close agreement with the calculated values.

The apparent inconsistency that arises if one compares the predicted and experimental failure modes is closely associated with the reason why the shear studs exhibit ductile behavior. The ductility is the result of high local stresses: the concrete is undergoing inelastic permanent deformations or crushing locally around the lower part of the stud, creating a void that permits the stud to deform (Fig. 3.11). Thus, even if the predicted strength appears to be based on a concrete failure, the overall shear connector behavior is still ductile because of the deformations occurring in the stud. The shear force and the moment in the stud have their maximum values at the weld connecting the stud to the beam flange and decrease rapidly with the distance from the weld. For studs with large length-to-diameter ratios the values may become negative, similar to the behavior of a cantilever supported on an elastic foundation.

3.3.3 Studs in a formed steel deck

The strength of shear connectors located in the ribs of a formed steel deck may be reduced from that in a flat soffit slab because of the influence of deck geometry. Empirical expressions for this reduction were developed by evaluating the results of numerous composite beam tests.[77] The reduced stud strength is obtained as a product of the nominal strength of a shear stud Q_n from Eq. (3.2) and a strength-reduction factor. For ribs oriented perpendicular to the beam, the stud strength-reduction factor R_{pe} is

$$R_{pe} = \frac{0.85}{\sqrt{N_r}} \frac{w_r}{h_r}\left(\frac{H_s}{h_r} - 1\right) \leq 1.0 \qquad (3.3)$$

where N_r = number of studs in one rib at a beam intersection
 w_r = average width of concrete rib
 h_r = nominal rib height
 H_s = length of shear stud after welding

When the ribs are parallel to the beam, the stud strength-reduction factor R_{pa} is given by

$$R_{pa} = 0.6 \frac{w_r}{h_r}\left(\frac{H_s}{h_r} - 1\right) \leq 1.0 \qquad (3.4)$$

Equations (3.3) and (3.4) were developed as a part of a Lehigh research program.[77] They have been in design specifications in the United States and abroad for many years, resulting in structures with satisfactory record of field experience. However, in recent years several researchers have reported that Eq. (3.3) is unconservative in certain configurations.[74,105,107] Modified calculation procedures have been proposed but no consensus has developed regarding the best design approach as a replacement for Eq. (3.3).

The reason for the discrepancy between recent experimental results and those predicted using Eqs. (3.2) and (3.3) is not clear. However, it is clear that a significant data base exists to substantiate the presently used procedures. A review of the data reported by Grant et al.,[77] Henderson,[74] and Klyce[107] reveals two important variables that may relate to the discrepancy. At least some of the tests reported by Grant et al. and all tests reported by Henderson were detailed with studs placed in pairs within a given rib. The single test reported by Klyce had two-thirds of the studs placed in pairs. Also, the deck used in the specimens of the test program at Lehigh University that represented the basic part of the much more extensive studies reported by Grant et al.[77] did not have a stiffener in the bottom flange of the steel deck. Both of these details, i.e., the use of pairs of studs per deck rib and the absence of the stiffener in the deck, appear to make the position of the shear stud within a rib of the deck less of a concern. These and other details are under investigation in several research studies in progress at the time of this writing.

Equations (3.3) and (3.4) were derived from tests of beams since beams simulate closely the behavior of shear connectors in practical applications. It can be argued, however, that an accurate evaluation of the shear connector strength must be made using carefully controlled push-out tests because the sensitivity of stud strength to various parameters is difficult to discern if the strength is back-calculated from beam test results. The best approach is a combination of the two types of specimens: use the push-out tests to evaluate a wide range of parameters and to formulate strength relationships, and the beam tests to check the applicability of the results to structural elements in practice.

3.3.4   Design criteria for shear connection

Equations (3.2) to (3.4), presented in the previous sections, represent the strength of headed shear studs and account for reductions due to the use of a steel deck. On the demand side of the inequality, the horizontal shear force required in positive-moment regions is the minimum of $0.85A_c f_c'$, $A_s F_y$, and ΣQ_n. In negative-moment regions, the required horizontal shear force is the minimum of $A_r F_{yr}$ and ΣQ_n, where only properly developed reinforcing bars can be included in A_r.

The required number of shear connectors must be placed between the point of maximum moment, either positive or negative, and the adjacent point of zero moment. Thus, for a simply supported uniformly loaded beam the required number of shear connectors must be placed between midspan and the beam end, the full required number on each side of midspan.

Because of the ductility of the headed studs, the connectors required between the points of maximum and zero moments may be distributed arbitrarily along the beam within some limits. Uniform spacing is the common practice. Minimum and maximum spacing limitations, described later in this section, must be satisfied. If the beam is subjected to concentrated loads, additional stud-distribution checks are necessary. Specifically, the number of shear connectors between a concentrated load and an adjacent point of zero moment must be adequate to develop the moment at the concentrated load. This flexibility in the placement of shear studs contributes favorably to the economy of composite beams.

One important parameter pertaining to stud placement has been overlooked previously but was identified in recent research studies: the position of the shear stud relative to the stiffener in the bottom flange of the steel deck. Most deck profiles manufactured in the United States have a stiffener in the middle of the bottom flange, thus making it necessary to weld shear studs off center (Fig. 3.12). Tests have shown differences in shear stud strengths for the two available locations. A stud placed on the side of the stiffener nearest the end of the span is stronger (strong position) than one placed on the side of the stiffener nearest the location of maximum moment (weak position).

The difference in strength might be attributed to the different thickness of concrete between the stud and the web of the deck that is nearest to midspan. Research has indicated that the strength of stud connectors in the weak position is not a function of concrete strength but rather depends more on the properties of the steel deck.[144] The problem can be minimized by specifying that the studs must be placed in the strong position; this would require coordination between the design engineer and the contractor installing the studs, and may not be realistic in many situations. Fortunately, the problem seems

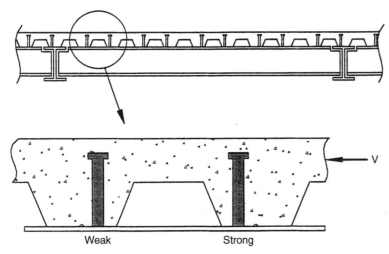

Figure 3.12 Weak and strong stud positions.[144]

to be critical only when there is just one stud per rib. It is recommended, therefore, to reduce the stud design strength by 25 percent from the value given by Eqs. (3.2) and (3.3) in cases where a rib contains only one stud.

Recommendations for spacing and lateral cover of shear connectors have been developed over the years on the basis of a combination of available test data and practical considerations. The distance between the surface of a shear connector and a free surface of concrete, that is, a surface not covered by steel decking, must not be less than 1 in, but a greater lateral cover is desirable. The maximum stud spacing should not be greater than the lesser of eight times the slab thickness or 36 in (0.91 m). Studs placed in a steel deck should be spaced a minimum of four stud diameters, center-to-center, in any direction. On the other hand, in installations without a steel deck, studs should be spaced a minimum of six stud diameters, center-to-center, along the length of the beam and four diameters, center-to-center, in the transverse direction.

Finally, tests have demonstrated[58] that when the stud diameter exceeds 2.5 times the plate thickness, the stud shear connector fails prematurely by tearing out of the plate. It is recommended that unless the stud is placed over the web of the supporting steel beam, a difficult requirement to ensure under field conditions, the stud diameter to flange thickness ratio should not exceed 2.5.

3.4 Design for Flexure

The design of structural members by LRFD places emphasis on the ultimate-strength-limit state. Composite beams are no exception, and thus the flexural design of these members requires accurate assessment of the strength of the individual components: the steel beam, the concrete slab, and the connection between them.

3.4.1 Cross-section forces

The steel beam and the concrete slab resist internal forces that are in equilibrium. Their characteristics are discussed in this article.

Steel beam.   The minimum strength of the steel beam for the case of full interaction can be represented by $A_s F_y$, where A_s is the area of the steel section and F_y is the nominal yield stress of the steel. Tests have shown that wide-flange steel beams are capable of reaching and exceeding their full plastic capacities (i.e., they can be considered compact) when used as composite beams with a concrete slab of a size sufficient to resist horizontal force equal to or exceeding $A_s F_y$. It should be noted, however, that once the concrete hardens the correct limit state in a composite beam is distortional buckling rather than the lateral torsional buckling which is the basis for current code limitations.[D91] Nevertheless, at least in part owing to ignoring the stiffening effect of the slab, American specifications[D91] are generally conservative. During construction, when the steel beam acts as a noncomposite section, the bracing effect of the decking and any bridging present are usually sufficient to prevent lateral torsional buckling problems.

When the effective portion of the slab is small or the degree of interaction is low, parts of the steel beam are in compression. Tests have shown that most steel beams can develop their yield capacity in tension and compression if local buckling of the web is avoided. The LRFD specification[D91] permits use of the full plastic capacity of the cross section as long as web slenderness h/t_w of the steel beam is less than $640/\sqrt{F_{yf}}$, where F_{yf} is the yield stress of the steel beam flange. In practice this is not a serious limitation since only one rolled section fails to meet this criterion, and the additional restraint of the slab adds some margin of safety. In summary, the force in the steel beam is easy to quantify and is probably the best known of the three components.

Another material characteristic that may need consideration in design is the effect the actual strength in excess of the minimum specified value may have on the ductility of a composite beam. The values used in design for F_y and f_c' are based on 5 percent exclusion rules; i.e., 95 percent of the materials have at least this strength and probably substantially more, while the values for shear studs are mean values; i.e., 50 percent of the studs are stronger. Thus, even though the strength of a beam is certain to equal or exceed the ultimate design moment M_u, the mode of failure may be controlled by the studs. In such a case the beam may respond to loading as one with partial interaction even when connectors are provided in the amount required for complete interaction. Thus a simple substitution of A572 Grade 50 steel for A36 steel may lead to a change in the mode of failure and possibly also to some loss of ductility.

Concrete slab.   The compressive strength of concrete is also seldom a problem. The compressive force in the slab can be taken as $0.85 A_c f_c'$, where A_c is the effective compression area, f_c' is the nominal concrete strength, and the 0.85 factor accounts for the idealized shape of the stress block and other variables. However, because the concrete is generally about 10 times weaker than

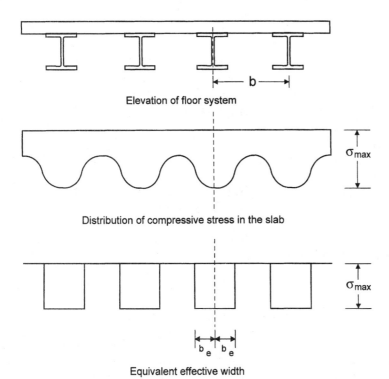

Elevation of floor system

Distribution of compressive stress in the slab

Equivalent effective width

Figure 3.13 Effective width definition.

the steel, a large area of the slab must be activated to balance the forces on the cross section. The problem is aggravated by the thin concrete slabs located above the steel ribs, often as little as 2 in (51 mm) thick.

The effective area of the slab A_c is the product of slab thickness and its effective width. Figure 3.13 shows a slab spanning several equally spaced beams. Because of shear lag effects, the elastic distribution of strains assuming perfect interaction between the beam and the slab is not uniform.[56,73,D52] The strains are large immediately above the beam and decrease with the distance from the beam, as is illustrated in Fig. 3.13. Assuming linear elasticity, the force F_t that can be carried by the slab attached to any given beam is

$$F_t = 2 \int_0^{A/2} \sigma_x t_s dy \qquad (3.5)$$

where A = beam spacing b
t_s = slab thickness
σ_x = stress in the slab

The effective width b_e can then be defined as the portion of the total width b that can carry the same total force assuming that the stress is uniform and its value is equal to that over the beam, i.e., σ_{max}:

$$b_e = \frac{F_t}{\sigma_{max} t_s b} \tag{3.6}$$

The value of b_e depends primarily on the type of loading and the ratio of beam spacing to beam length.[56] Based on many studies, the effective width on either side of a beam was generally taken in the past as one-half of the beam spacing ($b/2$), one-eighth of the span length ($l/8$), or eight times slab thickness. Tests and analysis indicate that the slab thickness seldom if ever governs and that there is no rational basis for this requirement. The AISC-LRFD specification[D91] requirements for effective slab width are based only on beam spacing, the span length, and the distance from the edge of the slab. Vallenilla[D52] has proposed recently that the effective width should also depend on the degree of composite action. He proposed $b_e = l/12$ for beams with less than 50 percent interaction and $b_e = l/8$ for beams with more than 50 percent interaction. An excellent discussion of this topic can be found in papers by Adekola[56] and Vallenilla.[D52]

3.4.2   Shear capacity at the interface

The design of composite beams is controlled primarily by the magnitude of horizontal shear force transferred between the concrete slab and the steel beam. This force transfer is usually provided for by headed stud or other types of shear connectors, all of which are characterized by similar load-slip behavior. Figure 3.10 shows a typical relationship between the horizontal shear and the horizontal displacement (slip) between the concrete slab and the steel beam for a headed shear stud obtained from a push-out test. It can be seen in Fig. 3.10 that the load-slip relationship is nonlinear from the beginning of loading. However, an elastoplastic approximation such as the one shown by the dashed lines in Fig. 3.10 can be used to describe the general characteristics of the interface. Three quantities, the shear stiffness k_s, the ultimate strength of the connectors Q_u, and the maximum slip s_{max}, are needed to characterize this elastoplastic curve. The value of k_s is useful in determining the serviceability characteristics, i.e., deflections and vibrations. The value Q_u is needed in determining the ultimate strength of the beam, and the value of s_{max} is important in evaluating the ductility of the system.

Figure 3.10 shows also one unloading cycle during a monotonic test to failure. At first, the unloading curve follows essentially the initial slope of the monotonic load-slip curve. However, at loads substantially less than the maximum reached before the start of the unloading, large slip reversal takes place, suggesting the presence of permanent deformations of the stud and particularly of the surrounding concrete. Under full load reversals, this pinching behavior results in redistribution of forces to less stressed connectors and may lead to significant loss of composite action and residual deflections.

The force transfer in a composite beam can be visualized by drawing free-

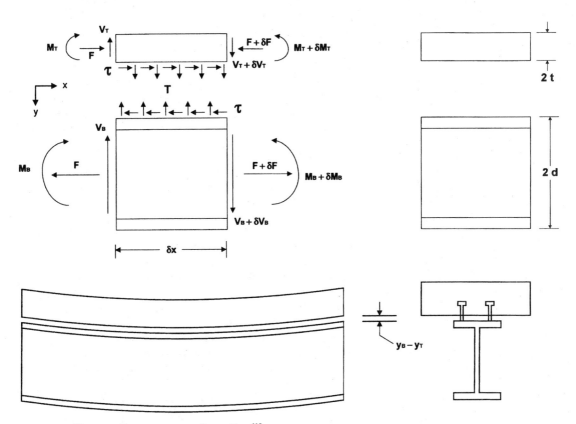

Figure 3.14 Forces acting on a composite section.[113]

body diagrams of the beam and the slab (Fig. 3.14) and writing equations of equilibrium of the components and the overall system. For the linear elastic case, i.e., barring any nonlinear behavior of materials and assuming that the slope of the load-slip curve for the studs is constant, it is possible to write a closed-form solution.[57,113,129,143,D34] The complete treatment of this case is given in App. A, where solutions for the forces and displacements are given for the cases of a single concentrated load, distributed load, and constant moment. The reader is encouraged to study App. A carefully, since the results are not always intuitive. For example, it should be noted that because of the lack of a continuous connection between the beam and the slab and other characteristics of the component elements of a composite beam, vertical separation can occur between the steel beam and the concrete slab, as has been demonstrated in tests of full-size composite beams.[28] This gives rise to vertical forces, and the need (1) to incorporate the axial stiffness of the connector k_t into the calculations and (2) to provide a vertical force-transfer mechanism, i.e., the heads of stud shear connectors.

3.4.3 Plastic strength for positive moments

Experiments performed on composite beams have shown that the true moment capacity of a section subjected to positive bending can be closely approximated by assuming that either the structural steel section is fully yielded or the concrete slab is stressed to $0.85f'_c$ through its full depth. The effective cross section for plastic analysis consists of the steel beam and the effective slab shown schematically in Fig. 3.15 together with a plastic stress distribution diagram. The compression force C in the concrete slab is the smallest of

$$C = A_s F_y \tag{3.7a}$$

$$C = 0.85f'_c A_c \tag{3.7b}$$

$$C = \Sigma Q_n \tag{3.7c}$$

where A_c = area of concrete slab within effective width
A_s = area of structural steel cross section
f'_c = specified compressive strength of concrete
F_y = minimum specified yield stress of steel
ΣQ_n = sum of nominal strengths of shear connectors between the point of maximum positive moment and the point of zero moment to either side

The effect of longitudinal slab reinforcement on the properties of the composite cross section is generally negligible. A possible exception may be the case where the compression force C is governed by the strength of the slab and the slab is heavily reinforced. In such case, the area of the longitudinal reinforcement within the effective width of the slab times the yield stress of the reinforcement may be added in determining C.

The depth of the concrete compression stress block a is equal to or less than the slab thickness. It is obtained from the equilibrium of horizontal forces acting on the slab (Fig. 3.15) as

$$a = \frac{C}{0.85f'_c b_e} \tag{3.8}$$

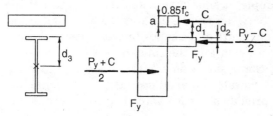

Figure 3.15 Plastic stress distribution for positive bending.[D91]

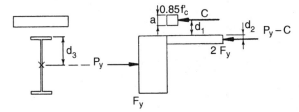

Figure 3.16 Modified plastic stress distribution.[D91]

where b_e is the effective width of the concrete slab. Replacing the stress distribution shown in Fig. 3.15 with the equivalent stress distribution shown in Fig. 3.16 leads to a simple, general solution of the problem. The nominal plastic resistance is obtained by adding the couples caused by compression C and tension P_y with respect to the compression force in the steel section[D91]:

$$M_n = C(d_1 + d_2) + P_y(d_3 - d_2) \qquad (3.9)$$

where P_y = tensile strength of steel section equal to $A_s F_y$
  d_1 = distance from centroid of compression force C in concrete to top of steel section
  d_2 = distance from centroid of compression force in steel section to top of steel section; for the case of no compression in the steel section $d_2 = 0$
  d_3 = distance from P_y to the top of the steel section

Equation (3.9) is applicable to steel sections symmetrical about one or two axes.

Normally, there is no reason not to use partial composite design for most commercial buildings. If a building is to be subjected to harsh fatigue loadings, such as lift trucks, fully composite construction and well-reinforced concrete slabs may be the prudent solution. Such, however, is not a common design situation. For nearly all composite floors partial interaction leads to the most economical designs.

The complete design of a partial composite section is not an easy task unless design aids[D50,D95] or a computer with a suitable design program are used. Three methods are presented here, an approximate method which can be used for preliminary designs and two exact methods which are based on the actual physical and geometrical properties of the composite section. The use of the word "exact" is inaccurate, as the methods are not really exact. The beam models used for the exact methods require that the actual properties of the beam be modified somewhat to account for the fillet areas between the web and the flanges of a rolled section.

Two different models of the beam section can be used (Fig 3.17). The model normally used has two equal flange areas each equal to the product of the flange thickness and flange width, and the web area is equal to the total beam area

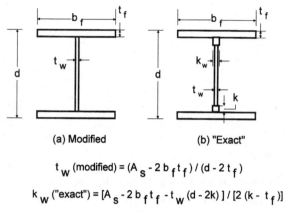

(a) Modified   (b) "Exact"

$$t_w \text{ (modified)} = (A_s - 2\,b_f t_f) / (d - 2\,t_f)$$

$$k_w \text{ ("exact")} = [A_s - 2\,b_f t_f - t_w (d - 2k)] / [2\,(k - t_f)]$$

Figure 3.17 Models for steel I beams.

less the two flange areas. The web thickness used for design is equal to the modified web area divided by the beam depth less twice the flange thickness (Fig. 3.17*a*). A more exact model can be used for computer programs. This model has two flange areas equal to the product of the flange width and depth. The web area is equal to the product of the web thickness and the beam web depth is equal to the distance between the inside faces of beam flanges less the *k* dimensions of the beam. There are two additional areas each with an area equal to one half of the total beam area less the two flange areas and the web area. These two areas can be taken as rectangular and are located between the flanges and the web in the position defined by the *k* distance dimension and the flange thickness of a beam at both the top and bottom. The use of this model results in a slightly more efficient design when the plastic neutral axis is located in the web of the composite section. This is the model used in the preparation of the Composite Beam Selection Tables in the LRFD manual[D95] and accounts for the slight difference found between the tables and manual calculations.

3.4.4 Design for positive bending

Three design examples are included to demonstrate approaches based on full and partial interaction. Both approximate and exact designs are given for partial interaction.

Full interaction. Find the maximum ultimate moment capacity of a W16×26 [$A_s = 7.68$ in² (50 cm²); $d = 15.69$ in (0.4 m)], $F_y = 36$ ksi (250 MPa), with a $3\frac{1}{4}$-in-thick (83-mm) lightweight concrete [$w = 115$ lb/ft³ (1.84 t/m³); $f_c' = 3.5$ ksi (24 MPa)] slab poured over a 3-in-deep (76-mm) composite steel deck using the AISC's LRFD specification.[D91] The orientation of the deck ribs is perpendicular to the beam. The beam span is 30 ft (9.1 m) and the spacing is 10 ft (3 m) on centers. Find the total number of $\frac{3}{4}$-in-diameter (19-mm) headed studs required to develop this ultimate moment.

1. Check compactness criteria

$$\frac{h_c}{t_w} = \frac{15.69 - 2(0.345) - 2(0.50)}{0.25}$$

$$= 56.0 < \frac{640}{\sqrt{f_y}} = 107$$

Therefore, a plastic section analysis is valid.

2. Determine effective width for typical interior beam

$$b_e = \frac{2l}{8} = \frac{2(360)}{8} = 90 \text{ in}$$

$$b_e = \frac{2b}{2} = \frac{2(120)}{2} = 120 \text{ in}$$

$$b_e = 90 \text{ in}$$

3. Determine C

$$C = A_s F_y = 7.68(36) = 276.5 \text{ kips}$$

$$C = 0.85 f'_c A_c = 0.85 \,(3.5)\,(90 \times 3.25) = 870.2 \text{ kips}$$

$$C = \Sigma Q_n - \text{assume it will not govern}$$

$$C = 276.5 \text{ kips}$$

4. Determine distances to centroid of forces

$$a = \frac{C}{0.85 f'_c \, b_e} = \frac{276.5}{0.85 \times 3.5 \times 90} = 1.03 \text{ in}$$

$$d_1 = \text{deck depth} + \text{slab thickness} - \frac{a}{2}$$

$$= 3 + 3.25 - \frac{1.03}{2} = 5.73 \text{ in}$$

$$d_2 = 0$$

$$d_3 = \frac{d}{2} = \frac{15.69}{2} = 7.84 \text{ in}$$

5. Compute ultimate capacity

$$M_n = 276.5 \times 5.73 + 276.5 \times 7.84 = 3752 \text{ in-kips}$$

$$= 312.7 \text{ ft-kips}$$

6. *Determine the design moment*

$$M_u = \phi M_n = (0.85)(312.7)$$

$$= 265.8 \text{ ft-kips}$$

7. *Determine required number of $\frac{3}{4}$-in-diameter shear studs*

$$Q_n = 0.5 A_{sc} (f'_c E_c)^{0.5} \leq A_{sc} F_u$$

$$= 0.5 \times 0.44 \times [3.5(115)^{1.5}(3.5)^{0.5}]^{0.5}$$

$$= 19.77 \text{ kips} < 0.44(60) = 26.4 \text{ kips}$$

Check for reduction due to deck geometry (Vulcraft 3 VLI deck):

$$h_r = 3.00 \text{ in}$$

$$H_s = (3 + 3.25 - 1.5) = 4.75 \text{ in}$$

$$w_r = [4.75 + 0.5(7.25 - 4.75)] = 6.00 \text{ in}$$

$$N_r = 1$$

$$R_{pe} = (0.85)\frac{6}{3}(\frac{4.75}{3}) - 1) = 0.99$$

$$Q_n = 19.77(0.99) = 19.6 \text{ kips}$$

$$N = \frac{C}{Q_n} = \frac{276.5}{19.6} = 14.1$$

Total required number of studs = 28.2. Use one stud per flute. Thus the stud design strength must be decreased by 25 percent for a total of 38 studs:

$$\Sigma Q_n = \frac{0.75(38)(19.6)}{2} = 279 \text{ kips} > C \qquad \text{O.K.}$$

Several design aids are available.[D50,D95] The AISC LRFD manual[D95] includes a series of tables (pp. 5-5 to 5-65) that simplify the design process. For this example, the distance from the top of the steel beam to the concrete flange force $d_1 = 5.73$ in. Entering the table on p. 5-28 with $Y_2 = 6$ in gives $M_u = 271$ ft-kips. Interpolating between $Y_2 = 6$ in and $Y_2 = 5.5$ in yields $Y_2 = 5.75$ in and $M_u = 266$ ft-kips, or the same answer as obtained from the above long-hand calculations.

Partial interaction, approximate approach.   Design a composite beam with partial interaction for ultimate design moment $M_u = 236$ ft-kips (320 kN-m). Assume the same properties as for the first example.

As shown in Fig. 3.7, the actual strength of a partially composite beam is somewhat higher than that given by a linear interpolation between the steel only and the full composite cases. For preliminary design purposes, therefore, the reduced number of studs may be calculated using the equation

$$N_{est} = \frac{N M_u - M_{min}}{M_{fc} - M_{min}}$$ (3.10)

where N_{est} = number of shear studs required for partial interaction
$\quad\quad N$ = number of shear studs for full interaction
$\quad M_{min}$ = minimum moment for estimating studs
$\quad\quad\quad = \phi P_y(0.5d)/12$
$\quad M_{fc}$ = flexural strength of a fully composite beam
$\quad\quad\quad = P_y e/12$

This formula is conservative only if the plastic neutral axis is in the steel flange or above. To begin the design, several sections are tried and listed in Table 3.1, where M_{fc} is calculated in the same way as ϕM_n in Sec. 3.4.5, N_d is the actual number used in design, and M_u is the exact capacity of the partially composite section.

From this preliminary design it is clear that the W16×26 is the most economical section and that the number of studs could be reduced from the preliminary estimate of 12 to perhaps as few as 10 studs per half-span.

Partial interaction, exact approach.   Using exact formulas, analyze the W16×26 from the preceding subsection. Assume the same properties as in Sec. 3.4.4.
$\quad$ 1. Determine C

$$C = A_s F_y = 7.68(36) = 276.5 \text{ kips}$$

$$C = 0.85 f'_c A_c = 0.85 (3.5) (90 \times 3.25) = 870.2 \text{ kips}$$

$$C = \Sigma Q_n = (10)(19.6) = 196 \text{ kips}$$

TABLE 3.1   Preliminary Design—Partial Interaction

Section	M_{min}	M_{fc}	N	N_{est}	N_d	M_u
W14×30	128	275	18.4	13.5	14	256
W16×26	119	266	14.1	11.5	12	253
W16×26	119	266			11	240
W16×26	119	266			10	233
W18×35	180	384	18.9	5.2	6	268

The units of M_{min}, M_{fc}, and M_u are ft-kips.
NOTE: For explanation of headings see Sec. 3.4.4.

2. *Determine distance to centroid of concrete force*

$$a = \frac{C}{0.85 f'_c b_e} = \frac{196}{0.85 \times 3.5 \times 90} = 0.73 \text{ in}$$

$$d_1 = \text{deck depth} + \text{slab thickness} - \frac{a}{2}$$

$$= 3 + 3.25 - \frac{0.73}{2}$$

$$= 5.89 \text{ in}$$

3. *Determine distance to centroid of compression in the steel* (see Fig. 3.17 and note $b_f = 5.50$ in for W16×26)

$$\frac{P_y - C}{2} = \frac{276.5 - 196}{2} = 40.3 \text{ kips}$$

Assume that d_2 is less than the flange thickness:

$$2d_2 = \frac{40.3 \text{ kips}}{(36 \text{ ksi})(5.5 \text{ in})} = 0.20 \text{ in}$$

Check that d_2 is in the flange as assumed:

$$2d_2 = 0.20 < t_f = 0.345 \text{ in} \qquad \text{O.K.}$$

$$d_2 = 0.10 \text{ in}$$

4. *Determine distance from P_y to top of the section*

$$d_3 = \frac{d}{2} = \frac{15.69}{2} = 7.84 \text{ in}$$

5. *Compute ultimate capacity*

$$M_n = (196)(5.89 + 0.10) + (276.5)(7.84 - 0.10)$$

$$= 3314 \text{ in-kips}$$

$$= 276.2 \text{ ft-kips}$$

6. *Determine the design moment*

$$M_u = \phi M_n = 0.85 \times 276.2$$

$$= 234.8 \text{ ft-kips}$$

TABLE 3.2   Composite Beam Economy Listing
for Wide-Flange Sections

W8×10	W18×40	W30×108
W10×12	W21×44	W30×116
W12×14	W21×50	W33×118
W12×16	W24×55	W33×130
W12×19	W24×62	W36×135
W14×22	W24×68	W40×139
W16×26	W24×76	W36×160
W14×30	W27×84	W40×167
W16×31	W30×90	W40×183
W18×35	W30×99	W40×192

This capacity is just short of the desired 236 ft-kips; say O.K. or redesign with 11 shear studs per half-span. Interpolating linearly in the tables in the LRFD manual will lead to a moment of 236 ft-kips.

The beam sections should be picked from an economy table arranged for plastically designed composite beam sections (Table 3.2). The measure for efficiency for composite beams designed on an ultimate-strength basis is simply the product of the beam area and the beam depth. This arrangement of sections is similar to but not identical to the economy table for flexure which appears in the AISC's LRFD Manual[D95] for noncomposite beams on pp. 4-15 to 4-25.

3.4.5   Partial interaction design with a cover plate

An existing floor system consists of A572 W21×44 beams spaced at 10 ft (3 m) and spanning 45 ft (13.7 m). The beams are connected with 30 $\frac{3}{4}$-in-diameter (19-mm) studs to the floor slab made of 3-in (76-mm) steel deck and 3.25-in (83-mm) topping of lightweight concrete with $f_c' = 4$ ksi (27.6 MPa). The floor system, originally designed for a $w_d = 2.35$ kips/ft (10.4 kN/m), needs to be checked for the storage loads required by a new tenant which increases the live loads by 50 lb/ft^2 (2.39 kN/m^2). If the existing system is inadequate, investigate cover plating the beam to increase the capacity.

1. Determine current capacity.   Taking the strength of one $\frac{3}{4}$-in stud reduced for the effects of lightweight concrete and steel deck geometry as 21.9 kips, the compressive force in the slab is limited by the available strength of shear connectors:

$$C = \Sigma Q_n$$

$$= 15 \times 21.9 \text{ kips/stud}$$

$$= 329 \text{ kips}$$

$$a = \frac{329}{0.85 \times 120 \times 4}$$

$$= 0.81 \text{ in}$$

$$Y_2 = 3.00 + 3.25 - \frac{0.81}{2}$$

$$= 5.85 \text{ in}$$

From the AISC manual, interpolate between $Y_2 = 6.0$ in and $\Sigma Q_n = 358$ kips ($M_u = 623$ ft-kips) and $Y_2 = 5.5$ in and $\Sigma Q_n = 260$ kips ($M_u = 561$ ft-kips). The capacity ϕM_n is roughly 603 ft-kips.

The required capacity computed for the current load $w_d = 2.35$ ft-kips is

$$M_u = \frac{2.35 \times 45^2}{8} = 595 \text{ ft-kips} < 603 \text{ ft-kips} \qquad \text{O.K.}$$

The additional 50 lb/ft^2 load translates into an additional factored load. The total factored load and the corresponding moment are

$$w_d = 2.35 + (0.050 \times 10 \times 1.6) = 3.15 \text{ kips/ft}$$

$$M_u = \frac{3.15 \times 45^2}{8} = 797 \text{ ft-kips}$$

The current capacity of 603 ft-kips is way short of the required 797 ft-kips, so a cover plate is needed.

2. *Assume a $\frac{1}{2} \times 7\frac{1}{2}$-in cover plate with $F_y = 50$ ksi and use the plastic stress distribution of Fig. 3.16.* In addition to the compressive force in the slab C, the following tensile and compressive forces acting on the steel section are present (Fig. 3.16):

P_{yp} = cover plate tensile yield force

$$= b_{cp} t_{cp} F_y = 7.5 \times 0.5 \times 50 = 187.5 \text{ kips}$$

P_{yr} = tensile yield force in the rolled shape

$$= (A_s - b_f t_f) F_y = [13.0 - (6.50 \times 0.45)] \times 50 = 504 \text{ kips}$$

P_{yf} = top flange compressive yield force

$$= b_f t_f F_y = 6.50 \times 0.45 \times 50 = 146.3 \text{ kips}$$

P_{yw} = compression yield force in the web

$$= 187.5 + 504 - 146.3 - 329 = 216.2 \text{ kips}$$

The depth of compression yielding in the web is

$$d_{wc} = \frac{216.2}{0.35 \times 2 \times 50} = 6.18 \text{ in}$$

Calculate the nominal capacity of the section by taking moments about the compressive force in the web:

$$M_n = \text{sum of yield forces multiplied by distance to the compressive force in the web}$$

Cover plate $= 188(0.25 + 20.66 - 0.45 - 3.09) = 3266$

Rolled shape $= 650(10.33 - 0.45 - 3.09) = 4414$

Top flange $= 293(0.225 + 3.09) = 971$

Slab $= 329(6.25 - 0.405 + 0.45 + 3.09) = 3088$

$$M_n = 3266 + 4414 + 3088 + 971 = 11{,}740 \text{ in-kips}$$

$$M_u = \frac{0.85 \times 11{,}740}{12} = 832 \text{ ft-kips} \qquad \text{O.K.}$$

3.4.6 Required number of studs

There is no direct way of determining the proper number of studs required for a partial composite section. A method of estimating is illustrated below. The method is generally conservative when the plastic neutral axis lies within the beam flange. When the plastic neutral axis is in the web of the steel section, the results may be unconservative. Any estimate made using Eq. (3.10) should be carefully checked.

Another method for estimating the number of studs required for a partial composite section is illustrated in Fig. 3.18. The figure pertains to a W16×26, $F_y = 36$ ksi (250 MPa), with 90 in (2.29 m) effective width of concrete flange, a $3\frac{1}{4}$-in-deep (83-mm) lightweight concrete slab of $f_c' = 3.5$ ksi (24 MPa) cast on a 3-in-deep (76-mm) composite steel deck. The calculated flexural strengths are plotted for the number of studs varying from 14 (fully composite) to the minimum recommended (4). The required number of studs for a given flexural strength is defined by the line between $M_{fc} = \phi P_y e/12$ which equals 266 ft-kips (361 kN-m) and $M_{min} = \phi P_y(d/2)/12$ which equals 154 ft-kips (209 kN-m). The plastic neutral axis is located in the web for four and six studs; for all other points it is located in the flange. One can observe that the moment capacity is reduced at an almost constant rate as long as the plastic neutral axis is located in the flange of the beam.

A number of different rolled shapes have been checked to verify the accuracy of Eq. (3.10). It appears that for light sections in any group the results are

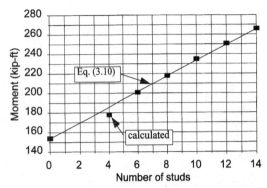

Figure 3.18 Minimum number of stud shear connectors.

very good, generally within 1 or 2 percent. As the sections get heavier, the estimated number of studs required becomes more conservative, up to 6 or 7 percent too high. If the plastic neutral axis is located in the web, the results are unreliable. It should be noted that in most cases for floor beams, the minimum number of studs required for minimum spacing will result in a section that places the plastic neutral axis in the flange of a rolled shape.

3.4.7 Elastic properties of partially composite beams

There are two elastic properties which may be needed for the design of partially composite sections. First, if an elastic stress analysis of the composite section is required, as in the case of checking for fatigue, the elastic section modulus must be known. If deflections are to be calculated, the effective moment of inertia of the partially composite section must be known. Approximate formulas for both follow:

$$I_e = I_s + \sqrt{\frac{\Sigma Q_n}{C_f}}\,(I_{tr} - I_s) \qquad (3.11)$$

$$S_e = S_s + \sqrt{\frac{\Sigma Q_n}{C_f}}\,(S_{tr} - S_s) \qquad (3.12)$$

where I_e = effective moment of inertia of a partially composite section
  S_e = effective section modulus of the partially composite section
  ΣQ_n = sum of the nominal strengths of shear connectors between the point of maximum moment and the point of zero moment to either side
  C_f = compression force in concrete for a fully composite section
  I_{tr} = moment of inertia of the fully composite uncracked transformed section
  I_s = moment of inertia of the steel section

S_{tr} = section modulus of the fully composite uncracked transformed section referred to the tension flange

S_s = section modulus of the structural steel section referred to the tension flange

It has been suggested that the values of the section modulus and the moment of inertia should be a direct ratio of $\Sigma Q_n/C_f$, thus reducing the value of the section modulus and the moment of inertia for a partially composite section. Because of the difficulty in calculating deflections accurately, this suggestion does not seem like a reasonable requirement for design.

3.4.8 Plastic strength for negative moment

Assuming that concrete has no tensile strength, the design of composite beams under negative moments reduces to the case of the steel section and the longitudinal steel reinforcement located in the slab within the effective slab width. The solution requires finding the plastic centroid of the cross section and computing moments about it. It is necessary to ensure that the steel section does not buckle locally, that the slab reinforcement is properly developed, and that appropriate shear connection is provided.

Referring to Fig. 3.19, the tensile force T in the reinforcing bars is the smaller of

$$T = A_r F_{yr} \tag{3.13a}$$

$$T = \Sigma Q_n \tag{3.13b}$$

where A_r = area of properly developed slab reinforcement parallel to the steel beam and within the effective width of the slab

F_{yr} = specified yield strength of the slab reinforcement

ΣQ_n = sum of the nominal strengths of shear connectors between the point of maximum negative moment and the point of zero moment to either side

The nominal plastic resistance of a composite section in negative bending may be expressed as follows:

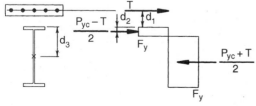

Figure 3.19 Plastic stress distribution for negative bending.[D91]

$$M_n = T(d_1 + d_2) + P_{yc}(d_3 - d_2) \qquad (3.14)$$

where P_{yc} = the compressive strength of the steel section $A_s F_y$
d_1 = distance from the centroid of the longitudinal slab reinforcement to the top of the steel section
d_2 = distance from the centroid of the tension force in the steel section to the top of the steel section
d_3 = distance from P_{yc} to the top of the steel section

3.4.9 Design for negative bending

Determine the negative moment capacity and elastic section properties for an A572 grade 50 W18×50 section with 10#5 grade 60 bars in the slab. Assume that the slab is 3 in (76 mm) thick on top of a 3-in (76-mm) deck, and that the bars have a 1-in (25-mm) cover.

1. Determine moment capacity.   Locate centroid of tension force in the beam:

$$T = A_r F_{yr} = 10 \times 0.31 \times 60 = 186 \text{ kips}$$

$$P_{yc} = A_s F_y = 14.7 \times 50 = 735 \text{ kips}$$

$$\frac{P_{yc} - T}{2} = \frac{735 - 186}{2} = 274.5 \text{ kips}$$

$$\text{Force in flange} = b_f t_f F_y = 7.495 \times 0.57 \times 50 = 213.6 \text{ kips} = F_f$$

$$\text{Force in web} = 274.5 - 213.6 = 60.9 \text{ kips} = F_w$$

$$a_w = \frac{F_w}{F_y \times t_w} = \frac{60.9}{50 \times 0.355} = 3.43 \text{ in}$$

Centroid of the compression force in the web:

$$d_2 = \frac{(F_f \times 0.5t_f) + [F_w \times (t_f + 0.5a_w)]}{F_f + F_w}$$

$$= \frac{(213.6 \times 0.5 \times 0.57) + [60.9 \times (0.57 + 0.5 \times 3.43)]}{274.5}$$

$$= \frac{60.9 + 139.2}{274.5} = 0.73 \text{ in}$$

$$d_3 = \frac{d}{2} = \frac{17.99}{2} = 9.00 \text{ in}$$

$$d_1 = 3 + 3 - 1 = 5 \text{ in}$$

Therefore:

$$M_n = [186(5 + 0.73)] + [735(9.00 - 0.73)] = 7140 \text{ in-kips}$$

$$= 595 \text{ ft-kips}$$

$$M_u = \phi M_n = 0.85 \times 595 = 506 \text{ ft-kips}$$

Note that this is very close to the positive-moment capacity of a similar partially composite beam with the plastic neutral axis in the web and $Y_2 = 4.5$ in, and is about 72 percent of the complete interaction capacity of a similar section.

2. *Determine the moment of inertia and elastic section modulus.* First determine the elastic centroid by adding moments about the bottom of the steel section:

$$\text{Slab bars} = 0.31 \times 10 \times (17.99 + 5.00) \quad = \quad 71.3$$

$$\text{Top flange} = 7.495 \times 0.57 \times 17.71 \qquad = \quad 75.7$$

$$\text{Bottom flange} = 7.495 \times 0.57 \times 0.285 \quad = \quad 1.2$$

$$\text{Web} = 16.85 \times 0.355 \times 9.00 \qquad = \quad 53.8$$

$$\text{Total} = 202.0 \text{ in}^3$$

$$\text{Centroid} = \frac{202}{3.1 + 14.7} = 11.35 \text{ in}$$

Distance between steel and composite centroid

$$11.35 - (0.5 \times 17.99) = 2.36 \text{ in}$$

$$\text{Slab bars} = 0.31 \times 10 \times \left(\frac{17.99}{2} + 5.00 - 2.36\right)^2 = \quad 419.7$$

$$\text{Steel beam} = \qquad\qquad\qquad\qquad\qquad\qquad\qquad = \quad 800.0$$

$$\text{Steel beam} = 14.7 \times (2.36)^2 \qquad\qquad\qquad\qquad = \quad 81.9$$

$$\text{Total} = 1302.0 \text{ in}^4$$

$$S_t = \frac{1302}{5 + 17.99 - 11.35} = 111.9 \text{ in}^3$$

$$S_b = \frac{1302}{11.35} = 114.7 \text{ in}^3$$

3.5   Serviceability

The commonly accepted span/depth ratios ($1000/F_y$ or $800/F_y$) and the usual check for live load ($l/360$) are generally sufficient to ensure adequate serviceability, since most structures are seldom loaded to their full service loads. In some cases, however, these commonly accepted limits do not give satisfactory results.

In particular, the long-term deflections due to creep and shrinkage need to be considered if spans are long, if a large portion of the live load is present over long periods of time, or if the materials used for the slab are sensitive to creep and shrinkage. The use of shallower and slender beams made possible by LRFD and the widespread use of lightweight aggregates certainly result in larger deflections and more vibration problems unless a careful assessment of serviceability criteria is made.

Another serviceability criterion which has not received much attention in the past but which could become more important in the future is excessive cracking of the slab. Cracks result from (1) settlement of plastic concrete, (2) volumetric instabilities, (3) structural action, and (4) unintended restraints.[G27] No guidelines are available as to the amount of cracking and crack width that may be allowed. In general these cracks do not endanger the safety of the structure, but many discussions between the owner, the designer, and the contractor arise because of this issue.

Floor vibrations have been extensively studied, and many guidelines to control their impact have been issued.[G26,G28] Problems with floor vibrations are usually associated with (1) a matching of the loading frequency with the frequency of the structure and (2) low damping characteristics. The vibration frequency depends primarily on (1) the superimposed mass, (2) the degree of restraint or continuity, (3) the stiffness of the beam, and (4) the span length. The span length is known, and the superimposed mass and stiffness of the beam can be calculated fairly well. The impact of the degree of end restraint or continuity can be very significant, but little or no data is available in this area. The same can be said for damping, with recommended values for composite floors ranging from 2 to 3 percent of critical.

3.5.1   Deflections

The exact calculation of deflections is complex even for a fairly simple structure like a simply supported composite beam. From the structural standpoint there are at least three main reasons for this complexity. First, loads change during the life of the structure and these changes cannot be predicted during the design stage. Second, the structural modeling cannot easily account for three-dimensional effects and unintentional structural continuity that is almost always present in structures. Third, the nonlinear characteristics of the connection provided by the shear studs are ignored. From the material standpoint the main complication that arises is the change in material properties (modulus of elasticity) with time due mainly to creep and shrinkage.

The computation of deflections in a structure can be subdivided into those for instantaneous deflections and those for long-term deflections. The former include the deflection when the slab is cast in an unshored floor or when shores are removed in a shored one, and the deflection due to a live load of short duration. The long-term deflection calculations may need to include deflections due to creep and shrinkage of the concrete, and changes of material properties with time.

Instantaneous deflections.   Procedures for calculating instantaneous deformations of composite beams are based on linear elastic analysis and nominal material properties. The main variable in these calculations is the moment of inertia ascribed to the composite beam. It is well known that, at least for deflection calculations, the current allowable stress design provisions[D67] assume an optimistic value for the effective width of a slab in a composite beam. Comparison with experimental results shows that using elastic moments of inertia based on this methodology underestimates deflections in the service range by 15 to 25 percent.[93,D52] The results of a linear elastic analysis can be improved by accounting for shear and the slip between the beam and the slab. Both of these factors are seldom if ever included in design calculations. The calculation of deflections by the LRFD specification is based on an ultimate-strength analysis, with a stress block smaller than that assumed in linear elastic transformed section analysis. In general the LRFD procedure limits the size of the concrete flange to the smallest of the total force on the steel section and the summation of the total force on shear studs. While this assumption of equivalent concrete flange is entirely reasonable in ultimate-strength calculations, the deflections under service loads are at significantly lower stress levels. Therefore, the use of a plastic moment of inertia for a computation in the elastic range is theoretically incorrect. On the other hand, the procedure typically results in better correlation with experimental results, since the plastic moment of inertia is 20 to 30 percent lower than the elastic one.

Long-term deflections.   Excessive deflection and cracking of composite floors shortly after buildings are finished are among the most common problems encountered in construction. Creep and shrinkage of the concrete slab are the most likely cause. Creep and shrinkage are generally treated together because they share some basic characteristics. First, the dimensional instabilities known as creep and shrinkage arise from the removal of absorbed water from the cement paste, and are partly reversible. Second, most of the factors that influence creep also affect shrinkage, resulting in very similar strain vs. time curves for both effects. Finally, the magnitude of creep and shrinkage strains in unrestrained concrete specimens is similar and equal to between 600 and 1000 microstrain.

To study the deflection behavior in service, four full-scale specimens were tested at the University of Minnesota.[D71] Each specimen consisted of a W18×35 beam with a 4.5-in-thick (114-mm) 96-in-wide (2.44-m) slab on a 3-in (76-mm) steel deck. The composite beams were 32 ft (9.75 m) long and were designed as fully composite with A36 steel and f'_c of 4 ksi (28 MPa), uti-

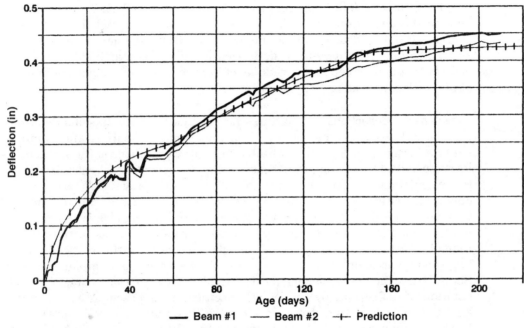

Figure 3.20 Predicted vs. measured shrinkage deflections adjusted for humidity.[D73]

lizing normal-weight concrete. Two specimens were used to monitor long-term shrinkage and creep (beams 1 and 2), while the other two were used to study the unshored vs. shored behavior (beams 3 and 4). Figure 3.20 shows the behavior of the first two beams. Beams 1 and 2 were identical except for the fact that at 28 days a sustained load equal to about 25 percent of the design live load was added to beam 1. The effect of shrinkage can be clearly seen, as the deflections continue to increase until around 200 days after casting. In contrast, the effect of creep is small, on the order of one-tenth of the shrinkage. Similar results have been reported from two studies conducted in Canada by Robinson[D47] and Kennedy[94] which indicate that the centerline deflection of typical simply supported composite beams and trusses due to drying shrinkage can approach $l/1200$ to $l/1000$.

In many cases deflections due to creep and shrinkage can be ignored if certain span-to-depth ratios are adhered to or if continuous construction is used. In continuous reinforced concrete construction creep and shrinkage generally act against one another and have about the same order of magnitude, and their net effect is to cancel each other and to produce small net deflections. In simply supported composite construction, on the other hand, the effects of creep and shrinkage are generally additive, and it is therefore unconservative to ignore their contribution.

When a floor slab is first cast two types of shrinkage, thermal and drying, occur. Thermal shrinkage is associated with the cooling of the member, while drying shrinkage is associated with the loss of moisture. For most practical situations in buildings, thermal shrinkage can be ignored. On the other hand, drying shrinkage can induce appreciable deflections. The amount of drying shrinkage will depend on the mix proportions, the age of the concrete, the ambient humidity, and the geometry of the member. The two most commonly used procedures for estimating drying shrinkage are those proposed by ACI Committee 209[G84] and by Comité Euro-Internationale du Béton (CEB).[G68] Both of these estimate the shrinkage strain as the product of some ultimate strain multiplied by a series of factors to account for the mix proportions, curing period, age of concrete, and surface-to-volume ratio of the member.

At least one simple method of predicting the amount of deflection due to shrinkage is available. The idea, first presented by Viest,[D15] involves replacing the shrinkage strain with a force acting at the centroid of the effective slab as shown in Fig. 3.21. The procedure requires that this force, acting eccentrically to the neutral axis of the member, be replaced with an equivalent moment applied at the ends of the section. The magnitude of ϵ_s (the drying shrinkage) can be obtained from tests, from the ACI or CEB procedures, or from an informed estimate.

The ACI and CEB procedures are tedious and require data that are in general unavailable to the designer. A more reasonable approach, and a long-accepted one, is to assume the shrinkage strain to be 200 microstrain as proposed by Viest[D15] and assume a simplified model such as that shown in Fig. 3.21.

Creep is a stress-relieving mechanism that results in increased shortening of the slab in compression and produces additional deflections of the composite beam. Creep is generally important when the ratio of dead load to live load is large or when a large portion of the live load is present for long periods of time. Current codes do not differentiate between short-term and long-term live loads. While codes do not specify what percentage of the live load

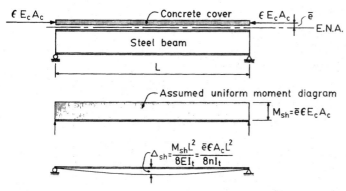

Figure 3.21 Calculation of shrinkage deflections.[D47] (*Canadian Institute of Steel Construction.*)

should be considered to be long-term, studies have shown that in the absence of better information, assuming about 25 percent of full live load to be long-term load is reasonable for most buildings.

The typical expression for creep computes the creep strain at time t as the product of a creep strain at a reference time $t = 0$, corrected by multipliers to account for ultimate creep, for the time at which creep strain is desired, the age of loading, relative humidity, volume-to-surface ratio, slump, amount of fines in the concrete mix, and air content. These calculations are valid for concrete under constant stress. Because the concrete shrinks and creeps with time, the computed creep strain must be adjusted. A simplified approach to this procedure has been proposed by Bažant,[G23] who uses the concept of an aging coefficient. The coefficient is used to find an effective modulus of elasticity for concrete. This new modulus of elasticity is then used to compute a modified modular ratio, and the creep deflection is calculated using elastic analysis formulas and the modified n and E values. Shown in Fig. 3.20 is a prediction made using an age-adjusted modulus approach that included careful modeling of the relative humidity conditions with time. The age-adjusted modulus seems to give very good predictions.

Effect of end restraint.   The degree of fixity at the end of a beam can have a significant impact on the total deflection. There is a large degree of continuity in most composite floors, including additional reinforcement over the column lines to decrease the size of cracks. Figure 3.22 shows the centerline deflections for a composite beam attached to a column with several different end restraints. For a connection consisting of double web angles and 8#4 reinforcing bars in the slab, the reduction in deflection was over 60 percent. For a connection made up of a large seat angle and the same amount of reinforce-

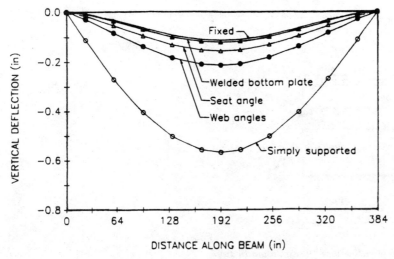

Figure 3.22 Influence of end restraint on deflections.

ment in the slab, the decrease was close to 70 percent. Finally, for a connection consisting of a welded bottom plate, web angles, and the same amount of slab reinforcing bars, the reduction in deflection was almost 80 percent.

3.5.2 Camber and shoring

The methods used for composite construction include a number of combinations of cambering and shoring. Most contractors prefer to use unshored construction with camber in the beams and girders to overcome dead-load deflections. It also appears that most designers now employ camber in the beams and possibly girders to overcome the effects of dead-load deflections. Others design for shored construction.

If shored construction is specified and shores are placed only at the center of the filler beams, the effects of initial stresses in the steel beams are partially offset. If the supporting structure cannot safely support the wet load of the new slab, shores may be placed at the $\frac{1}{4}$ or $\frac{1}{5}$ points of the filler beam span in order to minimize the effect of wet load on the supporting structure. One should note that when shoring is specified, once the shores are removed the entire dead load is supported by the composite section. This method has a distinct disadvantage: When the load is released, as the filler beams deflect, the chance of a crack's opening up at the centerline of the girder along a row of studs is increased. These cracks are often unsightly, and there is some question as to whether they have adverse effect on the strength of the composite section even though such an effect, if present, is likely to be small. If this method of construction is used, it is especially important to place crack control reinforcement over the supporting girders.

For unshored construction, camber is usually called for beams and sometimes for girders to overcome the dead-load deflections that are resisted by the steel section alone. One must be careful not to specify too much camber. If beams have too much camber, the shear studs may not have proper cover. For beams used in most buildings, the tolerance for overcamber is $\frac{1}{2}$ in (13 mm) and that for undercamber is zero inches. However, only about three quarters of the camber can be expected to remain after shipment of the steel to the site.[D67] Camber obtained by heat is more likely to remain unchanged than that obtained by cold bending. In addition to the problem of getting beams with the proper camber to the job site, the beam's end connections may offer restraint that reduces the calculated dead-load deflection. The most common practice is to require cambering for somewhat less than the calculated dead-load deflection.

In situations where the beams are neither cambered nor shored and the slab is poured to a constant elevation, an allowance for the extra concrete should be made. For a filler beam, the extra concrete does not reduce its capacity, as the extra depth is sufficient to provided adequate strength. However, the extra concrete may affect the design of girders and columns.

Additional information on shoring is given in Sec. 3.6.5 and on camber in Sec. 3.6.6.

3.5.3 Floor vibrations

Millions of square feet of composite floor systems have been built in the United States in the last 35 years. A few of these projects have experienced severe vibration problems caused by walking of the occupants. The problem has been addressed primarily by Murray[G26] and the Steel Joist Institute[D63] in the United States and by Allen[G28] and the Canadian Standards[G60] in Canada. Murray and Allen have recently joined efforts to produce a consistent set of recommendations.[D82]

Two criteria have been used in the United States in the past. One was promulgated by Wiss and Parmelee.[G25] Modifications to this standard were suggested in the Steel Joist Institute guide.[D63] Murray[G26] proposed a standard based on the percent of critical damping, the maximum initial amplitude of the floor system due to a heel drop excitation, and the first natural frequency of the floor system. The paper by Allen and Murray[D82] follows the standard of the International Organization for Standardization (ISO), which sets upper limits on peak acceleration for a given natural frequency (Fig. 3.23). Unfortunately, the natural frequency of most floor systems is in the range of the lowest acceptable accelerations.

Special care should be taken for long-span structures without obvious sources of damping such as floor-to-ceiling partitions. In this type of structure (e.g., large dance halls and open-space floors in department stores) if the frequency of the activity matches the natural frequency of the floor system, a resonant response may occur. The use of deeper floor beams and girders, addition of mass and damping devices, and supplementing simple connections with end restraints are examples of possible preventive or remedial measures. However, an increase in end restraints is of little help if the resonance occurs with only one bay loaded.

3.5.4 Cracking

Some cracking can be expected in almost all concrete slabs. In composite floor slabs, the cracks tend to occur directly over a line of studs, whether it be a filler beam or a girder. Even in shored systems the slab concrete is generally placed on an unshored steel deck. As a result only loads applied after the concrete has hardened increase the deck's initial deflection. The nature of a composite slab is that slip must occur between the steel deck and the concrete slab before the deck embossments engage the concrete. This slip and the accompanying deflection tend to create a crack over the filler beams. In most cases, welded wire fabric reinforcement of the slab is assumed to adequately control the size of these cracks. An alternate method is to place reinforcing bars over the filler beams. If a floor slab is subjected to moving vehicles such as lift trucks, the slabs should be designed as ordinary reinforced concrete.

In shored systems, it may be expected that some cracking will occur over the supporting girders. This is due to the dead-load deflection of the filler beams and other factors already discussed in Sec. 3.5.1. As stated earlier, there is no reason to expect that these cracks reduce the strength of the com-

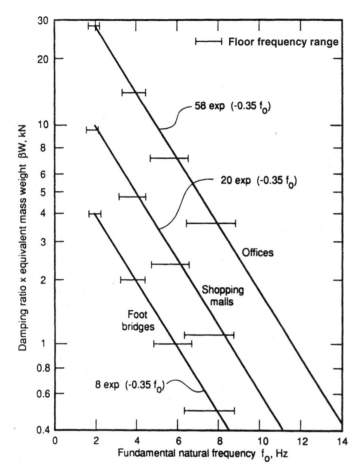

Figure 3.23 Floor accelerations.[D47] (*Canadian Institute of Steel Construction.*)

posite section significantly. In the case of the beams tested by Leon and Alsamsam[D73] one of the beams was unloaded after the maximum strength was reached and a large crack along the studs had formed. Upon reloading, this beam reached more than 85 percent of its maximum strength and exceeded its nominal plastic capacity.

In unshored systems the dead-load deflections affect only the steel beam section, not the composite section. Therefore, the tendency to crack is less severe than in shored systems. Nevertheless, it is recommended to place over the tops of girders reinforcing bars with an area equal at least to that of the usual temperature steel.[D91]

3.5.5 Knocking

Knocking is a problem caused by the abrupt slippage into bearing, under service loading, of fully tightened high-strength bolts. When the slippage occurs, a loud, sharp ringing or knocking sound is heard and a sharp floor vibration is felt. Occupants of buildings where this has occurred apparently find this phenomenon very disturbing and fear for their safety. Although at this time the extent of this problem is unknown, it is certain that knocking does not occur when the bolts are designed as slip-critical. The problem is under study by the Steel Buildings Committee of ASCE.[G73] The easiest way to prevent knocking is to install high-strength bolts snug-tight rather than fully tightened.

3.6   Other Design Considerations

3.6.1   Shear

In general the shear capacity of composite beams is not a governing criterion, but shear should be checked in any case. The prevailing practice is to assume that all shear in a composite beam is carried by the steel beam, so that the shear capacity is calculated as for a bare steel beam. An important exception are beams with substantial web penetrations common in both new and retrofitted structures. The design of beams with web openings is discussed in detail in Sec. 3.7.

Another case where shear is important relates to the shear strength of the slab when the ribs of the steel deck are parallel to the beam. If the ribs are high and narrow and the slab is thin, the horizontal shear capacity of the slab at the edge of the beam flange may be inadequate.[D47]

3.6.2   Floor assembly

Perhaps the first decision faced in the design of a composite beam is the selection of the floor assembly, that is, the selection of the type of concrete, whether lightweight or normal-weight; the depth and gage of the composite steel deck, typically 2- or 3-in-deep (51- or 76-mm) decks with gages ranging from no. 16 to no. 22; the thickness of concrete over the top of the steel deck, typically 2 to $4\frac{1}{2}$ in (51 to 114 mm); and whether the deck assembly is to be fireproofed or left unprotected. These questions are answered by consideration of a number of factors discussed below.

Experience has shown that it is usually more economical to leave the deck assembly unprotected and to make the concrete slab thick enough to achieve the 2-h fire rating required by most building codes. In such an assembly only the supporting steel beams must be sprayed with fireproofing. Buildings in high seismic zones, particularly of multifloor construction, may be an exception since in a lateral-load-resisting system it may prove more economical to reduce the floor dead load by using the thinnest acceptable floor slabs and spraying the whole deck assembly to achieve the 2-h fire rating. Fire assembly ratings for composite floor systems may be found in most steel deck manufacturer catalogs and in the Fire Resistance Directory published by Underwriters Laboratories, Inc.[G85] They are usually based on the total slab thickness including the depth of the steel deck and the thickness of concrete over the top of the deck.

The decision between 2- and 3-in-deep (51- and 76-mm) steel decks depends on the desired beam spacing and span length. Two-inch-deep decks can typically span 7 to 10 ft (2 to 3 m) while 3-in-deep decks can span 10 to 15 ft (3 to 4.5 m), depending on concrete thickness and deck gage. To span 10 ft, it is common to use a 2-in no. 18 gage steel deck combined with a lightweight concrete slab $3\frac{1}{4}$ in (83 mm) thick above the top of the ribs or an overall deck thickness of $5\frac{1}{4}$ in (133 mm), while a 3-in no. 16 gage composite deck with a total thickness of $6\frac{1}{4}$ in (159 mm) is common for a 15-ft span. These deck assemblies have an unprotected 2-h fire rating and are typically built without shores. For normal-weight concrete unprotected floor assemblies, popular alternatives are 2-in no. 20 gage decks spanning 7.5 ft (2.3 m) with a $6\frac{1}{2}$-in (165-mm) total slab thickness, and 3-in no. 16 and no. 18 gage decks spanning 10 and 12 ft (3 and 3.7 m), respectively, with a $7\frac{1}{2}$-in (191-mm) total slab thickness. Similarly as for lightweight concrete, the data are for unshored construction. Most deck manufacturers publish catalogs that aid in the deck selection for various types and thicknesses of slabs. Composite steel deck design criteria are published by the Steel Deck Institute.[D81]

Ponding of concrete caused by deck deflections between the supporting beams must always be accounted for in the selection of the composite steel deck and in the design of composite beams. It is customary to limit the steel deck deflection due to the weight of fresh concrete to the smaller of $l/180$, where l is the clear deck span, and $\frac{3}{4}$ in (19 mm).

3.6.3 Steel deck slab reinforcement

Composite deck slabs typically contain only nominal slab reinforcement because the steel deck itself is bonded to the concrete and provides for the positive moment. Temperature and shrinkage steel is customarily provided either as welded wire fabric or as reinforcing bars. The amount of such steel should not be less than about 0.00075 times the area of concrete above the deck, and 6×6 (15×15 cm) W1.4×W1.4 welded wire fabric is generally considered the lightest product usable for this purpose. Such quantity of steel controls cracking if placed near the top of the slab with $\frac{3}{4}$ to 1 in (19 to 25 mm) nominal cover. It is, however, quite common to provide more than twice this amount over the tops of composite beams and girders, more in the range of 0.0018 times the gross concrete area which is equal to the shrinkage and temperature steel required by the ACI building code. The purpose of this or even heavier reinforcement is to control more effectively the frequently inevitable negative-moment cracking that occurs randomly along the beam or girder length. While experience and limited research evidence suggest that such cracks have no significant effect on the strength of composite beams, the cracks can pose serviceability problems if not properly controlled. It is important to realize, however, that reinforcement cannot eliminate cracking of concrete, it can only control it.

3.6.4   Grade of structural steel

The selection of steel depends on local availability and cost of different grades. With the LRFD procedure for composite beams, it is very common for 50 ksi (345 MPa) grade steels to result in more economical designs than A36 steel. This trend applies to spans ranging from 25 to 50 ft (7.5 to 15 m). For lighter office-type loading (50 lb/ft^2 live load; 2.4 kN/m^2) and unshored construction, the size is often dictated by construction loading during concrete placement. For heavier mechanical or storage loads the design is usually governed by the strength or by live-load deflection of the composite beam. For shored construction, beam sizes are almost always controlled by live-load deflection, normally limited to $l/360$. The trend to higher-strength steels is being accelerated by the availability of dual certification steels (A36/A572) at little or no cost premium.

3.6.5   Shored vs. unshored construction

A number of factors affect the choice whether the composite deck, wet concrete, and other construction loads are to be supported by the bare steel beam alone or by temporary shoring. Should no temporary shoring be used, the steel beam must support all of these loads as well as its own weight. It is the customary practice to assume that all loads applied after the concrete has attained 75 percent of its 28-day strength are supported by the composite section.

In many practical cases of composite beam design for office live loads the size of the steel beam may be controlled by loads applied to the bare steel beam during construction. In such cases it seems reasonable to assume that a more economical design can be achieved if temporary shores are used to support the construction loads so that all design loads are resisted by the composite section. However, when the following factors are considered, it becomes apparent that this conclusion is not valid:

1. Theoretical studies and actual load tests have shown that the ultimate strength of a composite beam is the same whether shoring is used or not.

2. The cost of the shoring operation tends to offset any potential savings, even when the bare beam carrying the construction load controls composite beam design.

3. Shored composite beams have the disadvantage in that after the concrete hardens and the shoring is removed the slab takes part, through composite action, in carrying the dead loads. As a result, the composite beam is subjected to shrinkage and creep forces parallel to the beam. The net effect is a decrease in concrete slab stresses with a corresponding increase in the steel stresses as time progresses. Additional deflection is the practical consequence of the stress transfer. Although the additional time-dependent deflection may be compensated for by an increased initial camber, the stress transfer calls for increased sizes of the steel beams. Past experience shows that such increase more than offsets any potential savings, especially when the cost of shoring is considered. One justification for shored construction is the pre-

sumed advantage in controlling floor levelness. As this advantage is mitigated when long-time deflections are considered, the disadvantage brought on by creep and shrinkage assumes particular importance.

4. Apart from the extra cost incurred by shoring, the shoring operation itself can be difficult to effect in practice, particularly where settlement of the shoring is possible.

The conclusion from the above discussion suggests strongly that shored composite beam construction usually cannot be justified from the standpoint of either economy or practical execution.

3.6.6 Miscellaneous construction items

This section is focused on some of the practical problems that must be considered in the application of composite beam construction.

Support for slab reinforcement. One practical problem is cracking in the composite slab. Such cracks have often been very alarming to owners who tended to believe that the cracks represent serious structural problems. Composite slab cracks are caused by several factors including shrinkage and temperature forces built up in large concrete pours and by negative moments in the slab that occur over the tops of beams and girders. The latter cracks tend to parallel the axis of the beam or girder and in many instances can be as wide as $\frac{1}{8}$ in (3 mm) or more. Composite slabs in which the steel deck serves as positive reinforcement are usually designed as simply supported. Thus these negative-moment cracks are a natural stress-relief mechanism. The question with this type of crack is whether it decreases the capacity of shear connectors, since in many instances the crack runs through the line of studs. Although little specific research has been conducted on this problem, experience and the limited available evidence seem to show that the ultimate composite beam capacity is not impaired, at least not to any significant degree (Sec. 3.5.4).

Typically, composite slabs are very lightly reinforced by welded wire fabric that often is pushed to the very bottom of the slab during concrete placement and rests on the metal deck; thus its effectiveness in controlling slab cracks is drastically reduced. One remedy is to use a heavier welded wire fabric that can successfully be chaired up during the placement of concrete. Such practice reduces the size and extent of slab cracking. The negative-moment cracks over the beam and girders can be controlled by placing additional reinforcing bars extending 3 ft (0.9 m) or so on each side of the centerline. The bars should be chaired up with a 1-in (25-mm) top concrete cover and tied to longitudinal bars to control their spacing and position.

Construction joints. In pouring large areas of composite floors the contractor is often required to use construction joints to break up the pours into manageable sections, typically 7500 to 15,000 ft^2 (700 to 1400 m^2). The joints should be carefully placed to avoid any compromise to composite beam action.

It is prudent to place them no closer than 5 ft (1.5 m) from the longitudinal axis of a beam or girder and to cross the beam and girder axes near the center of their span. Such practice will ensure that the construction joint does not impair the flange action of the composite beam.

Beam camber. With the introduction of LRFD, there is a strong tendency toward smaller beams, particularly with the widespread use and economy of high-strength steel. For unshored construction and longer beam spans, where composite design can result in large savings, there is a need to compensate for the large bare beam deflection resulting from loads applied prior to commencement of composite action. Beam camber of 2 or $2\frac{1}{2}$ in (51 to 64 mm) is common for the longer spans, say 38 to 42 ft (12 to 13 m). Determining what camber is needed and the end product of beam cambering can be very inexact processes that may lead to field problems. The tendency to overestimate the dead load and underestimate connection restraint in simple beam connections often results in members that are overcambered, so that the beams are bowing upward after all dead load is in place.

There are two ways to place a concrete steel deck floor. One way is to specify a uniform slab thickness which conforms to the deflected supporting beam. The other way is to specify that the top of the slab be horizontal, resulting in a nonuniform slab thickness. Beam camber is obviously very important to the latter method because it can result in the final product's having a thinner slab than required and less than the specified cover over the top of the studs.

It is prudent to specify that camber shown on the drawings is the amount required at the time of erection and then monitor the loss of camber that inevitably occurs from the time the beam is cambered in the mill or fabricating shop and its arrival on the job site. The camber may have to be field-adjusted to ensure a level beam in the end.

Shear connector placement. Stud shear connectors can be welded to steel beams either in the field or in the shop using semiautomatic stud welding equipment. Shop-applied studs may be damaged during beam shipment and are also a safety hazard in the field during beam erection. Therefore, field welding of studs after erection of the steel is preferred. The ceramic ferrule used in the welding process should be removed from around the stud body prior to concrete placement. The AWS D1.1 Structural Welding Code[D99] contains general requirements for welding steel studs and stipulates specific requirements for

1. Mechanical properties of steel studs and requirements for qualification of stud bases

2. Workmanship, preproduction testing, operator qualification, and testing for application qualification

3. Fabrication and verification inspection of stud welding during production

It is important to prescribe connector placing guidelines for beams with concentrated loads. In the absence of such guidelines the field personnel is likely to install the studs with uniform spacing along the beam length. It is, of course, imperative that the stud placement in the field according to the guidelines is practical.

3.7 Openings in Webs

Web openings in composite beams can greatly enhance the economy of steel structures by allowing the use of shallower floor systems. Openings allow utilities to be passed through the webs of the steel members, reducing overall floor thickness and decreasing both the exterior surface and the interior volume of a building. The use of web openings during retrofit operations in existing structures provides owners and designers with extra flexibility in the placement of utilities, while having a minimum impact on usable building space. On the negative side, web openings can significantly reduce the shear and bending strength of a beam.

Over the past 25 years, a great deal has been learned about the behavior of both composite and noncomposite steel beams with web openings. The earliest design procedures treated composite and noncomposite members, with and without opening reinforcement, as four distinct problems.[D58,D60,D65,G19,G30,G35,G36,G45,G49] In most cases, the design procedures were highly conservative. Research efforts culminating in 1990,[79,80,104,D58] however, have established that the behavior of all structural steel beams with web openings is quite similar—independent of composite action or the presence of opening reinforcement. This has allowed for the development of the unified design approach presented here.

3.7.1 Behavior

This section gives a brief overview of the forces that act on a beam in the vicinity of a web opening and describes the response of the beam to these forces. Figure 3.24 illustrates the forces in a beam near an opening located in a region of positive bending. Above the opening, in the top tee, the member is subjected to a compressive force P_t, shear V_t, and secondary bending moments M_{tl} and M_{th}. In the region below the opening, in the bottom tee, the member is subjected to a tensile force P_b, shear V_b, and secondary bending moments M_{bl} and M_{bh}. Equilibrium at the opening results in the following relationships:

$$P_b = P_t = P \tag{3.15a}$$

$$V = V_b + V_t \tag{3.15b}$$

$$V_b a_o = M_{bl} + M_{bh} \tag{3.15c}$$

$$V_t a_o = M_{tl} + M_{th} \tag{3.15d}$$

$$M = Pz + M_{th} + M_{bh} - \frac{Va_o}{2} \tag{3.15e}$$

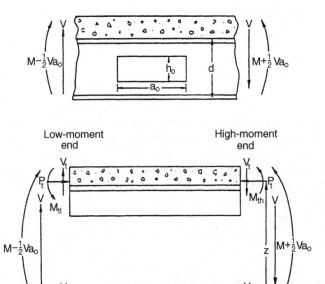

Figure 3.24 Forces around a web opening.[D68]

where a_o = opening length
$\quad z$ = distance between points about which secondary bending moments are calculated
$\quad M$ = primary bending moment at centerline of opening
$\quad V$ = shear at centerline of opening

The deformation and failure modes of beams with both solid and ribbed slabs depend strongly on the ratio of moment to shear M/V, at the opening. For a high moment-shear ratio, the opening deforms primarily in flexure, with the steel in tension below the opening and the concrete in compression (Fig. 3.25a). Depending on the size and location of the opening, the steel above the opening may be in tension or in both tension and compression. Shear and secondary bending play minor roles.

As the moment-shear ratio decreases, the shear and secondary bending moments increase, causing an increasing differential, or Vierendeel deformation, through the opening. The top and bottom tees usually exhibit a well-defined change in curvature, as shown in Fig. 3.25b. Secondary bending causes tension in the top of the section, at the low-moment end of the opening, resulting in transverse concrete cracks. Depending on the moment-shear ratio, the concrete at the high-moment end of the opening is either crushed or fails in diagonal tension due to prying action across the opening.

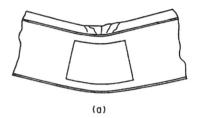

(a)

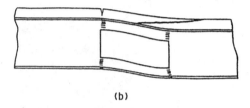

(b)

Figure 3.25 Deformation modes at web openings.[D68]

Figure 3.26 Slab cracking at high shear zones.[D68]

For beams with ribbed slabs in which the ribs are transverse to the steel member, failure is preceded by rib cracking over the high-moment end of the opening (Fig. 3.26). Rib cracking appears to be a manifestation of diagonal tension failure. Large amounts of slip take place between the concrete deck and the steel section over the opening, even for very high moment-shear ratios. This slip is sufficient to place the slab in compression at the low-moment end of the opening, although the adjacent steel is in tension.

Figure 3.27 Deck separation.[D68]

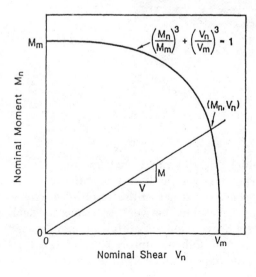

Figure 3.28 Interaction between shear and moment.[D68]

The concrete slab in composite members contributes significantly to the shear strength as well as the flexural strength of beams at web openings. This contrasts with the standard design practice for composite beams in which the concrete deck is used only to resist the bending moment and shear is assigned solely to the web of the steel section.

Failure at web openings in composite beams is, in general, quite ductile. Failure is preceded by major cracking in the slab, yielding of the steel, and large deflections of the member. Strains in the concrete remain low, long after the steel begins to yield. First yielding in the steel is not a reliable predictor of the strength of the section. Tests show that the load at first yield can vary from 17 to 52 percent of the failure load.[79,80,104] Peak loads are governed by failure of the concrete slab. For solid slabs, failure is due to crushing for openings with high M/V ratios, and to diagonal tension for openings with low M/V ratios. For beams with transverse ribbed slabs, failure is governed by a concrete failure around the studs, which may vary from a pullout failure at the high-moment end of the opening to a shear failure at the low-moment end of the opening and between the low-moment end and the point of zero moment. For beams with longitudinal ribs, longitudinal shear failure occurs with the stem of the rib separating from the upper portion of the slab.

Shear connectors above the opening and between the opening and the support strongly influence the capacity at the section. As the capacity of the shear connectors increases, the strength at the opening increases. The increased capacity can be obtained by increasing either the number of shear connectors or the capacity of the individual connectors.

Separation of the slab from the steel section, referred to as bridging, occurs primarily in beams with transverse ribbed slabs (Fig. 3.27). Bridging takes place more readily as the slab thickness increases.

The interaction between bending and shear at a web opening is relatively weak. As illustrated in the interaction diagram in Fig. 3.28, the shear capacity is largely unaffected by moment until the moment capacity approaches the peak strength of the section.

Construction loads, as high as 60 percent of member capacity, do not affect the strength at web openings.[83]

3.7.2 Design

In North American practice, the strength of composite beams with web openings is determined using moment-shear interaction diagrams. A few detailed research models generate moment-shear diagrams point by point.[79,80,83,104] For design, however, it is preferable to generate an interaction diagram (Fig. 3.28) by establishing the maximum moment capacity M_m and the maximum shear capacity V_m and connecting these points with a curve or series of curves that accurately represent the interaction between bending and shear. A number of different representations have been developed following this procedure.[79,84,D58,D69] These representations agree on the methods used to calculate M_m, but differ on the methods used to calculate V_m and the curve connecting M_m to V_m.

Based on the work of Darwin and Donahey,[D58] Darwin and Lucas[D69] developed a procedure that is both accurate and easy to apply. Their model pertains to both composite and noncomposite members with or without opening reinforcement. For composite members, the slabs may be solid or ribbed, and the ribs may be either parallel (longitudinal ribs) or perpendicular (transverse ribs) to the steel member. The model was compared with tests of 35 composite beams, 22 having ribbed and 13 solid slabs. The overall mean ratio of the test to predicted strength was 1.039, with a coefficient of variation of 0.092; the corresponding values for beams with ribbed slabs were 1.002 and 0.073, and those for beams with solid slabs were 1.101 and 0.090.[127,D69]

For the comprehensive design procedure for composite beams with web openings the reader is referred to three excellent publications.[D68,D78,D79] The procedure is applicable to rectangular and circular web openings, both unreinforced and those reinforced with horizontal bars welded to the web below and above the opening.

3.8   Composite Joists and Trusses

3.8.1   Description and use

Composite trusses are another form of composite flexural member. When the trusses are simply supported, the concrete slab resists the compressive force of the internal couple while the bottom chord of the truss resists the tensile force. As for composite beams, the vertical or transverse shear is assumed to be carried by the steel web system. The slab is usually cast on a steel deck and is connected to the top flange of the supporting steel truss by shear connectors.

Composite trusses are used principally in the floors of high-rise buildings where their unique advantages can be exploited effectively. Table 3.3 lists a sample of buildings built during the last few decades with composite trusses or composite open-web steel joists in the United States and Canada. The table provides data on a few major characteristics of the composite steel members. The composite open-web steel joists generally are spaced more closely on centers, because of their limited flexural capacity, than the trusses designed for a particular application. Both can provide long clear spans, as shown in the table, ranging from about 35 to 80 ft. Span to overall depth ratios of composite trusses of 14 to 20 have been used, the first at Principal Plaza in Edmonton and the second at Sears Tower in Chicago.[C54] Maximum flexibility of office layouts is obtained with column-free floor space between the central core and the perimeter columns.

Composite trusses designed for a specific building would tend to be more expensive, because of fabrication costs, than composite rolled beams, assuming the latter were capable of the same clear spans. However, fabrication costs are reduced on a unit basis where significant numbers of identical trusses are required for a number of identical floors. Camber is easily obtained by jigging the trusses in fabrication. Thus, when unshored construction is used and camber is provided for the total dead load that acts before

TABLE 3.3 **Buildings with Composite Joists and Trusses**

Year	Building system	City	Number of floors	Floor type	Span, ft	Spacing, ft	Details
1972	World Trade Center	New York	110	OWSJ	60	3.3	
1972	Amoco Building	Chicago	80	Truss	60	10	WT chords L diagonals
1973	Stelco Tower	Hamilton	26	OWSJ	41	4.9	
1973	Fourth Financial Center	Wichita	10	Truss	80	15	WT chords L diagonals
1974	Sears Tower	Chicago	109	Truss	75	15	WT chords
1974	Guardian Royal Exchange	Toronto	23	OWSJ	41	7.5	
1977	Oxford Square Towers	Calgary	33, 37	OWSJ	39	6.6	
1978	Republic Plaza	Denver	56	Truss	43	10	L chords L diagonals
1978	Edmonton Centre 3	Edmonton	29	Truss	35	9.8	
1981	Edmonton Centre 5	Edmonton	32	Truss	35	9.8	
1983	City Corp. Plaza	Los Angeles	40	Truss	45	15	WT chords L diagonals
1983	Principal Plaza	Edmonton	29	Truss	39	9.8	HSS chords
1984	303 W Madison	Chicago	27	Truss	50	10	WT chords L diagonals
1984	Quaker Center	Chicago	38	Truss	42	15	WT chords L diagonals
1989	AT&T Building	Chicago	67	Truss	48	15	WT chords L diagonals
1990	One Financial Place	Toronto	31	Truss	39	9.8	HSS chords
1990	BCE Place, Canada Trust	Toronto	55	Truss	46	9.8	WT chords
1990	Hamilton Centre	Regina	15	Truss	36	9.8	HSS chords
1991	1000 De La Gauchetiere	Montreal	47	Truss	49	9.8	WT top chord 2L bottom chord
1992	BCE Place II	Toronto	44	Truss	46	9.8	WT chords
1992	First Century Tower	Toronto	19	Truss	44	9.8	HSS chords

the concrete sets, the concrete can be screeded to a flat plane. Furthermore the web openings in the trusses can accommodate ductwork for heating, air conditioning, and other services with relative ease and thereby reduce the ceiling-to-floor depth. When even larger openings are required, it is not difficult to provide a Vierendeel panel in regions of low shear with chord stiffening as required. Ribbed steel deck supports the weight of wet concrete and other loads between the trusses during construction and then acts compositely with the concrete in carrying further applied loads from truss to truss. The composite trusses with significant contribution from the concrete slab are relatively stiff.

Rapid construction is possible, particularly with unshored construction. For the ultimate-limit state, which probably controls the design of most elements of the truss, the concrete floor slab acts as the compression chord of the truss. The internal lever arm is maximized with all the tension steel at the level of the bottom chord. The web steel mass is reduced, as compared to that in a beam with a solid web, with the transverse or vertical shear being most efficiently carried by concentrating the steel in axially loaded web members. Composite trusses therefore provide a lightweight floor framing system by combining the virtues of trusses with composite action.

It should be pointed out, though, that each and every element of a truss is critical. To obtain the desired ductile mode of failure of yielding of the bottom chord, other less ductile modes must be prevented. Experimental studies in Canada[78,133,D38] and the United States[96,99,102] indicate that either failure of a compression diagonal or shear stud failures can significantly impact the performance of these members. While the ultimate load obtained was close to or greater than that predicted, the ductility was limited in some cases. Brattland and Kennedy[133] went so far as to recommend that truss diagonals, shear connectors, and connections be designed for forces corresponding to the yield load in the bottom chord multiplied by the ratio of F_u/F_y of the bottom chord material. This is equivalent to reducing the resistance factor for the other components in the inverse proportion. Alternatively they suggested to assign reduced resistance factors to members subject to brittle fracture modes, an approach similar to that generally accepted for connections. A recently proposed composite joist specification[D101] suggested lowering the strength-reduction factor for diagonal compression members from 0.85 to 0.75 to reduce the probability of their premature failure.

3.8.2   Selection of steel member type

Other factors aside, the number of trusses required is minimized when the span of the concrete slab acting compositely with the metal deck is maximized. Repetitive usage of the basic composite truss unit in buildings with extensive floor areas means that alternative steel members and configurations for the composite trusses can be studied in detail to determine the most suitable one for the particular building. For the architect, suitability is related to form—long clear spans with acceptable ceiling-to-floor depths. For the mechanical engineer, the needs are space for ducting and services. For the structural engineer, the serviceability and ultimate-limit states must be satisfied. For the fabricator-erector, ease of fabrication and erection which translate into economy of construction are crucial. Consultation with potential fabricators can be valuable in determining which shapes to use.

The data in Table 3.3 indicate that tees (WT), hollow structural sections (HSS), and double angles (2L) have been used frequently for chords of steel trusses. Combinations of web and chord member sections are listed in Table 3.4 in the ascending order of cost, as given by Chien and Ritchie,[D47] for the three basic web configurations of Pratt, Warren, and Warren with verticals. The web

TABLE 3.4   Combinations of Chord and Web Members in Composite Trusses

Rank*	Member	Web configuration	
		Pratt	Warren[†]
1	Chords	HSS	HSS
	Webs	Ls	2Ls
	Warren verticals		L, HSS, rounds
2	Chords	T	T
	Webs	L, 2Ls	L, 2Ls
	Warren verticals		L, HSS, rounds
3	Chords	2Ls	2Ls
	Webs	HSS	HSS
	Warren verticals		HSS
4	Chords	HSS	HSS
	Webs	HSS	HSS
	Warren verticals		HSS

*Ranked in the order of ascending cost.
[†]Without or with verticals.

members are connected to the chords without gussets for reasons of simple fabrication and economy.

Apart from cost, factors influencing the choice of members and the web configuration include:[D47]

1. Shorter, more efficient compression web members in Pratt web systems

2. Larger web openings in Warren web systems

3. Shorter panel lengths of the top chord for bending due to transverse loads in a Warren system with verticals

4. The depth of the chord available to make web-chord connections

5. The smaller number of web components when single angles are deemed satisfactory or when Warren web systems are used

With the availability of computer-aided design and analysis software, the designer has the opportunity to compare several options within the limits of the architectural and mechanical constraints.

The triangular layout shown diagrammatically in Fig. 3.29a with the axes of web members intersecting as closely as possible to the axis of the top chord appears natural and indeed reduces in-plane joint eccentricity moments for the case when the unshored bare steel truss is supporting the weight of wet concrete and attendant construction loads. The alternative layout in Fig. 3.29b with the projected axes of the web members intersecting at the mid-depth of the cover slab was proposed by Brattland and Kennedy,[133] who argued that this triangulation was consistent with the ultimate behavior of the truss when the cover slab forms the compression chord. Evaluation of test results of trusses with this triangulation by Maurer, Woldegiorgis, and Kennedy[150,152] shows that a pin-jointed truss analysis is consistent with measured axial strains; i.e., the composite truss behaved as if the web members

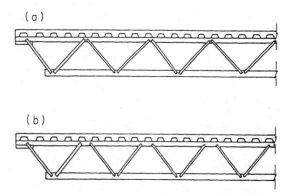

Figure 3.29   Alternate layout of composite trusses.

extended to the middepth of the cover slab. For the ultimate-load condition the diagonal web members are both steeper and shorter and therefore carry the shear more efficiently than those of Fig. 3.29a. This advantage has to be weighed against the possible increase in size of the steel top chord due to the joint eccentricity moments developed particularly in the unshored construction phase. Limited calculations suggest that the configuration of Figure 3.29a is better for trusses with T chords and that of Fig. 3.29b for trusses with HSS chords. This appears to be related to the greater flexural efficiency of hollow structural tubes as compared to tees.

3.8.3   Resistance at ultimate load

In LRFD, structures and their components are designed to meet the ultimate-limit state requirements during construction and the life of the structure, and the serviceability-limit states during the life of the structure. The ultimate-limit states considered for design therefore depend on the method of construction. As unshored construction is generally used, it is assumed to be the method of construction in what follows. For shored construction the designer can deduce what limit-states design checks can be omitted.

It is common practice to proportion or size as many elements of the truss as possible for the in-service factored (ultimate) load condition and then to check for other loading conditions including serviceability. The selection of the top chord of the steel truss is an exception: It is based on conditions during construction.

Flexural resistance.   As no rules are given in the 1993 AISC-LRFD manual[D95] for the design of composite trusses, the limited number of rules developed specifically for composite trusses or joists in the Canadian steel design standard Limit States Design of Steel Structures[G86] and a proposed new American specification[D101] served as a basis for the recommendations presented here. Both documents assume (1) that full shear connection must be provided between the concrete slab and the steel top chord, (2) that the neutral axis must lie in the slab, and further (3) that the area of the steel top chord is neglected in determining the ultimate moment resistance. The required factored shear connector resistance is therefore based on the factored tensile resistance of the bottom chord. The requirement for 100 percent connection is a conservative interpretation of Robinson et al.,[D38] who showed that at least 75 percent connection was required if the top chord was not to fail by buckling in compression and if it were to develop tensile strains eventually. With greater than 75 percent connection, the initial compression strains in Robinson's test reversed and tensile strains developed. In two tests with about 50 percent connection failure occurred by buckling of the top chord. In one case the buckling followed failure of the arc spot welds, the only connection between the steel deck and the top chord and therefore between the concrete slab and the top chord. In this test the overall ductility was also severely limited.

Thus the simple expedient of requiring 100 percent shear connection helps to ensure ductile behavior related to straining of the bottom chord. It is obtained by precluding failure of the top chord by buckling downward with the concomitant overloading of the shear connectors in tension as well as their failure.

With the requirement that the plastic neutral axis lie in the concrete slab, neglecting the area of the steel top chord in determining the tensile force of the internal couple is a further conservative simplification (Fig. 3.30). Robinson et al.,[D38] Brattland and Kennedy,[133] and others[96,99,102] report that significant tensile straining of the top chord occurred, although it was recognized that, with the small lever arm to the compressive force in the slab, the contribution of the top chord to the ultimate-moment resistance was small. Neglecting this contribution, the top chord is seen to act, at the ultimate-limit state, principally as a longitudinal connector between the shear studs and the steel web members.

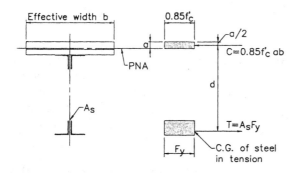

Cross Section   Stresses at Section

Figure 3.30 Equilibrium for composite truss sections.[D47] (*Canadian Institute of Steel Construction.*)

The factored tensile force of the internal couple of the composite truss is based on the gross area of the bottom chord because, with welded connections, the net area A_n is equal to the gross area A_s. In the new proposed American specification,[D101] the tensile resistance is the lesser of the factored yield force T_{rg} on the gross section and the factored fracture load T_{rn} on the net section:

$$T_{rg} = \phi_t A_s F_y \qquad (3.16)$$

$$T_{rn} = 0.85\ \phi_t A_n F_u \qquad (3.17)$$

in which ϕ_t, the resistance factor, is taken as 0.90.

Equating the two resistances gives a ratio of 1.25 for F_u/F_y. With F_u/F_y ratios of low- and medium-strength steels in the range of 1.3 to 1.5, Eq. (3.17) corresponding to yielding of the gross cross section will control for welded tension members. As much of the steel used for joists has recently moved to mini-mill dual-grade A36/A572 material, whose F_u/F_y is lower than for traditional mild steels, the 0.85 factor in Eq. (3.17) may need to be adjusted to prevent tensile fracture from governing the design.

The depth a of the compression stress block in the concrete slab is found by equating the concrete compressive force to the tensile resistance of the bottom chord:

$$0.85 \phi_c b_e a f_c' = \phi_t A_s F_y \qquad (3.18)$$

where A_s is the area of the bottom chord of the truss. The depth a must be less than the thickness of concrete above the ribs to ensure that compression does not govern the design.

The factored moment resistance is then

$$M = Td = \phi A_s F_y d \qquad (3.19)$$

where d is the distance from the tensile force in the bottom chord to the compressive force in the slab.

Equations similar to Eqs. (3.16) through (3.19) are used in the Canadian standard.[G86] However, the Canadian standard is based on partial safety factors using ϕ_s of 0.90 for yielding and fracture of steel and ϕ_c of 0.6 for crushing of concrete. The latter recognizes the greater variability in concrete strength as evidenced in its probability density function. Thus the Canadian specification results in an additional safety margin against compressive failure of concrete.

Shear resistance.   The transverse shear manifests itself in axial forces in the web members which may also develop both in-plane and out-of-plane end moments depending on the joint geometry. In-plane moments develop when the members at a joint do not intersect at a point (Fig. 3.31). Secondary moments develop when the truss joints rotate when the truss deflects. Azmi[65] and Korol et al.[G47] show that the secondary moments dissipate with inelastic

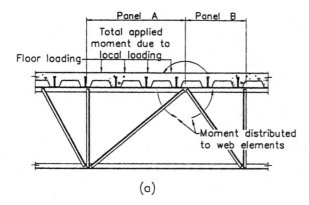

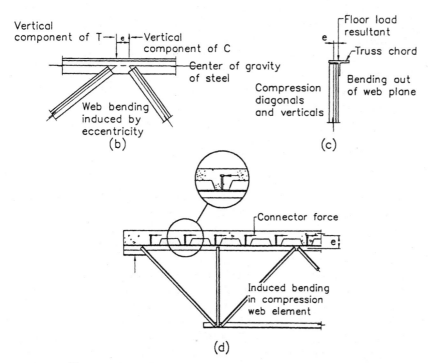

Figure 3.31 Eccentricities in composite truss connections.[D47] (*Canadian Institute of Steel Construction.*)

end rotations, and therefore it is recommended that the secondary moments not be included in the member end stress resultants. A plane frame analysis of a rigidly jointed truss would give both the joint eccentricity and secondary moments in all the truss members. The use of such moments for design would be conservative.

Shear studs can be modeled as short links at each connector location. Careful examinations after the load tests revealed that, when shear connectors fail in bending rather than in shear, their upper end rotates in the concrete (Fig. 3.11). The bending stiffness characteristics of the shear connections can be determined empirically from load-slip curves obtained in push-out tests duplicating the proposed composite truss slab, metal deck, and top chord. When the shear studs are modeled elastically, the distribution of shears in the studs at ultimate-load condition, when the shears tend to become uniform because of inelastic redistribution of loads, is not modeled well.

Out-of-plane joint moments develop, for example, when each member of a double-angle web member is connected by one leg only. Brattland and Kennedy[133] and Woldegiorgis and Kennedy[152] show that about two-thirds of the out-of-plane moment is resisted in the joint itself and only one-third acts on the end of the member.

A valid strategy for the design of such members is to determine the net in-plane joint eccentricity moments, without secondary moments, and estimate the out-of-plane joint moments. These are then resolved about the principal axes, and the member is designed using appropriate biaxial load-moment interaction diagrams. As the member-end stress resultants are being used in the analysis, it is appropriate to use the center-to-center distance as the effective length. Arguments could be made for using the clear distance between connections, as suggested by Chien and Ritchie.[D47]

The principles presented above can be applied with proper modifications to other types of web members.

3.8.4   Web-to-chord welded connections

These are all gussetless connections. Brattland and Kennedy[133] recommended that double angle–to–chord connections be designed for the axial load and the in-plane joint eccentricity moment that coexists at the ultimate-limit state. Out-of-plane moments are not considered, as proposed by Blodgett.[G15] This approach is substantiated by the facts that the welds need provide only the tensile component with the compressive component carried in bearing, and also that the interaction diagram for welds subject to transverse and longitudinal shear[G58] is quite convex. A computer program has been developed[G62] and modified by Kennedy[123] to determine the ultimate strength of fillet weld groups of arbitrary geometry when subject to axial load and moment based on the concept of rotation about an instantaneous shear center and, of course, modeling the inelastic behavior.

3.8.5   Resistance during construction

Having sized the web members and bottom chord for the total factored occupancy loads, the top chord is the only member likely to be critical during construction. In unshored construction two loading stages should be checked. During deck placement, while the construction loads may be relatively small, the unsupported length of the top chord for lateral torsional buckling is either the distance between bridging lines or the entire span of the truss. Bending moments of the top chord due to distributed gravity loads are likely to be relatively small.

With the steel deck, shear studs, and slab reinforcement in place, the steel truss with a laterally supported top chord now has to support the weight of the deck, reinforcement, wet concrete, and construction loads. Chien and Ritchie[D47] propose construction loads to be used at this stage. This loading is likely the critical stage for the top chord as it is subject to axial loads acting as the top chord of the steel truss, in-plane joint eccentricity moments and bending moments due to the deck, wet concrete, and construction loads acting transversely. At this stage, if the in-plane joint eccentricities using the web configuration of Fig. 3.29b are too severe, leading to an increased size of the top chord, the configuration of Fig. 3.29a should be considered. As the top chord is constrained to deflect in-plane, appropriate interaction equations to check the cross-sectional strength and in-plane bending strength should be used.

3.8.6 Deflections

Suggestions for approximate calculations of truss deflections are given below.

Live-load deflections. Short-term live-load deflections can be found using appropriate values for the short-term modulus of elasticity of the concrete in compression and, as discussed previously, for the elastic properties of the studs. Alternatively, the following approximate procedures of Brattland and Kennedy,[133] calibrated to their test results, can be used:

1. Determine the moments of inertia of the steel truss I_s and of the composite truss I_t based on the area of the steel chords and transformed concrete cover slab area.
2. Divide each of these values by 1.10, as an allowance for the flexibility of the web stiffness, giving values I_s' and I_t' respectively.
3. Compute the effective moment of inertia as $I_e = I_s' + 0.77\,(I_t' - I_s')$ to account for the flexibility of the studs and interfacial slip.
4. When cold-formed hollow structural sections are used for the steel truss chords, multiply the effective moment of inertia I_e by 0.80 to obtain deflections at the specified load level. This allows approximately for the nonlinear stress-strain curve of these sections which is exacerbated by residual stresses.

Shrinkage deflections. The composite truss deflects downward as the concrete shrinks. Brattland and Kennedy[133] proposed an equilibrium model based on the free-body diagram and the shrinkage strain variation shown in Fig. 3.32. Because Branson's method[41] is also based on equilibrium and strain compatibility the two methods are equivalent provided that the same values are used for the free shrinkage strain and modulus of elasticity of the concrete.

3.8.7 Floor joists design

Design a composite joist to span 36 ft (11 m) and carry a uniformly distributed dead load of 80 lb/ft² (3.83 kN/m²) and live load of 100 lb/ft² (4.79 kN/m²). Assume construction dead loads of 60 lb/ft² (2.87 kN/m²) and live

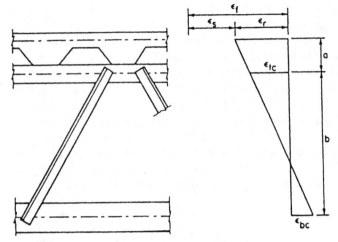

Figure 3.32 Strain distribution in a composite truss.

loads of 30 lb/ft² (1.44 kN/m²). Use F_y = 50 ksi (345 MPa) and normal-weight concrete with f'_c = 4 ksi (27.6 MPa), and assume a 2-in (51-mm) deck with a 4-in (102-mm) topping. Use double-angle members if possible.

1. Determine loads. Assume a 10-ft spacing for the composite joists:

$$w_u = \frac{(1.2 \times 80 + 1.6 \times 100) \times 10}{1000} = 2.56 \text{ kips/ft}$$

$$w_s = \frac{(80 + 100) \times 10}{1000} = 1.80 \text{ kips/ft}$$

$$w_c = \frac{(1.2 \times 60 + 1.6 \times 30) \times 10}{1000} = 1.20 \text{ kips/ft}$$

2. Design bottom chord based on ultimate strength

$$M_u = \frac{2.56 \times 36^2}{8} = 415 \text{ ft-kips}$$

$$= 4980 \text{ in-kips}$$

Assume a joist depth of 21 in so that the total depth d_t is

$$d_t = 21 + 2 + 4 = 27 \text{ in}$$

Assume that the distance between the centroids of the tension and compression force is less, say 0.5 in at the top (compression force in the slab) and 1 in at the bottom (centroid of double angles to be used as bottom chord). Thus

$$d = 27 - 0.5 - 1 = 25.5 \text{ in}$$

The required force T_s, equivalent to T_{rg} and T_{rn} in Eqs. (3.17) and (3.18), is

$$T_s = \frac{4980}{25.5} = 195.2 \text{ kips}$$

The required area, using $\phi = 0.9$, is

$$A_g = \frac{195.2}{0.9 \times 50} = 4.34 \text{ in}^2$$

Try 2L $3\frac{1}{2} \times 3\frac{1}{2} \times \frac{3}{8}$ ($A_g = 4.97 \text{ in}^2$, $y_{bc} = 1.01 \text{ in}$, $y_p = 0.355 \text{ in}$, and $r_z = 0.687 \text{ in}$). Check slenderness requirements assuming maximum panel lengths will be about 40 in long:

$$\frac{l}{r_z} = \frac{40}{0.687} = 58 < 240 \qquad \text{O.K.}$$

Check actual tension forces:

$$T_g = 4.97 \times 50 = 248.5 \text{ kips (yield)}$$

$$T_n = 0.85 \times 4.97 \times 65 = 274.6 \text{ kips (fracture)}$$

Therefore, yield governs and $T_s = 248.5$ kips.

3. *Check ultimate strength.*   Find governing effective width:

$$b_e = \frac{l}{4} = \frac{36}{4} = 9 \text{ ft}$$

or

$$b_e = \text{joist spacing} = 10 \text{ ft}$$

Therefore, $b_e = 9 \text{ ft} = 108 \text{ in}$.
  Calculate depth of the compressive block:

$$a = \frac{248.5}{0.85 \times 4 \times 108} = 0.68 \text{ in}$$

$$d = \text{joist depth} + \text{slab thickness} - \frac{a}{2} - y_p$$

$$= 21 + 6 - \frac{0.68}{2} - 0.355$$

$$= 26.31 \text{ in}$$

$$M_u = \phi \, M_n = 0.9 \times 248.5 \times 26.31 = 5880 \text{ in-kips} \qquad \text{O.K.}$$

4. Design top chord. This will be based on the construction loads, with the thickness of the top chord t_{tc} governed by the requirement that it be greater than the stud diameter divided by 2.5. Using $\frac{3}{4}$-in-diameter studs, the minimum thickness

$$t_{tc} \geq \frac{0.75}{2.5} = 0.30 \text{ in}$$

Under the construction loads the joist will act as a steel truss alone, with the decking acting as out-of-plane lateral bracing. Thus it should be designed as a beam-column and checked according to Chap. H of the LRFD-AISC specification:[D91]

$$M_u = \frac{1.2 \times 36^2}{8} = 194.4 \text{ ft-kips} = 2333 \text{ in-kips}$$

Assume that the distance between the centroid of the top and bottom angle is

$$d_{cs} = \text{joist depth} - y_{bc} - y_{tc}$$

$$= 21 - 1.01 - 1 \text{ (assumed)}$$

$$= 18.99 \text{ in}$$

$$C_{tc} = \frac{2333}{18.99} = 122.9 \text{ kips}$$

and the required gross area of the top chord is

$$A_g = \frac{122.9}{0.9 \times 50} = 2.73 \text{ in}^2$$

Try 2L $3 \times 3 \times \frac{3}{8}$ ($A_g = 4.22$ in², $y_{bc} = 0.888$ in, and $r_z = 0.587$ in). In making this selection the designer should bear in mind that the section will carry moments and will have to be checked as a beam-column, so it is not advisable to select a section that just meets the axial requirements. To check this section as a beam-column an analysis must be run, using the top and bottom chord as continuous members and the web members as pinned-end ones. Assuming the end panels to be 36 in long and the remaining nine panels to be 40 in long, the analysis indicates an axial load of 121 kips and a moment of 15 kip-in

The bending resistance of this member, by Chap. H,[D91] is

$$\phi M_n = \phi M_y = 0.9 \, S_x \, F_y = 0.9 \times 1.67 \times 50 = 75.2 \text{ kip-in}$$

The axial resistance interpolating from the tables in the manual is

$$\phi P_n = 163 \text{ kips}$$

From Eq. H1-1A:[D91]

$$\frac{121}{163} + \frac{8}{9} \frac{15}{75.2} = 0.74 + 0.18 = 0.92 < 1.00 \qquad \text{O.K.}$$

Check for fillers:

$$\frac{l}{r_x} = \frac{40}{0.922} = 43.4$$

$$\frac{l}{r_z} = \frac{40}{0.587} = 68.1$$

Use 1 filler between panel points to force buckling about the x axis to govern.

5. *Design a typical web member.* The final composite joist configuration is shown in Fig. 3.33. From the structural analysis described above, the axial load in member W3, the critical compression load was 46.7 kips. The tables in the AISC LRFD manual are based on $\phi = 0.85$. Thus the force for these members should be modified:

$$P_u = \frac{46.7 \times 0.85}{0.75} = 52.9 \text{ kips}$$

For the length $kl = 22.8$ in of member 3, try 2L 2 $\times$ 2 $\times$ ¼:

$$\phi P_{nx} = 71 \text{ kips}$$

$$\phi P_{ny} = 63 \text{ kips with two connectors}$$

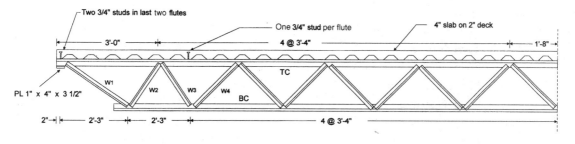

BC = 2L 3 1/2 x 3 1/2 x 3/8

TC = 2L 3 x 3 x 3/8

W1 - W4 = 2L 2 x 2 x 1/4

Figure 3.33 Composite joist design example.

6. *Design shear connectors.* In order to ensure the ductility of the system, i.e., that substantial yielding takes place before the shear connection fails, an overstrength factor of 1.3 is recommended. In addition, since single studs will be placed in each flute, an additional reduction of 0.75 must be made ($Q_n = 0.75 \times 21.9 = 16.4$ kips). Thus:

$$N = \frac{1.3\,(4.97 \times 50)}{16.4} = 19.7$$

Use one $\frac{3}{4}$-in stud per flute except in the last two flutes, where double studs should be placed.

3.8.8 Floor truss design

Design typical 38-ft-span (12-m) composite floor truss. Truss spacing is 15 ft (4.57 m) on center. Refer to Fig. 2.9 for the general arrangement of floor trusses. No shoring. Use 1-h fire separation between floors. AISC LRFD design.

Materials

Truss chord members: A572 grade 50 (345 MPa yield)

Truss web members: A36 (248 MPa yield)

Metal deck: 3-in (76-mm) trapezoidal composite metal deck

Concrete slab: $2\frac{1}{2}$ in (64 mm) over top of steel deck; $f_c' = 4$ ksi (28 MPa) lightweight concrete; concrete density = 110 lb/ft^3 (17.3 kN/m^3)

Loads

Truss weight	4
Deck + slab	41
Concrete fill allowance	5
Total dead load	50 lb/ft^2
Suspended ceiling, electrical, mechanical, plumbing	8
Partition allowance	20
Total superimposed D	28 lb/ft^2
Office live load	50 lb/ft^2
Construction L	20 lb/ft^2

Truss arrangement. Out-to-out depth of WT6 truss chords is 31 in (0.79 m). Double-angle web members. Vierendeel opening at midspan to accommodate primary air-distribution loop.

Design approach.   Employ hand calculations to determine preliminary sizes of chord members, web members, and shear studs based on strength considerations only. Fully (100 percent) composite design. Verify member sizes, floor deflections, cambers, and vibration characteristics utilizing computer analysis model.

1. Size bottom chord.   Bottom chord size is normally controlled by full design load.

$$w_u = \text{uniform factored design load}$$

$$= (1.2D + 1.6L) \times \text{tributary width}$$

$$= [1.2(50 + 28) + 1.6(50)] \times \frac{15}{1000}$$

$$= 2.60 \text{ kips/ft}$$

$$M_u = \text{moment}$$

$$= \frac{w_u l^2}{8}$$

$$= 2.60 \times \frac{38^2}{8}$$

$$= 470 \text{ ft-kips}$$

$$d_{cc} = \text{distance between WT6 chord centroids}$$

$$= 31 - (2 \times 1.30)$$

$$= 28.4 \text{ in}$$

$$T_u = \text{axial tension in chord}$$

$$= \frac{M_u}{d_{cc}}$$

$$= \frac{470 \times 12}{28.4}$$

$$= 199 \text{ kips}$$

$$A_{bc} = \text{required bottom chord area}$$

$$= \frac{T_u}{\phi_t F_y}$$

$$= \frac{199}{0.90 \times 50}$$

$$= 4.42 \text{ in}^2$$

Use WT6 × 15 with cross-sectional area $A = 4.40$ in^2.

2. Size top chord.   Top chord size is normally controlled by strength at the Vierendeel panel during construction as a noncomposite member in combined axial compression plus bending. It is assumed that the metal decking provides adequate lateral restraint perpendicular to the truss plane. Two construction load cases should be considered due to the presence of the center panel: full load on the entire span and construction live load on only half of the span. For the case of full load on the entire span:

$$w_u = [1.2(50) + 1.6(20)] \times \frac{15}{1000}$$

$$= 1.38 \text{ kips/ft}$$

$$M_u = \frac{1.38 \times 38^2}{8}$$

$$= 249 \text{ ft-kips}$$

$$P_u = \text{axial compression in chord}$$

$$= \frac{249 \times 12}{28.4}$$

$$= 105 \text{ kips}$$

$$M_{um} = \text{bending moment at midspan of Vierendeel panel chord}$$

$$= \frac{1.38 \times 5^2}{24} \times 12$$

$$= 17.3 \text{ in-kips} \qquad \text{(stem in tension)}$$

$$M_{ue} = \text{bending moment at end of Vierendeel panel chord}$$

$$= \frac{1.38 \times 5^2}{12} \times 12$$

$$= 34.5 \text{ in-kips} \qquad \text{(stem in compression)}$$

Try WT6 × 17.5.

Calculate compression strength about *x-x* axis (continuously braced about *y-y* axis).

Check slenderness of stem in compression.

$$d/t = \text{width/thickness ratio}$$

$$= 6.25/0.300$$

$$= 20.8$$

$$\lambda_r = \frac{127}{\sqrt{F_y}}$$

$$= \frac{127}{\sqrt{50}}$$

$$= 18.0 < 20.8 \qquad \text{stem is slender}$$

Calculate reduction coefficient Q_s from Eq. (A-B5-9) in Ref. D91:

$$Q_s = 1.908 - 0.00715(d/t)\sqrt{F_y}$$

$$= 1.908 - 0.00715 \times [(20.8) \times \sqrt{50}]$$

$$= 0.856$$

Calculate λ_c with $K = 1.0$, $l = 60$ in, $r = r_x = 1.76$ in.

$$\lambda_c = \text{column slenderness parameter}$$

$$= \frac{Kl(F_y/E_s)^{0.5}}{\pi r}$$

$$= \frac{1.0 \times 60 \times (50/29{,}000)^{0.5}}{1.76\pi}$$

$$= 0.451 < 1.5$$

Calculate design compression strength.

$$\lambda_c\sqrt{Q} = 0.451 \times \sqrt{0.856} \qquad (Q = Q_s)$$

$$= 0.417 < 1.5$$

Designating $A = \lambda_c^2$,

$$F_{cr} = \text{critical column stress}$$

$$= Q(0.658^{QA})\,F_y$$

$$= 0.856 \times (0.658^{0.856 \times 0.451 \times 0.451}) \times 50$$

$$= 39.8 \text{ ksi}$$

$$\phi_c P_n = \phi_c A_g F_{cr}$$

$$= 0.85 \times 5.17 \times 39.8$$

$$= 175 \text{ kips} \qquad (778 \text{ kN}) > 105 \text{ kips} \qquad \text{O.K.}$$

Calculate flexural strength $\phi_b M_n$:

$$\phi_b = \text{resistance factor for flexure } (= 0.90)$$

$$M_n \leq 1.0\, M_y$$

where M_y = moment at first yield

$$\phi_b M_n = \phi_b M_y$$
$$= \phi_b Q_s F_y S_x$$
$$= 0.9 \times 0.856 \times 50 \times 3.23$$
$$= 124 \text{ in-kips}$$

Check combined axial compression and flexure with Eq. (H1-1a) in Ref. D91:

$$\frac{P_u}{\phi_c P_n} + \frac{8M_u}{9\phi_b M_n} \leq 1.0$$

$$\frac{105}{175} + \frac{8 \times 34.5}{9 \times 124} = 0.600 + 0.247 = 0.847 < 1.0 \qquad \text{O.K.}$$

Use WT6 × 17.5.

3. Size web members.   Design first tension diagonal member at support.

$$l = \text{diagonal length}$$
$$= (28.4^2 + 36.0^2)^{0.5}$$
$$= 45.9 \text{ in}$$

$$V_u = \text{shear at support under full load on entire span}$$

$$= \frac{2.61 \times 38}{2}$$

$$= 49.6 \text{ kips}$$

$$T_u = \text{tension in diagonal}$$

$$= 49.6 \times \frac{45.9}{28.4}$$

$$= 80.2 \text{ kips}$$

$$A_t = \text{required area of tension diagonal}$$

$$= \frac{T_u}{\phi_t F_y}$$

$$= \frac{80.2}{0.90 \times 36}$$

$$= 2.48 \text{ in}^2$$

Use 2L 3 × 3 × ¼ with $A = 2.88$ in².
Design first compression diagonal at support.

$$l = (28.4^2 + 31.5^2)^{0.5}$$

$$= 42.4 \text{ in}$$

$$P_u = 49.6 \times \frac{42.4}{28.4} \times \frac{0.85}{0.75}$$

$$= 83.9 \text{ kips}$$

Use AISC LRFD manual column capacity tables for double angles.[D95]

$$\phi_c P_n = 90 \text{ kips} > 83.9 \text{ kips} \quad \text{O.K.}$$

Use 2L 3 × 2 × ⅜.
The design of the remainder of the web members follows in a similar manner based on the shear force present at the location under consideration.

4. Calculate number of shear studs required for full composite action. The horizontal shear force between the point of maximum moment and the support is the lesser of the following:

1.
$$H = \text{horizontal shear force}$$

$$= 0.85 f_c' A_c$$

$$A_c = \text{effective concrete area}$$

$$= \frac{38}{4} \times 12 \times 2.5 = 285 \text{ in}^2$$

$$H = 0.85 \times 4.0 \times 285 = 969 \text{ kips}$$

2.
$$H = A_s F_y$$

$$A_s = \text{area of bottom chord} = 4.40 \text{ in}^2$$

$$H = 4.40 \times 50 = 220 \text{ kips} \qquad \text{governs}$$

TABLE 3.5 Floor Joist Deflections

Loading	Deflection Δ		l/Δ
	in	mm	
Construction	0.23	5.8	2000
Dead load	0.63	16	720
Superimposed dead load	0.12	3.1	3800
Live load	0.23	5.8	2000
Total service load	0.98	25	465

NOTE: l = span length 38 ft (11.58 m).

$$Q_n = \text{strength of a single shear connector} = 21.9 \text{ kips}$$

$$0.75 = \text{reduction factor for one stud per rib}$$

$$N = \text{required number of shear studs} = \frac{2H}{Q_n}$$

$$= \frac{2 \times 220}{21.9 \times 0.75} = 26.8$$

Use 27 stud shear connectors.

5. Computer analysis and design verification.   Computer analysis was performed to verify the member sizes determined above and overall deformation characteristics of the floor truss system. The analysis was performed on two separate models representing construction (steel truss and metal deck only—no slab) and final (composite) conditions. The resulting deflections are listed in Table 3.5.

3.9 Stub Girder Systems

The stub girder system was developed in response to a need for new and innovative construction techniques that could be applied to certain parts of all multistory steel-framed buildings. Originated by Colaco in the early 1970s,[D28,D32] the design concept aimed at improving construction economy through the integration of the electrical and mechanical service ducts into the part of the building volume that is occupied by the floor framing system of the building (Fig. 3.34). The stub girder system makes extensive use of relatively simple shop fabrication techniques, basic elements with limited fabrication needs, simple connections between the main floor system elements and the structural columns, and composite action between the concrete floor slab and the steel load-carrying members. The result is a floor system with better strength, stiffness, and ductility characteristics. This system leads to a reduction in the amount of structural steel that traditionally had been needed for the floor framing. When coupled with the use of continuous, usually composite transverse floor beams and the shorter erection time that was needed for the stub girder system, attractive construction cost savings result. Since its

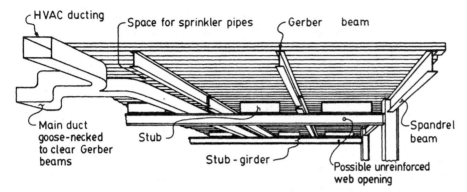

Figure 3.34 Stub girders.[D47] (*Canadian Institute of Steel Construction.*)

development and introduction, the stub girder floor system has been used for a variety of steel-framed buildings in the United States, Canada, and Mexico, ranging in height from 2 to 72 stories.

3.9.1 Description of the floor system

The main element of the stub girder system is a special girder, fabricated from standard hot-rolled wide-flange shapes, that serves as the primary framing element. Hot-rolled wide-flange shapes are also used as transverse floor beams, running in a direction perpendicular to the main girders. The girder must be and the floor beams usually are designed for composite action; the latter are normally analyzed as continuous beams.

Figure 3.35 shows the elevation of a typical stub girder. The girder shown makes use of four stubs, oriented symmetrically with respect to the midspan

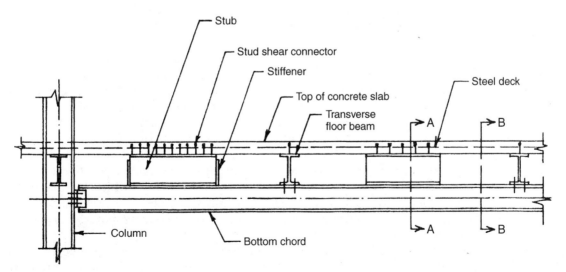

Figure 3.35 Elevation of a stub girder.

of the member. The locations of the transverse floor beams are assumed to be the quarter points of the span, and the supports are simple. In practice many variations of this layout may be found, to the extent that the girders utilize any number of stubs, although three to five seems to be the most common. The locations of the stubs may differ significantly from the symmetrical case, and the exterior (or end) stubs may be placed at the very ends of the bottom chord. However, this is not difficult to address in the modeling of the girder, and the essential requirements are that the forces that develop as a result of the choice of girder geometry be accounted for in the design of the girder components and the adjacent structure. These forces are used in the design of the various elements, as distinguished from the idealized code criteria that are currently used for many structural components.

All of the above choices are made by the design team, and depend on the service requirements of the building as seen from the architectural, structural, mechanical, and electrical viewpoints.

Figure 3.35 illustrates the main structural components of the stub girder, as follows:

1. Bottom chord

2. Exterior and interior stubs

3. Transverse floor beams

4. Formed steel deck

5. Concrete slab with longitudinal and transverse reinforcement

6. Stud shear connectors

7. Stub stiffeners

8. Beam-to-column connection

The bottom chord should preferably be a hot-rolled wide-flange shape of column-type proportions, often in the W12 to W14 series of wide-flange shapes. Other chord cross sections, including tees and tubes, have been considered.[C59] Tee shapes and rectangular tubes have certain advantages as far as welded attachments and fire protection are concerned, respectively. However, these other shapes also have significant drawbacks. The rolled tube, for example, cannot accommodate the shear stresses that develop in certain regions of the bottom chord. Rather than using a tee or a tube, therefore, a smaller W shape (in the W10 series, for example) is most likely the better choice under these conditions.

The steel grade for the bottom chord, in particular, is important, since several of the governing regions of the girder are located within this member, and tension is the primary stress resultant. It is therefore possible to take advantage of higher-strength steels, and 50 ksi yield stress material is generally the choice.

The floor beams and the stubs are mostly of the same size W shape and are normally selected from the W16 and W18 series of shapes. This is directly influenced by the size(s) of the mechanical ducts that are to be used, and input from the mechanical engineer is essential at this stage. Although it is not strictly necessary that the floor beams and the stubs use identical shapes, it avoids a number of problems if such a choice is made. At the very least, these two components of the floor system should have the same height.

The concrete slab is the top chord of the stub girder. It is made from either lightweight or normal-weight concrete, although if lightweight is readily available, even at a modest cost premium, it is preferred. The reason is that it is an advantage to reduce the dead load of the floor, especially since the shores that will be used are strongly influenced by the concrete weight. Further, the shores must support several stories before they can be removed. In other words, the stub girders must be designed for shored construction, since the girder requires the slab to complete the system. In addition, the bending rigidity of the girder is substantial, and a major fraction is contributed by the bottom chord. The reduction in slab stiffness that is prompted by the lower value of the modulus of elasticity for the lightweight concrete E_c is therefore not as important as it may be for other types of composite bending members.

The strength of the concrete is usually not less than 3 to 4 ksi (20 to 27 MPa), although the choice also depends on the limit state of the stud shear connectors. No studies have addressed whether it is possible to take advantage of the very high strength concretes that are now used in high-rise and other forms of construction. However, apart from certain long-span girders, some local regions in the slab, and the desired mode of behavior of the slab-to-stub connection (which limits the maximum f'_c value that can be used), the strength of the stub girder is not controlled by the concrete. Consequently, there appears to be little that can be gained by using high-strength concrete.

The steel deck should be of the high-bond variety, and a number of manufacturers produce suitable types. Normal deck heights are 2 and 3 in (51 and 76 mm). The deck ribs are run parallel to the longitudinal axis of the girder, since this allows for the preferable form of deck support on the transverse floor beams. This also increases the top chord area, which lends additional stiffness to a member that can span substantial distances. Finally, the parallel orientation provides a continuous rib trough directly above the girder centerline, improving the composite interaction of the slab and the girder. Owing to fire protection requirements, the thickness of the concrete cover over the top of the deck ribs is either $4\frac{3}{16}$ in (106 mm) for normal-weight concrete or $3\frac{1}{4}$ in (83 mm) for lightweight concrete. This eliminates the need for applying fire protective material to the underside of the steel deck.

Stud shear connectors are distributed uniformly along the length of the exterior and interior stubs, as well as on the floor beams. The number of connectors is determined on the basis of the computed shear forces that are developed between the slab and the stubs. This is in contrast to the current design practice for simple composite beams, which is based on the smaller of the ultimate axial load-carrying capacity of the slab and the steel beam.[D67,D91] The latter approach is not applicable to members where the cross section varies significantly along the length (nonprismatic beams). The computed shear force design approach also promotes connector economy, in the sense that a much smaller number of shear connectors is required in the interior shear transfer regions of the girder.[87,D41,D43]

The stubs are welded to the top flange of the bottom chord with fillet welds. In the original applications of the system, the design called for all-around welds;[D28,D32] subsequent studies demonstrated that the forces that are developed between the stubs and the bottom chord are concentrated toward the end of the stubs.[D41,D43] The welds should therefore be located in these regions.

The type and locations of the stub stiffeners that are indicated for the exterior stubs in Fig. 3.35, as well as the lack of stiffeners for the interior stubs, represent one of the major improvements that were made to the original stub girder designs. Based on extensive research,[D41,D43] it was found that simple end-plate stiffeners were as efficient as the traditional fitted ones, and in many cases the stiffeners could be eliminated at no loss in strength and stiffness to the overall girder.

Figure 3.35 shows that a simple shear connection is used to attach the bottom chord of the stub girder to the adjacent structure. This is the most common solution, especially when a duct opening needs to be located at the exterior end of the girder. If the support is an exterior column, the slab will rest on an edge member; if it is an interior column, the slab will be continuous past the column and into the adjacent bay.

The stub girder has sometimes been used as part of the load-resisting system of steel-framed buildings.[C58,D44] Although this has certain disadvantages insofar as column moments and the concrete slab reinforcement are concerned, the girder does provide significant lateral stiffness and ductility for the frame. As an example, the maintenance facility for Mexicana Airlines at the Mexico City International Airport, a structure utilizing stub girders in this fashion,[D44] survived the 1985 Mexico City earthquake with no structural damage.

Expanding on the details that are shown in Fig. 3.35, Fig. 3.36 illustrates two typical cross sections of stub girders, and Fig. 3.37 shows a complete girder assembly with lights, ducts, and suspended ceiling. Of particular note for the cross-sectional details are the longitudinal reinforcing bars. These add flexural strength as well as ductility and stiffness to the girder, by helping the slab to extend its service range.

It is important to observe that the longitudinal rebars are commonly placed in two layers (Fig. 3.36), with the top one just below the heads of the stud shear connectors. Also, the lower longitudinal rebars must be raised above the deck proper, using chairs or other means. This assures that the bars are adequately confined.

In addition, transverse rebars are important for adding shear strength to the slab, and they also help in the shear transfer from the connectors to the slab. The transverse bars also increase the overall ductility of the stub girder, and placing the bars in a herringbone pattern leads to a small improvement in the effective width of the slab.

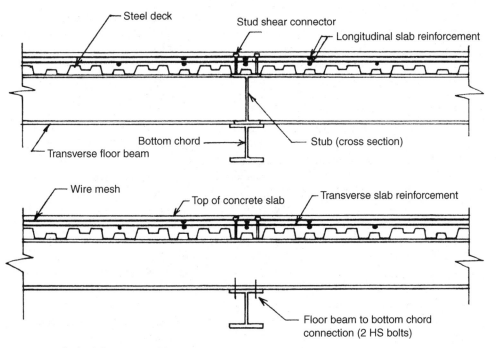

Figure 3.36 Stub girder cross sections.

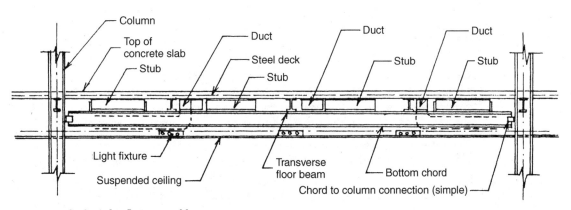

Figure 3.37 Stub girder floor assembly.

3.9.2 Preliminary design

Using the ultimate-strength approach for the preliminary design, it is not necessary to make any assumptions as regards the stress distribution over the depth of the girder, other than to adhere to the strength model that was developed for normal composite beams. The stress distribution will vary anyway along the span because of the openings.

The ultimate-strength model of Hansell et al.,[D37,D56] which is also the one used for the AISC LRFD specification,[D91] assumes that when the ultimate moment is reached, all or a portion of the slab is failing in compression, with a uniformly distributed stress of 0.85 f_c'. The steel in the cross section is simultaneously plastified in tension. Equilibrium is therefore maintained, and the internal stress resultants are easily determined using first principles. Tests have demonstrated excellent agreement with theoretical analyses that utilize this approach.[87,D37,D41,D43]

The best solution makes use of an LRFD procedure, where the load and resistance factors are chosen in accordance with the current LRFD specification.[D91] With the appropriate values, it is also directly applicable in other specification jurisdictions. In this case, therefore, the applicable ϕ factor is given by the AISC LRFD specification, for the case of gross cross-section yielding. This is because the preliminary design mostly is needed to find the bottom chord size, and this component is primarily loaded in tension.[87,D41,D43] The load factors of the LRFD specification are those of the ASCE load standard,[G88] for the combination of dead plus live load.[D91]

Reduced live loads should be used wherever possible. This is especially advantageous for stub girder floor systems, since the spans, and therefore the tributary areas, tend to be large. The ASCE load standard[G88] makes use of a live-load reduction factor that is significantly simpler to use and also less conservative than that of earlier codes. A word of caution is in order: Since it is difficult to retrofit the girder, it is advisable to provide some reserve strength at ultimate in the concrete slab.

3.9.3 Choice of component sizes

Some examples have been given in the preceding sections for the choices of chord and floor beam sizes, deck height, and slab configuration. These were made primarily on the basis of acceptable geometries, deck size, and fire protection requirements, to mention some examples. However, construction economy is critical, and the following guidelines will assist the potential user:

1. Economical span lengths for the stub girder range from 30 to 50 ft (9 to 15 m), although the preferable spans are 35 to 45 ft (10 to 14 m). Although 50-ft (15-m) girders are erectable, they approach the limit where the dead load becomes excessive, which has the effect of making the slab govern the design.

2. Depending on the type and configuration of steel deck that has been selected, the floor beam spacing should generally be maintained between 8 and 12 ft (2.4 and 3.6 m), although larger values have been used. The decisive factor is the ability of the deck to span the distance between the floor beams.

3. The performance of the stub girder is not particularly sensitive to the stub lengths that are used, as long as these are kept within reasonable limits. Usually the exterior stub controls the behavior of the stub girder. As a practical guideline, the exterior stubs are normally 5 to 7 ft (1.5 to 2.1 m) long; the interior stubs are considerably shorter, normally around 3 ft (0.9 m), but components up to 5 ft (1.5 m) long are known to have been used.

4. When the stub lengths are chosen, it is necessary to bear in mind the actual purpose of the stubs and how they carry the loads on the stub girder. That is, the stubs are loaded primarily in shear, which is why the interior stubs can be so much shorter than the exterior ones.

5. The shear connectors that are welded to the top flange of the stub, the stub web stiffeners, and the welds between the bottom flange of the stub and the top flange of the bottom chord are crucial to the function of the stub girder system. For example, the first application of stub girders utilized fitted stiffeners at the ends and sometimes at midlength of all of the stubs. Subsequent research demonstrated that the midlength stiffener did not perform any useful function and that only the exterior stubs needed stiffeners in order to provide the requisite web stability and shear capacity.[D41,D43] Regardless of the span of the girder, it was found that the interior stubs could be left unstiffened, even when they were made as short as 3 ft (0.9 m).[82,87]

6. Similar savings were realized for the welds and the shear connectors. In particular, in lieu of all-around fillet welds for the connection between the stub and the bottom chord, the studies showed that a significantly smaller amount of welding was needed, and often only in the vicinity of the stub ends. However, specific weld details must be based on appropriate analyses of the stub, considering overturning moment, weld capacity at the tension end of the stub, and adequate ability to transfer shear from the slab to the bottom chord.

3.9.4 Modeling of stub girders

The original work of Colaco[D28,D32] utilized a Vierendeel modeling scheme for the stub girder to arrive at a set of stress resultants, which in turn were used to size the various components. Elastic finite-element analyses were performed for some of the girders that had been tested, mostly to examine local stress distributions and the correlation between test and theory. However, it was recognized early that the finite-element solution would not be a practical design tool.

Other studies have examined the use of approaches such as nonprismatic beam analysis[D43] and variations of the finite-element method.[82] The latter have continued to prove impractical for usage. The nonprismatic beam solution is relatively simple to apply, although it is not as accurate as the Vierendeel approach. It tends to overlook some important local effects and overstates service load deflections.[D41,D43]

There are no "simple" methods of analysis that can be used to find the bending moments, shear forces, and axial forces in Vierendeel girders. Once the preliminary sizing has been accomplished, a computer solution is required for the girder. In general, all that is required for the Vierendeel evaluation is a two-dimensional plane frame program for elastic structural analysis. This gives moments, shears, and axial forces, as well as deflections, joint rotations, and other displacement characteristics. The stress resultants are

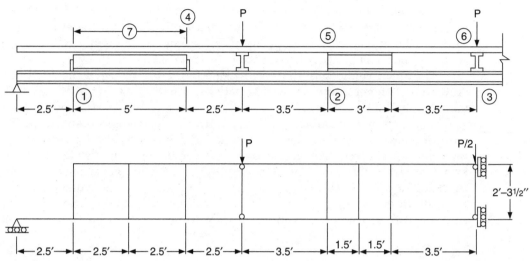

Figure 3.38   Vierendeel model for a stub girder.

used to size the girder and its elements and connections; the displacements reflect the serviceability of the stub girder.

Once the stress resultants are known, the detailed design of the stub girder can proceed. A final run-through of the girder model should then be done, using the components that were chosen, to ascertain that the performance and strength are sufficient in all respects.

As an illustration of the Vierendeel modeling of a stub girder, the girder itself is shown in Fig. 3.38 together with the Vierendeel model. The girder is the same as the one that will be used for the design example in Sec. 3.9.8. The example utilizes a girder with four stubs that is symmetric about midspan; therefore, only one half is illustrated.

The bottom chord of the model is assigned a moment of inertia equal to the major-axis I value I_x for the wide-flange shape that was chosen in the preliminary design. The bending stiffness of the top chord equals that of the effective-width portion of the slab. This should include the contributions of the steel deck as well as the reinforcing steel bars that are located within this width. In particular, the influence of the deck is important.

The effective width of the concrete slab is determined on the basis of the criteria in the AISC LRFD specification. It is noted that these were developed on the basis of analyses and tests of prismatic composite beams. The approach has been found to give conservative results.[D41,D43]

In the computations for the slab, the cross section is conveniently subdivided into simple geometrical shapes. The individual areas and moments of inertia are determined on the basis of the usual transformation from concrete to steel, using the modular ratio $n = E_s/E_c$, where E_s is the modulus of elasticity of the steel and E_c is that of concrete. The latter must reflect the density of the concrete that is used, and can be computed from Eq. (3.2a). The shear connectors that attach the slab to the top flange of the stub effectively are required to develop 100 percent interaction, since the design is based on the computed shear forces rather than the axial capacity of the steel beam or the concrete slab, as is used for prismatic beams in the AISC specifications.[D67,D91] However, it is neither common nor proper to add the moment of inertia contribution of the top flange of the stub to that of the slab, contrary to what is done for the bottom chord. The reason for this is that dissimilar materials are joined, and some local concrete cracking, compaction, and eventually crushing can be expected to take place around the shear connectors.

The discretization of the stubs into vertical Vierendeel girder components is relatively straightforward. Considering the web of the stub and any stiffeners (Fig. 3.39), if applicable, the moment of inertia about an axis that is perpendicular to the plane of the web is calculated. Detail calculations are illustrated in the design example in Sec. 3.9.8.

Several studies have aimed at finding the optimum number of vertical members to use for each stub. Generally, however, the strength and stiffness of the stub girder are only insignificantly affected by this choice, and a number between 3 and 7 is usually chosen. As a rule of thumb, one vertical per foot (30 cm) length of stub is suitable.

In the model, the verticals are placed at uniform intervals along the length of the stub, usually with the outside members close to the stub ends. Figure 3.38 illustrates the approach. The overall solution for the stub girder is not sensitive to the placement of the verticals. As for end conditions, these vertical members are assumed to be rigidly connected to the top and bottom chords of the Vierendeel girder.

One vertical member is placed at each of the locations of the floor beams. This member is assumed to be pinned to the top and bottom chords, as shown in Fig. 3.38, and its stiffness is conservatively set equal to the moment of inertia of a plate with a thickness equal to that of the web of the floor beam, and a length approximately the same as the beam depth. See Sec. 3.9.8 for details.

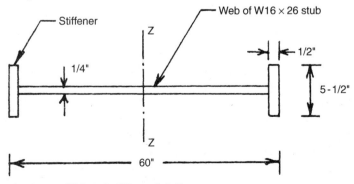

Figure 3.39 Stub and stiffener details.

The Vierendeel model shown in Fig. 3.38 indicates that the portion of the slab that spans across the opening between the exterior end of the exterior stub and the support for the slab has been neglected. This is realistic, considering the relatively low rigidity of the slab in negative bending.

Figure 3.38 also shows the support conditions that are used as input data for the computer analysis. In the example, the symmetrical layout of the girder and its loads make it necessary only to analyze one half of the span. For the girder that is shown, it is known that only vertical displacements can take place at midspan; horizontal displacements and end rotations are prevented at this location. At the far ends of the bottom chord only horizontal displacements are permitted, and end rotations are free to occur. It is noted that the reactions that are found are used to size the support elements. This includes the bottom chord connections and the column.

The results of the structural analysis of the stub girder of Fig. 3.38 are shown in Fig. 3.40 in terms of the overall bending moment, shear force, and axial force distributions based on the Vierendeel model given in Fig. 3.38. Figure 3.38 provides the layout details of the stub girder that help to identify the locations of the key stress resultant magnitudes with the corresponding regions of the girder. The forces are the same as those in the design example in Sec. 3.9.8.

Given these distributions, the design of the stub girder and its various components can now be done. This must also include deflection checks, even though research has demonstrated that the overall design will never be gov-

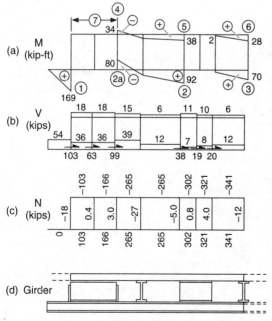

Figure 3.40   Result of Vierendeel analysis.

erned by deflection criteria.[82,87] However, since the girder has to be built in the shored condition, the girder is often fabricated with a camber, approximately equal to the dead-load deflection.[87,D47] In other cases the camber is introduced in the field during the installation of the shores.

3.9.5 Final design

In general, the design of the stub girder and its many components must consider overall member strength criteria as well as local checks. For most of these, the AISC specifications[D67,D91] give detailed requirements that suffice to address the needs. Further, although LRFD and ASD are equally applicable in the design of the girder, LRFD is recommended as the more appropriate method.

In several important areas there are no standardized rules that can be used in the design of the stub girder, and the designer must rely on rational engineering judgment to arrive at satisfactory solutions. This applies to the parts of the girder that have to be designed on the basis of computed forces, such as the shear connectors, the stiffeners, the stub-to-chord welds, and the slab reinforcement. The modeling and evaluation of the capacity of the central portion of the concrete slab are also subject to interpretation. However, the design recommendations that are given in the following paragraphs are based on a wide variety of practical and successful applications.

Figures 3.38 and 3.40a show certain circled numbers at various locations throughout the span of the stub girder. These reflect the sections of the girder that are the most important, for one reason or another, and are the ones that must be examined to determine the required member size, etc. These are the governing sections of the stub girder, and are itemized as follows:

1. Points 1, 2, and 3 indicate the critical sections for the bottom chord.

2. Points 4, 5, and 6 indicate the critical sections for the top chord, i.e., the concrete slab.

3. Point 7, which is a region rather than a specified point, indicates the critical shear transfer region between the slab and the exterior stub.

Bottom chord. The size of the bottom chord is almost always governed by the stress resultants at midspan, or point 3 in Figs. 3.38 and 3.40. This is why the preliminary design procedure is focused almost entirely on determining the required chord cross section at this section.

As the stress-resultant distributions in Fig. 3.40 show, the bottom chord is subjected to combined positive bending moment and tensile force at point 3, and the design check must consider the beam tension member behavior in this area. The design requirements are given in the AISC LRFD specification.[D91]

The combined effect of bending and tension must also be evaluated at point 2, the exterior side of the interior stub. The local bending moment in the chord is generally larger here than at midspan, but the axial force is smaller. Only a computation can confirm whether point 2 will govern in lieu of point 3.

Further, although the location at the interior side of the exterior stub (point 2a) is rarely a critical one, the combination of negative moment and tensile force should be evaluated.

At point 1 of the bottom chord, the exterior end of the exterior stub, the axial force is equal to zero. Here the bottom chord must be checked for pure bending, as well as shear. The shear force evaluation is actually quite important at this point, since this is where it reaches the maximum value.

The preceding applies only to a girder that uses simple end supports. When it is part of the lateral load-resisting system, axial forces will exist in all parts of the chord. These must be resisted by the adjacent structural members.

Concrete slab.   The top chord carries varying amounts of bending moment and axial force, as illustrated in Fig. 3.40, but the most important areas are indicated as points 4 to 6. The axial forces are compressive in the concrete slab; the bending moments are positive at points 5 and 6 but negative at point 4. As a result, this location is normally the one that governs the performance of the slab, not the least because the reinforcement in the positive-moment region includes the substantial cross-sectional area of the steel deck.

The full effective width of the slab must be analyzed for combined bending and axial force at all of the points 4 through 6. Either the composite beam-column criteria of the AISC LRFD specification[D91] or the criteria of the reinforced concrete structures code of ACI[D80] may be used for this purpose.

Shear transfer regions.   Region 7 is the shear transfer region between the concrete slab and the exterior stub, and the combined shear and longitudinal compressive capacity of the slab in this area must be determined. A similar shear transfer region is found between the slab and the interior stub, but the shear force is always smaller here.

Several studies have shown that the slab in region 7 will fail in a combination of concrete crushing and shear.[87,D41,D43] The shear failure zone usually extends from corner to corner of the steel deck, over the top of the shear connectors. This also emphasizes why the placement of the longitudinal reinforcing steel bars in the central flute of the steel deck is important, as well as the location of the transverse bars: Both groups should be placed just below the level of the top of the shear connectors (see Fig. 3.36). The welded wire mesh reinforcement that is used, mostly to control shrinkage cracking in the slab, also assists in improving the strength and ductility of the slab in this region.

Design of stubs for shear and axial load.   The shear and axial force distributions indicate the governing stress resultants for the stub members. It is important to note that since the Vierendeel members are idealized from the real (i.e., continuous) stubs, bending is not a governing condition. Given the sizes and locations of the individual vertical members that make up the stubs, the design checks are easily made for axial load and shear.

The areas and moments of inertia of the verticals are known from the modeling of the stub girder. Figure 3.40 also shows the shear and axial forces in the bottom and top chords, but the design for these elements has been addressed elsewhere in this chapter and in Chap. 4.

The design checks that are made for the stub verticals will also indicate whether there is a need for stiffeners for the stubs, since the evaluations for axial-load capacity should first be made on the assumption that no stiffeners are used. However, experience has shown that the exterior stubs always must be stiffened; the interior stubs, on the other hand, are usually satisfactory without stiffeners, although exceptions can occur.

If stiffeners are required, it is important to remember that the purpose of such elements is to add to the area and moment of inertia of the web, to resist the axial load that is applied. There is no need to use bearing stiffeners, since the load is not transmitted in this fashion. The most economical solution is to make use of end-plate stiffeners of the kind that is shown in Fig. 3.36. Extensive research evaluations showed that this was the most efficient and economical choice.[87,D41,D43]

The vertical stub members are designed as compression members, using the column design criteria of the AISC specification.[D91] For a conservative solution, an effective length factor of 1.0 may be used. However, it is more realistic to utilize a K value of 0.8 for the verticals of the stubs, recognizing the end restraint that is provided by the connections between the chords and the stubs. The K factor for the floor beam verticals must be 1.0, owing to the pinned ends that are assumed in the modeling of these components.

Stud shear connectors. The shear forces that must be transferred between the slab and the stubs are given by the Vierendeel girder shear-force diagram. These are the factored shear-force values which are to be resisted by the connectors. The example shown in Fig. 3.40 indicates the individual shear forces for the stub verticals. However, in the design of the overall shear connection, the total shear force that is to be transmitted to the stub is used, and the stud connectors are then distributed uniformly along the stub. The design strength of each connector is determined in accordance with the LRFD specification,[D91] including any deck-profile reduction factor.

Floor-beam connections to slab and bottom chord. The floor beam is represented in the Vierendeel model as a pinned-end compression member. It is designed using a K factor of 1.0, and the floor-beam web by itself is almost always sufficient to take the axial load. However, the floor beam must be checked for web crippling and web buckling under shoring conditions.

No shear forces are transferred from the beam to the slab or the bottom chord. At least in theory, therefore, any attachment device between the floor beam and the other components should not be needed. However, owing to the requirements for construction stability, as well as the fact that the floor beam usually is designed for composite action normal to the girder, fasteners are needed. In practice, these are not actually designed; rather, one or two stud shear connectors are placed on the top flange of the beam, and two high-strength bolts are used to attach the lower flange to the bottom chord. This system has proved to be satisfactory in all circumstances.

Connection of bottom chord to supports. In the traditional use of stub girders, the girder is supported as a simple beam, and the bottom chord end connections need to be able to transfer vertical reactions to the supports. The latter structural elements may be columns, or the girder may rest on corbels or other types of supports that are part of the concrete core of the building.

Any one of the simple (shear-type) beam connections may be used to connect the bottom chord to a column or corbel or similar bracket. It is important to ascertain that the chord web shear capacity is sufficient, including block shear.

The slab may be supported on an edge beam or similar element at the exterior side of the floor system. In the interior of the building the slab will be continuously cast across other girders and around columns; this will almost always lead to some cracking, both in the vicinity of the columns as well as along beams and girders. With suitable placement of floor slab joints, this can be minimized, and appropriate transverse reinforcement for the slab will reduce if not eliminate the longitudinal cracks.

Deflections. The service-load deflections of the stub girder are needed for several purposes. First, the overall dead-load deflection is used to assess any camber requirements. Because of the long spans of typical stub girders, as well as the flexibility of the framing members and the connections during construction, it is important to end up with a floor system that is as level as possible by the time the structure is ready to be occupied.

Second, it is essential to bear in mind that each girder will be shored against a similar member at the level below the current construction floor. This member, in turn, is similarly shored, albeit against a girder whose stiffness is greater, owing to the additional time of curing of the concrete slab. This has a cumulative effect for the structure as a whole, and the dead-load deflection computations must take this response into account.

In other words, the support for the shores is a flexible one, and deflections therefore will occur in the girder as a result of floor system movements of the structure at levels other than the one under consideration. Although this is not unique to the stub girder system, the span lengths and the interaction with the frame accentuate the influence on the girder design.

The welding of the stubs to the top flange of the bottom chord causes bending of the bottom chord during fabrication. This effect should be considered in the design of the girder.

Depending on the structural system, it is also likely that the flexibility of the columns and the connections will add to the vertical displacements of the stub girders. The deflection calculations should incorporate these effects, determining displacements as they occur in the frame. Thus the curing process for the concrete might be considered, since the strength development as a function of time is directly related to the value of E_c.

Live-load deflections must be determined to assess the serviceability of the floor system under normal operating conditions. However, several studies have demonstrated that such displacements will be significantly smaller than the $l/360$ requirement that is normally associated with live-load deflections.[82,87,D43,D47]

3.9.6 Stub girders for lateral load systems

The stub girder was originally conceived only to serve as part of the vertical load-carrying system of structural frames, and the use of simple connections came from this development. However, recognizing that a deep, long-span member can be very effective as a part of the lateral load-resisting system for a structure, several applications have been made to incorporate the stub girder into moment frames and similar systems. The projects of Colaco in Houston[C58] and Martinez-Romero[D44] in Mexico City were successful for a number of reasons, although the designers noted that the cost premium could be substantial.

In the case of the Colaco structure, his applications reduced drift substantially, as expected, but made for a much increased complexity of the beam-to-column connections and the reinforcement needs of the slab around the columns. Thus the exterior stubs were moved to the far ends of the girders, and moment connections were designed for the full depth. For the Mexico City building, the added ductility was a prime factor in the survival of the structure during the 1985 earthquake.

It must also be recognized that the lack of room for perimeter mechanical ducts may also be undesirable. This can only be addressed by the mechanical engineering consultant. As a general rule, a designer who wishes to use stub girders as part of the lateral load-resisting system should examine all structural effects but also incorporate nonstructural considerations such as are prompted by ductwork and electronic communication needs.

3.9.7 Influence of method of construction

A number of construction-related considerations have already been addressed. The most important ones relate to the fact that the stub girders must be built in the shored condition. The placement and removal of the shores may have a significant impact on the performance of the member and the structure as a whole. In particular, too early shore removal may lead to excessive deflections in the girders at levels above the one where the shores were located. This is a direct result of the low stiffness of "green" concrete. It can also lead to "ponding" of the concrete slab, producing larger dead loads than accounted for in the original design. Finally, larger girder deflections can be translated into an "inward-pulling" effect on the columns of the frame. This is known to have happened in at least two construction projects, where it led to problems for the erection of the structure. However, this phenomenon is clearly a function of the framing system.

On the other hand, the use of high-early-strength cement and similar products can reduce this effect significantly. Further, since the concrete usually is able to reach about 75 percent of the 28-day strength after 7 to 10 days, the problem is less severe than originally thought.[87,D41,D47] In any case, it is important for the structural engineer to interact with the general contractor, in order that the influence of the method of construction on the girders as well as the frame can be quantified, however simplistic the analysis procedure may be.

Owing to the larger loads that can be expected for the shores, either the latter must be designed as structural members or the design must at least be evaluated by the structural engineer. The size of the shores is also influenced by the number of floors that are to have these supports left in place.

As a general rule, when stub girders are used for multistory frames, the shores should be left in place for at least three floor levels. Some designers prefer a larger number; however, any choices of this kind should be based on computations for sizes and effects. Obviously, the more floors that are specified, the larger the shores will have to be. There is also a possibility that the lowest girder that is used for support will be overloaded.

3.9.8 Stub girder design

Figure 3.41 shows the layout of a stub girder for which the preliminary sizes are needed. Other computations have already given the sizes of the floor beam, the slab, and the steel deck. The span of the girder is 40 ft (12.2 m), the distance between adjacent girders is 30 ft (9.1 m), and the floor beams are located at the quarter points. The steel grade remains to be chosen (36 or 50 ksi yield stress steel; 248 or 345 MPa); the concrete is lightweight, with $w = 120$ lb/ft^3 (1.92 t/m^3) and a compressive strength of $f_c' = 4$ ksi (27.6 MPa). The estimated dead load is 74 lb/ft^2 (3.6 kN/m^2), while the nominal live load is 50 lb/ft^2 (2.4 kN/m^2). The reduced live load is 30 lb/ft^2 (1.5 kN/m^2).

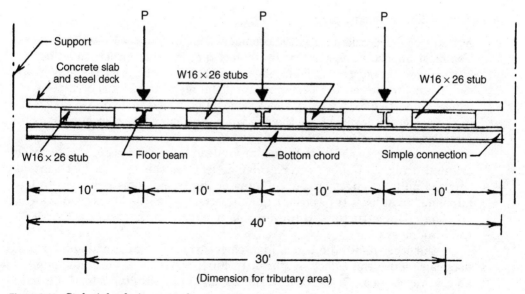

Figure 3.41 Stub girder design example.

1. Factored distributed loads (for $1.2D + 1.6L$ combination)

$$\text{Dead load } D = 74 \times 1.2 = 88.8 \text{ lb/ft}^2$$

$$\text{Live load } L = 30 \times 1.6 = 48.0 \text{ lb/ft}^2$$

$$\text{Total} = 136.8 \text{ lb/ft}^2$$

2. Concentrated load at each floor beam location

$$P = 136.8 \times 30 \times 10 = 41.0 \text{ kips}$$

3. Maximum factored midspan moment

$$M_{max} = (1.5 \times P \times 20) - (P \times 10) = 820 \text{ kip-ft}$$

4. Estimated interior moment arm. The moment arm for the full stub girder at centerline can be estimated as

$$d = \text{depth of bottom chord (assume } \tfrac{1}{2}\text{W14}) = 7.0 \text{ in}$$

$$= \text{depth of floor beam (assume W16)} \qquad = 16.0 \text{ in}$$

$$= \text{deck height (assumed)} \qquad\qquad = 3.0 \text{ in}$$

$$= \text{distance to concrete centroid (assumed)} = 1.5 \text{ in}$$

$$\text{Total} = 27.5 \text{ in}$$

In general for the stub girder system, the interior moment arm typically varies between 25 and 30 in (64 and 76 cm), depending on the heights of the bottom chord, floor beams and stubs, steel deck, and concrete slab.

5. Slab and bottom chord axial forces F. These are the compressive and tensile stress resultants:

$$F = \frac{M_{max}}{d} = \frac{820 \times 12}{27.5} = 357.9 \text{ kips}$$

6. Required cross-sectional area of bottom chord A_s

$$A_s = \frac{M_{max}}{d\phi F_y}\frac{4}{3}$$

where $\phi = 0.9$ and the (4/3) give an arbitrary increase in area to account for the fact that the final Vierendeel analysis yields higher forces than this simplified approach.[87,D47]

$$A_s = \frac{820 \times 12 \times 4}{27.5 \times 0.9 \times F_y \times 3}$$

For $F_y = 36$ ksi

$$A_s = 14.73 \text{ in}^2$$

For $F_y = 50$ ksi

$$A_s = 10.60 \text{ in}^2$$

If 36-ksi steel is chosen for the bottom chord of the stub girder, wide-flange shapes W12×50 and W14×53 are suitable. If 50-ksi steel is the choice, the sections may be W12×40 or W14×38. Obviously the final decision must be made by the structural engineer. However, since the W12-series shapes save approximately 2 in in floor-system height per story of the building, this could make for significant savings if the structure is 10 to 15 stories tall or taller.

Therefore, try W12×40 using A572 steel.

7. *Stub selection.* Figure 3.39 shows the stub and stiffener configuration for a typical case. The stub is a 5-ft-long W16×26 with $5\frac{1}{2} \times \frac{1}{2}$-in end-plate stiffeners. This selection is arbitrary. It is based on the considerations discussed in the previous text.

8. *Modeling of the stub.* The moment of inertia about the z-z axis is given by

$$I_x = \frac{0.25 \times 60^3}{12} + 2 \times 5.5 \times 0.5 \times 30^2 = 9450 \text{ in}^4$$

Depending on the number of vertical Vierendeel truss members that will represent the stub in the model, the bending stiffness of each is taken as a direct fraction of the value of I_x. For the girder shown in Fig. 3.38, where the stub is modeled as three vertical members, the magnitude of I_x is found as 9450/3 = 3150 in⁴.

The cross-sectional area of the stub, including the stiffeners, is similarly divided between the verticals. The total area is 20.25 in² so that each vertical has an area of 6.75 in².

For the framing beams, $t_w = 0.25$ in; the beam depth is 15.69 in. This gives a moment of inertia of $[(15.69 \times 0.25^3)/12] = 0.02$ in⁴. The cross-sectional area is (15.69 × 0.25) = 3.92 in².

Carrying out the analysis (Fig. 3.40), the following results are obtained:

Exterior stub verticals:

Shear forces, kips	103	63	99
Axial forces, kips	−18	0.4	3

Interior stub verticals:

Shear forces, kips	38	19	20
Axial forces, kips	5	0.8	4

Floor beam verticals:

Exterior: Axial force $= -39$ kips

Interior: Axial force $= -12$ kips

Shear forces are zero in these members. The totals are:

Exterior stub:

$$\text{Total shear force} = V_{es} = 103 + 63 + 99 = 265 \text{ kips}$$

Interior stub:

$$\text{Total shear force} = V_{is} = 38 + 19 + 20 = 77 \text{ kips}$$

9. Design of shear connectors.   The nominal strength Q_n of the stud shear connectors is given by Eq. (3.2). For stub girders ¾ in is currently the largest stud diameter that can be used.[D67,D91] For concrete with $w = 120$ lb/ft^3 and $f_c' = 4$ ksi, $E_c = 2630$ ksi. With ¾-in-diameter studs, the nominal shear capacity is $Q_n = 22.7$ kips. The required number of shear connectors can now be found, using the total stub shear forces V_{es} and V_{is}.

Exterior stub:

$$N = \frac{V_{es}}{Q_n} = 11.7$$

Use twelve ¾-in-diameter stud shear connectors, placed in pairs and distributed uniformly along the length of the top flange of each of the exterior stubs.

Interior stub:

$$N = \frac{V_{is}}{Q_n} = 3.4$$

Because of the small number, there will be only one stud connector in any one rib. Thus the strength of the connectors must be reduced by 25 percent and the required number of connectors increased to 3.4/0.75 = 4.5.

Use five ¾-in-diameter stud shear connectors, placed singly and distributed uniformly along the length of the top flange of each of the interior stubs.

10. Design of welds between stub and bottom chord.   The welds that are needed to fasten the stubs to the top flange of the bottom chord are primarily governed by the shear forces that are transferred between these components of the stub girder. The shear-force distribution gives these stress resultants. Thus the factored forces V_{es} and V_{is} are used to size the welds.

In addition to the shear forces, axial loads also act between the stubs and the chord; these may be compressive or tensile. Referring to the example of Fig. 3.40, it is seen that the only axial force of note occurs in the exterior vertical of the exterior stub; the other loads are very small compressive or tensile forces. Unless a significant tensile force is found in the analysis, it will be a safe simplification to ignore the axial forces insofar as the weld design is concerned.

The primary shear forces that have to be taken by the welds are developed in the outer regions of the stubs, although it is noted that in the case of Fig. 3.38, the central vertical elements in both stubs carry forces of some magnitude (63 and 19 kips, respectively). However, this distribution is a result of the modeling of the stubs; analyses of girders where many more verticals were used[D43,D47] have confirmed that the major part of the shear is transferred at the ends. The reason is that the stub is a full shear panel, where the internal moment is developed through stress resultants that act at points toward the ends, in a form of bending action. Tests have also verified this characteristic of the girder behavior.[D43] Finally, concentrating the welds at the stub ends will have significant economic impact.[87,D41,D43]

In view of these observations, the most effective placement of the welds between the stubs and the bottom chord is to concentrate them across the ends of the stubs and along a short distance of both sides of the stub flanges. For ease of fabrication and structural symmetry, the same amount of welding should be placed at both ends, although the forces are always smaller at the interior ends of the stubs. Such U-shaped welds were used for a number of the full-size girders that were tested, with very limited localized yielding in the welds.

Prior to the research that led to the change of the welded joint design,[D41,D43] the stubs used all-around fillet welds for the exterior as well as the interior elements. The improved, U-shaped detail provides for weld-metal savings of approximately 75 percent for interior stubs and around 50 percent for exterior stubs.

For the sample stub girder, W16×26 shapes are used for the stubs. The total forces to be taken by the welds are:

Exterior stub: $V_{es} = 265$ kips

Interior stub: $V_{is} = 77$ kips

The fillet weld size must be smaller than the thickness of the stub flange, which is 0.345 in. Selecting E70XX electrodes and $\frac{5}{16}$-in fillet welds, the total weld length for each stub l_w equals two times $(b_f + 2l)$ since U-shaped welds of length $(b_f + 2l)$ are placed at each stub end. The total weld lengths required for the stub girder in question are determined as follows.

Exterior stub: $$l_w = \frac{V_{es}}{0.707\, a_w \phi_w F_w} = 38.1 \text{ in}$$

Interior stub: $$l_w = \frac{V_{is}}{0.707\, a_w \phi_w F_w} = 11.1 \text{ in}$$

where the fillet weld size $a_w = \frac{5}{16}$ in, the resistance factor $\phi_w = 0.75$, and the strength of the weld $F_w = 0.6F_{EXX} = 0.6(70) = 42$ ksi for E70XX electrodes (AISC LRFD specification,[D91] Table J2.5).

The total required U-weld lengths at each stub end are 19.1 in for the exterior stub and 5.6 in for the interior stub. The flange width of the W16×26 is 5.50 in. Thus the following weld lengths are chosen:

$$l_u = 5.50 + 2 \times 7.0 = 19.5 \text{ in} > 19.1 \text{ in} \qquad \text{O.K.}$$

for the exterior stub and

$$l_u = 5.50 + 2 \times 2.0 = 9.5 \text{ in} > 5.6 \text{ in} \qquad \text{O.K.}$$

for the interior stub.

The length of the returns is a matter of judgment. The interior stub requires almost no weld other than the one across the flange. However, at least a minimum weld return of ½ in should be used.

4

Composite Columns

4.1 Basic Concepts

The basic function of *columns* is the delivery of vertical forces to the base of the structural frame. Traditionally, the column cross section has been chosen by using the most economical arrangement of materials to resist only required axial loads. But columns can be more than compression members. Columns that are connected to beams with moment-resisting connections which help restrain deflections of floor members as well as lateral drift of the overall structure must be designed as beam columns. Their cross section must be chosen for both axial and flexural demands.

Concrete is a material with reliable compressive strength and low cost per square inch of the cross section. However, an axially loaded structural member without lateral restraint requires not only strength but also flexural stiffness when axial forces must be delivered over significant distances. The stability of slender columns is a measure of material stiffness rather than material strength. *Steel,* which has 5 to 8 times the stiffness and strength of concrete, is the more efficient structural material for slender columns. In many modern building applications, structural columns are neither slender nor stocky. Instead, most required column proportions are intermediate between these two extremes. Very large compression members in high-rise buildings are often built as elevator shafts, fireproof stairwells, or even extremely large concrete-filled steel tubes. These large columns are characterized by stocky segments between adjacent floors. Such supercolumns, laterally braced by the floors, can be used efficiently at higher average service load levels than those acceptable in smaller, more slender columns.

Two basic types of composite columns are used in buildings: those with the steel section encased in concrete and those with the steel section filled with concrete.

Encased composite columns consist of structural shapes surrounded by concrete. The concrete requires vertical and horizontal bar reinforcement to sustain the encasement of the steel core. Shear connectors may be needed as well to ensure interaction and force transfer between the steel shape and the concrete encasement. Stud shear connectors transfer forces between the steel and concrete through attachment by welds to the steel shape and by bearing against the surrounding concrete.

Filled composite columns may be the most efficient application of materials for column cross sections. Their steel shell can be a pipe or tubing or a hollow section fabricated from plates. It provides forms for the inexpensive concrete core and increases the strength and stiffness of the column. In addition, because of its relatively high stiffness and tensile resistance, the steel shell provides transverse confinement to the contained concrete, making the filled composite column very ductile with remarkable toughness to survive local overloads. Since the concrete core is contained and confined by the steel shell, interaction between the steel and concrete is assured. However, it may be desirable in some cases to provide additional bearing surfaces for shear transfer such as studs or bars welded inside the shell near the connections of the columns to the floor beams.

4.2   Types of Composite Compression Members

Four types of compression members are encountered in composite construction: encased composite columns, filled composite columns, composite concrete walls, and plated composite walls. The design of composite columns is covered in the AISC-LRFD specification[D91] and in the ACI building code,[D100] and seismic design of composite shear walls is addressed in the recommendations developed by the Building Seismic Safety Council (BSSC).[D96]

A composite column is defined in the AISC-LRFD specification[D91] as "a steel column fabricated from rolled or built-up steel shapes and encased in structural concrete or fabricated from steel pipe or tubing and filled with structural concrete"; and in the ACI building code[D100] as a concrete compression member "reinforced longitudinally with structural shapes, pipe or tubing with or without longitudinal bars." The AISC specification is more restrictive than the ACI code in that it limits its rules to columns in which the cross-sectional area of the shape, pipe, or tubing is at least 4 percent of the column gross section. Columns with smaller percentages of structural shapes are characteristic of reinforced concrete and thus should be designed according to ACI rules.

Composite walls are reinforced concrete walls with additional steel shapes or plates. Walls with additional shapes, referred to in this book as *composite concrete walls,* contain one or more encased steel shapes, usually located at the ends of the wall. Walls with steel plates, referred to as *plated composite walls,* are defined in the BSSC recommendations[D96] as "consisting of steel plates with concrete encasement on one or both sides that provides out-of-plane stiffening to prevent buckling of the steel panel." The design of composite walls as an element of lateral resistance is presented in Sec. 5.5, Shear Wall Design. Another type of plated composite wall is of sandwich construction consisting of two exterior steel plates and a concrete core. Applications of plated composite walls include structures built as protection against blast loadings.[34]

The encasement of structural steel sections with concrete began very early with concrete used to protect the section against fire and to increase the load-carrying capacity. In current practice, lightweight, spray-on fire protection is used in lieu of concrete. Nevertheless, concrete continues to be applied as encasement around steel sections, primarily for the following purposes:

- Flexural stiffening and strengthening of compression elements in the perimeter of tube-type high-rise buildings and in portal frames

- Exposed concrete finish required by architects for aesthetic reasons

- Protection of columns from traffic impact, as in truck loading areas or in buildings where fork lifts and other mobile machinery are used

- Increasing capacity of axially loaded column

- Fire protection

When concrete is used as encasement for applications in which axial loads or required moments are relatively light, the concrete usually is not utilized structurally. Justifying the cost of fabricating both a steel shape and a tied reinforcement as component parts of the same compression member requires special service demands.

The following types and applications of composite compression members are used in practice:

1. Encased composite columns supporting gravity loads in multistory buildings, primarily as axially loaded members as shown in Fig. 4.1. The steel section is designed to carry the construction weight of the steel frame erected several levels ahead of the concrete work plus the weight of concrete floors cast before the concrete encasement provides additional flexural stiffness to the steel shape. Transverse ties in the concrete or studs ensure shear transfer and interaction between the shape and the concrete encasement. Concrete helps to support all loads applied thereafter.

2. Encased composite columns as parts of lateral force resisting rigid frames as indicated in Fig. 4.2. Similar to the gravity load composite columns, relatively small wide-flange steel sections are included in a large reinforced-concrete section for use in exterior frames of tall buildings. The steel section of the column permits standard shear and moment connection mechanisms between the column core and the steel of composite floor beams. Most commonly used are closely spaced columns and relatively deep spandrel beams that comprise a flexurally stiff and efficient lateral framing system for control of drift in tall buildings. Known as partial tube structures, these frames have proved to be economical and have provided flexural and axial stiffness adequate to control lateral drift in tall buildings.

3. Composite transition columns to transfer axial load from steel columns of upper levels of steel framing to reinforced concrete columns below as suggested

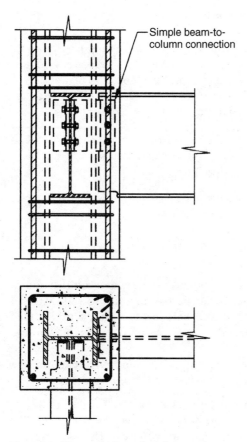

Simple beam-to-column connection

Figure 4.1   Encased composite column.

in Fig. 4.3. This type has been used in buildings that have a reinforced-concrete frame for the lower floors and steel frames above, as might occur for steel office buildings over a concrete parking garage. The composite column is used for this transition in order to avoid a large-sized base plate for the steel columns above the concrete structure. The structural steel section in the composite column is the same as the steel column at the lowest level of the steel frame. The overall concrete section dimensions preferably should be the same as the reinforced concrete column dimensions below the composite column. The composite column may be extended one or more floors, depending upon the magnitude of the axial load. At the base of the steel section, a minimal-sized base plate, which may be an inch wider and deeper than the steel section, is utilized to transfer the construction loads prior to casting and hardening of the concrete of the composite column. Transition columns can be used also for the transition from a steel frame beneath to a concrete frame above.

4. Filled composite columns as illustrated in Fig. 4.4. The concrete in the core of the steel pipe column provides additional strength, toughness, and

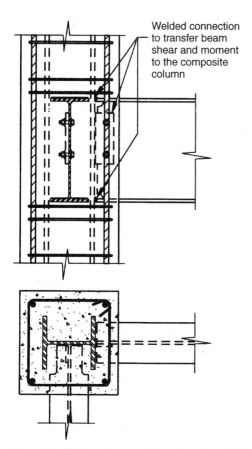

Welded connection
to transfer beam
shear and moment
to the composite
column

Figure 4.2 Encased composite column in rigid
frames.

stiffness to the steel column. This type of composite column generally is used
when the structural steel elements are exposed for architectural reasons, and
some economy is realized as concrete formwork is eliminated. For multistory
buildings in which the steel column needs to be fireproofed, structural engineers may design a bar-reinforced concrete core to support the full required
axial load without help from the steel shell during a major fire. The total
composite section, including the steel shell, can be utilized with its additional
stiffness to control lateral drift of the overall structure. Filled composite
"supercolumns" have been used in high-rise buildings, sized generally for
their stiffness when steel shells are filled with high-strength concrete ($f_c' > 8$
ksi). Filled composite columns provide damping in the order of 1.5 to 2 percent in response to dynamic loads.

5. Composite concrete walls indicated by the plan view in Fig. 4.5 are used
as shear walls in steel buildings to provide lateral stiffness as well as vertical
support for the steel floor framing. More than one steel section in the wall

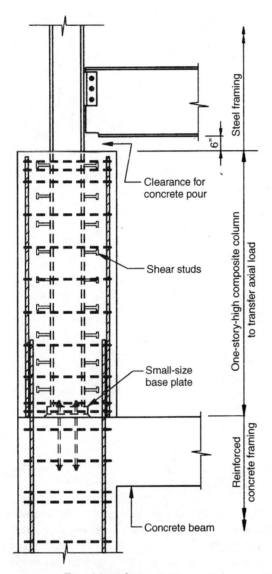

Figure 4.3 Transition column.

may be provided, depending upon the floor framing. Common locations for composite walls include elevator shafts and stairways in multistory buildings, although composite shear walls can be placed between any columns in a structure. As in encased composite columns, the steel section in the composite wall construction can be designed to provide a means of support for the erection of several floors ahead of the forming and casting required for the complete composite concrete wall. The procedure expedites construction schedules and thus has the potential for reducing overall construction cost.

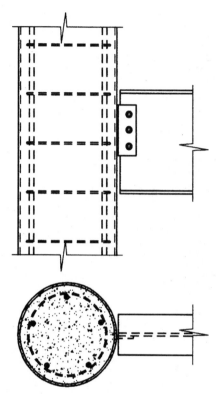

Figure 4.4 Filled composite column.

6. Plated composite walls combine steel plates with concrete that either encases the steel plate or provides a core for two surface plates (Fig. 4.6). The plates must be bonded to the concrete with positive anchorage devices such as studs, channels, or angles. The concrete core stabilizes the steel plates against local buckling, and the steel plates provide stiffness and strength for the composite sandwich. Plate-reinforced composite walls are ductile and provide high resistance to in-plane compressive and shear forces. Those with outside plates possess a high resistance to penetration by high-velocity small missiles and have been used for protection against blast forces. Those with encased plates have been applied in structures located in areas of high seismicity.

4.3 Behavior of Composite Columns

4.3.1 Response to load

Composite columns respond to load as a combination of the response of plain concrete and the response of bare steel. Generally, composite interaction is synergistic; i.e., it enhances the performance of the whole to something superior to the sum of the component parts.

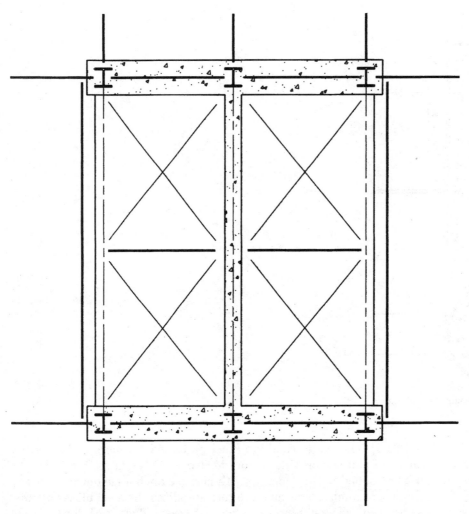

Figure 4.5 Composite concrete walls.

Plain concrete in standard control cylinders or cubes subjected to small strains resists compression load as an elastic solid until its matrix of mortar and coarse aggregate fractures. As an elastic solid, concrete exhibits a Poisson ratio one-third to one-half as high as that of steel, and it has a Young's modulus that is a function of the density and compressive strength of the concrete. The LRFD Manual[D95] gives the following empirical expression for Young's modulus of concrete E_c:

$$E_c = w1.5\sqrt{f_c'} \tag{4.1}$$

where w = density of concrete, lb/ft^3
$\quad\;\; f_c'$ = compressive strength of concrete, ksi

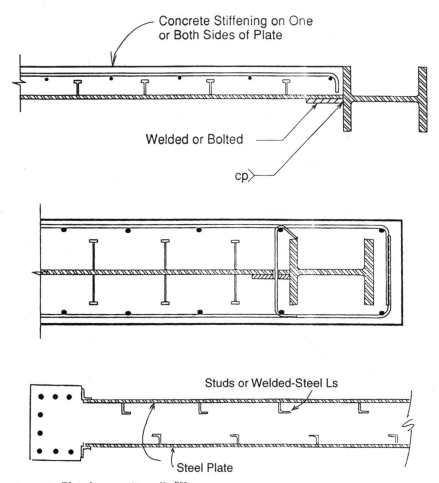

Figure 4.6 Plated composite walls.[D96]

The matrix of mortar and coarse aggregate fractures initially at points of maximum tensile stress.[G14] As the load is increased beyond initial fracture of the heterogeneous material, cracking progresses along ragged lines of tensile fracture. After internal cracking at stresses in the order of $0.5f_c'$, the effective stiffness E_c begins to decrease and the apparent Poisson ratio for concrete is greater than 0.5, as internally fractured concrete occupies more volume than the original uncracked concrete.

Under sustained compression, internal macroscopic fracturing of plain concrete will continue slowly to extend. Compressive deformations increase without corresponding increases in the compression stress as concrete appears to flow, or "creep," from beneath compressive loads. The rate of creep increases with the stress level but decreases with time. After sustained loads are removed, there is an immediate elastic recovery, but the recovery of creep deformations occurs very slowly and is never complete. Plain concrete shrinks with drying and expands with moisture. Its volume can vary with changes in atmospheric moisture. A detailed discussion of volume changes due to creep and shrinkage is presented in Sec. 4.5.2.

Bare structural steel can fail in compression owing to instability or to compression stresses reaching the steel yield stress F_y. Instability may cause either overall or local elastic buckling, i.e., buckling at nominal stresses less than the yield stress F_y. Instability also may result in transverse deformations causing local fiber stresses to reach the material yield limit F_y; inelastic buckling may follow. The Young's modulus of steel is virtually constant at 29,000 ksi (200,000 MPa) for all compressive stresses less than the yield stress F_y.

The stiffness of an uncracked composite section is the sum of the stiffnesses of each component part, both for axial force and for flexure. For axial force,

$$EA = E_s A_s + E_c A_c \qquad (4.2a)$$

and for flexural force,

$$EI = E_s I_s + E_c I_c \qquad (4.2b)$$

Shear bond between concrete and steel. The surface of rolled steel shapes and tubes is smooth. In composite steel and concrete elements, any adhesion or bond between smooth faces of steel and concrete is easily broken.[50] However, the coefficient of sliding friction between smooth faces of steel and concrete can be taken in the order of 0.5. Thus, in the presence of pressure normal to the smooth interface between steel and concrete, a shear stress at least as high as one-half the normal stress can be transferred between the steel and concrete. Pressure normal to the smooth interface exists always in concrete-filled shells deformed by bending. In contrast, even in regions of flexural curvature, the concrete encasement of structural shapes creates pressure against the encased shape only if the concrete is confined laterally to bear against the steel shape. Although concrete located inside the flanges of wide-flange shapes is effectively constrained so that shear is transferred along the inside surfaces of the steel shape,[92] lateral confinement by ties is required for all concrete-encased steel shapes designed in accordance with AISC-LRFD and ACI-318 regulations.

Locally, in regions near connections to floor beams or bracing members, it may be necessary to supplement steel-concrete bond with shear studs or bars welded to the structural shape. The transfer of shear into concrete at connections to floor beams is discussed in subsequent sections of this chapter.

4.3.2   Encased composite columns

The flexural stiffness of structural shapes encased in concrete is governed largely by the concrete encasement. Prior to flexural cracking, the flexural stiffness EI of encased composite columns can be estimated as the product of the Young's modulus E_c [Eq. (4.1)] and the moment of inertia I_g for the gross concrete outline of the section. Steel reinforcement and structural shapes inside the concrete gross section increase the stiffness of the cross section, but frequently the extra stiffness from steel is less than the deviation of the actual E_c from that computed from Eq. (4.1). Under sustained loading, the creep of concrete in effect reduces E_c, and any flexural tension cracking reduces the effective amount of concrete in a section. If the flanges of a large steel shape are encased in relatively thin concrete cover of 3 in (76 mm) or less, the flexural stiffness $E_s I_s$ of the steel shape about its own major axis should be added to the flexural stiffness of the concrete section. Even in cases for which the flanges of a large steel shape are encased in a relatively thin concrete cover of 3 in or less, the elastic stiffness of the composite member prior to initial flexural cracking can be taken as $E_c I_g$.

Measured flexural stiffness for bending about the major axis of a W8×40 steel shape encased in a 16 × 16-in (41 × 41-cm) concrete section without axial load is illustrated in Fig. 4.7.[140] Also shown are stiffness values computed as $E_c I_g$; $0.5 E_c I_g$; ACI Eq. 10-14;[D66] ACI Eq. 10-11;[D66] E_m, from LRFD Eq. 12-2[D91] used in place of E_c times the moment of inertia computed from the steel area A_s times the LRFD-modified radius of gyration r_m^2; and E_c times the moment of inertia of the transformed composite cracked section. In ACI Eqs. 10-11 and 10-14, the coefficient for the effect of creep was taken as zero. Flexural stiffness

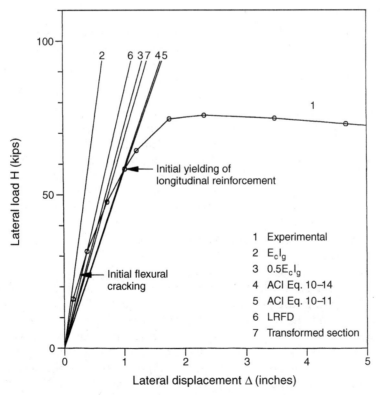

Figure 4.7 Flexural stiffness of encased composite beam.[140]

based on $0.5E_cI_g$ has an average value of 0.92 times the experimental secant stiffness corresponding to initial yielding. Statistical analysis of the lateral load-displacement response of additional composite column test specimens indicated that an effective flexural stiffness of $0.5E_cI_g$ provided a reasonable estimate of the secant stiffness corresponding to the observed initial yielding of the longitudinal reinforcement. Thus the secant stiffness of $0.5E_cI_g$ can be used as an approximate lower-bound estimate of the elastic interstory drift associated with no yielding of steel in encased composite columns.

Shear transfer takes place through bond between the steel shape and the concrete encasement as long as the encasement is retained around the steel shape. The encasement can be maintained with a grid of reinforcing bars in the concrete surrounding the steel shape. For nonseismic applications, the size and spacing of steel reinforcement in the surrounding grid correspond to minimum reinforcement in tied reinforced-concrete columns. Near the beam-to-column joints for earthquake-resistant columns, the spacing between bars in the grid should not exceed 4 in (100 mm). Transverse ties in the grid can be considered as a contributing factor to the transverse shear strength of a composite column with an encased shape. Additional shear transfer can be achieved with headed studs, channels, or angles welded to the steel shape.

4.3.3 Filled composite columns

Steel pipes and tubes filled with concrete possess a flexural stiffness governed largely by the steel shell. Compression strength of the column is at least as great as the sum of the strength of the bare shell and the strength of the unconfined concrete. When a concentric load is applied so that both the concrete and the steel are strained uniformly, the Poisson ratio of the steel causes the shell to expand laterally somewhat more than the concrete fill until the applied compression force creates concrete stresses large enough to cause internal microcracking and an expanding volume of concrete. Internal microcracking associated with an expanding concrete volume initiates at stresses higher than $0.5f'_c$. After internal cracking begins, subsequent loads cause lateral expansion of concrete that is restrained by the steel shell. Eventually, the steel shell reaches its yield stress from longitudinal compression combined with transverse tension. Inelastic outward buckling of the shell wall takes place, and concrete, no longer contained by the shell, crushes locally as the column fails.

Triaxial confinement from the steel shell can increase the effective strength of concrete. Theoretically, triaxial confinement should increase the strength enough to triple the nominal concentric capacity of concrete inside the circular steel shell. However, the longitudinal stiffness E_c of contained, microcracked concrete reduces dramatically. If the column length were more than three times its diameter, the longitudinal stiffness of the shell would be inadequate to resist inelastic buckling at compression loads that exceed the capacity determined without any increase in f'_c from lateral confinement. In more slender columns, the regions of increased concrete strength due to confinement would be so soft that longitudinal stiffness could not prevent inelastic buckling. Some design codes permit stocky column compression strength estimates that recognize values of f_c' effectively higher than the specified cylinder strength.[G70A] When the height-to-thickness ratio exceeds 2, the safe limit strength under concentric longitudinal loading is equal to the sum of material capacities as long as the concrete-filled shell does not fail from elastic or inelastic buckling before the material strength limit is reached.

Truly concentric loads are rare. Some eccentricity of longitudinal force is probably present in practically all columns at all times. Eccentric compression involves flexure in addition to axial force. In the presence of curvatures caused by bending, the steel walls of filled shells press against the contained core of concrete, ensuring some shear transfer along the contact surfaces. An unbroken bond between the steel tube and the contained concrete would satisfy the usual boundary condition that there is one strain profile in the column as flexural curvature develops. However, test results from concrete-filled tube specimens with a lubricated inside surface were compared with results from specimens without the lubrication, and no differences in the behavior were found. Concrete showed no discernible adhesion to steel.[50] Filled composite columns behaved as if slip could take place along the contact surface whether or not the surface had been lubricated before the concrete was cast.

Some absence of shear transfer at the interface has a positive effect on column performance. Complete adhesion of steel to concrete is a constraint which may result in less resistance to force than that which can be developed if some slippage takes place. Both materials must assume the same curvature, but their neutral axes need not coincide. Slippage between the concrete core and the steel shell wall permits the neutral axis of concrete to migrate toward the tension face, while lateral confinement from the shell wall helps compression face concrete to resist longitudinal stress at strains higher than the limit strains expected without such confinement. The migration of the neutral axis for concrete toward the tension face delays tension cracking and permits more compression force to be resisted by concrete. Some flexural resistance is lost while axial resistance increases and there is only a marginal increase in limit strength of the composite column. However, column ductility is improved significantly.

Tests of the shear strength of concrete-filled shells indicate that intentional slippage, caused by a lubricant between concrete and the shell wall, allows more shear to be resisted and larger shear deformations to develop than those observed from specimens with slippage prevented.[110] With some slippage, the concrete adjusts effectively to act as a series of compression struts with shell walls responding as tension ties that resist shear forces.

Connections to filled composite columns. Transfer of forces at connections of floor members to the steel shell can be accomplished with gusset plates for shear attachment to floor members or with a steel bearing plate at the top of a filled composite column. Such a cap plate must contain a hole through which concrete can be placed. Floor beams can penetrate completely through large shells filled with concrete. Vertical shear forces are transferred through direct bearing of the floor beam flanges against the shell and against the concrete. Flexural forces with associated curvature of the composite column will force shell walls to bear against the concrete core with enough pressure to transfer effectively shear between the wall and the core. If local transverse pressure is considered inadequate for the transfer of shears at the floor beam connection, or if the shell wall is relatively flexible, studs can be welded inside the shell to stiffen and stabilize the thin shell wall and also to transfer vertical shear directly into concrete.

Shear plates welded to the exterior surface of shells transfer vertical shear effectively into the shell wall. Locally, there may be enough curvature at the connection to develop effective shear transfer of vertical forces into the concrete core, as is indicated in Fig. 4.8a. If the shell wall is too thin to develop an entire vertical shear and bending reaction, a shear plate may be extended through the column, as indicated in Fig. 4.8b, or external horizontal stiffener plates can be used to strengthen the wall, as shown in Fig. 4.8c. The holes in the shear plate of Fig. 4.8b create concrete dowels that are helpful in developing bearing and shear transfer to the concrete core. The extension of the shear plate through the tube as shown in Fig. 4.8b provides bearing surfaces between steel and concrete both at the bottom edge of the plate and at the bearing edges of the holes in the steel plate. The limit strength of concrete in bearing against steel should be taken no greater than f_c' with a resistance factor $\phi = 0.65$. Moment connections of the type shown in Fig. 4.8c are suggested. The top ring plate is recommended for continuity in lieu of single-flange plates welded to the wall of the shell if the tube is too flexible to transfer significant flange forces across the column between beam flanges.

Shear strength. The shear strength of a filled composite column can be taken as the sum of limit shear capacities of concrete and of the shell walls. Confined by the shell, concrete helps to resist the shear force by acting as a series of compression struts pushing against the compression and tension surfaces of the shell while sidewalls of the shell serve as tension struts. The ACI building code[D100] effectively limits the shear strength of stirrup-reinforced concrete to five multiples of the nominal shear capacity of plain concrete. If this limit is exceeded, concrete crushes in diagonal compression. However, the walls of the steel shell can resist shear without help from concrete. Taking one-half the total steel area as the effective shear area of round or square tubing, i.e., the area of steel oriented in the plane of bending, the shear strength of steel alone V_s can be estimated as

$$V_s = 0.3 A_s F_y = 0.3 \rho_s A_g F_y \tag{4.3}$$

where A_s = area of steel shell
$\quad\quad F_y$ = yield strength of steel
$\quad\quad \rho_s = A_s/A_g$
$\quad\quad A_g$ = gross area of concrete-filled shell

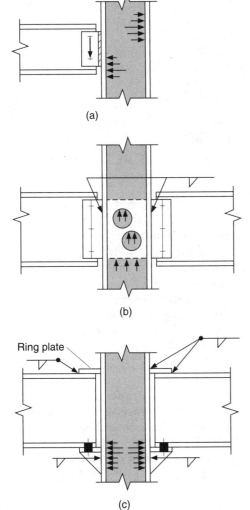

(a)

(b)

Ring plate

(c)

Figure 4.8 Steel beam to filled composite column joint. (a) Bending creates forces between tube and core. (b) Shear plate through tube. (c) Horizontal stiffening of tube.

The wall of the steel shell reinforces the concrete fill in a manner similar to the tension tie stirrups reinforcing the web of a concrete beam. As a tension tie, the shell wall can resist shear at full yield strength F_y, whereas the limit shear stress in the shell walls, without any help from concrete, must not exceed the shear strength of steel, usually taken as $0.6F_y$. The total shear capacity can be taken as the steel "stirrup" strength required with concrete plus the steel shear strength which is available after the "stirrup" area has been deducted from total shear area of tube walls. The total nominal shear strength V_n for square or round tubes filled with concrete can be estimated as

$$V_n = 5v_c A_{cv} + [0.6(\tfrac{1}{2} A_s F_y - 5v_c A_{cv})]$$

$$= 2v_c A_{cv} + 0.3 A_s F_y$$

When the area A_{cv} is assumed to be one-half of the actual area of the encased concrete and the shear strength of concrete v_c is taken as $2\sqrt{0.001 f_c'}$,

$$V_n = [\rho_s F_y + 0.21(1 - \rho_s)\sqrt{f_c'}]\, 0.3\, A_g \qquad (4.4)$$

where the units of V_n are kips, of F_y and f_c' are kips per square inch, and of the gross column area A_g are square inches. The effective shear area of rectangular tubes is the area of steel in the tube walls parallel to the plane of the shear.

Fire resistance.   Laboratory tests of the fire-resisting behavior of filled composite columns indicate that concrete acts as a heat sink. The dissipation of heat from steel into concrete delays the rate of temperature increase in the steel tubing. Procedures have been developed for a finite-difference method of estimating the temperature at points on and within concrete-filled composite columns in an environment of increasing temperature.[G42] Stress-strain characteristics for steel and concrete at each temperature state can be used to determine force-moment-curvature response and the resulting strength to support required loading as temperature increases. Computer programs have been developed for such thermal analyses in response to standardized temperature-time curves acceptable to U.S. and Canadian building codes.

Fire endurance is more reliable if longitudinal bar reinforcement is used inside the filled tubes as the bars help the concrete core sustain stiffness after the steel shell softens in intense heat. When the longitudinal reinforcement is at least 1 percent but less than 3 percent of the concrete area, the fire resistance of the column may be estimated as a function of the shape and outside dimension of the column cross section, the effective column length, and the magnitude of the service load.[M24]

4.4   Design Rules

4.4.1   Background

Design rules for composite columns are included in the AISC-LRFD specification[D91] and in the ACI building code.[D100] Both provide methods for evaluating the strength of the cross section and of the effects of slenderness. Both apply to encased structural shapes and to concrete-filled structural pipe and tubing as well as fabricated shells. The LRFD rules are based on procedures analogous to steel design. Applied to encased or filled round or rectangular composite column shapes, analytic expressions for strength, stiffness, and slenderness effects lead directly to values of axial-load capacity as well as beam-column capacity. The ACI rules for composite columns follow the same procedures as for bar reinforced-concrete columns. The ACI code requires a strain compatibility analysis at the limit state of loading, and it does not permit column design without at least a minimum eccentricity of the required axial loads. Consequently, general formulations of column capacity cannot be developed to satisfy the ACI building code so that the use of design aids becomes necessary.

Procedures of the AISC-LRFD specification are recommended for design of composite columns of regular cross section. The AISC-LRFD rules may be used for axially loaded columns as well as for eccentrically loaded columns. Expressed in the form of strength equations, these rules are applied more easily than the rules of the ACI building code. AISC-LRFD rules specifically require that at least 4 percent of the composite section be comprised of structural steel shape, tube, pipe, or shell. Composite sections with less structural steel are considered to perform as if they were bar-reinforced columns, and the ACI building code is recommended for design of such sections. The ACI building code is recommended as well for sections of such irregular shape that AISC-LRFD formulations would not apply.

Eurocode 4, a comprehensive European model code for the design of composite members and systems,[D94] contains criteria for composite columns. It is similar in scope to the American specifications. However, the European rules prescribe detail information and procedures that are considered in the United States to be the prerogative of the design engineer.

4.4.2 Axial compression

It is a common practice to connect steel beams to steel columns with simple shear connections that permit the beam ends to rotate without significant resistance. While simple shear connections provide some rotational restraint, such restraint can be neglected, as it is insignificant with respect to the flexural stiffness of the beam itself. Accordingly, simple shear connections are proportioned only for the beam-end reaction or shear. The concrete in an encased composite column offers some additional bending restraint that may be neglected when columns are designed to support only vertical load reactions from beams. Columns can be designed as loaded only in axial compression if they support only vertical or gravity loading.

Design for axial compression requires consideration of cross-section capacity as well as slenderness effects. Slenderness can result in buckling of a column under concentric axial force. Buckling of very slender columns is a phenomenon based on the elastic flexural stiffness of the column. Buckling of less slender columns involves combined elastic and postelastic flexural deformations.

Under uniaxial compressive stress, concrete spalls and fails when longitudinal strain reaches about 0.18 to 0.20 percent. Cross-section strength P_0 is the sum of axial-load capacities of the materials that make up the cross section. Thus, for steel that yields at strains no greater than 0.2 percent,

$$P_0 = A_s F_y + A_r F_{yr} + 0.85 A_c f'_c \qquad (4.5)$$

where P_0 = cross-section capacity in uniaxial compression
$\quad A_s$ = area of structural shape in cross section
$\quad A_r$ = area of longitudinal reinforcement in cross section
$\quad A_c$ = area of concrete in cross section
$\quad F_y$ = yield strength of structural shape steel
$\quad F_{yr}$ = yield strength of longitudinal reinforcement
$\quad f'_c$ = strength of concrete from standard cylinder tests

Slender columns fail under loads less than P_0 because of buckling. Elastic (Euler) buckling strength P_E of very slender columns can be expressed as

$$P_E = \frac{\pi^2 EI}{(Kl)^2} \qquad (4.6)$$

where Kl = effective column length
$\quad EI$ = effective flexural stiffness of column cross section

Effective flexural stiffness of a composite cross section may be estimated on the basis of the transformed area of an uncracked section. Section transformation involves adjustment of the actual width of one material into a transformed effective width perpendicular to the plane of bending. The adjustment is in proportion to the modular ratio $n = E_s/E_c$ of steel and concrete. Thus for a section transformed into equivalent steel, the width of all concrete must be divided by n, and the product $E_s I_{tr}$ represents the flexural stiffness of the composite section. For a section transformed into equivalent concrete, the width of all steel must be multiplied by n in order for the product $E_c I_{tr}$ to represent the flexural stiffness of the composite section.

Short or stocky composite columns fail when the limit strength of steel and concrete is reached, as expressed by Eq. (4.5). For longer columns, if concrete stress exceeds $0.5f'_c$ to $0.6f'_c$, buckling failure is inelastic, and the columns are considered to be of intermediate length. Very slender columns fail in elastic buckling. Elastic buckling occurs only for columns which are so slender that the average concrete stress at failure remains elastic. This is the case for concrete stresses less than $0.5f'_c$ to $0.6f'_c$.

The design strength of two concentrically loaded composite columns, determined according to the LRFD specification, is shown in Fig. 4.9 as a function of slenderness. Details for obtaining each curve are given in App. B. One of the columns is a W8×40 steel shape encased in 16 × 16-in (0.41 × 0.41-m) concrete and the other a 10 × 10-in (0.25 × 0.25-m) concrete-filled tube. For $Kl = 0$, the design strength is equal to ϕP_0. For stocky and intermediate slenderness, the design strength decreases at a rate that increases as the effective length Kl increases. For slender columns the strength decreases at a decreasing rate. The three characteristic segments of a typical strength-slenderness curve have the following limits:

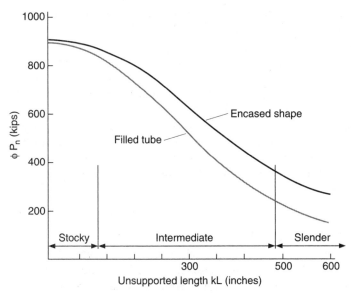

Figure 4.9   Axial strength and column length.

1. Stocky columns: $\phi P_n \geq 0.9 P_0$
2. Intermediate columns: $0.9 P_0 > \phi P_n \geq 0.6 P_0$
3. Long columns: $\phi P_n < 0.6 P_0$

Shanley[G10] demonstrated that a lower bound of the strength-slenderness function for columns of a homogeneous material is defined if the slope of the stress-strain curve for the material E_t were substituted for E in Eq. (4.6). If all components of a steel column had a truly elastic rather then plastic response to load, the strength-slenderness function would remain at a constant stress limit equal to F_y until the slenderness is so large that P_E from Eq. (4.6) equals P_0 from Eq. (4.5). Equation (4.6) would apply to all columns with slenderness exceeding this value. All structural-steel shapes contain residual internal stresses that result from nonuniform cooling after rolling, fabrication, erection, and other causes. As the residual stresses are the result of many unpredictable factors, their magnitude and distribution for any specific piece of steel is unknown. Steel shapes with the thickest flanges tend to have the highest levels of residual stresses. As a consequence of the residual stresses, no structure exhibits truly elastoplastic behavior, and strength-slenderness curves similar to those in Fig. 4.9 assume lower positions as the residual stresses increase. Recommendations of Eurocode 3[G82] contain three primary and two secondary strength-slenderness curves assigned to different categories and uses of steel shapes.

   The specific shape of column curves that most accurately reflect the relationship between thrust capacity and column slenderness for various types of composite cross sections has been studied.[131] However, for composite columns the variability of the concrete stiffness obscures variations that the steel forms and shapes might produce among strength-slenderness functions. In recognition of the extreme scatter in the available test data and large uncertainty concerning the magnitude and distribution of residual stresses in any completed structure, only one conservative curve is included in the LRFD specifications.[D91] The LRFD column curve is discussed in Sec. 4.4.5, and application details are contained in App. B.

Design for concentric axial force generally begins with an estimate of the relative slenderness of the composite member. On the basis of the estimated slenderness, some reduction of the value P_0 can be used with Eq. (4.5) to determine the necessary trial areas of steel, bar reinforcement, and concrete in the composite column.

4.4.3 Bending and axial load

Bernoulli's hypothesis that strains vary linearly with the distance from the neutral axis about which bending occurs can be applied in the analysis of bending for composite sections. Stress is proportional to strain until load creates stresses above the proportional limit of the material. Increasing load causes strains to increase more rapidly than the corresponding stresses for both steel and concrete, and a plastic distribution of stresses is approached. The limit strength of most concrete-encased composite columns is attained at crushing and spalling of the encasement. Before concrete spalls, the encasement restrains postyield compression buckling of longitudinal bars as well as of the compressed parts of encased shapes.

Loss of encasement is accompanied by buckling of longitudinal bars, fracture of transverse bars, local postyield buckling of the steel shape, and overall failure of the section. Thus failure of composite cross sections occurs when concrete crushes. The ACI code specifies the maximum usable strain of concrete in compression as 0.3 percent. With a limit strain of 0.3 percent on the extreme fibers plus the location of the neutral axis, a failure strain profile can be described for any particular section. Stresses consistent with each strain can be computed, and axial and flexural forces that result from the stresses can be integrated to determine the value of the nominal axial load P_n and the moment M_n associated with the failure strain profile. The locus of such points P_n and M_n for various positions of the neutral axis defines a capacity thrust-moment function known as the interaction diagram for the section. The stresses in steel shapes and the reinforcing bars are taken as the product of strain ϵ and modulus of elasticity of steel E_s until ϵE_s exceeds F_y; for all strains greater than F_y/E_s, steel stress equals F_y.

Any stress-strain function resembling measured behavior can be used for concrete, but a rectangular stress block is a common and simple representation of the distribution of the pressure on concrete at failure. As a result of recent research on high-strength concrete,[G80] a stress block with the stress equal to $\alpha_1 f_c'$ and the depth of the block equal to β_1 times the distance between the maximum compressed concrete fiber and the neutral axis has been recommended. For f_c' expressed in ksi units, the coefficients α_1 and β_1 may be taken as

$$\alpha_1 = 1.01 - \frac{f_c'}{50} \qquad (4.7a)$$

$$\beta_1 = 0.91 - \frac{f_c'}{70} \qquad (4.7b)$$

with the maximum and minimum values of both coefficients equal to 0.85 and 0.7, respectively. It is assumed that concrete resists no tension. Analytical evaluation of cross-section strength by the procedure thus defined can be applied to any composite cross section, but the procedure is tedious. Computer codes for accomplishing the strength analysis are needed for practical design applications.

An approximate evaluation of the limit strength of a composite section with normal-strength concrete, i.e., $f_c' \leq 10$ ksi (69 MPa), can be accomplished by hand,[C70] and the results are adequate for most applications. The procedure, based on plastic stress distribution, is illustrated in App. B for two cross sections referred to in the subsequent text as the demonstration sections:

1. A W8×40 rolled shape of A36 steel encased in a 16-in-square (0.4-m) concrete section of $f_c' = 3.5$ ksi (24 MPa)
2. A 10 × 10 × ¼-in (254 × 254 × 6-mm) tube, of $F_y = 46$ ksi (317 MPa) A500 steel, filled with $f_c' = 5$ ksi (34 MPa) concrete

The procedure requires calculation of four sets of coordinates on the $P_n - M_n$ diagram as follows:

1. Compute P_{n0} from Eq. (4.5).
2. Assume a plastic distribution of stress with strength of concrete equal to zero in tension and $0.75f_c'$ in compression. Then locate a neutral axis for zero axial force by equating the tension yield force in steel about middepth to the force in the compressed concrete. In App. B, the distance from middepth to the plastic neutral axis is called z when $P_n = 0$. Compute compression forces on steel above z and tension forces on steel below z. These forces are equal to and opposite one another.
3. Compute the value of M_n about middepth as the sum of moments on the cross section when the neutral axis is distance z above middepth.
4. Compute the total force P_{n2} and total moment M_{n2} about middepth when the plastic neutral axis is at middepth.
5. Compute the total force P_{n1} and total moment M_{n1} about middepth when the plastic neutral axis is at distance z below middepth.
6. Connect the coordinates to complete the strength interaction diagram for the cross section.

The thrust-moment interaction diagram computed by the plastic analysis procedure detailed in App. B is plotted in Fig. 4.10 (heavy line). All combina-

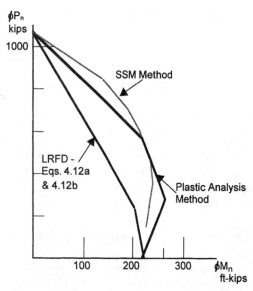

Figure 4.10 Thrust-moment interaction diagrams.

tions of thrust P and moment M inside the interaction diagram represent force values for which the strength of the section is adequate.

4.4.4 Biaxial bending

An analysis of the capacity of a cross section based on the premise that a failure occurs when a concrete fiber reaches a certain limiting strain can be applied with the neutral axis oriented at various angles that need not be parallel to any principal axis. An axial force and moment capacity interaction surface similar to that shown in Fig. 4.11 can be generated. If inelastic response of concrete is represented with an accurate stress-strain function, that procedure produces the most accurate analysis of section strength under biaxial loading. However, the procedure is laborious even when used for only one interaction curve, and defining an interaction surface requires several interaction curves.[G32] The procedure is too tedious for practical applications without the aid of a computer program.

For a specified axial force, the strength of a section in biaxial bending can be approximated by observing that the sum of the ratios of the required moment to the nominal uniaxial moment capacity about the two principal axes must be equal to unity:[G25A]

$$\left(\frac{M_{ux}}{M_{nx}}\right)^{\alpha} + \left(\frac{M_{uy}}{M_{ny}}\right)^{\alpha} = 1 \qquad (4.8)$$

where M_{ux} = required moment capacity for bending component in the plane of the x axis

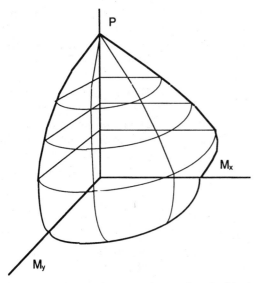

Figure 4.11 Strength interaction surface for biaxially eccentric loading.

M_{uy} = required moment capacity for bending component in the plane of the y axis

M_{nx} = nominal bending strength with bending only in the plane of the x axis

M_{ny} = nominal bending strength with bending only in the plane of the y axis

α = a number between 1 and 2 defining the shape of the biaxial moment contour

The AISC-LRFD specification[D91] in effect uses Eq. (4.8) with the exponent α equal to 1.0. Ratios between the required and actual bending strength considered individually for bending about each principal axis are added to produce the interaction contour that is a straight line. The LRFD procedure is safe, as it underestimates actual capacity to resist biaxially eccentric compression load.

Test results for reinforced-concrete columns under biaxially eccentric loading[G32] indicate that strength predictions with Eq. (4.8) and $\alpha = 2$ are as accurate as the strength predictions for uniaxial bending based on the rectangular stress block for concrete. The same reliability should apply for encased composite columns, although sufficient test data are not available.

4.4.5 AISC-LRFD specification

The AISC specification[D17] has included provisions for the design of composite beams with shear connectors since 1961. Design requirements for composite columns were introduced in 1986 with the first edition of the AISC-LRFD specification.[D56] The method adopted for composite columns was developed under the auspices of an ACI-AISC-AISI liaison committee[D40] in the form of an allowable stress design procedure. The intent of the liaison committee was to develop methods that would give similar estimates of strength with the ACI building code and with the AISC specification.

The concept of applying AISC column design methodology to composite columns by the use of modified properties was first presented by Furlong[D35] in 1976. Modified yield stress F_{my}, modified modulus of elasticity E_m, and modified radius of gyration r_m were incorporated into an allowable stress design procedure that was published by Task Group 20 of the Structural Stability Research Council[D40] in 1979. An extensive statistical study[D42] of the available test data on composite columns followed under the leadership of Galambos at Washington University in St. Louis, Mo., and the modified properties were adopted into an LRFD procedure which became a part of the 1986 AISC-LRFD specification.[D56]

Since it is common practice for steel and composite beams to be attached to composite columns with shear plates that transmit virtually no moment, the LRFD specification for composite columns recognizes and permits design of axially loaded columns without bending. The LRFD rules include also provisions for slender columns and beam columns and for consideration of frame stability.

Axial strength.   The compression strength of composite column cross sections can be estimated accurately as the sum of the compressive capacities of each component part, the structural shape or tube, the longitudinal reinforcement, and the concrete. Superposition of component capacities is a reliable procedure if each of the components maintains stiffness to resist increasing strains until the nominal capacity of all components is reached. In such case, the nominal strength of the cross section P_n is equal to P_0 given by Eq. (4.5).

Design strength of composite columns is determined from the same equations as those applicable to bare steel columns except that the formulas are entered with modified properties F_{my}, E_m, and r_m. The axial design strength is computed as

$$\phi_c P_n = 0.85 A_s F_{cr} \tag{4.9}$$

where A_s is the area of the structural steel shape, pipe, or tube and F_{cr} is the critical stress of the column given by Eqs. (4.10):

$$F_{cr} = (0.658^A)\, F_{my} \qquad \text{for } A \le 2.25 \tag{4.10a}$$

and

$$F_{cr} = \frac{0.877}{A}\, F_{my} \qquad \text{for } A > 2.25 \tag{4.10b}$$

where $A = \lambda_c^2 = (Kl/\pi r_m)^2 (F_{my}/E_m)$
F_{my} = modified yield stress
$\lambda_c = (Kl/\pi r_m)\sqrt{F_{my}/E_m}$ (4.10c)
K = effective length factor
l = laterally unbraced length of the column
r_m = modified radius of gyration about the axis of buckling
E_m = modified modulus of elasticity

The modified properties F_{my}, E_m, and r_m account for the effects of concrete and longitudinal reinforcing bars. The modified radius of gyration r_m is the larger of (1) the radius of gyration of the steel section r and (2) 30 percent of the thickness of the gross composite section in the plane of bending. The modified values F_{my} and E_m are given by the following equations:

$$F_{my} = F_y + \frac{c_1 F_{yr} A_r}{A_s} + \frac{c_2 f_c' A_c}{A_s}$$ (4.11a)

and

$$E_m = E_s + \frac{c_3 E_c A_c}{A_s}$$ (4.11b)

where F_y = yield strength of structural steel $\leq$ 60 ksi (414 MPa)
F_{yr} = yield strength of longitudinal reinforcing bars $\leq$ 60 ksi (414 MPa)
A_r = total area of longitudinal reinforcing bars
A_s = area of structural steel shape, pipe, or tube
A_c = area of concrete
f_c' = design strength of concrete
E_s = modulus of elasticity of steel
E_c = modulus of elasticity of concrete
c_1, c_2, c_3 = numerical coefficients listed in Table 4.1

Dividing both sides of Eq. (4.5) by the area of structural steel A_s transforms the equation into an effective composite stress F_{my}. Coefficients c_1, c_2, and c_3 are higher for filled composite columns than for encased composite columns. With the steel encasement always available to provide lateral confinement to concrete in filled composite columns, there is no uncertainty that the contained concrete will reach at least as much strength as that reached by concrete in

TABLE 4.1   Numerical Coefficients for Design of Composite Columns

Composite column type	Numerical coefficients		
	c_1	c_2	c_3
Concrete-filled tubes	1.0	0.85	0.4
Concrete-encased shapes	0.7	0.6	0.2

unconfined standard concrete cylinders used to determine f_c'. In contrast, there is less certainty that an unconfined concrete encasement can attain stress as high as $0.85f_c'$. If the unconfined concrete fails to reach $0.85f_c'$, the longitudinal reinforcement it stabilizes may not reach its yield stress F_{yr} either. The values of c_1 and c_2 for encased composite columns are 70 percent of the values for filled composite columns, reflecting the higher degree of uncertainty.

Slenderness effects.   Slenderness can be expressed analytically for columns as a measure of the member flexural stiffness EI/l. The straightforward application of a modulus of elasticity, a cross-section moment of inertia, and an effective length, customary for the design of bare structural-steel columns, cannot be used for composite and reinforced-concrete members. The relative contribution of each component does not remain constant throughout loading. Concrete cracks in flexural tension, it is less homogeneous than steel, and its stiffness decays at strain less than the yield strain of steel. The degree of stiffness available from bending of concrete contained within a pipe or tube is higher than that which can be anticipated from unconfined concrete. The overall stability of filled composite columns is affected much more by the steel shell than by the concrete core. Conversely, the overall stability of an encased composite column is influenced more significantly by concrete than by steel.

To account for the uncertainty regarding the contribution of concrete to the buckling strength of a composite column, Eq. (4.11b) includes the numerical coefficient c_3 equal to 0.4 for filled composite columns and 0.2 for encased composite columns. These coefficients are consistent with values recommended in the ACI building code[D100] for flexural stiffness EI in estimates of inelastic buckling loads. The ACI code expressions include a parameter for the softening influence of creep of concrete that is subjected to sustained compressive loading. The influence of creep may be neglected in the presence of large areas of steel, which does not creep. Every composite column designed in accordance with LRFD[D91] must have a structural-steel area at least equal to 4 percent of the gross column cross section. The influence of creep as well as the influence of concrete cracking have been accommodated adequately by the values of c_3 given in Table 4.1.

The application of Eqs. (4.9), (4.10), and (4.11) for the determination of axial column capacity is straightforward, but as a part of an iterative process of selecting and checking trial sections, it is very tedious. The reader is referred to the AISC *Manual of Steel Construction for LRFD*[D95] that includes extensive tables for both encased and filled composite columns loaded axially, and to Steel Design Guide Series 6,[D74] which contains comprehensive tables for design of encased composite columns subjected to axial load and bending.

The conventional definition of a radius of gyration cannot be applied rigorously to composite cross sections. However, an index of cross-section width to resist flexure is needed as a measure of slenderness. The radius of gyration of a solid rectangle is about 30 percent of its depth, and the radius of gyration of a box or wide-flange shape can approach 50 percent of the depth of the section. The steel shape and the concrete portion of composite cross sections contribute to resistance against flexural displacement. If the steel predominates, the radius of gyration of the steel is appropriate for the whole section. If flexural deformation is resisted primarily by concrete, the radius of gyration for concrete is appropriate for slenderness calculations. In either case an effective radius of gyration for the composite section will be somewhat greater than the larger of the values for each material taken separately. Until a more rigorous definition is found, it is recommended that the larger of the radius of gyration values for steel or concrete be used in calculating the slenderness index l/r_m for values λ_c in Eq. (4.10c).

Limitations. Concrete loses stiffness at strains near 0.2 percent and may not be fully effective for stabilizing steel at strains higher than 0.2 percent, which translates into steel-stress values of about 60 ksi (414 MPa). The yield stress F_y of structural steel and F_{yr} of reinforcing bars used in calculating the strength of composite columns should not exceed 60 ksi. It is further recommended that the concrete strength f_c' be limited to 10 ksi (69 MPa) and smaller, since tests are available for only very few composite columns with f_c' in excess of 10 ksi.[D35,D42] A lower limit of $f_c' = 2.5$ ksi (17 MPa) is recommended in order to encourage a degree of quality control commensurate with this readily available and familiar grade of structural concrete.

Moment capacity without axial load. The nominal flexural strength M_n of a column cross section may be determined from the plastic state of stress as presented in App. B or from an analysis of flexural strength at the ultimate state of strain. For simplicity, the LRFD commentary[D56] offers an approximate equation for moment capacity of doubly symmetric sections. The sum of flexural capacities for component parts includes the plastic moment capacity of the steel shape, the yield moment of reinforcement assuming that three of eight bars are on opposite faces of the section, and a moment capacity for which compression concrete is considered reinforced at middepth by longitudinal bars and the web of the steel shape:

$$M_n = ZF_y + \tfrac{1}{3}(h_2 - 2c_r)A_rF_{yr} + \left(\frac{h_2}{2} - \frac{A_wF_y}{1.7f_c'h_1}\right)A_wF_y \qquad (4.12)$$

where A_w = web area of steel shape plus any longitudinal bars at center of section

Z = plastic section modulus of steel shape
h_1 = concrete width perpendicular to the plane of bending
h_2 = concrete thickness in the plane of bending
c_r = thickness of concrete cover from center of bar to the edge of section in the plane of bending

Axial load and bending. For composite columns symmetrical about the plane of bending, the interaction of compression and flexure should be limited by the following bilinear relationship:

$$\frac{P_u}{\phi_c P_n} + \frac{8M_u}{9\phi_b M_n} \leq 1.0 \qquad \text{for } P_u \geq 0.2\phi_c P_n \qquad (4.13a)$$

$$\frac{P_u}{2\phi_c P_n} + \frac{M_u}{\phi_b M_n} \leq 1.0 \qquad \text{for } P_u < 0.2\phi_c P_n \qquad (4.13b)$$

where P_u = factored axial force
$\qquad M_u$ = factored moment increased for slenderness effects
$\qquad P_n$ = nominal thrust capacity including slenderness effects
$\qquad M_n$ = ultimate moment capacity without axial force
$\qquad \phi_b$ = resistance factor for bending = 0.85
$\qquad \phi_c$ = resistance factor for compression = 0.85

For columns of zero slenderness, Eqs. (4.13a) and (4.13b) represent the same type of interaction limit as that obtained from the plastic analysis of the cross section.

The strength of the two demonstration sections of App. B was computed from Eqs. (4.13a) and (4.13b) for the full range of combinations of thrust P and moment M. The resulting interaction curve is plotted in Fig. 4.10 as a line of intermediate thickness. For thrust without bending, LRFD reduces to the same equation as that for the plastic analysis so that the heavy and the intermediate lines start from the same points on the vertical axis. For all other combinations of thrust and moment the two methods differ. LRFD values are consistently conservative except for the case of tubular cross sections subjected predominantly to bending. The conservative nature of the LRFD equations is the result of a deliberate choice for simplicity. Details for application of the LRFD procedure are given in App. B.

Axial force and biaxial bending.   For symmetrical members, the LRFD specification[D91] permits computing the flexural strength ratio $M_u/\phi M_n$ separately about each of the two major axes, and adding these two components to the axial-force component. Such linear superposition of flexural strength ratios has the effect of producing the same results for biaxially loaded cases as that obtained from Eq. (4.8) with the exponent $\alpha = 1$. The LRFD procedure therefore underestimates the capacity to resist biaxially eccentric loads. Since the capacity of biaxially loaded filled steel tube columns depends predominantly on the capacity of the steel tube, the use of the LRFD interaction equation is recommended for such columns.

Bar reinforcement for encased composite columns.   Concrete encasement of a steel shape in a composite column should be reinforced with both longitudinal and transverse bars spaced not more than two-thirds of the width of the shorter column side. The bars should have an area not less than 0.007 in²/in (0.2 mm²/mm) of bar spacing. Clear edge cover over bars must be at least 1.5 in (38 mm).

4.4.6 ACI building code

Rules of ACI 318-95[D100] require all columns to be designed as beam columns, since floor-to-column connections in concrete are considered to be monolithic and continuous, transferring both shear and moment at joints. A moment-magnification procedure is used to account for the effects of column slenderness. The moment magnifier δ is expressed as

$$\delta = \frac{0.6 - 0.4 M_{u1}/M_{u2}}{1.0 - P_u/\phi P_c} \tag{4.14}$$

with M_{u1} = the smaller required moment applied at one end of the column

M_{u2} = the larger required moment applied at the opposite end of the column; the ratio M_{u1}/M_{u2} is positive if both moments compress the same face

P_u = required factored axial load on the column

P_c = elastic Euler buckling index for the column = $\pi^2 EI/(Kl)^2$

ϕ = capacity-reduction factor taken as 0.7 for encased shapes and as 0.75 for concrete-filled tubes

Kl = effective length of column

Stiffness EI for the Euler buckling index is determined as

$$EI = \frac{0.40 E_c I_g}{1 + \beta_d} \tag{4.15a}$$

or

$$EI = \frac{0.2 E_c I_g + E_s I_s}{1 + \beta_d} \tag{4.15b}$$

where β_d = ratio of the required permanent axial load to the required total axial load, usually taken as $1.4 P_D/P_u$

Equation (4.15b) will produce EI values higher than those from Eq. (4.15a) for concrete-filled tubes, and the reverse is true generally for encased light shapes.

The ACI building code[D100] requires that all columns be designed for at least a minimum eccentricity of axial force expressed in inches as

$$e_{min} = 0.6 + 0.03h$$

where h is the overall depth of the column in inches.

A capacity-reduction factor $\phi = 0.70$ is given for concrete-encased shapes and $\phi = 0.75$ for concrete-filled steel tubes and pipes. In addition, the axial resistance is limited to 80 percent of the theoretical squash load P_0 for encased shapes and 85 percent of P_0 for concrete-filled steel tubes and pipes.

The superposition of component capacities gives the value of P_0 in the form of Eq. (4.5). Thus, for concrete-encased steel shapes,

$$P_u \leq 0.8\phi P_0 = 0.56 P_0 \qquad (4.16)$$

and for concrete-filled steel tubes and pipes

$$P_u \leq 0.85\phi P_0 = 0.72 P_0 \qquad (4.17)$$

Biaxially eccentric loading. The response to loading of a composite cross section, for any orientation of the neutral axis, can be obtained assuming the same strain compatibility and rectangular concrete stress block as those for uniaxial bending. As this procedure is tedious, the Commentary to ACI 318-95[D100] suggests as adequate a biaxial-strength analysis that satisfies an interaction surface similar to the upper part of Fig. 4.11. The analysis is based on the following relationship:[G12]

$$\frac{1}{P_i} = \frac{1}{P_x} + \frac{1}{P_y} - \frac{1}{P_0}$$

with P_i = capacity for biaxially eccentric axial force
P_x = axial force capacity for eccentricity e_x in the plane of the x axis
P_y = axial force capacity for eccentricity e_y in the plane of the y axis
P_0 = axial force capacity for concentric load (the squash load)

Bar reinforcement for encased composite columns. ACI code[D100] permits placement of any steel shape inside a section that is reinforced with bars satisfying requirements for tied columns. The yield stress in calculations of the encased shape should not be taken greater than 60 ksi (414 MPa). Tied columns must contain longitudinal bars with an area at least 1 percent and not more than 8 percent of the gross area of the section.

The lateral spacing of longitudinal bars should not exceed ½ the length of the shorter side of the section. Lateral ties should extend completely around the structural-steel core and should have a diameter at least 2 percent of the length of the longer side of the section but need have a diameter no larger than ⅝ in (16 mm). The vertical spacing of lateral ties cannot exceed one-half the length of the shortest side of the section, 16 diameters of longitudinal bars or 48 diameters of lateral ties.

4.5   Special Considerations

4.5.1   Differential axial shortening

Buildings with vertical members of different materials and stresses, some composite and others of reinforced concrete or structural steel, undergo differential axial shortening. For buildings exceeding about 20 stories in height, predicting the axial shortening is necessary to ensure level floors and to prevent damage to nonstructural elements. Axial shortening of columns and walls can be analyzed in three categories including elastic change due to loads, change caused by shrinkage, and change from creep. The elastic shortening due to construction loads also needs to be computed for composite members involving steel erection columns encased in concrete at a later stage of construction. ACI Committee 209 report[G65] and a report by Fintel, Ghosh, and Iyengar[G50] are the sources of information for the following discussion.

Characteristic properties of constituent materials must be established before differential shortening can be determined. Average values for concrete are given in Sec. 4.5.2. If specific local test data are available, they should be used instead of the average values. Since differential shortening includes response to specific loading, the construction sequence for each member must be known or assumed. In the case involving steel erection columns which are later encased in concrete, the steel frame generally is erected 8 to 16 floors ahead of the concrete encasement. In the case of a core shear wall system with composite exterior columns, the concrete core wall is generally constructed ahead of the exterior columns.

Shortening of steel columns is computed as $\Delta_s = Pl/AE$. Several computer programs are in existence for the procedure presented by Fintel, Ghosh, and Iyengar.[G50] A sample of computed movements for an interior steel column in an 80-story building is shown in Fig. 4.12a and for an exterior composite column in Fig. 4.12b. The final curves for both the exterior composite column and an interior steel column are shown in Fig. 4.12c.

Length of fabricated components can be modified as a means of compensation for differential axial shortening. Analysis is generally made on a 10-floor basis; i.e., the steel columns are adjusted every 10 floors to compensate for the differential movement. A table of the adjusted steel column lengths is developed and provided to the contractor. An example for the 75-story Texas Commerce Plaza in Houston is shown in Table 2.3. It should be noted that foundation movements were included in the calculations in order to obtain proper column adjustments.

In cases where the composite column or wall is connected to an adjacent vertical member by rigid connections to deep floor beams or trusses, the analysis must include the indeterminate flexural restraint to vertical movement. In the case of story-high outrigger truss or wall, secondary stresses in the outrigger element can be minimized if most of the axial shortening of the composite vertical member is allowed to take place before its connection to the outrigger truss or wall is completed.

4.5.2   Time-dependent properties of concrete

Concrete is a material that undergoes both irreversible and reversible changes with time. Irreversible gains in strength and stiffness occur with time, and reversible volume changes due to shrinkage and to fluctuations of temperature vary with time. Volume changes due to creep are partially reversible.

Strength and stiffness.   Concrete gains strength and stiffness with age after it is cast and cured. The rate of gain decreases with time such that it is quite low within 1 month after casting. However, it is not uncommon to observe in

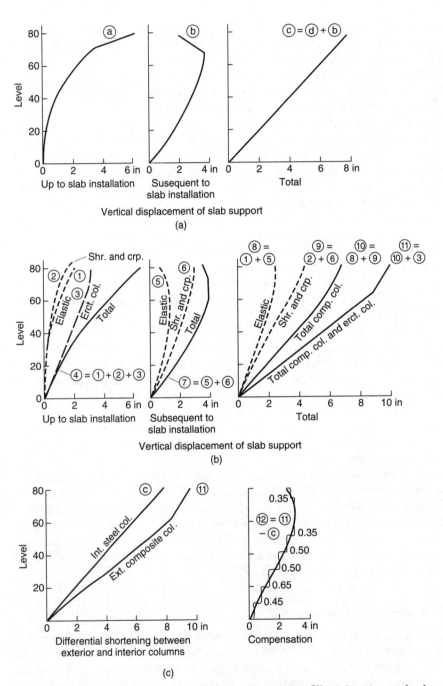

Figure 4.12 Column length changes in an 80-story building.[G50] (*a*) Interior steel column. (*b*) Exterior composite column. (*c*) Differential shortening.

a few years that the strength is 20 to 40 percent greater than the required 28-day strength. It is essential that consideration be given to actual values of f_c' at early ages if estimates are needed of column shortening during construction. ACI Committee 209[G39] developed the following relationships for the rate of strength gain for concrete made with type I cement:

$$f_{ct}' = \frac{f_{c28}' t_d}{4 + 0.85 t_d} \qquad (4.18)$$

where f_{ct}' = compressive strength of concrete at time t_d
$\quad\;\; f_{c28}'$ = compressive strength of concrete at 28 days
$\quad\;\; t_d$ = time in days after casting

For concrete made with type III cement, the coefficients 4 and 0.85 are replaced with 2.3 and 0.92, respectively. The Committee 209 report[G39] was issued before research data became available on high-strength concrete. Thus Eq. (4.18) may not be valid for concrete with f_c' greater than 10 ksi (69 MPa).

The time dependence of Young's modulus is given by substituting the actual cylinder strength at time of loading f_{ct}' into Eq. (4.1):

$$E_{ct} = w^{1.5}\sqrt{f_{ct}'} \qquad (4.19)$$

where w is the unit weight of concrete given in lb/ft³ and f_{ct}' is concrete compressive strength at the time of loading computed from Eq. (4.18). Modulus E_{ct} and strength f_{ct}' are taken in ksi.

Shrinkage.   Concrete volume fluctuates with changes in moisture and humidity, increasing as moisture increases and decreasing as moisture decreases. Volume changes with moisture are recoverable as each moisture state is restored. The thinner a concrete component is, the more its ambient moisture can change. A size-effect factor K_{vs} for shrinkage is expressed in terms of the volume to surface area ratio V/S:

$$K_{vs} = \frac{0.037(V/S) + 0.944}{0.177(V/S) + 0.734} \qquad (4.20a)$$

A relative humidity influence factor K_h for shrinkage can be taken for $40 \le H_r \le 80$ as

$$K_h = 1.40 - 0.10 H_r \qquad (4.20b)$$

and for $80 \le H_r \le 100$ as

$$K_h = 3.00 - 0.03 H_r \qquad (4.20c)$$

where H_r is the annual average ambient relative humidity given in percent.

Time-dependent shrinkage factor K_t in terms of concrete age in days after casting can be estimated as

$$K_t = \frac{t_d}{t_d + 26e^{(0.36V/S)}} \tag{4.20d}$$

The overall limit or long-time shrinkage strain of concrete can be taken as 0.0008 for purposes of providing allowances for volume change in structural concrete to minimize harmful effects on the adjacent architectural components or attachments. Thus the estimated linear shortening strain ϵ_s due to shrinkage of a composite column can be estimated as

$$\epsilon_s = 0.0008K_{vs}K_hK_t \tag{4.21}$$

Creep. When subjected to sustained compression, concrete creeps; i.e., its density is increasing as its volume is being reduced. Creep strain is linearly related to elastic strain for stresses less than $0.5f_c'$. For higher stresses, creep is nonlinear, increasing rapidly for stresses above $0.75f_c'$. The commentary to ACI 318-95[D100] indicates that in estimating flexural deflections it is appropriate to take twice the initial strain as the limiting creep strain on plain concrete. In order to design clearance allowances for creep deflections under sustained load, ACI Committee 209[G39] suggests that an acceptable value for long-time sustained load creep is 2.35 times the initial elastic strain.

More specific estimates of creep displacements can be made if data are available regarding the age t_i at time of loading, the duration t_d of load in days, the member volume-to-surface area ratio V/S, and the relative humidity H_r. The effects of these four variables are obtained with the help of the following four coefficients:

1. C_{ti} for the age of concrete t_i

$$C_{ti} = 2.3(t_i)^{0.25} \tag{4.22a}$$

2. C_{vs} for member size or shape

$$C_{vs} = \frac{0.044 \ (V/S) + 0.934}{0.10(V/S) + 0.85} \tag{4.22b}$$

3. C_h for relative humidity

$$C_h = 1.40 - 0.01H_r \tag{4.22c}$$

4. C_t for time under sustained load

$$C_t = \frac{t_d^{0.6}}{10 + t_d^{0.6}} \tag{4.22d}$$

Estimated shortening strain ϵ including creep under sustained load after an initial elastic strain ϵ_i becomes

$$\epsilon = \epsilon_i C_{ti} C_{vs} C_h C_t \tag{4.23}$$

Application. A computational procedure, based on Eqs. (4.19), (4.21), and (4.23) and outlined by Fintel, Ghosh, and Iyengar,[G50] can be used to determine column shortening during construction of tall buildings.

4.5.3 Seismic resistance

If buildings are to survive a major earthquake with lateral forces large enough to cause inelastic structural response of framing members, the members must possess sufficient ductility and toughness to absorb the imparted energy by undergoing several cycles of large deformations without loss of strength. Seismic design of structural members should ensure retention of strength through several reversals of displacements 4 to 6 times larger than the displacement at initial yielding of the structural component. A steel tube or pipe provides filled composite columns with an effective containment for concrete fill resulting in a ductile structural response to large flexural deformations. Similar containment can be provided for concrete encasement of structural shapes by closely spaced ties. Consequently, specific seismic design requirements focus on details of construction and assembly in addition to the clearly necessary provisions of required strength.

Until 1994 no authoritative guidance was available in the United States regarding the seismic design of composite members and structures. The 1994 edition of the BSSC/NEHRP Recommended Provisions[D96] presented the first step toward satisfying the need for guidance. It includes a new Chap. 7 entitled Composite Steel and Concrete Structure Design Requirements. Articles 7.5.3 and 7.5.4 deal with encased and filled composite columns, and Art. 7.4.7 deals with composite shear walls. A list of references is included in the document.

Strength considerations. Analyses of the strength of composite columns in accordance with AISC-LRFD and ACI 318 provisions, and a plastic analysis of a composite column cross section have been described in Sec. 4.4. Another analysis of strength under eccentric loading applicable to symmetric cross sections has been shown[140] to produce capacity predictions that are in agreement with experimental results. The method is based on the superposition of the individual nominal strengths of the separate steel and reinforced concrete sections, leading to a moment–axial load interaction surface for the composite cross section. The procedure, called the superposed strength method,[D54] is a limit-strength analysis similar to the allowable-stress method included in the Japanese standard for composite column design.[D57]

The superposed strength is obtained from the following equations:
For $P_{ct} \le P \le P_{c0}$ or $M \ge M_{s0}$,

$$P = P_{ct} \tag{4.24a}$$

$$M \le M_c + M_{s0} \tag{4.24b}$$

For $P > P_{nc}$ or $M < M_{s0}$,

$$P \le P_{nc} + P_{st} \qquad (4.25a)$$

$$M = M_{s0} \qquad (4.25b)$$

For $P < P_{ct}$ or $M < M_{s0}$, with tensile axial force,

$$P \ge P_{ct} + P_{st} \qquad (4.26a)$$

$$M = M_{ss} \qquad (4.26b)$$

where P = compressive force
P_{nc} = limit compressive strength of reinforced concrete portion
P_{ct} = limit tensile strength of reinforced concrete portion subjected to tension alone, taken negative
P_{c0} = limit compressive strength of reinforced concrete portion subjected to compression alone
P_{st} = limit compressive strength of steel portion
M = bending-moment resistance
M_c = limit flexural strength of reinforced concrete portion
M_{s0} = limit flexural strength of steel portion subjected to bending alone
M_{ss} = limit flexural strength of steel portion

A thrust-moment interaction curve based on the superposed-strength method (SSM) is shown in Fig. 4.10 as a light line for the $10 \times 10 \times \frac{1}{4}$-in (254 $\times$ 254 $\times$ 6-mm) filled tube. The calculation procedure is described in App. B. The SSM curve shown in Fig. 4.10 reflects ACI values of strength; i.e., all strength factors ϕ were taken in calculations equal to 0.85. The comparison shows that the superposed-strength method gives results very close to those obtained from the plastic analysis (heavy line). It was pointed out in Sec. 4.4.5 that LRFD gives conservative results for combined thrust and bending. As this conservatism for the intermediate cases of combined loading is at times excessive, the use of the superposed-strength method is preferable. The superposed-strength method is particularly convenient when design tables or charts are available for both structural steel shapes and reinforced concrete.

Reinforcing details. Concrete encasement of steel shapes must be reinforced with longitudinal and transverse reinforcing bars. The size and location of bars for nonseismic applications serves primarily to maintain the concrete encasement around the steel shape until failure strain of about 0.3 percent is reached under monotonically increasing load. Most structural steel shapes and reinforcing bars yield at strains less than 0.3 percent.

Seismic applications require significantly more reinforcement of the concrete encasement than that required for nonseismic applications. Under cyclic lateral loading composite column ductility is highly dependent on the confinement of the concrete core surrounding the encased steel section. The confinement in encased composite columns is provided by closely spaced stir-

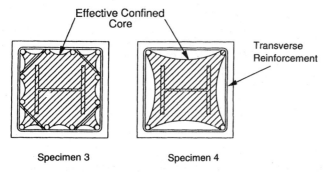

Figure 4.13 Effective confined core.[140]

rups. Other factors influencing confinement include the size and distribution of longitudinal reinforcement, the presence of intermediate cross ties, and the yield stress of the transverse reinforcement. Figure 4.13 shows as a cross-hatched area the effective zone of confinement for the inner core of concrete. The outer cover of concrete may spall off near critical sections during major earthquakes, exposing the longitudinal and transverse reinforcement. Spalling usually occurs at the base of a ground-floor column where a plastic flexural hinge has formed. Transverse ties, if allowed to bulge outward, permit the inner core of concrete to deteriorate under cyclic loading. Buckling of the longitudinal reinforcing bars may lead to similar deterioration. The result of a loss of the inner core is a degradation in column capacity and ductility.

To provide adequate confinement to the concrete, the following criteria for the amount of transverse reinforcement have been found satisfactory. They are based on New Zealand provisions for reinforced concrete:[G40]

$$A_{sh} \geq 0.3 s_t h_c \frac{f_c'}{F_{yh}} \left(\frac{A_g}{A_{ch}} - 1 \right) \left(0.5 + 1.25 \frac{P_u}{\phi f_c' A_g} \right) \qquad (4.27a)$$

$$A_{sh} \geq 0.12 s_t h_c \frac{f_c'}{F_{yh}} \left(0.5 + 1.25 \frac{P_u}{\phi f_c' A_g} \right) \qquad (4.27b)$$

where A_{sh} = cross-sectional area of transverse reinforcement (including cross ties) within spacing s_t and perpendicular to dimension h_c

s_t = spacing of transverse reinforcement measured along the longitudinal axis of the structural member

h_c = cross-sectional dimension of column core measured center-to-center of confining reinforcement

f_c' = specified compressive strength of concrete

F_{yh} = specified yield strength of transverse reinforcement

A_g = gross area of section

A_{ch} = cross-sectional area of reinforced core of a section measured out-to-out of transverse reinforcement

P_u = applied axial load
ϕ = resistance factor equal to 0.70

The influence of axial force reflected by the bracketed term in Eqs. (4.27) is omitted from seismic requirements of ACI 318-95,[D100] which requires the following lower limit instead:

$$A_{sh} \geq \frac{0.09s_t h_c f_c'}{F_{yh}} \qquad (4.28)$$

In addition, to inhibit longitudinal bar buckling, the maximum tie spacing s_{max} should satisfy the following condition:

$$s_{max} \leq 0.25h_c \leq 4 \text{ in} \qquad (4.29)$$

ACI provisions for reinforcement detailing related to bar bending, tail lengths, and development length are suitable for composite columns.

The hysteretic response of two encased composite column specimens, specimen 1 not satisfying Eq. (4.28) and specimen 3 in compliance with Eq. (4.28), is shown in Fig. 4.14.[140] The superior response of specimen 3 is clearly evident. Its stable hysteretic loops are in marked contrast to the rapidly degrading loops of specimen 1.

Bond interaction between concrete and steel.   Curvature along the length of an encased steel shape is the same as that of the encasing concrete if curvature compatibility exists along the column. A lack of bond between the interface of the steel shape and the surrounding concrete results in a migration of the concrete neutral axis toward the tension face. The length along which significant inelastic response occurs under severe cyclic loading is limited to one depth of the section.

At the base of the column the steel shape and the longitudinal reinforcement must be well anchored in order to allow the development of inelastic curvature at the composite column base. A detail that places the steel shape base plate below the surface of the footing is given in Fig. 4.15. It is preferred because column-to-base plate welds are subjected to less deformation than those on a surface base plate of Fig. 4.16 where the base plate is located on the top of the footing.

Experiments[140] involving cyclic loading have shown that specimens with enhanced bond, through the use of shear studs on the outside surface of the flanges, do not perform significantly better than specimens without such bond enhancement. The cyclic stiffness and strength of a specimen with shear studs are shown in Fig. 4.17 to be essentially the same as those of a specimen without shear studs.

Transverse-shear behavior.   Special attention must be given to provide sufficient transverse reinforcement within the plastic hinge region at the joints of

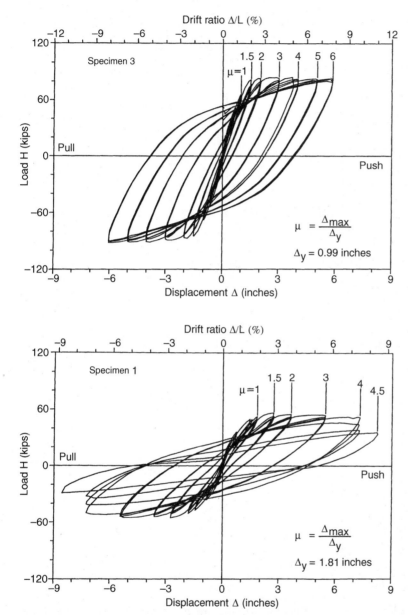

Figure 4.14 Lateral load-displacement response.[140]

columns to confine the concrete core. Transverse-shear reinforcement also enhances bond between the steel section and the concrete encasement by providing confining pressure while maintaining the concrete core. Although the encased steel shape alone has a relatively large shear capacity, the reinforced concrete encasement can help resist some of the total applied shear.

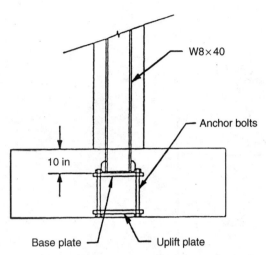

Figure 4.15 Composite column with base plate submerged in footing.[140]

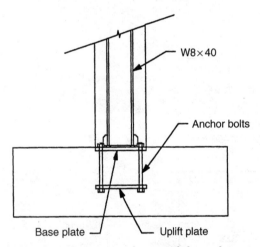

Figure 4.16 Composite column with base plate at surface of footing.[140]

ACI 318-95[D100] recommendations provide an estimate for the shear resistance capacity of concrete columns under axial load as

$$V_c = 2\left(1 + \frac{P_u}{2A_g}\right)bd\sqrt{0.001f_c''} \qquad (4.30)$$

where V_c = nominal shear resistance, kips
$\quad P_u$ = applied axial load, kips
$\quad A_g$ = gross area of section, in²
$\quad f_c'$ = concrete compressive strength, ksi

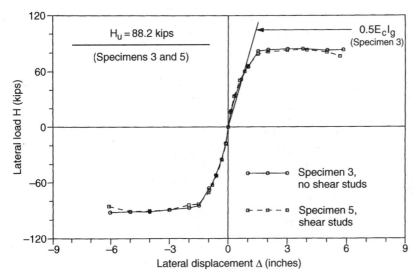

Figure 4.17 Envelope of lateral load-displacement response.[140]

b = cross-section width, in

d = depth of tensile reinforcement relative to extreme concrete compressive fiber, in

For encased composite columns the width b used in Eq. (4.30) should be replaced with an effective width b_E of concrete that is restricted to concrete uninterrupted by the steel shape and that is measured perpendicular to the plane in which shear is resisted, as is indicated by the shaded areas shown in Fig. 4.18.

Cyclic load reversal tests[140] have shown that the shear strength of composite columns with steel shapes encased in concrete is not always the sum of shear capacity for component parts. Total shear H applied to a composite column can be assigned to steel shape V_s, to concrete V_c, and to ties V_t. Under service loading, in which the displacement ductility μ is less than 0.7, the relatively high shear stiffness of concrete retains most of the applied service load shear, with a small contribution coming from the encased shape and no appreciable contribution from the transverse ties. The curves in Fig. 4.19 illustrate that after concrete cracks in shear at 25.8 kips (115 kN) a softening occurs in the shear stiffness of the concrete, causing a redistribution. After shear cracking, the encased steel shape resists most of the applied shear. Under cyclic loading, the ultimate shear capacity V_u of the composite column should be taken as equal to V_s of the steel section alone.

4.6 Design Examples

4.6.1 Encased column strength

A concrete section 20×20 in (0.5×0.5 m) is to support a factored axial force P_u = 2350 kips (10.5 MN) through a clear height Kl = 14 ft (4.3 m). With f'_c = 5 ksi (34 MPa) and grade 60 (414 MPa) reinforcement equal to 8 percent of

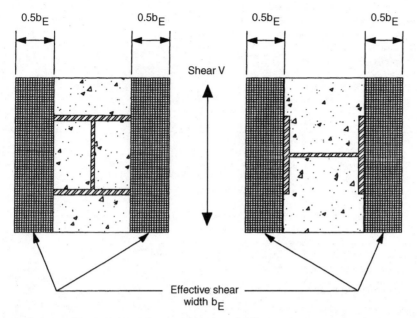

Figure 4.18 Shear in encased composite columns.[140]

the gross area A_g, the largest ϕP_n that the reinforced concrete section can carry is computed from Eq. (4.17a) using P_0 from Eq. (4.5):

$$\phi P_n = 0.56(A_s F_y A_r F_{ry} + 0.85 f_c' A_c)$$

$$= 0.56[0 + (0.08 \times 400 \times 60) + (0.85 \times 5 \times 0.92 \times 400)]$$

$$= 1951 \text{ kips}$$

Since 1951 kips is not adequate, select an A572 grade 50 W shape for the composite column.

AISC LRFD Manual[D95] contains tables listing the strength of composite columns (pp. 5-73 to 5-143). The tables are used below for rapid selection of the composite section. Enter Manual[D95] p. 5-93 with $Kl = 14$ ft to select a W12×120 shape in the 20 × 20-in concrete section with 4#9 longitudinal bars to support the load of 2350 kips.

4.6.2 Encased column design

Select a W10 A572 grade 50 (345 MPa) shape to support a braced frame construction load $P_u = 375$ kips (1.67 MN) for an unbraced length of $Kl = 16$ ft (4.9 m). Subsequently, an 18 × 18-in (0.46 × 0.46-m) square composite section must support an axial force $P_u = 1340$ kips (5.96 MN) and a moment $M_u = 205$ ft-kips (278 kN-m) when $Kl = 14$ ft (4.3 m) and $f_c' = 8$ ksi (55 MPa).

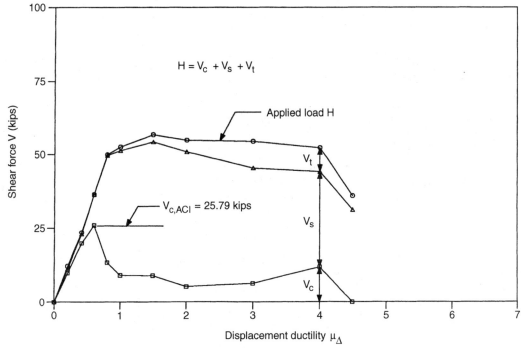

Figure 4.19 Shear behavior of an encased composite column.[140]

Use Manual[D95] p. 3-27 to select a W10×49 for the construction column load of 375 kips for Kl = 16 ft. Check the core size in the 18 × 18-in composite column by using Manual p. 5-108.

For the W10×49, ϕM_n = 379 ft-kips and with Kl = 14 ft, ϕP_n = 1720 kips. $P_u/\phi P_n$ = 0.78 > 0.2; therefore, Eq. (4.13a) applies:

$$\frac{P_u}{\phi P_n} + \frac{8}{9}\frac{M_u}{\phi_b M_n} = \frac{1340}{1720} + \frac{8}{9}\frac{205}{379} = 1.26 > 1$$

The section is not adequate.

Try a W10×60 steel shape embedded in 18 × 18-in concrete section reinforced with 8#10 longitudinal grade 60 bars instead of 4#8 (Fig. 4.20):

$$A_s = 17.6 \text{ in}^2 \qquad A_r = 8(1.27) = 10.16 \text{ in}^2$$

$$A_c = 18(18) - 17.6 - 10.16 = 296 \text{ in}^2$$

Eq. (4.11a):

$$F_{my} = 50 + 0.7(55)\frac{10.16}{17.6} + 0.6(8)\frac{296}{17.6} = 153 \text{ ksi}$$

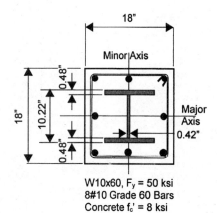

18"

Minor Axis

0.48"

10.22"

18"

0.48"

Major
Axis
0.42"

W10x60, F_y = 50 ksi
8#10 Grade 60 Bars
Concrete f_c' = 8 ksi

Figure 4.20 Cross section
for example in Sec. 4.6.2.

Eq. (4.1):

$$E_c = 145^{1.5}(\sqrt{8}) = 4940 \text{ ksi}$$

Eq. (4.11b):

$$E_m = 29{,}000 + (0.2)4940\,\frac{296}{17.6} = 45{,}600 \text{ ksi}$$

Compute P_n from Eq. (4.9). Using Eq. (4.10a), where

$$r_m = 0.3 \times 18 = 5.4 \text{ in} > 4.39 \text{ in}$$

$$A = \left[\frac{14(12)}{5.4\pi}\right]^2 \times \frac{153}{45{,}600} = 0.329$$

Therefore, $\lambda_c < 1.5$ and

$$F_{cr} = (0.658^{0.329})153 = 133 \text{ ksi}$$

$$\phi P_n = 0.85(17.6)133 = 1990 \text{ kips}$$

Compute M_n from Eq. (4.12). The steel strength at middepth of the composite section includes the area of the web and 2#10 bars:

$$A_w F_y = 0.420[10.22 - 2(0.680)]50 + 2(1.27)55 = 326 \text{ kips}$$

$$Z F_y = 74.6(50) = 3730 \text{ in-kips} = 311 \text{ ft-kips}$$

$$\tfrac{1}{3}(h_2 - 2c_r)F_{yr}A_r = \tfrac{1}{3}[18 - 2(2.5)]55(10.16) = 2421 \text{ in-kips} = 202 \text{ ft-kips}$$

$$\left(0.5h_2 - \frac{A_w F_y}{1.7f_c'h_1}\right)A_w F_y = \left[9 - \frac{326}{1.7(8)18}\right]326 = 2500 \text{ in-kips} = 208 \text{ ft-kips}$$

$$\phi M_n = 0.85(311 + 202 + 208) = 613 \text{ ft-kips}$$

$$\frac{P_u}{\phi P_n} + \frac{8}{9}\frac{M_u}{\phi M_n} = \frac{1340}{1990} + \frac{8}{9}\frac{205}{613} = 0.971 < 1$$

W10×60 with 8#10 bars is satisfactory.

4.6.3 *P/M* diagram for an encased column

The composite column shown in Fig. 4.21 must support several different load combinations of P_u and M_{ux}. LRFD procedures cannot be used, as the W14×61 (34 cm × 28 kg) has an area less than 4 percent of the gross area of the composite section. Limit-strength interaction graphs are needed.

Design aids are readily available for reinforced concrete columns (ACI handbook,[G69] CRSI handbook,[G44] and computer software). Coordinates of an interaction curve for strength of the reinforced concrete alone can be taken from such sources, while the thrust-moment capacity of steel shapes is readily determined from plastic analysis. The two graphs can be added graphically to produce a graph for the composite section.

Coordinates for interaction curves generated by computer[G60A] are listed in Table 4.2. The lines in Fig. 4.22 marked "reinforced concrete alone" were con-

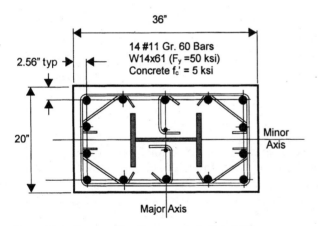

Figure 4.21 Cross section for example in Sec. 4.6.3 .

TABLE 4.2 **Coordinates for Interaction Curves**

ϕP_n, kips	ϕM_{nx}, ft-kips	ϕM_{ny}, ft-kips
2750	755	509
2500	975	660
2000	1316	898
1500	1526	1052
1000	1600	1107
500	1474	985

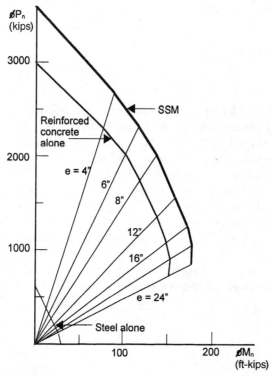

Figure 4.22   Interaction diagrams by superposed-strength method.

structed from the tabulated coordinates. The lines for "steel alone" give the plastic moment capacity multiplied by resistance factor $\phi = 0.85$. Rays along the lines of coordinates can be added. In this case rays from the origin to the "W14×61 alone" were added to the "reinforced concrete alone" coordinates to produce the interaction curves for the composite section labeled SSM for superposed-strength method.[D54]

4.6.4   Filled pipe column design

Design a concrete-filled round pipe column with $F_y = 35$ ksi (240 MPa) and $f'_c = 5$ ksi (34 MPa) to support a required axial load $P_u = 186$ kips (827 kN) and zero moment for an unsupported effective length $Kl = 14$ ft (4.3 m). This design is completed easily with the LRFD Manual[D95] load tables for composite columns, pp. 5-111 to 5-114. The table on p. 5-114 for $f'_c = 5$ ksi shows $\phi P_n = 190$ kips for a 6-in standard pipe with a wall thickness of 0.280 in, for an effective length of 14 ft.

4.6.5 Filled pipe column design without tables

Rework design example from Sec. 4.6.4 without the use of design tables. Steel pipe shapes generally comprise at least 15 percent of a composite section, and since steel yield strength is $(35/5) = 7$ times as great as concrete strength, estimate that the pipe will resist about 80 percent of the total required P_u, and guess that the modest 186-kip load for a 14-ft length will result in a slenderness ratio such that ϕF_{cr} will be near $0.5F_y$.

Then $0.5F_y A_s \approx 0.8P_u$ or $A_s \approx 0.8(186)/(0.5 \times 35) = 8.50$ in^2. For round columns, $A_s \approx \pi dt = 8.5$ in^2 and $dt \approx 2.7$ in^2. The following combinations result in $dt = 2.7$ in^2:

$$t = \tfrac{1}{4}\text{ in} \quad \text{and} \quad d = 10.8\text{ in}$$

$$t = \tfrac{3}{8}\text{ in} \quad \text{and} \quad d = 7.2\text{ in}$$

$$t = \tfrac{1}{2}\text{ in} \quad \text{and} \quad d = 5.4\text{ in}$$

From among the available pipe sizes, try 6-in standard pipe for which $d = 6.625$ in, $t = 0.280$ in, $A_s = 5.58$ in^2, and $r = 2.25$ in.

Check the selection using Eqs. (4.9) and (4.10):

$$A_c = (6.625 - 2 \times 0.28)^2\,\frac{\pi}{4} = 28.9\text{ in}^2$$

Eq. (4.11a):

$$F_{my} = F_y + 0.85f_c'\,\frac{A_c}{A_s} = 35 + 0.85(5.0)\frac{28.9}{5.58} = 57\text{ ksi}$$

Eq. (4.1):

$$E_c = w^{1.5}\sqrt{f_c'} = (145)^{1.5}\sqrt{5} = 3900\text{ ksi}$$

Eq. (4.11b):

$$E_m = E_s + \frac{0.4E_cA_c}{A_s}$$

$$= 29,000 + \left(0.4 \times 3900 \times \frac{28.9}{5.58}\right) = 37,080\text{ ksi}$$

$$\lambda_c = \frac{Kl}{r\pi}\sqrt{\frac{F_{my}}{E_m}} = \frac{14(12)}{2.25\pi}\sqrt{\frac{57.0}{37,080}} = 0.932$$

$$A = \lambda_c^2 = 0.932^2 = 0.869$$

For λ_c less than 1.5, Eq. (4.10a) applies. The design strength is obtained from Eq. (4.9) as

$$\phi P_n = 0.85A_s F_{cr} = 0.85A_s(0.658^A)F_{my}$$

$$= 0.85(5.58)(0.658^{0.869})57.0 = 188\text{ kips}$$

which is greater than the required 186 kips. Standard 6-in pipe with wall thickness of 0.28 in is satisfactory.

4.6.6   Filled-tube beam-column design

Design a square, concrete-filled steel tube column to support the loads tabulated below. This column is a part of a braced frame, and the load case for maximum moment bends the column into reverse curvature. The unbraced length Kl = 16 ft 8 in (5.08 m), f_c' = 5 ksi (34 MPa), and F_y = 46 ksi (317 MPa). There is no moment magnification.

Load	Axial force		Moment	
	kips	(kN)	ft-kips	(kN · m)
Dead	170	(756)	14	(19)
Roof	28	(125)	0	(0)
Live	86	(383)	33	(45)

$$\text{Required } P_u = 1.2D + 1.6L + 0.5L_r$$

$$= 1.2(170) + 1.6(86) + 0.5(28) = 356 \text{ kips}$$

$$\text{Required } M_u = 1.2(14) + 1.6(33) + 0.5(0) = 70 \text{ ft-kips}$$

The tables in the LRFD Manual[D95] are used for rapid selection of a trial cross section. For the required axial load alone, a 17-ft column with 8 × 8 × ¼ tube (Manual p. 5-123) can resist 356 kips. However, that cross section has a design moment of only 75.6 ft-kips. Since the column is near its limit capacity both for axial force and for moment, a larger section is required to satisfy Eqs. (4.13) for combined axial load and bending. Try to find a section with axial and flexural capacities about twice the required values. For a 10 ×10 × ⁵⁄₁₆ tube 17 ft long, listed on p. 5-123, the axial design strength is given as 629 kips and the flexural design strength as ϕM_n = 148 ft-kips.
Check the adequacy of this section using Eq. (4.13a):

$$\frac{P_u}{\phi P_n} + \frac{8}{9}\frac{M_u}{\phi M_n} = \frac{356}{629} + \frac{8}{9}\frac{70}{148} = 0.986 < 1.0$$

For Kl = 16 ft 8 in, an interpolation on p. 5-123 of the AISC Manual[D95] yields an axial design strength ϕP_n = 633 kips. The flexural design strength remains at ϕM_n = 148 ft-kips. Thus the 10 × 10 × ⁵⁄₁₆ tube is acceptable.

An alternate approach is contained in the ACI 318-95 building code.[D100] Referring to Fig. 4.23, in which the neutral axis is shown at the distance of 8.78 in below the inside edge of the top wall of the tube (9.09 in below the top surface of the tube), the loads required by ACI are

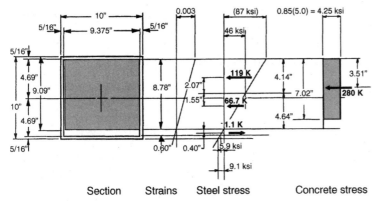

Figure 4.23   ACI method for section strength.

$$P_u = 1.4D + 1.7L = 1.4 \times 170 + 1.7(28 + 86) = 432 \text{ kips}$$

$$M_u = 1.4 \times 14 + 1.7 \times 33 = 76 \text{ ft-kips}$$

Details of strain compatibility analysis with a neutral axis located 9.09 in from the compression edge of the cross section are shown in Fig. 4.23. Concrete strength is represented with a rectangular stress block for which α_1 = 0.85 and $f_c' = 5$ ksi.

Force summary		Thrust, kips	Arm, in	Moment, in-kips
$P_{s1} = 46(10)(\%_{16})$	=	143.8	4.81	691
$P_{s2} = 46(\%_{16})2(4.14)$	=	119.0	2.62	312
$P_{s3} = (\frac{1}{2})46(\%_{16})2(4.64)$	=	66.7	−1.00	−67
$P_{s4} = \frac{1}{2}(−5.9)(\%_{16})2(0.60)$	=	−1.1	−4.49	5
$P_{s5} = (−7.5)(\%_{16})10$	=	−23.4	−4.81	112
$P_{c1} = 0.85(5)9.38(7.02)$	=	279.9	1.18	330
Sum		584.9		1383

The sum of axial forces equals 585 kips and moments about the centroid equal 1383 in-kips. The ACI ϕ factor for concrete-filled tube columns is 0.75. Thus the values $\phi P_n = 0.75(585) = 439$ kips and $\phi M_n = 0.75(1383/12) = 86$ ft-kips are found to be greater than the required $P_u = 432$ kips and $M_u = 76$ ft-kips. The section is shown to be acceptable.

4.6.7   Filled-pipe column strength

Determine the axial load capacity of a concrete-filled steel pipe with $F_y = 60$ ksi (414 MPa), $f_c' = 8$ ksi (55 MPa), outside diameter = 8 in (20 cm), and pipe wall thickness = 0.25 in (6.4 mm). The unsupported length $Kl = 16$ ft (4.9 m).

This example is similar to the example in Sec. 4.6.4, except that no column-load table is available. Note that there is an upper limit of 60 ksi (414 MPa) for F_y.

Determine geometric and material properties using LRFD rules.

$$A_s = (8^2 - 7.5^2)\frac{\pi}{4} = 6.09 \text{ in}^2$$

$$A_c = 7.5^2\,\frac{\pi}{4} = 44.2 \text{ in}^2$$

$$I_s = (8^4 - 7.5^4)\frac{\pi}{64} = 45.7 \text{ in}^4$$

$$r_m = r_s = \sqrt{I_s/A_s} = \sqrt{\frac{45.7}{6.09}} = 2.74 \text{ in}$$

$$F_{my} = 60 + 0 + \frac{0.85(8.0)44.2}{6.09} = 109.4 \text{ ksi}$$

$$E_m = 29{,}000 + (0.4)145^{1.5}(\sqrt{5})\frac{44.2}{6.09} = 40{,}300 \text{ ksi}$$

Use Eqs. (4.9) and (4.10) to determine ϕP_n:

$$\lambda_c = \frac{16 \times 12}{2.74\pi}\sqrt{\frac{109.4}{40{,}300}} = 1.162$$

$$\lambda_c^2 = 1.162^2 = 1.350 = A < 2.25$$

$$F_{cr} = (0.658^{1.350})109.4 = 62.2 \text{ ksi}$$

The axial load capacity of this concrete-filled steel pipe is

$$\phi P_n = 0.85(62.2)6.09 = 322 \text{ kips}$$

4.6.8 Filled-tube beam-column strength

If a required axial load $P_u = 112$ kips (498 kN) is acting on an $8 \times 8 \times \frac{1}{4}$-in ($200 \times 200 \times 6.4$-mm) tube column filled with 5-ksi (34-MPa) concrete, what magnitude of moment M_u can be sustained? Assume an unbraced length of 16 ft 8 in (5.08 m) and a yield stress $F_y = 46$ ksi (317 MPa) for the tube. Use beam-column interaction Eqs. (4.13).

From AISC Manual[D95] the plastic section modulus of the tube is $Z = 21.9$ in³. Use sidewalls as the web area of the composite section:

$$A_w = 2 \times 7.5 \times 0.25 = 3.75 \text{ in}^2$$

For the nominal moment M_n use the plastic moment capacity of the composite cross section:

$$M_p = ZF_y + A_w F_y \left(0.5h - \frac{A_w F_y}{1.7 f_c' b}\right)$$

$$= 21.9 \times 46 + 3.75 \times 46 \times \left(0.5 \times 8 - \frac{3.75 \times 46}{1.7 \times 5 \times 8}\right)$$

$$= 1260 \text{ in-kips}$$

From AISC Manual[D95] p. 5-123, the axial design strength of the concrete-filled tube is obtained by interpolation as $\phi P_n = 361$ kips. Since

$$112 > 0.2 \phi P_n = 0.2 \, (361) = 72.2 \text{ kips}$$

Eq. (4.13a) applies. Solve for the magnitude of moment M_u that this beam column can sustain in addition to the axial load P_u:

$$M_u = 0.85 \times 1260 \times \left(1 - \frac{112}{361}\right) \times \frac{9}{8} = 831 \text{ in-kips} = 69.3 \text{ ft-kips}$$

Lateral Resisting Systems

5.1 Function of Bracing

Bracing of a building, simply stated, provides strength and stiffness to resist forces in the horizontal direction such as wind and seismic loads. Furthermore, it provides out-of-plane stability to the columns and walls which support the building's gravity loads.

Buildings are always designed for gravity loads with a floor system strong enough to carry the design loads to the columns or bearing walls and stiff enough not to deflect excessively or be bouncy and flexible to disturb occupants. In other words, the design for gravity loads must satisfy all vertical-load issues. But design must also consider horizontal-load issues. First, there are the questions of stability. The design must provide enough strength and stiffness in the horizontal plane so that the structural floor system braces all columns and walls to prevent them from buckling. The bracing system must be sufficiently strong and stiff so that it supplies stability bracing for the columns at each floor level. In addition, the floors and the roof function as horizontal diaphragms that interconnect all vertical elements at each framing level. Second, there are the lateral loads: The bracing has to be adequate to resist wind forces and seismic movements. The normal process in design of a building is selecting a system to resist wind and seismic forces, designing it, and ensuring that the selected lateral-force-resisting system is adequate for stability bracing of the building.

When discussing bracing and lateral-force resistance, the phrase "design for wind and seismic forces" is frequently used. To implement a design properly, it is essential to have a clear understanding of this phrase. The design is made for the greater of wind and seismic forces according to the applicable building code or a site-specific study accepted by the responsible building official. Wind forces are based on wind exposure. Seismic forces are based on the seismicity of the region, the mass of the building, and the lateral-force-resisting system. The greater of the two sets of forces is used for the design of the lateral-force-resisting system. However, building codes recognize that actual seismic forces can be significantly greater than the code-prescribed values. Thus seismic design includes not only strength requirements but also material limitations and special provision for member proportioning and detailing. The purpose of these additional provisions is to assure that the members and joints have the necessary ductility as well as strength. Therefore, when designing a building located in a seismic region, even when the wind forces govern the strength design, the detailing and proportioning requirements for seismic resistance must also be satisfied.

The stiffness that the bracing system imparts to a building limits the drift or interstory displacement under wind and seismic loading, in addition to its role in providing building stability. Seismic code provisions have drift limitations for code-specified seismic forces. Generally, the stiffer a building, the less damage to nonstructural components, such as curtain walls and partitions, in a strong earthquake. There are also limits on drift for wind forces which are typically based on experience and engineering judgment rather than specified in codes. In tall multistory buildings, practical limits on drift center around the perception of motion by the occupants. It is discomforting to occupants to be enjoying a nice dinner only to have the water or wine in their glass sloshing or to be trying to sleep when the building creaks and groans as partitions and other nonstructural elements adjust to a deflected building shape. For more information on drift limitations based on human perception, the reader is referred to Ref. D82.

5.2   Types of Bracing

Bracing systems for a building consist of bracing elements in vertical and horizontal planes. Vertical bracing is provided by the primary bracing elements of the building: moment-resisting frames, diagonally braced frames, or structural walls also referred to as shear walls. Horizontal bracing elements include floor and roof diaphragms or horizontal diagonal bracing that interconnects columns and walls at each floor level. The horizontal and vertical bracing should be properly interconnected in order to transfer all lateral forces from their point of origin through the horizontal bracing to the vertical bracing and into the base of the structure. A complete load path throughout the structure interconnecting all elements of the bracing system is an essential ingredient of a successful bracing system.

Composite structures are often conceived to create efficient and economical bracing systems to resist lateral forces. Steel and reinforced concrete structural systems have their functional and economic advantages and disadvantages. Composite systems of concrete and steel can often combine the advantages of the two different systems and create a building that is more structurally efficient and less expensive. Bracing or lateral resistance drives the design of high-rise structures, and composite structures are often selected for such buildings. Similarly, composite bracing systems are often advantageous for low- and midrise buildings.

The remainder of this chapter provides information on typical composite bracing systems, both vertical and horizontal. Other chapters of this book cover in detail the design of individual elements and joints. The purpose of this chapter is to highlight the importance of bracing systems to the design of composite buildings and to emphasize important design considerations for composite bracing systems. In the following sections, emphasis is given to seismic resisting systems since the detailing of those systems is more critical for earthquake resistance. All of the systems mentioned are generally acceptable for wind resistance.

5.3 Moment-Resisting Frames

Moment-resisting frames have traditionally been the most common lateral-force-resisting system in the areas of high seismicity because of their limited interference with other building systems and their potential for large ductility under seismic loading. Past seismic code provisions have distinguished between "special" and "ordinary" moment frames of both steel and reinforced concrete construction. Special moment frames, which must meet additional detailing requirements to provide ductile inelastic response, are designed for lower force levels than ordinary moment-resisting frames. Recently, a third class called partially restrained moment-resisting frames has been identified and is being researched for use in seismic design. This system, which relies on the flexibility of the beam-to-column connections for inelastic energy dissipation, has been proposed in both steel and composite systems.

Explicit design of composite moment-resisting frames in seismic areas of the United States began to develop during the late 1980s. Previous design procedures typically did not incorporate composite column elements or consider the composite action of the concrete slabs with steel beams. About this time, the design profession began to explore possibilities of combining reinforced concrete and steel in seismic design using methods which take maximum advantage of the properties of both materials. In many cases, these early designs focused on combining steel beams with composite steel and concrete columns, with the lateral force design generally being controlled by wind forces. In some instances, the steel column section was solely used for erection purposes, with a large concrete section provided for the required stiffness and strength to resist the lateral forces in tall buildings. A number of other possible combinations exist for providing moment-resisting frames to resist lateral loads, the use (or lack of use) of which has been driven by economic considerations. Few such buildings have been constructed in high seismic regions in the United States, although the practice is more popular in Japan. The development of these composite systems has generally taken place in practice. Recent research in both the United States and Japan indicates that properly detailed elements and connections in composite frames can provide acceptable performance even under reverse cyclic loading which could occur under severe seismic excitation.

Little or no guidance has been provided by existing building codes. No code provisions were available prior to 1993 regarding the system and detailing requirements. As a result, the designer of composite moment framing systems has been left to rely on engineering judgment, paying particular attention to configuration and detailing issues. Future codes will undoubtedly develop and incorporate composite construction into the provisions for lateral-force-resisting systems, such as moment-resisting frames. The development of such provisions for seismic design has begun by the Building Seismic Safety Council (BSSC). In 1993, BSSC developed recommendations for seismic design of composite steel and concrete construction. They were incorporated into the 1994 **NEHRP Recommended Provisions for Seismic Regulations for New Buildings.**[D96] These provisions and the accompanying commentary served as the basis for the discussion of the design of lateral-force-resisting systems which follows. Design for wind or other lateral forces would follow similar procedures, with the major differences being in the need to provide ductile element and connection detailing specifically in areas of high seismicity.

5.3.1 Identification of moment frames

Three potential classes of composite moment-resisting framing systems can be identified: (1) partially restrained moment-resisting frames, (2) ordinary moment-resisting frames, and (3) special moment-resisting frames. These three potential systems are parallel to the potential moment-resisting frame systems presently identified for use in steel construction. Each of these systems and its potential use in seismic design is discussed briefly in the following paragraphs.

Partially restrained frames.   Partially restrained steel moment-resisting frames have been used since the earliest days of steel construction. The elements of these early frames were typically connected with top and bottom clip angles which provide a moment resistance well below that which would be required to develop the full capacity of the beam section which frames into the joint. When provided as a complete gravity-load-resisting system in conjunction with infilled frames of masonry construction, this system has demonstrated good performance in a number of earthquakes.[G4] During the mid-1900s, typical practice for moment-resisting frame construction changed to a system in which the connections were intended to develop the full moment capacity of the beams. Recent developments in steel research have indicated that acceptable seismic performance may be achievable in moment frame systems, which are only partially restrained and rely on the ability of the connections themselves to dissipate energy during severe seismic shaking.[138] These developments have led to the proposal for the incorporation of this system into future seismic design provisions for steel construction.

Partially restrained composite moment frame systems were developed in parallel with steel partially restrained frames. As defined by Zandonini and Leon,[D77] composite partially restrained moment frames consist of structural-steel columns and composite steel beams connected with semirigid composite connections. Such connections (Fig. 2.6) consist of the standard steel web connection, an attachment of the lower beam flange to the column, and the reinforcement in the floor slab connected to the steel beams with shear connectors. Other composite systems which provide partially restrained systems are possible but have not been developed to date. An application of composite girders with partial restraint for wind-load design was reported by Wexler.[D90]

Composite action between the steel beam and the floor slab can result in a favorable distribution of strength and stiffness in both negative- and positive-moment beam regions. Such construction can also provide for redistribution of forces within the beam and frame when inelastic action takes place. Laboratory tests on beam-column subassemblages indicated that properly detailed, partially restrained composite connections can undergo large deformations without fracturing. In providing a ductile connection with a design capacity below that of the members framing into the joint and the panel zone, such a system should provide good performance under large inelastic deformation cycles. Partially restrained systems also have the potential advantage of being subjected to lower seismic forces than comparable fully restrained systems owing to the lengthening of the natural period of vibration and the energy which is dissipated by the connections, effectively increasing the system damping ratio. This type of advantage has also been postulated for partially restrained steel frames.[138]

Initial developments of the composite partially restrained system were intended to address applications in regions of low or moderate seismicity. With appropriate analysis and detailing, it may also be possible to use this system in areas of high seismicity for some applications. Seismic design provisions limit the height for which this system may be used unless special analysis procedures are incorporated to justify applications in taller buildings. No limit is required if this system is used as part of a dual system with braced steel or composite frames.[D93]

Ordinary frames. Ordinary moment-resisting frames in steel or concrete construction have been incorporated into seismic design codes for a number of years. The term "ordinary" refers to systems in which the elements are not designed or detailed to provide the maximum potential ductility during inelastic cyclic response. In an effort to provide acceptable performance of these systems, the lateral design forces are increased significantly over those required of "special" moment-resisting frame systems, in order to reduce the potential ductility demand. Because of the limited ductility which is available in ordinary moment-resisting frames, seismic building codes have restricted their use in areas of high seismicity and in tall buildings.[G71] Where permitted in areas of low seismicity, these systems are often economical, since the cost of providing the additional base shear strength can easily be exceeded by the expense of providing the ductile elements and connections required of special moment-resisting frames.

A number of possible combinations are available to develop a composite ordinary moment-resisting frame system. These include steel or composite beams combined with either steel, reinforced concrete, or composite columns. The most commonly used system to date has included steel beams and composite columns. This system may consist of encased or filled composite columns. In encased composite columns, the structural steel element is often used primarily for erection purposes.

The connections in composite ordinary moment-resisting frames are generally intended to develop the full moment capacity of the steel beam members. Various connection details may be used, such as those shown in Figs. 5.1 and 5.2. A large number of large-scale laboratory tests on connections of these types have been performed in the United States[116,145] and Japan under both monotonic and cyclic loading. These tests have demonstrated that with proper detailing, such connections can provide performance comparable to that of steel or reinforced concrete connections. Filled concrete columns (Fig. 5.3) have been used less frequently, with fewer tests reported, although the force-transfer mechanisms are similar to those of the connections shown in Fig. 5.2.

To be consistent with seismic design provisions for steel or reinforced concrete ordinary moment-resisting frame systems, present design requirements for composite moment-resisting frame systems limit their use to areas of low seismicity in buildings over certain height limits.[D93] With further testing, incorporation into design practice and proven performance in future earthquakes, some of the limitations on the use of this system may be reduced.

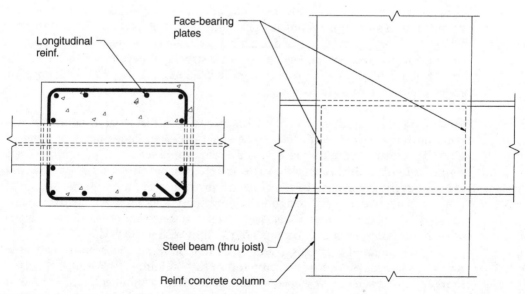

Figure 5.1 Steel beam to reinforced concrete column connection.

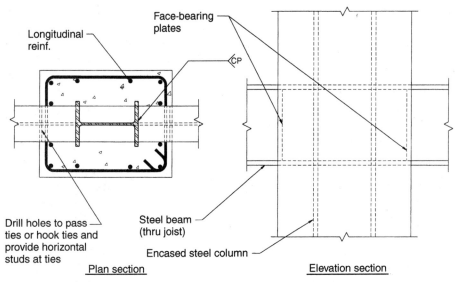

Figure 5.2 Steel beam to encased composite column connection.

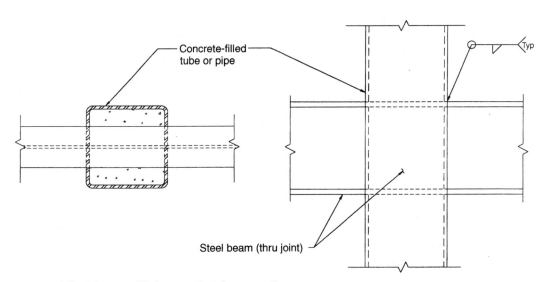

Figure 5.3 Steel beam to filled composite tube connection.

Special moment-resisting frames. The third type of moment-resisting framing system used to resist seismic forces is termed special moment-resisting frame. The term "special" refers to systems where the elements and connections are designed and detailed to provide a maximum amount of ductility and toughness, implying excellent energy dissipation and seismic performance during severe earthquake shaking. Recognizing this ductility, seismic codes allow the design base shear for special moment-resisting systems to be less than or equal to that of any other system included in these codes.

Because of the acknowledged ductility and the limited interference with architectural and other building requirements, special moment-resisting frames, especially in steel, have been a commonly used structural system for resisting lateral forces. The extensive detailing requirements for reinforced concrete to qualify as a special moment-resisting frame have resulted in more limited use in building design practice in areas of high seismicity.

Composite special moment-resisting framing systems are similar to the configurations previously discussed for ordinary moment-resisting frames. Analogous to steel or concrete systems, more stringent detailing provisions are required to increase the system ductility and toughness of the composite special moment-resisting frame, with the commensurate reduction in design lateral forces. The intent of such provisions is to confine inelastic hinging to the beams, while the columns and connections remain essentially elastic. Tests in Japan have demonstrated that beam-to-column connections can be detailed such that little damage to the connection occurs adjacent to beams subjected to large inelastic rotations.[145] As a result, the design base shear value prescribed for this system is similar to special moment-resisting frame systems of steel or reinforced concrete, and no limitations have been placed on their usage.

The Northridge, Calif., earthquake of 1994 caused cracks in the welds and connections of numerous structural steel buildings designed with special moment-resisting frames. Similar joint weld failures were observed in the 1995 Kobe, Japan, earthquake. An extensive research program is underway to further define the failure mechanisms and develop suitable solutions. Composite special moment-resisting frames are subject to the same potential failure mechanisms and solutions. For guidance, see Ref. G91 and subsequent work from the same coordinated research program.

5.3.2 Partially restrained frames

Procedures for the design of partially restrained composite moment frames as defined in the previous section have been developed and published.[121,124,136,D89] Standardized guidelines are under development by the ASCE Task Committee on Design Guide for Composite Semi-Rigid Connections. This section summarizes the published procedures.

Analytical considerations. Only a nominal amount of slab steel at the columns is needed to transform a simple connection into a rather stiff semirigid joint. The additional required slab reinforcing bars, shear connectors, and seat angles provide both significant additional strength and stiffness to the frame system. The semirigid behavior of the beam-to-column connections reduces significantly the lateral drift of these frames.

The contribution of the beam-to-column connection flexibility discussed above must be incorporated into the lateral force analysis of these systems. The simplest method for incorporating this effect in the lateral frame analysis is to model connections as linear springs with an effective stiffness reduced from the initial elastic stiffness to account for the inelastic nature of the connection moment-curvature relationship. A simple method for accounting for this effect was presented by Bjorhovde.[D45] Incorporating the effective connection stiffness into the frame analysis will obviously affect the building period and lateral deflections and, to a lesser extent, the distribution of member forces. Frame stability analyses must also consider the effective stiffness of connections in determining the rotational restraint at the ends of columns. Including these effects with typical effective buckling-length procedures should result in satisfactory column design for low-rise construction. For structures taller than four stories, geometric and connection nonlinearities should be included in the lateral drift and stability analyses.[121]

The moments of inertia of composite beams composed of steel wide-flange sections and a concrete floor slab are significantly different for negative and positive bending. Under cyclic lateral forces, such as those caused by seismic ground motion, the beam bending-moment diagram (and therefore stiffness) will change during the response. The use of either the positive or negative composite beam moment of inertia alone will lead to significant errors in the calculation of the frame stiffness.[121] A weighted average of the two values has been demonstrated to result in acceptable accuracy. This weighted average is based on the following equation:[121]

$$I_c = 0.6\,I_{Lp} + 0.4\,I_{Ln} \tag{5.1}$$

where I_c = moment of inertia of composite section
I_{Lp} = lower-bound moment of inertia for positive bending
I_{Ln} = lower-bound moment of inertia for negative bending

The lower-bound values can be obtained from the AISC LRFD Manual.[D95]

Element design. As noted in the previous section, the effect of the connection stiffness must be included in the lateral frame analyses of partially restrained composite frames. The element moment and shear diagrams determined from these analyses can be used with standard member design procedures. Composite beam design can be accomplished using the procedures presented in Chap. 3. For low-rise applications, steel columns may be designed using standard AISC LRFD design equations, with proper consideration of bending moments developed through the semirigid connections. The rotational connection restraint must be properly considered in determining the effective column lengths. For taller buildings, analyses which consider geometric nonlinearities should be incorporated in the design of frame columns.

Connection design. The connection detail typically considered for partially restrained composite moment frames consists of a bottom seat angle, a double angle or shear tab for the web, and stud connectors with added slab reinforcement to deliver top flange forces. Section 6.5.2 includes a complete description of the design considerations and calculations for semirigid composite connections for gravity-load design, and a design example is presented in Sec. 6.5.3. Discussion of semirigid connection design for partially restrained moment-resisting frames is included in Sec. 6.5. According to Sec. 6.5.3 it is advisable to attempt to detail these connections so that the positive- and negative-moment sections have roughly the same stiffness. This can be accomplished by providing seat angle and web connections which are on the order of 50 percent stronger than that required for negative moments.

The joint rotations in connection design should be limited to approximately 0.02 radian. If the frame analyses indicate larger rotations, the connection plates must be stiffened by increasing the amount of slab reinforcement and providing heavier seat angles and web connections.

5.3.3 Ordinary frames

The beam and column elements of composite ordinary moment-resisting frames may consist of one of a number of possible combinations of structural steel, reinforced concrete, and composite sections. The analysis and design detailing of the frame members is quite similar to that required of steel or concrete moment-resisting frames. Force transfer between the elements of a composite frame is somewhat unique and deserves special attention, since in general the connections are designed to be stronger than the weakest element (generally the beams) framing into the joint.

Analytical considerations. In general, the analytical procedures to be used in the design of composite ordinary moment-resisting frames are identical to those employed in the design of structural steel or reinforced concrete frames. Elastic properties of composite elements can be transformed into equivalent properties of one material for stiffness analyses using standard procedures. Since the size of composite columns in certain types of these frames can become quite large for stiffness considerations, it may be more accurate to include a finite rigid joint size into the frame model. Additional accuracy can be obtained by including the shear stiffness of the joints. But, since the connections are typically required to be stronger than the members framing into the joint, in many cases inclusion of an elastic spring to represent the joint stiffness will not be necessary to obtain the accuracy required for design.

Element design. As noted above, the design of elements in composite ordinary moment-resisting frames is not significantly different from the procedures for structural steel and reinforced concrete elements. In fact, the design and detailing of structural steel beams and columns in these ordinary moment-resisting frames can generally be based on the requirements of one of the commonly used seismic design codes, such as Chap. 27 of the Uniform Building Code,[G71] the NEHRP seismic design provisions,[D96] or the AISC seismic design provisions.[G78] Composite beams can be designed according to the procedures presented in Chap. 3.

It has been suggested and implemented into the Canadian seismic design requirements that reduced capacities should be used for these shear connectors in composite beams of moment-resisting frames, since they will be subjected to cyclic forces. This would be more important in special moment-resisting frames where the expected ductility demand on the elements and connections is higher. A reduction of 10 to 25 percent appears to be reasonable where the studs are expected to be subjected to severe cyclic loading.[D96] Such a reduction is recommended for all applications of shear connectors in these composite frames.

The design of composite columns can generally follow the procedures presented in Chap. 4. Encased composite columns should have a minimum ratio of structural steel to gross column area of 4 percent, as required in the AISC LRFD provisions. The shear strength of these columns generally ignores the contribution of the concrete.[D61] Contribution of the shear strength of the reinforcing ties is based on an effective shear width b_w of the section, as noted in Fig. 5.4.[D96] For filled composite columns, it is conservative to neglect the contribution of the concrete to the shear strength of the column. For conditions where shear strength becomes critical, it may be possible to treat the element as a reinforced concrete column with the steel tube considered as the shear reinforcement. Transfer of forces between the structural steel and reinforced concrete portions of the section should be made through shear connectors, ignoring the contribution of bond or friction, using calculation procedures such as those presented in Chap. 6.

The design and detailing of reinforced concrete columns in these frames should be similar to those of intermediate or special moment frames of reinforced concrete. Conservative detailing practices (i.e., incorporating the special moment frame requirements) are recommended for these frames in high seismic zones since there is little research in the use of intermediate detailing of concrete columns in these applications.[D96] This recommendation may be relaxed in the future if research indicates that the composite beam and beam-column connection details can be designed to perform better and more reliably than similar elements in reinforced concrete moment frames.

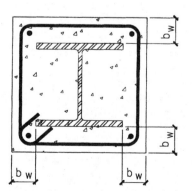
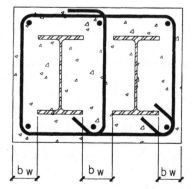

Figure 5.4 Effective widths for encased composite columns.

Connection design.   Section 6.4.1 includes description of the design considerations and calculations for moment-resisting connections between steel or composite beams and composite or reinforced concrete columns. Section 6.4.7 presents similar information for moment-resisting connections between steel or composite beams and steel columns.

In ordinary moment-resisting frames, the typical procedure is to design the connections to develop the strength of the connected members. In seismic design, it is generally desirable to avoid inelastic action in the frame connections unless the joints can be detailed with sufficient ductility. Consideration of all contributions to member strength must be included in determination of connection strength. Contributions which should be considered include the strengthening effect of the composite action of a steel beam and concrete slab in the joint regions.

Transfer of loads between structural steel and reinforced concrete elements of a composite moment-resisting frame should be made only through shear friction and direct bearing. Reliance on bond and adhesion forces should not be considered because of the cyclic nature of the lateral loading. In addition, where shear friction equations are used in the calculation of connection transfer forces, it has been recommended that a 25 percent reduction on the typical shear-friction capacities be imposed for buildings in areas of high seismicity.[D96]

Panel zone strength calculations for composite frames with fully encased steel columns may typically be taken as the sum of the steel and reinforced-concrete capacities. Recommendations for transverse reinforcement in the joint region of composite frames have been presented by Deierlein et al.[116] and Kanno.[145] Reinforcing bar development lengths similar to reinforced concrete moment frame construction should be provided in the detailing of these joints.

5.3.4   Special moment-resisting frames

The design approach for composite special moment-resisting frames is basically the same as that previously discussed for composite ordinary moment-resisting frames. The attempt to provide the maximum possible frame ductility, toughness, and energy-dissipation capacity are the major differences between the special and ordinary moment-resisting frame systems. These differences result in more stringent provisions for element and joint detailing. Generally these frames are designed to limit inelastic action to the beams, with the intent of preventing or at least severely restricting any potential yielding in columns and connections.

Analytical considerations.   The discussion of analytical procedures for ordinary moment-resisting frames in the previous section also applies for composite special moment-resisting frames.

Element design.   The design of elements in composite special moment-resisting frames should incorporate all the procedures and requirements for ordinary moment frames described above, and add more stringent requirements in order to obtain the expected increased member ductility and toughness.

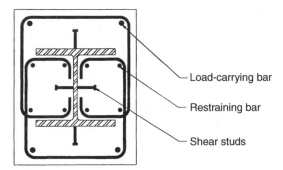

Figure 5.5 Closed-hoop detail for an encased composite column.

For composite systems which incorporate steel and reinforced concrete columns, all the typical design and detailing provisions for special moment-resisting frames of the two materials should be followed. For all systems, consideration of the strong column–weak beam approach should be included in the design. For composite columns, transverse reinforcement requirements should be equivalent to those required of reinforced concrete columns in special moment-resisting frames. Special details may be required to meet the intent of closed-hoop and cross-tie requirements for composite columns with a structural steel core. An example of a closed-hoop detail for an encased composite column is shown in Fig. 5.5.

Steel and composite beams should be designed to meet the more restrictive $b_f/2t_f$ and d/t_w compactness limits and the lateral bracing requirements of steel special moment-resisting frames. The additional restrictions are necessary to increase the resistance to local and lateral torsional buckling, allowing the beam elements to develop their fully plastic flexural capacity. However, these more restrictive requirements are not needed for steel flanges connected to the concrete slab with shear connectors since such flanges cannot fail in lateral torsional buckling and their local buckling is substantially inhibited by the presence of shear connectors and the concrete slab.

Connection design. Design considerations for connections in composite special moment-resisting frames are similar to those for ordinary moment-resisting frames. In special moment-resisting frames, the connection capacity should always be designed strong enough to develop the strength of the connected beams.

5.4   Braced Frames

Braced frames have traditionally been the most common lateral-force-resisting system with the exception of areas of high seismicity. These frames resist lateral forces primarily through axial stresses in the frame members that serve as elements of a vertical truss. Resisting lateral forces through this mechanism generally provides excellent lateral stiffness characteristics.

As a result, braced frames are generally more economical than moment-resisting frames. Their use is at times limited because of the potential interference of braces with other building systems or with architectural requirements.

The majority of braced frame construction is of structural steel, although there have been some examples of concrete braced frames in taller buildings designed to resist wind loads. Until recently, steel braced frame construction has consisted almost exclusively of concentric bracing, where the centerlines of the various members which frame into a joint meet at a single point. The ductility of concentric bracing systems has been considered to be limited by seismic design codes, because they rely on inelastic buckling of the brace elements to resist large overloads.

During the 1970s and 1980s, a new form of braced frame was developed which attempts to combine the excellent ductility of moment-resisting frames with the high stiffness of concentrically braced frames. This system, commonly known as eccentrically braced frames, consists of bracing elements which are deliberately offset from the centerline of beam-column joints. The short portion of beam between braces or between the brace and the column is referred to as the link beam. The link beams of an eccentrically braced frame are designed to act as ductile fuses which dissipate large amounts of energy during seismic overloads. As a result, the design of brace elements can be performed so as to preclude the possibility of brace buckling. With proper choice of the brace eccentricity, i.e., of the length of the link beams, the stiffness of this system can approach that of a concentrically braced frame. The ability to combine the ductility of moment frames and the stiffness of concentrically braced frames has led to increasing use of the system in areas of high seismicity. Special provisions for the design of eccentrically braced steel frames were first included is seismic building codes in 1988.[G54]

Braced frames of composite construction have been common in areas of low and moderate seismicity. Most of these buildings have included encased composite floors, composite columns, and steel braces. Composite columns are rarely used in buildings less than about 20 stories high. Very tall buildings are sometimes supported on a few supercolumns composed of large-diameter fabricated circular steel shells filled with high-strength concrete to provide the required lateral stiffness. Smaller-diameter concrete-filled steel tubes have also been used for bracing elements in an attempt to improve the local buckling resistance of the steel tube walls. Research indicates that the concrete filling of tubes with high diameter-to-thickness ratios improves the inelastic performance of such members.[G51] Composite elements can also be incorporated into the eccentrically braced frame system, although no practical applications are known at present.

Parallel to the previous discussion for composite moment-resisting frames, there were no building code provisions for the design of composite braced frame systems. The BSSC developed recommendations for seismic design of such frames; they have been included in the 1994 NEHRP Seismic Design Requirements for Buildings.[D96]

5.4.1 Identification of braced frames

Composite braced frame systems can be separated into those with concentric and those with eccentric bracing. As with moment frames, composite braced frames are similar to steel braced frames.

Concentrically braced frame. Concentrically braced steel frame construction is the most common form of steel framing. The earliest applications began to appear with the inception of steel framed construction and often included braces composed of built-up sections. Such bracing often was used to resist lateral forces in tower portions of larger steel frame buildings with masonry infills. Later applications consisted of typical steel beam and column wide-flange sections used in combination with various brace sections, such as wide-flange sections, tubes, double channels, or double angles. Connections between the steel frame and the bracing elements is usually accomplished by welding or high-strength bolting to vertical gusset plates.

Composite concentrically braced frames include a number of possible combinations of steel, reinforced concrete, and composite elements. All early applications of these composite systems have been in regions of low or moderate seismicity. Composite braces of either concrete-filled steel tubes or concrete-encased steel braces may be combined with steel frame elements. Composite columns may also be used in conjunction with composite floors and steel bracing members. Such a system is used frequently in tall buildings, where the composite columns become quite large to provide the required lateral stiffness.

As noted previously, the lateral deformation of concentrically braced frames, both steel and composite, is generally considered to be limited for seismic loadings because of the deterioration of energy-dissipation capacity which typical brace elements exhibit during repeated inelastic cycles. For small or moderate earthquakes where the braced frame elements remain essentially elastic, the response of these frames can be expected to be satisfactory. Measures such as filling steel tubes with concrete have proved to be able to inhibit the onset of local buckling and thereby improve the cyclic response of the brace elements. Design of connections should be similar to that of steel braced frames, where the connections are intended to develop the capacity of the brace elements. Where composite elements are used, the connection design must consider the increased capacity caused by the addition of concrete to the steel bracing elements.

Eccentrically braced frame. After approximately 10 years of experimental and analytical research, the seismic design of steel eccentrically braced frames was included in the 1988 Uniform Building Code.[G54] The ductile response of the link elements has resulted in the system's being designed for loads similar to those required for special moment-resisting space frames. The system has been used widely in California for various types of structures, with most applications in the low- to midrise range of building height. Similar applications in regions of low and moderate seismicity have been made, where the designs capitalized on the potential simplifications of the member connections which can be realized with eccentric bracing.

Little experience exists in the application of composite eccentrically braced frames, but the use of structural steel link elements, which are designed and detailed to meet the requirements of eccentrically braced steel frames, in conjunction with composite brace or column elements would appear to be a system which would have seismic resistance equivalent to an all-steel system. As a result, the 1994 NEHRP provisions[D96] recommended the same R and C_d values for steel and composite eccentrically braced frames, where R is the response-modification coefficient and C_d the deflection-amplification factor. Connections in composite frames should be designed for capacity similar to steel systems to ensure that the inelastic action takes place in the link beams.

5.4.2 Concentrically braced frames

The beam, column, and brace elements of a composite concentrically braced frame may consist of one of a number of possible combinations of structural steel, reinforced concrete, and composite sections. The analysis, design, and detailing of the frame members is quite similar to that required of concentrically braced steel frames. Force transfer between the elements of a composite braced frame is unique and deserves special attention, since the connections are generally designed to force inelastic action into the diagonal brace members.

Analytical considerations.   In general, the analytical procedures to be used in the design of composite concentrically braced frames are identical to those employed for similar structural steel systems. Elastic properties of composite elements can be transformed into equivalent properties of one material for stiffness analyses using standard procedures. Since the size of composite columns in certain types of these frames can become quite large, for stiffness considerations it may be more accurate to include a finite rigid joint size into the frame model. Since the connections are typically required to be stronger than the members framing into the joint, the inclusion of an elastic spring to represent the joint stiffness is generally not necessary for design purposes. Where composite brace elements include concrete intended to stiffen steel sections, the effects of the concrete on brace stiffness must be considered in the frame model.

Element design.   As noted above, the design of elements in composite concentrically braced frames is similar to the design of corresponding elements in other systems. The design of steel beams, columns, and braces in these frames can be generally based on the requirements of one of the commonly used seismic design codes, such as the AISC Seismic Design Provisions,[G78] Chap. 27 of the Uniform Building Code,[G71] or the NEHRP Seismic Design Provisions.[D96] Composite beams can be designed according to the procedures presented in Chap. 3. Reduction in the capacity of shear connectors should also be considered, as was previously discussed in Sec. 5.3.3.

The design of composite columns can generally follow the procedures presented in Chap. 4. Encased composite columns should have a minimum ratio of structural steel to gross column area of 4 percent. Transfer of forces between the structural steel and reinforced concrete portions of the section should be made through shear connectors, ignoring the contribution of bond or friction. The capacity design of reinforced concrete columns should meet the requirements for columns in ordinary moment-resisting frames. The detailing of both composite and reinforced concrete columns should provide ductility comparable to that of composite ordinary moment-resisting frames. This potentially conservative approach is warranted since there has been little research on such elements. Such requirements may be relaxed by the results of future research.

Composite brace design in concentrically braced frames must recognize that these elements are expected to provide the inelastic action during large seismic overloads. Braces which are concrete-encased steel elements should include reinforcing and confinement steel sufficient to provide the intended stiffening effect even after multiple cycles which have induced brace buckling. As a result, it is recommended that these elements meet detailing requirements similar to those of composite columns. Composite braces in tension should be designed considering only the structural steel unless test results justify higher strengths.

Connection design.   Section 6.7.2 includes descriptions of the design considerations and calculations for connections between steel braces and composite columns. Similar approaches may be followed for composite brace elements. The general intent of the connection design is to provide strength to develop the capacity of the braces in tension or compression. For composite brace sections, the additional strength of the concrete must be considered, since it would be unconservative to consider only the strength of the structural steel section. Brace buckling and the resulting large rotation demands which could result at the brace ends should be considered in connection detailing.

Transfer of loads between structural steel and reinforced concrete elements of a composite braced frame should be made only through shear friction and direct bearing. Reliance on bond and adhesion should not be considered because of the cyclic nature of the lateral loading. In addition, where shear-friction equations are used in the calculation of connection transfer forces, it has been recommended that a 25 percent reduction on the typical shear-friction capacities be imposed for buildings in areas of high seismicity.[D96] Examples of connections between braces and composite or reinforced concrete columns are shown in Figs. 5.6 through 5.8.

5.4.3   Eccentrically braced frames

The beam elements of composite eccentrically braced frames will generally consist of structural steel elements, although some research in Europe by Kanz et al. has investigated the use of concrete fireproofing for these members.[135] Any concrete encasement of the beam elements should not extend into the link regions where large inelastic action is developed. The column and brace elements of these frames could be composed of either structural steel or composite steel and concrete sections. The analysis, design, and detailing of

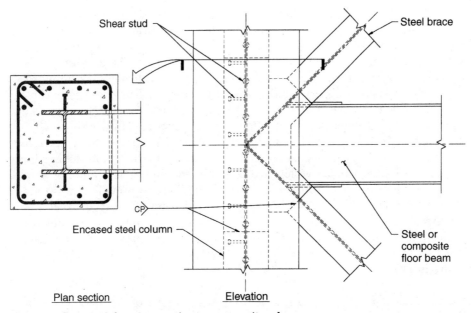

Figure 5.6 Concentric brace connection to a composite column.

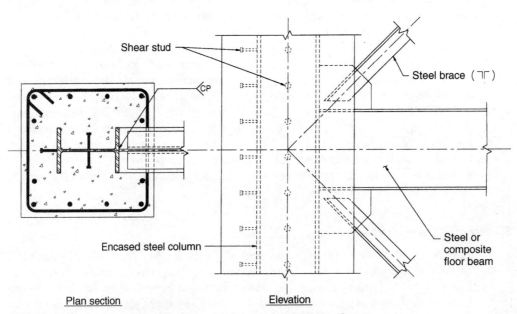

Figure 5.7 Alternate connection of a concentric brace to a composite column.

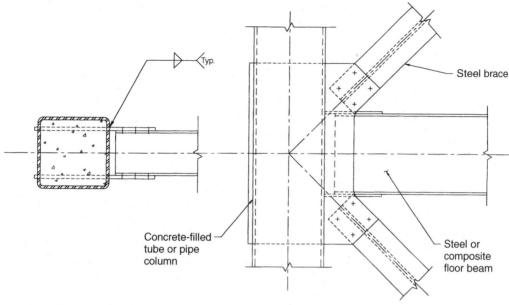

Typ.

Steel brace

Concrete-filled
tube or pipe
column

Steel or
composite
floor beam

Figure 5.8 Concentric brace connection to a filled tube.

the frames is quite similar to that required of steel eccentrically braced
frames. Since the force transfer mechanisms between the elements of a composite frame rely on bearing and shear friction, special attention must be
paid to the design of these connections if they are to focus the intended
inelastic action to the ductile link members.

Analytical considerations. In general, the analytical procedures to be used in the
design of composite eccentrically braced frames are identical to those employed
for similar structural steel systems. Elastic properties of composite elements
can be transformed into equivalent properties of one material for stiffness
analyses using standard procedures. Since the size of composite columns in certain types of these frames can become quite large, for stiffness considerations it
may be more accurate to include a finite rigid joint size into the frame model.
Since the connections are typically required to be stronger than the members
framing into the joint, the inclusion of an elastic spring to represent the joint
stiffness is generally not necessary for design purposes. Where composite brace
elements include concrete intended to stiffen steel sections, the effects of the
concrete on brace stiffness must be considered in the frame model.

Composite action of the concrete slab with the structural steel link beam
section may become significant in determining the initial capacity of the link
section, which should be considered in sizing the brace and column elements.
Tests by Ricles and Popov demonstrated that this effect diminishes in subsequent inelastic cycles but still may require consideration for longer links
which yield in bending.[119]

Element design.   As noted above, the design of elements in composite eccentrically braced frames is very similar to the design of corresponding elements in other systems. The design of steel beams, columns, and braces in these frames can be generally based on the requirements of one of the commonly used seismic design codes, such as the AISC seismic design provisions,[G78] Chap. 27 of the Uniform Building Code,[G71] or the NEHRP seismic design provisions.[D96] Reduction in the capacity of shear connectors should also be considered, as was previously discussed in Sec. 5.3.3.

The design of composite columns can generally follow the procedures presented in Chap. 4. Design loads must consider the maximum load which can be generated by yielding and some strain hardening of the link beam elements, similar to those required for steel columns in these frames. Encased composite columns should have a minimum ratio of structural steel to gross column area of 4 percent as required in various provisions unless they are designed as reinforced concrete columns. Transfer of forces between the structural steel and reinforced concrete portions of the section should be made through shear connectors, ignoring the contribution of bond or friction. The capacity design of reinforced concrete and encased composite columns in these frames should meet the requirements for columns in ordinary moment-resisting frames. The detailing of both encased composite and reinforced concrete columns should provide ductility comparable to that of intermediate moment-resisting frames. This potentially conservative approach is warranted since there has been little research on such elements. In addition, for higher-performance categories the 1994 NEHRP provisions[D96] recommend that these columns meet the transverse reinforcement requirements of special moment-resisting frames. This requirement is extended to all performance categories when the link element is located adjacent to the column.

Composite brace design in eccentrically braced frames must recognize that these elements are intended to remain essentially elastic during large seismic overloads, since they are designed to be strong enough to yield the link beam elements. The design strength of these braces must consider the yielding and significant strain hardening which can occur in properly designed and detailed link elements. Both axial and bending forces generated in the braces by the strain-hardened link beams must be considered. Braces which are concrete-encased steel elements or reinforced concrete should therefore be designed to meet detailing requirements similar to columns, as discussed above. Composite braces in tension should be designed considering only the structural steel, unless test results justify higher strengths.

Connection design.   Section 6.7.2 includes descriptions of the design considerations and calculations for connections between steel braces and composite columns. Similar approaches may be followed for composite brace elements. The general intent of the connection design is to provide strength to develop the capacity of the link-beam elements. For composite brace sections, the additional strength of the concrete must be considered, since it would be unconservative to consider only the strength of the structural steel section. Where the shear link is not adjacent to the column, the connections between

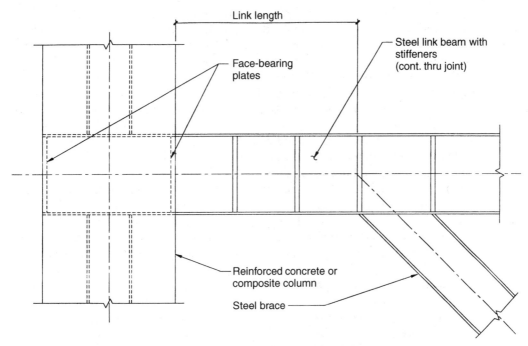

Figure 5.9   Eccentric brace connection to an encased composite column.

the braces and columns are similar to those in composite concentrically braced frames. Where the shear link is adjacent to the columns, the connections should be detailed similar to composite beam-column connections in special moment-resisting frames or between steel coupling beams and concrete wall piers in composite wall elements. An example of such a connection detail is shown in Fig. 5.9. The large rotation demands which could result at the ends of the link beams should always be considered in detailing the connections of composite eccentrically braced frames.

Transfer of loads between structural steel and reinforced concrete elements of a composite braced frame should be made only through shear friction and/or direct bearing. Reliance on bond and adhesion should not be considered because of the cyclic nature of the lateral loading. In addition, where shear-friction equations are used in the calculation of connection transfer forces, it has been recommended that a 25 percent reduction on the typical shear-friction capacities be imposed for buildings in areas of high seismicity.[D96]

5.5   Shear-Wall Design

5.5.1   Composite shear walls

Composite shear walls can take many forms, but a few basic common systems are found in composite structures. The most common composite shear wall consists of a structural steel frame in which some bays are filled with a reinforced-concrete wall encasing adjacent structural steel columns and beams.

In essence, this is a reinforced concrete shear wall with structural steel boundary elements. This shear-wall system is discussed further in Sec. 5.5.2.

A similar composite shear wall can be formed with a structural steel frame and masonry installed between some of the columns to form a composite shear-wall system. Historically, the high-rise buildings of the late 1800s and early 1900s in the United States consisted of structural-steel frames with semirigid connections or possible wind gussets all encased in massive masonry exterior walls creating, in effect, a composite shear-wall system. This type of building performed very well in the 1906 San Francisco earthquake and formed the philosophical basis for the dual system of modern seismic codes. These historic composite buildings have also performed well under wind exposure.

Structural steel beams are also used to couple tall, slender piers to form a stiffer composite shear-wall system with window openings (Fig. 5.10). The steel coupling beam is subjected to high shear and high moment at each end, requiring a moment-resisting connection to the column and probably a moment-resisting connection of the beam on the other side of the column within the shear-wall pier. A very strong shear connection is usually also required. A computer analysis provides an insight regarding the forces in the coupling beam and the effectiveness of the beam, as is described in the following paragraph for a multistory building with a composite wall system similar to that shown in Fig. 5.10.

If the coupling beams in Fig. 5.10 were pin-connected at each end or were very flexible, as might be provided by a floor slab connection, the coupling

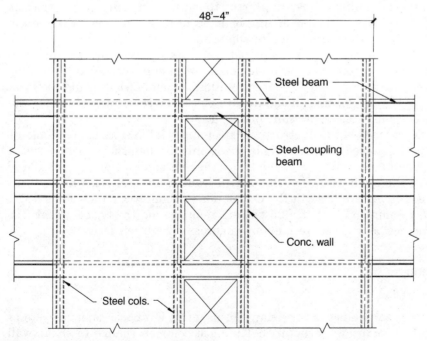

Figure 5.10 Composite shear-wall elevation.

beam would be ineffective and the two wall piers would resist lateral loads independently. As the walls deflect laterally, the floor slab or flexible beam undergoes considerable deformations which can lead to damage. If the coupling beams are very stiff, they can fully couple the two piers and make them work as a single wall resisting lateral forces. The coupled piers are considered next as a single wall with overturning moments resisted by the two outermost columns of the system. A free-body diagram cut through the midspan of the coupling beams gives an indication of the forces that they must resist. If the coupling beams are less stiff, a portion of the lateral forces will be resisted by the overall system and a portion by the individual elements. The advantage of modern computer programs is that they permit experimentation by changing the stiffness of the coupling beams and thus arriving at an optimum solution for each individual situation encountered in design.

Another composite shear-wall system is a building with a reinforced concrete shear-wall core, possibly constructed by slip forming, combined with structural steel floor construction including moment-resisting frames around the perimeter of the building. This type of building relies on the reinforced concrete shear-wall core and the moment-resisting perimeter frames as its bracing. Whereas each element may not be of composite construction, the building relies on the composite performance to brace the building. Computer models properly representing each system provide guidance in design. Usually the shear-wall core is stiffer and more effective in the lower stories while the moment-resisting frame is stiffer and more effective in the upper stories of the building. This requires attention to diaphragm design to gradually transfer the horizontal forces from the perimeter frames to the central core.

5.5.2 Concrete walls with steel boundaries

Composite shear walls consisting of reinforcing concrete walls connected to structural steel framing are a common composite system. The principal point illustrated in this section is the attention to design details that is necessary for properly functioning systems.

A composite shear wall consisting of a single bay wall encasing structural-steel framing is illustrated in Fig. 5.11. The concrete wall resists horizontal shear due to wind or earthquake while the structural steel columns resist the vertical overturning forces. At ultimate loads, the concrete wall will also add to the overturning resistance. If the floor beams on either side of the wall have moment-resisting connections, then they will transfer some of the overturning force out to the next column, depending on their stiffness and the geometry of the wall. The beams also serve as collectors, collecting the horizontal forces from the floor diaphragm and delivering those forces to the shear wall. Thus the connections of the beams to the column must be able to resist these horizontal forces.

Figure 5.12 illustrates a typical condition at the floor beam. The concrete wall has been offset to one side of the column centerline so the concrete wall can be poured. If the wall is centered on the column line, the beam makes it

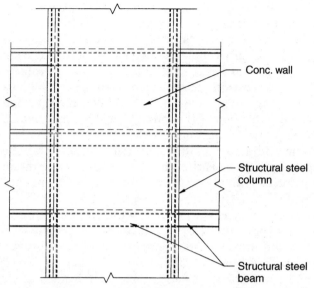

Conc. wall

Structural steel
column

Structural steel
beam

Figure 5.11   Single-bay composite shear-wall elevation.

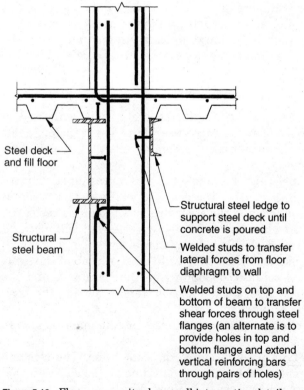

Steel deck
and fill floor

Structural
steel beam

Structural steel ledge to
support steel deck until
concrete is poured

Welded studs to transfer
lateral forces from floor
diaphragm to wall

Welded studs on top and
bottom of beam to transfer
shear forces through steel
flanges (an alternate is to
provide holes in top and
bottom flange and extend
vertical reinforcing bars
through pairs of holes)

Figure 5.12   Floor—composite shear-wall intersection detail.

very difficult to place the concrete unless the wall is very thick, which usually is not the case. A steel ledger is provided to support the steel deck adjacent to the wall until the concrete wall is poured. Studs are welded to the ledger. Once the wall is placed, it is stiffer than the ledger and the normal way to resist floor loads and prevent separation at the floor-to-wall connection takes place. Welded studs are also provided on the steel beam connected to the column to transfer horizontal floor diaphragm forces to the shear wall (see Sec. 5.6.3 for more discussion on this requirement). Finally, the shear stresses in the concrete wall must be properly transferred through the floor construction. The steel flanges of the floor beam break the continuity of the concrete wall and reduce the effective width of the wall to resist shear stresses without making special provisions. Welded studs on the top of the top beam flange and the bottom of the bottom beam flange (Fig. 5.12) provide this supplementary shear-transfer mechanism. Alternatively, the top and bottom flange of the beam to be embedded within the wall can be drilled with aligned holes at regular spacing so the vertical reinforcing steel of the wall can pass through pairs of holes, providing continuity for shear transfer. When placing concrete, construction joints can be suitably located to facilitate the contractor's sequence of concrete pours and special care is needed to properly vibrate the concrete at the beam to prevent voids from being created beneath the beam flanges.

In some cases, it is more appropriate to center the wall on the column. In such cases, the wall may be installed as shotcrete without encasing either the structural-steel floor beam or the column. When this condition exists, welded studs must be installed on both the beam and the column to transfer all forces at the perimeter of the shear panel. The design of such shear transfers is usually based on shear friction. Consideration should be give to either using very long headed studs that will effectively transfer forces between the reinforcing bars of the shear panel or using threaded reinforcing bar dowels installed as welded studs. Since shear friction requires contact between concrete and steel, special attention should be given to the top panel connection at the beam soffit, as slight consolidation of the shotcrete or poor workmanship may result in a continuous crack or voids. Repairs such as epoxy injection are frequently necessary to ensure good performance.

Figure 5.13 shows the detail of an encased column at the edge of a concrete wall. Welded studs are installed on the column to transfer the vertical shear forces and overturning forces to the structural steel column. In some cases, it may be desirable to only partially encase the column, as placing concrete all around the column can be difficult owing to the floor beams and steel decking above. Assuming that the steel column resists all of the overturning forces, it can be considered the boundary member for seismic loads, and closely spaced reinforcing ties will not be necessary. When the steel column serves as the shear-wall boundary member, for either wind or seismic loads, it will quite possibly be subject to uplift or tension loads. In such cases, special detailing considerations must be given to the steel column splices, as the normal lightly bolted or partial-penetration weld column splice used for milled bearing surfaces for compression may not be suitable for tension reversals. When

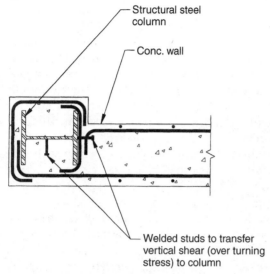

Figure 5.13 Detail at column in a composite shear wall.

these connections are subjected to tension, the nominal column splice is the weak link in the member. For seismic conditions where overloads are expected, the nominal connection acts like a notch and can fail if its tensile capacity is exceeded. For such cases, full-penetration welded column splices are appropriate despite their cost.

Welded studs or dowels are generally used for shear transfer between concrete and structural steel. Other devices acting as lugs, such as flat bars, angles, or other steel shapes, can be welded to the steel member with the shear acting as a bearing force on the lug with adequate welds to transfer the force in the lug to the structural steel member. In such details, the eccentricity between the center of bearing on the lug and the weld to the structural steel member must be considered, as it will influence the thickness of steel on the lug and the welds to the structural steel member. If the structural steel member has a thin web or flange, the eccentricity might cause local overstress in the web or flange, suggesting that more lugs or lugs of a different configuration are preferable.

5.5.3 Concrete-encased steel plates

In rare cases, when extremely high shear forces must be resisted by a wall, it becomes practical to use a shear wall with a steel plate web rather than reinforced concrete. Examples where such construction has been used include high-rise buildings where all lateral forces must be transferred to the core at the base of the building and multistory hospitals in California where strict seismic codes attempting to keep these facilities operational after major earthquakes result in very high lateral forces.

Although many details are possible for such conditions, a likely scenario is represented by structural steel framing surrounding the steel plates with the whole steel assembly encased in reinforced concrete. The steel framing consists of columns and floor beams which not only resist gravity loads but the columns act also as boundary members resisting overturning forces. The shear-wall web is a steel plate welded to the columns and beams. A simple practical detail would be to provide a short piece of steel plate continuously fillet welded in the shop to the beams and columns as a tab. The shear-wall steel plate can then be installed after the beams and columns with erection bolts to the tab. Field fillet welds can then be installed between steel plate and tabs. If the plates need to be installed in pieces because of size in shipping or erection, splices can be simple fillet welds to a common back-up plate. If there are openings in the wall, additional steel boundary members or flanges may be appropriate.

To prevent buckling of the steel plate when it is loaded, the completed steel assembly can be encased in reinforced concrete. This also fireproofs the steel. The encasement should be thick enough to provide the stiffness needed to prevent buckling and should be properly reinforced for strength. Common details would include a regular pattern of welded studs on each side of the plate or a regular pattern of holes in the plate to pass reinforcing bars hooked at each end. This provides a composite sandwich so the entire thickness is effective at preventing buckling. As forces can be quite high in such systems, special attention to details is particularly important with this type of construction.

5.6 Horizontal Diaphragms

5.6.1 Diaphragms

Floor and roof diaphragms are often one of the most overlooked elements in building design, but their performance is essential for any successful building. They interconnect all columns at each level, provide a horizontal transfer of forces to bracing elements, and provide stability bracing to columns that are not a part of the lateral-force-resisting system. In many buildings, they do this well even when neglected in the design process. But composite structures tend to be tall structures or ones with special elements concentrating bracing so that proper design of horizontal diaphragms is usually quite important.

Diaphragm design is no different in composite buildings than in conventional structural steel or reinforced concrete buildings. The same basic principles apply and will not be repeated here. The following sections discuss only several special considerations of force transfer unique to composite structures.

Information on the design of floor diaphragms for regions of high seismicity may be found in Ref. G58A, which is illustrated with several practical examples. It should be also noted that in view of the frequent use of computer analyses, simulation of diaphragms as finite elements is fairly common in the design practice.

5.6.2 Concrete-filled steel deck diaphragms

Most steel decking systems have been designed and tested for gravity loads, with the steel decking designed to resist independently construction loads and the wet concrete fill. The steel deck usually has embossments or deformations which have been pressed into the sheet during its manufacture into decking so that once the concrete hardens, the two will work compositely, with the decking acting as bottom tension reinforcement and the concrete resisting compression. Since these systems are proprietary, it is necessary to consult the manufacturers' literature for rated loads and other information. The design of these systems is addressed by the Steel Deck Institute.[G52]

When considering the diaphragm design, it is important to remember that the concrete fill is the stiffest part of the system in the horizontal plane so the shear stresses are primarily resisted by concrete. Thus, for force transfer between a steel column and the diaphragm, forces must first transfer to the beam through the beam-to-column connection and then to the concrete fill, either through welded studs or through puddle welds to the steel deck and through bond and the embossments of the decking to the concrete fill. Each of these transfers must be adequate for the intended forces. It is essential in design to always keep all load paths in mind and ensure complete load paths in the design and detailing. When the concrete fill on the steel deck connects directly to the concrete of shear walls or steel-encased composite concrete beams, reinforcing dowels between the two can be used for direct transfer.

Special construction considerations are also necessary for studs welded to steel beams through the steel decking. The steel decking is sometimes galvanized, and the zinc of the galvanizing can result in poor-quality welds.

When the published literature of the steel deck manufacturer gives capacities for diaphragm action less than needed, the concrete fill can be increased in thickness and adequately reinforced so the concrete alone can resist the horizontal diaphragm stresses, using the metal deck only as a form for concrete placement and as tension reinforcing of the composite floor slab as it spans between adjacent floor beams.

5.6.3 Diaphragm chords and collectors

As with any horizontal diaphragm, the load paths can usually best be seen by drawing the floor slab like a beam in each direction separately and applying all forces in and out of the slab and then analyzing the diaphragm like a beam. In this manner, the chord and collector forces can be determined.

In composite structures, it is usually easy to utilize members already present to serve as chords and collectors. For example, the perimeter framing usually is more than adequate for chord forces, so the only issues are ensuring that the perimeter framing members have adequate connections at the columns for the tension of the diaphragm chord together with other loads the connection must resist.

Figure 5.14 shows a simplified floor plan of a floor diaphragm with two composite shear walls at each end which brace the building in the narrow

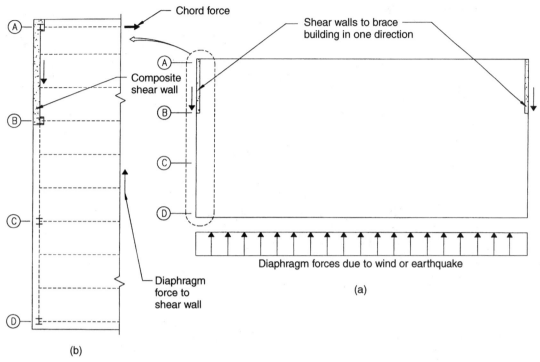

Figure 5.14 Transfer of diaphragm force to shear walls. (a) Floor diaphragm. (b) Free-body diagram of one diaphragm end.

direction. The diaphragm forces are either the tributary wind or seismic forces acting on the floor. Figure 5.14 shows a free-body diagram of the end of the floor diaphragm. The diaphragm will have a reasonably uniform shear flow as it nears the end. The total force divided by length gives a force per unit length that must be transferred from the concrete fill to the structural steel perimeter beam as discussed in Sec. 5.6.2. Assuming that the building has three bays of equal length, the collector force at the face of the shear wall at line *B* will be two-thirds of the total force to be transferred to the shear wall. The perimeter beam undoubtedly is strong enough to resist this tension collector load. The beam-to-column connection at line *B* must resist this collector force in combination with other design loads at that location. The beam-to-column connection at line *C* must resist half the collector load at line *B* (one-third of the total force) plus all other design loads. The beam within the shear wall from lines *A* to *B*, shown in Fig. 5.14, must have a sufficient number of studs to transfer the collector force from the structural steel beam to the concrete web of the composite shear wall. While this example is extremely simplified, it illustrates the method of determining the load-path analysis and the attention to detail that needs to be considered in composite structures.

5.6.4   Floor diaphragm design

Assume a building floor plate 200 by 100 ft (60 by 30 m) with composite shear walls at both ends as shown in Fig. 5.15. The floor is 3-in (76-mm) steel deck with 3¼-in (83-mm) lightweight concrete fill. Check diaphragm for seismic zone 4 or wind with net average pressure of 30 lb/ft² (1.43 kN/m²). The story height is 14 ft (4.3 m). Concrete strength is 4 ksi (28 MPa).

Determine critical load.

Seismic:

$$w_d = 0.4W = 0.4 \times 100 \text{ lb/ft}^2 \times 100 \text{ ft} = 4 \text{ kips/ft}$$

Wind:

$$w_d = 14 \text{ ft} \times 30 \text{ lb/ft}^2 = 0.42 \text{ kip/ft} \qquad \text{Seismic governs}$$

Diaphragm shear design.

$$V_{max} = \frac{w_d l}{2} = \frac{4 \times 200}{2} = 400 \text{ kips}$$

Check diaphragm shear on concrete fill alone.

$$V_u = 1.4 V_{max} = 1.4 \times 400 = 560 \text{ kips}$$

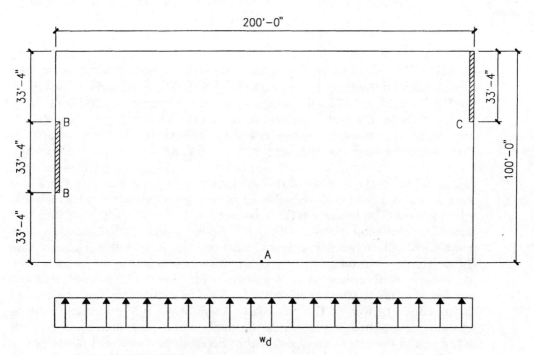

Figure 5.15   Floor diaphragm for Sec. 5.6.4.

Assuming 4.75 in average slab thickness, the area of concrete slab per unit width is

$$A_c = 100 \times 12 \times 4.75 = 5700 \text{ in}^2$$

$$\text{Average shear stress} = \frac{560}{5700} = 0.098 \text{ ksi}$$

$$\text{Concrete shear strength} = 2\phi\sqrt{0.001f_c'} = 2 \times 0.85 \times \sqrt{0.001 \times 4}$$
$$= 0.108 \text{ ksi} > 0.098 \text{ ksi} \quad \text{O.K.}$$

If the concrete strength alone is insufficient, refer to test data of the steel deck manufacturer or add reinforcing in the fill slab.

Chord force design. Check maximum chord force at the diaphragm edge (point A in Fig. 5.15):

$$M_{max} = \frac{w_d l^2}{8} = \frac{4 \times 200^2}{8} = 20,000 \text{ ft-kips}$$

For simplicity, assume chords are at the edge:

$$T_{max} = \frac{20,000}{100} = 200 \text{ kips}$$

Assume steel at the frame edge takes the entire force:

$$\text{Required } A_s = \frac{200}{0.6 \times 50} = 6.67 \text{ in}$$

However, code allows a one-third increase for seismic loading, so the 200 kips tension should be combined with gravity-load requirements and multiplied by 0.75. Compare this requirement with gravity-only requirements and design for the larger. Connections must also be designed for the 200-kip tension. Alternatively, add continuous reinforcing steel to the steel deck fill.

Collector force design

$$V_{max} = 400 \text{ kips at each end, assumed to be uniformly distributed}$$

At points B, collector force is $(33.3/100) \times 400 = 133$ kips
At point C, collector force is $(66.7/100) \times 400 = 267$ kips
These forces need to be combined with gravity forces as described above for chord forces.

5.6.5 Design of a floor diaphragm with an opening

Assume the same basic building configuration and dimensions as in Sec. 5.6.4, but at the second floor a shear wall from above is discontinued and the

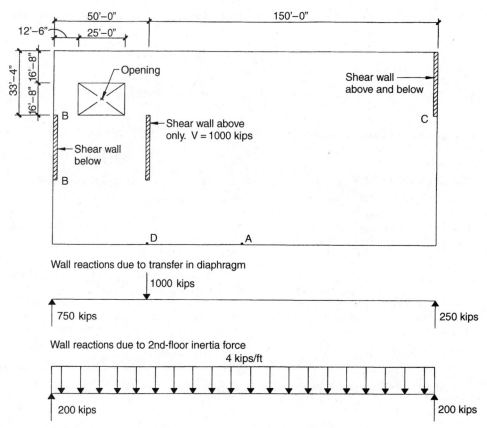

Figure 5.16 Floor diaphragm for Sec. 5.6.5.

force must be transferred by the diaphragm to the end shear walls below (Fig. 5.16).

Wall reactions due to the diaphragm transfer and due to the second floor inertia force are shown also in Fig. 5.16.

Chord force at *A*

$$M_a = 20,000 + \frac{1000 \times 50 \times 100}{200} = 45,000 \text{ ft-kips}$$

where 20,000 ft-kips is M_{max} from Sec. 5.6.4.

$$T_a = \frac{45,000}{100} = 450 \text{ kips}$$

Design chord at *A* for this force as in Sec. 5.6.4.

Chord force at *D*.   Consider free-body diagram (Fig. 5.17) just at the left edge of the wall above.

$$V = 950 + 200 = 1150 \text{ kips}$$

$$T_d = \frac{(1150 \times 50) - (4 \times 50 \times 25)}{100} = 525 \text{ kips}$$

Design chord at *D* for 525 kips as described in Sec. 5.6.4.

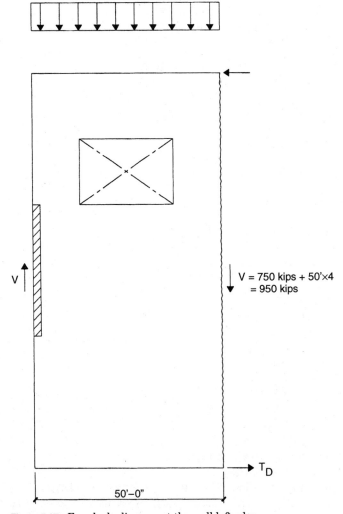

Figure 5.17 Free-body diagram at the wall left edge.

Check shear in diaphragm at opening:

$$V = 1150 - (12.5 \times 4) = 1100 \text{ kips}$$

Distribute shear proportionally to area or length:

$$V_u = \frac{1.4 \times 1100}{83.3 \times 12 \times 4.75} = 0.324 \text{ ksi}$$

This exceeds concrete shear strenth; therefore, add sufficient reinforcing steel in concrete fill to provide strength. In normal buildings when large force transfers pass through a diaphragm, the concrete will be made thicker.

Check local chord forces at opening.

In 16-ft 8-in length at top

$$V = \frac{16.7}{83.3} 1100 = 220 \text{ kips}$$

Assuming local point of inflection at center of opening, the moment and the local tensile force at the face of the opening are

$$M_{fo} \approx \frac{220 \times 25}{2} = 2750 \text{ ft-kips}$$

$$T_{fo} \approx \frac{2750}{16.7} = 165 \text{ kips}$$

If resisted by reinforcing steel in concrete fill

$$T = 1.4 \times 165 = 230 \text{ kips}$$

$$A_r = \frac{230}{0.9 \times 60} = 4.27 \text{ in}^2$$

Use 7#7 bars with $A_r = 4.20 \text{ in}^2$.

Collectors at opening parallel to walls:

$$F \approx \frac{1100}{100} 8.3 = 91.3 \text{ kips}$$

$$A_r = \frac{1.4 \times 91.3}{0.9 \times 60} = 2.37 \text{ in}^2$$

Use 4#7 bars with $A_r = 2.40 \text{ in}^2$.

Force in collector at B is 1150/3 = 383 kips.

Drag at wall above is 1000/3 = 333 kips.

The results are summarized in Fig. 5.18. Chord forces shown (e.g., 433 kips at the bottom corner of the right-hand-side shear wall) must be designed into floor framing in addition to gravity loads.

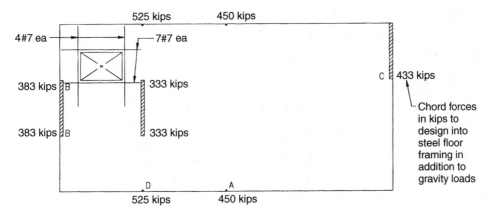

Figure 5.18 Chord forces.

5.7 Composite Systems for Retrofit

5.7.1 Seismic retrofit

There is an increasing effort in recent years to retrofit existing structures for improved performance, especially for improved response for lateral forces. This trend is most prevalent in regions of high seismicity where building owners desire to strengthen their buildings for improved performance in future earthquakes. Very significant changes have occurred in seismic design criteria over the past 20 years in the United States, and many buildings built before the early 1970s may be quite vulnerable to severe damage and even partial or complete collapse in a significant earthquake. Some jurisdictions have enacted regulations requiring retrofit of buildings with certain framing systems for compliance with specified standards. Unreinforced masonry bearing wall buildings were the initial target. Other programs can be expected for unreinforced masonry infill buildings and certain types of reinforced concrete buildings, specifically those relying on nonductile moment-resisting frames for lateral resistance.

Composite systems are frequently the result of these retrofits of the lateral-force-resisting structure. Steel diagonal bracing is often added to the masonry or concrete building, and it is necessary for the design to achieve a satisfactory level of performance of this mix of materials. One of the major factors influencing the selection of these composite systems is economy: The new steel diagonals and any steel shapes added to the existing beams or columns often must provide an economically viable solution. The added steel members are relatively light. Thus a retrofit scheme using steel members has minimal impact on the foundations and minimizes foundation reconstruction, which can be extremely expensive.

Criteria for retrofit of the lateral force system can vary considerably. Some mandatory programs have prescriptive requirements that must be met. Many retrofits are voluntary by the owner, and the criteria must be developed by the

Figure 5.19 University Hall at the University of California at Berkeley. (© *Jane Lidz 1992 for Degenkolb Engineers.*)

engineer for the owner's approval. The criteria must include providing ductile members, connections, and details as much as resisting a specific lateral force criteria. Considerable professional engineering judgment by the design engineer is always a necessary ingredient to a successful seismic retrofit solution.

Many examples could be shown to illustrate this type of construction. Figure 5.19 shows University Hall at the University of California at Berkeley, which was retrofitted in the early 1990s. The original building was completely of reinforced concrete construction. The building was constructed in the 1950s. There were a few nominal interior shear walls in the transverse direction, but the rest of the lateral force depended on the exterior concrete frames consisting of stiff 7-ft-deep (2.1-m) spandrel beams and 24-in-square (0.61-m) columns. Inelastic performance under strong ground shaking of the original building would be absorbed by the short stiff columns which, when they fail, could lead to collapse. The strengthening solution consisted of stiffening the partially exposed basement and first floor with concrete shear walls and adding the steel braced frame seen in Fig. 5.19. The analysis for this design modeled both the original concrete frame and the new steel bracing, and determined that after cracking reduced the high initial stiffness of the concrete frame, the steel bracing was stiff and strong enough to protect the concrete frame from excessive deformation and distress. The steel bracing was designed with ductile, full-strength connections. The steel columns of the new bracing were designed to support tributary building loads as a redundant system. As the concrete columns separated from the new bracing, anchored steel plates were added to provide partial confinement of the nominally tied columns.

Many other examples of this type of composite construction could be cited. In all cases, it requires an analysis which allows cracking of the concrete or masonry structure to allow the generally more flexible steel bracing system to function. The analysis must be reviewed to ensure that the cracking will not be detrimental to the performance of the structure under severe lateral loads. If the review indicates that cracking will be excessive, then another solution is usually required that will provide a stiffer retrofit solution. It is very important that the designer considers the composite response of such retrofit schemes to ensure their compatibility and success.

5.7.2 Retrofit for vertical loads

When a steel column needs to be strengthened for additional vertical load-carrying capacity, two techniques are generally available: an all-steel retrofit or a composite retrofit. The all-steel retrofit involves welding steel plates either to the flange faces or across the tips of the flanges to form a box. In either case, since the existing column is heavily loaded, the column temperature during the welding operation must be carefully controlled.

The other option is to provide a concrete encasement of the existing steel column as shown in Fig. 5.20. A composite retrofit increases the dead load on the foundation, and hence the foundation capacity must be checked. The design capacity of the retrofitted column is determined by the LRFD procedure for composite columns. The construction execution involves the removal of the existing fireproofing, placement of shear studs on the flanges and the web of the steel column, placement of the longitudinal bars and ties, and finally concrete placement. Two conditions need careful detailing. When the longitudinal column bars are always in compression, weldable reinforcing bars can be welded to the base plate provided the base plate and the grout beneath it can transmit the load. If the load transmission through the plate is not possible or if the longitudinal reinforcing bars are in tension and the anchor bolt

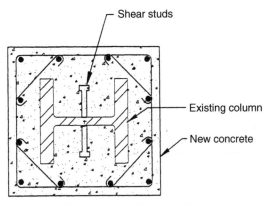

Figure 5.20   Cross section of the retrofitted column.

capacity is inadequate, it is preferable to drill and dowel the reinforcing bars into the existing foundation for the tension capacity. The other consideration is the differential axial shortening due to the shrinkage and creep of concrete. This applies primarily to tall structures or structures where only a few columns are being retrofitted. Detailed calculations are required to obtain the cumulative differential axial shortening over the height of the building in the composite retrofitted columns versus the all-steel unretrofitted columns.

5.7.3   Retrofit for wind loads

The science of wind engineering has been developed since the failure of the first Tacoma Narrows bridge in 1940. Newly acquired wind-load data led to

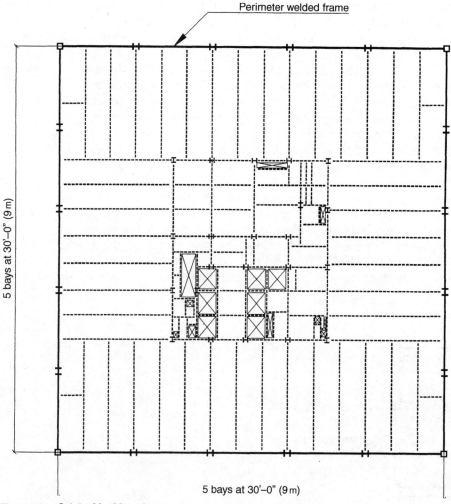

Figure 5.21   Original building frame.

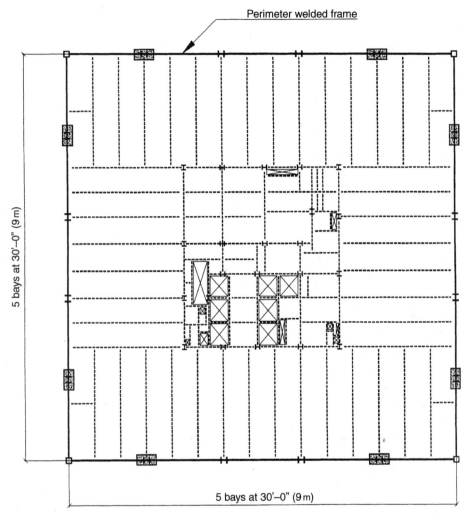

Figure 5.22 Composite retrofit.

increases in the wind loads specified in most building codes. Moreover, the wind effects such as building sway and motion perception are better understood. Sway guidelines are given in the Canadian code[G64A] and motion perception limits in the ISO standards.[G44A] Consequently, some older buildings have to be retrofitted for higher wind loads, sway, or perception of motion.

The use of a composite retrofit fulfills the basic requirements. Composite retrofit of columns gives higher axial and bending capacity required for higher wind loads. The additional stiffness due to composite action reduces the sway and lowers the fundamental period of the building. Furthermore, the additional mass and damping reduce the motion perception.

An example of a wind-load retrofit of an existing 47-story steel-framed

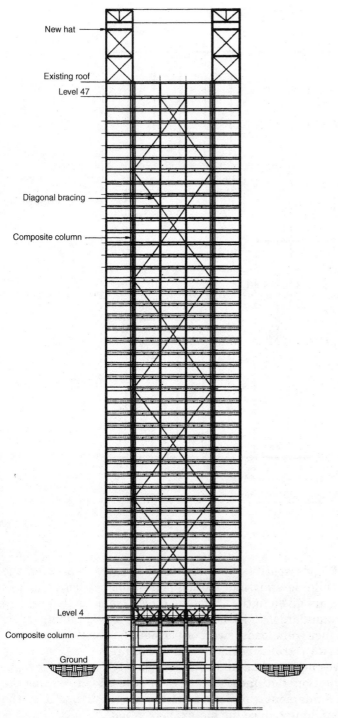

Figure 5.23   Elevation of the retrofitted building.

building built in 1971 is described below. The original plan of the building is shown in Fig. 5.21. The lateral resistance of the original building was provided by welding the exterior spandrel girders to the exterior columns which are spaced at 30 ft (9 m) on centers. The original structure was designed for strength only based on the existing code wind loads of 20 lb/ft^2 (1.0 kPa) up to 60-ft (18-m) height, and 30 lb/ft^2 (1.5 kPa) above that level. The building was purchased in 1994 by a major corporation. It was decided to retrofit the building for the corporate requirements and for the latest building code provisions and industry practice on sway and motion perception.

Six schemes were examined for the structural retrofit of the building. The final selected system was to provide a total of eight composite supercolumns with nine-story tall diagonal bracing as shown in Figs. 5.22 and 5.23. At the lower levels, all exterior columns from the mat foundation at the fourth basement level to the fourth floor in the tower were made composite as shown in Fig. 5.23. The composite frame at these levels transferred the wind load down to the foundation. Expansive cement was used in the columns to minimize shrinkage, and the diagonals were loose bolted until the supercolumns were topped out. The composite retrofit proved to be the most economical of all the alternates studied and also had the fewest construction problems.

6

Design of Joints

6.1 Basic Considerations

Connections or joints are potentially the most critical and possibly the least understood parts of the structural frame. The main role of connections is to transfer forces between members and to maintain the integrity of the structure under the applied loads. Usually several elements of the structure meet at a connection, and the combination results in a complex behavior. Portions of a connection may be stressed beyond the elastic range, and redistribution of forces may occur even at service load levels. In these cases, flexibility and ductility are necessary to maintain a satisfactory joint performance. Many structural failures occur not because of any shortcomings in the analysis or because of inadequate member design, but rather because of inattention to joint behavior and design. Even when the member forces are accurately known, often they are not fully understood. Most current codes and specifications, particularly those based on the probabilistic limit states design approach, recognize connections as the potential weak links in the structure and therefore require a larger margin of safety for connections than for members.

Current state of practice for design of composite connections of any type must of necessity rely heavily on judgment of the individual design engineer and on the available information for structural steel[G24,G87] and reinforced concrete[G75,G77] connections. Research directly addressing composite connections in the United States has been meager; only limited investigations have been performed. Further, even when research data are available for a certain type of connection, the geometry and size range needed for practical applications often fall well outside the range of test parameters.

The necessary prerequisites of a successful connection design are the knowledge of structural mechanics, ability to formulate a rational equilibrium model, intuition in visualizing and predicting the flow of forces through the joint, and careful identification of potential failure modes. After understanding the potential joint behavior the designer must proportion the connection elements accordingly, keeping in mind the practical needs of fabrication and construction.

Generally, the following items must be checked in the design of each joint:

Flexure

Shear

Bearing

Joint confinement

Anchorage of reinforcement

Shear-transfer devices

6.1.1 General design criteria

All composite connections must meet a variety of design and performance criteria outlined below.

Strength. Composite joints must be designed for the interaction of multidirectional forces which the members transfer to the joint including axial loads, bending, shear, and torsion. These forces are a consequence of the effects of externally applied loads as well as those resulting from creep, shrinkage, temperature changes, and settlements. All load combinations should be considered that could produce the most severe force distribution at the joint including the effects of member eccentricities. Connection design should distinguish between cases of lateral loading due to wind and those due to seismic forces. Under wind loading, the structural response is assumed to remain essentially elastic. For seismic loading, design is based on the premise that under severe earthquakes the structure, particularly at connections, will undergo inelastic cyclic loading. For seismic loading and other cases where inelastic response is envisioned, the connection should be designed to resist moments and shears associated with plastic hinging of adjacent members, where appropriate to the connection type.

Service. Composite connections must also be proportioned to assure satisfactory behavior under service loads. The designer must make certain that joint rotation in moment connections at service loads does not result in unacceptable deflections or drift that could cause cracking or other distress in one or more building elements.

Ductility. The ability of a connection to accommodate large deformations while maintaining load without failure must be checked. It is particularly important in joints subjected to cyclic inelastic deformations such as those caused by earthquakes. Ductility is achieved by proportioning connection elements for steel yielding prior to concrete failure.

Construction. Composite joints should allow for simple, problem-free fabrication and rapid construction. This point is specially important for composite connections containing concrete and large amounts of reinforcing steel or other hardware.

In sizing structural elements, minimum acceptable dimensions may not produce the best solution. Elements should be proportioned in such a way that congestion is kept to a minimum, the reinforcing steel is properly anchored, and concrete can be placed with relative ease. Large-scale connection details should be shown on the engineering drawings. Clearances and tolerances must be considered and provisions should be made for adjustments and easy access in the field.

Beam and brace widths should be different in the two orthogonal directions to avoid reinforcing-steel interference. Furthermore, beams should be narrower or wider than the columns to allow the beam bars to pass the column bars. The use of connection stubs is recommended wherever practical for proper anchorage of reinforcing bars. Finally, superplasticizers should be used in concrete to facilitate placement and compaction whenever appropriate.

6.1.2 General design procedure

The following steps outline a procedure applicable to the design of composite connections:

1. Establish equilibrium model.
2. Identify potential failure modes.
3. Check design strength (including flexure, shear, shear friction, and bearing).
4. Design joint reinforcement (including ties, stiffener plates, bearing plates, shear-transfer devices, and bar development length).
5. Check serviceability.
6. Draw connection to scale.

The list is a broad outline of potential factors that may be important. Depending on the particular type of structure, not all joint designs require consideration of each of these items.

6.1.3 Types of joints

Many of the most commonly used connections, including several types for which research has just recently been completed or is still ongoing, are discussed in the following sections. The connection types are listed below with a brief description of each. Detailed discussion and design examples are included in Secs. 6.2 through 6.7.

A recommended detail for the base plate connection of a composite column, that is, a column consisting of a concrete-encased steel shape, is described in

Sec. 6.2. A design example is included. Also discussed is a suggested detail for the base of a composite column in high seismic zones.

A detail for a composite column splice used in multistory buildings is described in Sec. 6.2.4.

The design of various types of beam-to-column connections that are commonly used in composite construction is covered in Secs. 6.3, 6.4, and 6.5. Included are standard double-angle web or framed beam web connections, single-plate shear connections or shear tabs, tee framing shear connections, moment-resisting connections of steel or composite beams to composite or concrete columns, standard moment-resisting steel or composite beams to steel wide-flange columns, semirigid composite beam connections, and stub girder connections.

The design and detailing of steel wide-flange link beams embedded in concrete walls is presented in Sec. 6.6. This type of connection couples shear walls or columns and shear walls in mid- and high-rise building construction.

Of the several other types of connections encountered in practice the following four are discussed in Sec. 6.7:

Transition composite columns which transfer loads between two different structural systems in a building where the upper floors have steel columns and the lower floors have either concrete or composite columns

Steel brace connections to composite concrete-encased steel H shape columns in braced cores of mid- or high-rise buildings

Steel brace connections to concrete-filled tube columns also used in mid- and high-rise buildings

Steel and composite column connections to composite floor slabs

6.2   Column Base and Splices

Three items are presented in this section. The first two pertain to the design of the base for a concrete-encased steel shape column, one subjected to wind or low to moderate seismic loads and the other to high seismic loads where a plastic hinge may form. The third item is a discussion of splices for composite columns.

6.2.1   Base design for wind or low seismic load[D74]

A base plate for the encased steel section of a composite column (Fig. 6.1) should normally have the minimum dimensions needed to accommodate the anchor bolts that hold the plate to the foundation during the erection phase. The base plate must not interfere with dowels coming up from the foundation to the splice with the longitudinal vertical bars of the composite column. A sufficient number of dowels must be provided to transmit column load in excess of the acceptable bearing load P_b on the foundation:

$$A_d F_{yd} \ge P_b$$

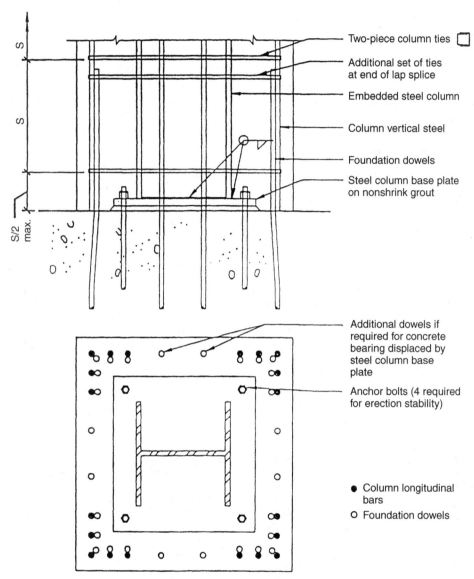

Figure 6.1   Composite column base plate.[D74]

where $P_b = \phi_c 0.85 f_c'(A_g - A_1)$

A_d = total cross-sectional area of dowels

A_g = total cross-sectional area of composite column

A_1 = area of base plate of encased column

f_c' = concrete strength of foundation

F_{yd} = yield stress of dowel bars

ϕ_c = 0.85; resistance factor for axially loaded composite columns

6.2.2   Column base design

Design the base plate of an 18×18-in (0.46×0.46-m) composite column with an encased W10 × 54 of $F_y = 50$ ksi (345 MPa), $f_c' = 8$ ksi (55 MPa), and 4#8 grade 60 longitudinal bars. Factored axial load $P_u = 1000$ kips (4.45 MN), $Kl = 31$ ft (9.4 m). Use $f_c' = 3$ ksi (21 MPa) for footing. Assume $(A_2/A_1)^{1/2} = 2$. See Fig. 6.2 for nomenclature. For base plate design procedures, refer to the second edition of the AISC LRFD Manual,[D95] pp. 11-54 to 11-64, and to the Steel Design Guide Series 6,[D74] pp. 27 to 28.

The base plate is designed for the portion of the factored axial load resisted by the W10×54.

$$b_f = 10.03 \text{ in}$$

$$d = 10.09 \text{ in}$$

$$t_f = 0.615 \text{ in}$$

$$A_s = 15.8 \text{ in}^2$$

$$F_{yr} = 60 \text{ ksi}$$

$$A_r = 4 \times 0.79 = 3.16 \text{ in}^2$$

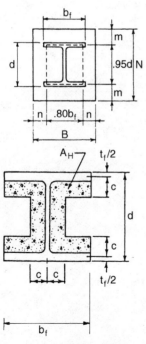

P_o = Factored load contributory to **area enclosed** by steel shape, kips

P_s = Factored axial load resisted by steel shape, kips

A_1 = Area of base plate, in^2

A_2 = Full cross–sectional area of concrete support, in^2

A_H = Area of H-shaped portion of base plate in light columns, in^2

F_y = Specified minimum yield stress of steel, ksi

f_c' = Specified compressive strength of concrete, ksi

t_p = Thickness of base plate, in

ϕ_c = Resistance factor for concrete = 0.6

ϕ_p = Resistance factor for base plate = 0.9

Figure 6.2 Nomenclature for design example.[D74]

Try base plate 12 × 12 in.

1. Compute axial load carried by W10×54 based on the contribution of W10×54 to the total column capacity

$$F_{my} = F_y + c_1 F_{yr} \frac{A_r}{A_s} + c_2 f_c' \frac{A_c}{A_s}$$

$$= 50 + \left(0.7 \times 60 \times \frac{3.16}{15.8}\right) + \frac{0.6 \times 8(18 \times 18 - 15.8 - 4 \times 0.79)}{15.8} = 151.1 \text{ ksi}$$

Portion of factored axial load resisted by W10×54 is

$$P_s = \frac{1000 \times 50}{151.1} = 330.9 \text{ kips}$$

2. Compute m and n

$$m = \frac{N_p - 0.95d}{2} = \frac{12 - 0.95 \times 10.09}{2} = 1.207$$

$$n = \frac{B_p - 0.8b_f}{2} = \frac{12 - 0.8 \times 10.03}{2} = 1.988 \qquad \text{governs}$$

3. Concrete bearing stress

$$\phi_c 0.85 f_c' \left(\frac{A_2}{A_1}\right)^{0.5} = 0.6 \times 0.85 \times 3 \times 2 = 3.06 \text{ ksi}$$

4. Check concrete bearing under base plate

$$\frac{P_s}{B_p N_p} = \frac{330.9}{12 \times 12} = 2.298 \text{ ksi} < 3.06 \qquad \text{O.K.}$$

5. Compute factored load corresponding to the area enclosed by W10×54

$$P_0 = \frac{P_s b_f d}{B_p N_p} = \frac{330.9 \times 10.03 \times 10.09}{12 \times 12} = 232.6 \text{ kips}$$

6. Compute area of H-shaped region

$$A_H = \frac{P_0}{0.6 \times 1.7 \times f_c'} = \frac{232.6}{0.6 \times 1.7 \times 3} = 76.0 \text{ in}^2$$

7. *Compute c*

$$A_H = d \times b_f - (d - t_f - 2c)(b_f - 2c)$$

$$76.0 = 10.09 \times 10.03 - (10.09 - 0.619 - 2c)(10.03 - 2c)$$

$$(9.47 - 2c)(10.03 - 2c) = 25.2$$

$$4c^2 - 39c + 69.8 = 0$$

$$c = \frac{39 - \sqrt{1521 - 1117}}{8} = 2.363 \text{ in}$$

8. *Compute base plate thickness.* Designating as A the larger of the parameters m and n,

$$t_p = A \times \left(\frac{2P_s}{0.9F_y B_p N_p} \right)^{1/2}$$

$$= 1.988 \times \left(\frac{2 \times 330.9}{0.9 \times 50 \times 12 \times 12} \right)^{1/2} = 0.635 \text{ in}$$

$$t_p = c \left(\frac{2P_o}{0.9F_y A_H} \right)^{1/2}$$

$$= 2.363 \times \left(\frac{2 \times 232.6}{0.9 \times 50 \times 76.0} \right)^{1/2} = 0.872 \text{ in}$$

Use $\frac{7}{8}$-in plate.

9. *Design dowels to foundation.* Allowable compression transfer by concrete:

$2\phi_c 0.85 f_c'$ (column area $-$ base plate area)

$$= 2 \times 0.6 \times 0.85 \times 3(18 \times 18 - 12 \times 12) = 551 \text{ kips}$$

Required compression transfer by concrete:

$$1000 - 330.9 = 669 \text{ kips} > 551 \text{ kips}$$

Dowels are required.
Required area of dowels:

$$A_d(\text{req'd}) = \frac{669 - 551}{0.85 \times 60} = 2.31 \text{ in}^2$$

$$A_d(\text{min}) = 0.005A_g = 0.005 \times 18 \times 18 = 1.62 \text{ in}^2 \qquad (\text{ACI 318-95, Chap. 15})$$

$$\text{Use 4\#7: } A_s = 4 \times 0.60 = 2.40 \text{ in}^2 > 2.31 \qquad \text{O.K.}$$

Embed dowels 22 bar diameters (for 3-ksi concrete) into foundation (ACI 318-95, Chap. 12):

$$22 \times 0.875 = 20 \text{ in}$$

Dowel projection into column = 30 bar diameters (ACI 318-95, Chap. 2):

$$30 \times 0.875 = 27 \text{ in}$$

6.2.3   Base design for high seismic load

Unless a composite column is designed and detailed as a true hinge or pin connection, which is a fairly difficult and impractical detail, it is very likely that a plastic hinge will form in the column under a severe seismic event. Inasmuch as such a plastic hinge can adversely affect the stability of the structure after numerous earthquake cycles, it is desirable to develop a detail that protects this critical zone of the column. Such a detail is proposed in Fig. 6.3.

The concept presented in Fig. 6.3 shows a steel jacket fillet welded to the top and bottom of a steel base plate. The jacket is cast into the foundation concrete to transmit shear and moment at the column base, leaving a void inside the jacket below the base plate except for such concrete as may enter the void through the open bottom of the jacket. Reinforcing dowels are welded to the four outside faces of the jacket inside the foundation concrete to help dissipate the shear and bearing forces. The steel jacket serves to confine the concrete at the vulnerable base zone and increase column ductility.

The embedded steel WF column and column vertical bars are cast into the floor slab and the concrete filling the steel jacket above the base plate. Anchor bolts are used to attach the base plate to the foundation and help carry vertical uplift forces as required. This detail has a large capacity to dissipate energy while protecting the critical column base zone from inelastic cyclic reversals of large earthquake motions.

6.2.4   Column splices

A typical detail for splicing an embedded steel H shape is shown in Fig. 6.4. The embedded steel H shape is normally spliced 3 ft (0.9 m) above the finish floor line using standard AISC column splice details. If wind controls the design and seismic forces are small, this connection is usually a compression splice depending on the size of the column and the forces it carries. For high seismic areas it is desirable that the splice connection develop the tensile capacity of the composite section.

The requirements for splicing vertical longitudinal reinforcing bars for composite columns should follow the rules applicable to reinforced concrete columns as specified in Chap. 12 of the ACI 318-95 Code.[D100] Two additional comments are needed for composite columns. First, additional vertical longitudinal restraining bars (LRFD Specification I2.1.b) should be used between the corners where the continuous load-carrying bars are located in composite

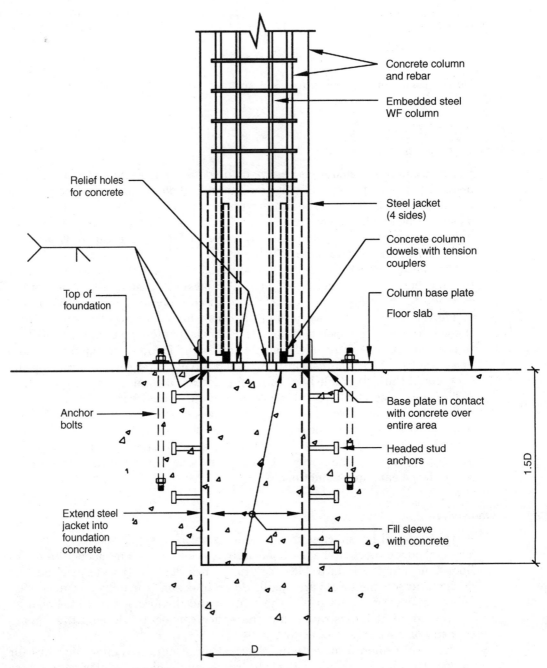

Figure 6.3 Base plate detail for high seismic zones.

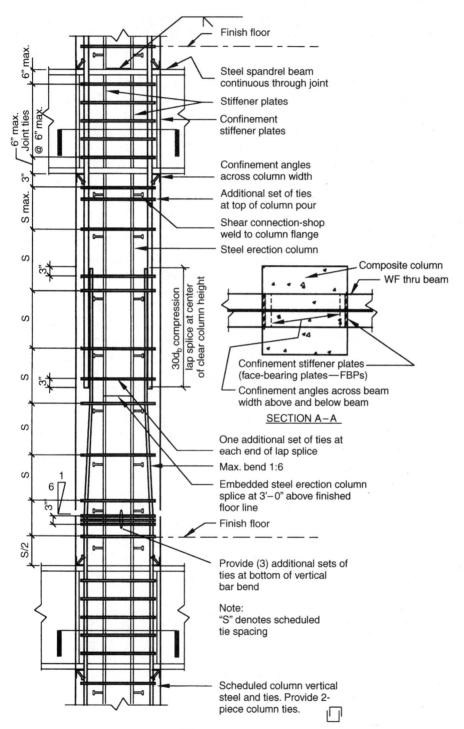

Finish floor

Steel spandrel beam continuous through joint

Stiffener plates

Confinement stiffener plates

Confinement angles across column width

Additional set of ties at top of column pour

Shear connection-shop weld to column flange

Steel erection column

Composite column
WF thru beam

Confinement stiffener plates (face-bearing plates—FBPs)

Confinement angles across beam width above and below beam

SECTION A–A

One additional set of ties at each end of lap splice

Max. bend 1:6

Embedded steel erection column splice at 3'–0" above finished floor line

Finish floor

Provide (3) additional sets of ties at bottom of vertical bar bend

Note:
"S" denotes scheduled tie spacing

Scheduled column vertical steel and ties. Provide 2-piece column ties.

6" max.
6" max.
Joint ties @ 6" max.
3"
S max.
S
S
S
S
S
3"
3"
3"
S/2
6
1

$30d_b$ compression lap splice at center of clear column height

Figure 6.4 Composite column splice.[D74]

frame construction. These bars usually cannot be continuous because of interruption with intersecting frame members at the floor line. They are often required to satisfy the spacing requirements for vertical longitudinal bars given in Sec. I2.1.b of the AISC LRFD specification.

Second, it is suggested to locate vertical bar splices in high-rise composite frame construction at the middle of the column clear height. This point is usually near the inflection point (zero moment) where the more economical compression lap splices or compression butt splices may be used. The more expensive tension lap or tension butt splices may be required if splices are made at the floor line. In high seismic areas, bars are always spliced at column midheight.

6.3   Beam-to-Column Shear Connections

Various types of beam-to-column shear connections that are used in modern composite construction are presented in this section. The behavior of a connection is characterized by its moment-rotation curve, which shows the moment as a function of the angle change between the beam and the column (Fig. 6.5). The stiffness of the connection is given by the slope of the moment-rotation curve. Connections are characterized as rigid (type FR—fully restrained) and semirigid or simple (type PR—partially restrained). The connection may be classified as either full-strength ($M > M_p$) or partial-strength ($M < M_p$) connection.

Shear connections of composite beams to steel columns are shown in Figs. 6.6 through 6.8. As the concrete slab is terminated short of the connection, it has no effect on the response to loading. In connections to composite columns, the concrete embedment restrains both the beam rotations and local buckling of the embedded steel elements. However, no guidelines are available at present for quantifying these restraints.

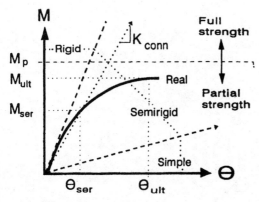

Figure 6.5 Connection behavior.[97]

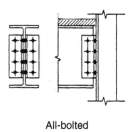

All-bolted

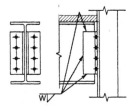

Bolted/welded, angles welded to supported beam

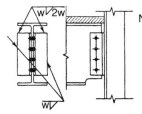

Note: (1) Weld returns on
top of angles per
LRFD Specification
Section J2.2b.
(2) Concrete slab
not shown
in cross sections.

Bolted/welded, angles welded to support

Figure 6.6   Double-angle web connection.[G79]

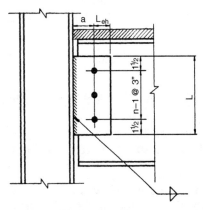

Minimum plate thickness	
n	$t_{p\,min}$, in
2–5	1/4
6–7	5/16
8	3/8
9	7/16

Figure 6.7   Single-plate shear connection.[G79]

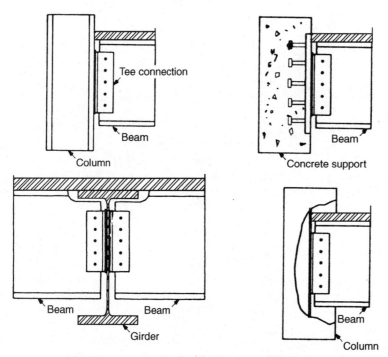

Figure 6.8 Typical applications of tee connections.[G56]

6.3.1 Double-angle connections

One of the simplest and most common types of beam-to-column connections is the double-angle web connection, also referred to as the framed beam connection (Fig. 6.6).[D95] It is commonly designed as a simple connection—that is, the connection restraint is ignored. It is assumed that under gravity loads the ends of the beams are connected for shear only and are completely free to rotate. Three additional conditions should be observed in the design of double-angle connections:

1. The connections and connected members should be adequate to carry the factored gravity loads as simple beams.

2. The connections and connected members should be adequate to resist the factored lateral loads.

3. The connections should have sufficient inelastic rotation capacity to avoid overloading fasteners or welds under combined factored gravity and lateral loading.

In the vast majority of applications, any restraint provided by the composite steel deck slab or its reinforcement is ignored in the design. The design of double-angle web connections is covered in the AISC Manual.[D95]

6.3.2 Single-plate connections

One connection that has gained considerable popularity in recent years is the single-plate shear connection often referred to as the shear tab.[G55] Used primarily to transfer beam-end reaction to the supporting element, it is efficient and easy to fabricate. The connection consists of a plate shop welded to the supporting element at one edge and field bolted to the beam web. Figure 6.7 shows a typical application of a single-plate shear connection. A design procedure for the shear tab is presented in this subsection and illustrated with a design example in Sec. 6.3.3.

The AISC LRFD specification[D91] has the following provision for simple shear connections:

> Except as otherwise indicated in the design documents, connections of beams, girders or trusses shall be designed as flexible, and are permitted to be proportioned for the reaction shears only. Flexible beam connections shall accommodate end rotations of unrestrained (simple) beams. To accomplish this, some inelastic but self-limiting deformation in the connection is permitted.

Single-plate connections not only should have sufficient strength to transfer the end shear reaction of the beam but should also have enough rotation capacity to accommodate the end rotation demand of a simply supported beam. In addition, the connection should be sufficiently flexible so that beam end moments become negligible. Thus, like any shear connection, single-plate shear connections should be designed to satisfy the dual criteria of shear strength and rotational flexibility and ductility.

Limit states. The following limit states are associated with the single-plate framing connections:

Shear failure of bolts

Yielding of gross area of plate

Fracture of net area of plate

Fracture of welds

Bearing failure of beam web or plate

Each of these limit states is addressed in the following design procedure.

Design procedure. Analyses of experimental results and information available on the actual behavior of shear connections are the basis for the design procedure. The single-plate framing connections covered by these procedures consist of a plate bolted to a beam web and welded to a support on one edge of the plate.

In design of a single-plate framing connection, the following requirements should be satisfied:

1. The connection should have only one vertical row of bolts and the number of bolts should be not less than two or more than nine.

2. Bolt spacing should be equal to 3 in (76 mm).

3. Edge distances should be equal to or greater than $1.5d_b$.

4. The distance from bolt to weld line should be equal to 3 in.

5. Material of the shear plate should be A36 steel to facilitate yielding.

6. Attachment should be fillet welds made with E70XX or E60XX electrodes.

7. Thickness of the single plate should be less than or equal to $d_b/2 + g$.

8. The ratio of l_p/a_{bw} of the plate should be greater than or equal to 2 to prevent local buckling of the plate.

9. ASTM A325 and A490 bolts may be used.

In the above a_{bw} = distance from bolt line to weld line
$\quad\quad\quad\quad\quad d_b$ = bolt diameter
$\quad\quad\quad\quad\quad g$ = $\frac{1}{16}$ in (1.6 mm)
$\quad\quad\quad\quad\quad l_p$ = plate length parallel with bolt and weld lines

The design procedure is valid for composite and noncomposite beams, standard or short slotted holes fully tightened or snug-tight bolts, and for all grades of beam steel and all loadings.

Bolts are designed for the combined effects of direct shear and a moment due to the eccentricity e_b of the reaction from the bolt line. The eccentricity e_b for single-plate connections covered by these procedures can be assumed to be equal to 3 in (76 mm), which is the distance from bolt line to weld line. The value is conservative when the single plate is welded to a rigid support. The value is more realistic when the supporting member is a relatively flexible element.

More realistic values for e_b can be calculated from Eqs. (6.1) and (6.2):
If the single plate is welded to a rotationally rigid element, e_b is obtained from

$$e_b = [(n_b - 1)c] - a_{bw} \tag{6.1}$$

where n_b = number of bolts
$\quad\quad\quad c$ = 1.0 in
$\quad\quad\quad e_b$ = eccentricity, in

If the single plate is welded to a rotationally flexible element, e_b is the larger value obtained from Eqs. (6.1) and (6.2):

$$e_b = a_{bw} \tag{6.2}$$

By using methods outlined in Table 8-18 of the AISC LRFD Manual, the bolts can be designed for the combined effects of shear V and moment equal to Ve_b.

Design of plate. The plate is designed to yield under the effect of direct shear. This is done to encourage timely yielding of the plate and release of beam end moment. Actually the plate yields under the combined effects of a large shear and a relatively small bending moment.

The proposed design equation is

$$V_p = \phi 0.6 F_y l_p t_p$$

where V_p = vertical shear capacity of connection plate
ϕ = 0.90
t_p = thickness of the connection plate

The plate must be made of A36 steel to facilitate an early yielding of the plate. To facilitate bearing yielding of the bolt holes, it is recommended that the thickness of the plate be equal to or less than $0.5d_b + g$, where $g = \frac{1}{16}$ in (1.6 mm).

To avoid edge failures, it is recommended that the horizontal and vertical edge distances be equal to or greater than $1.5d_b$. It is also recommended that the vertical edge distance should not be less than 1.5 in (38 mm) regardless of the bolt diameter. In the tests that were the basis of the design procedure, the bolt spacing was equal to 3 in (76 mm) and the maximum number of bolts was nine. Therefore, until more research is conducted on different bolt spacings and larger number of bolts, it is recommended that the proposed design procedure be used only with a bolt spacing of 3 in (76 mm) and the number of bolts less than or equal to nine.

Another failure mode that needs to be considered is local buckling of the bottom portion of the single plate. To avoid this failure mode, it is recommended that l_p/t_p be less than 64 for A36 steel single plates used in these connections.

In addition to plate yielding, bearing yielding, and edge distance deformations, another possible failure mode of the plate is shear fracture of the net section. Research indicated that shear fracture of the net section occurs along a vertical plane close to the edge of the bolt holes rather than along the bolt centerline plane. The following equation can be used to predict the shear capacity of the net section:

$$R_{ns} = \phi t_p [l_p - 0.5 n_b (d_b + g)] 0.6 F_u$$

where $\phi = 0.75$.

Design of bolts. Bolts are designed to resist combined effects of the applied shear force and bending moment that exist along the bolt line. The shear force is equal to the reaction of the beam. The moment can be obtained from

$$M_b = V e_b$$

The value of the eccentricity e_b is given by Eqs. (6.1) and (6.2). To design bolts for the combined effects of shear and moment, the methods given in the AISC LRFD Manual can be used.

Design of welds. The welds can be designed for the combined effects of shear and bending moment. The shear force V is equal to the beam reaction and the bending moment is given by

$$M_w = Ve_w$$

The value of the eccentricity e_w is given by the larger value obtained from

$$e_w = n_b c \quad \text{and} \quad e_w = a_{bw}$$

where n_b is the number of bolts, $c = 1.0$ in, and a_{bw} is the distance from the bolt line to the weld line in inches. However, to avoid a brittle failure of welds, it is recommended that the welds be designed to develop the strength of the plate. In shear tab connections, bolts, plate, and welds are subjected to a shear force and a moment. To ensure that the plate yields before the welds, the shear-moment interaction curve of the plate should lie inside the shear-moment interaction curve for the welds. The M-V interaction curve for rectangular cross sections such as shear tabs can be approximated by the equation of a circle given by

$$\left(\frac{V}{V_{yp}}\right)^2 + \left(\frac{M}{M_{pp}}\right)^2 = 1.0$$

where $V_{yp} = F_y t_p l_p$, shear yield strength of the plate
$M_{pp} = F_y t_p l_p^2/4$, plastic moment capacity of the plate
$M = Ve_w$, applied moment
t_p = plate thickness

The above interaction equation for welds is established with values given in Tables 8-38 through 8-45 of the AISC LRFD Manual.[G87] The values corresponding to $k = 0$ should be used. With this procedure, one can assume an eccentricity, calculate V and M, and plot the M-V interaction curve for weld failure. The curve can be approximated conservatively by a circle.

To ensure that the failure surface for the weld lines is greater than the failure surface for the plate, the following should be satisfied:

$$\left(\frac{V}{V_{yw}}\right)^2 + \left(\frac{M}{M_{pw}}\right)^2 > \left(\frac{V}{V_{yp}}\right)^2 + \left(\frac{M}{M_{pp}}\right)^2$$

where $V_{yw} = 2(0.5F_{EXX})0.707D_w l_w$, shear yield strength of a weld
$M_{pw} = 2(0.5F_{EXX})0.707D_w l_w^2/4$, plastic moment capacity of weld throat section
D_w = fillet weld size
l_w = weld length
F_{EXX} = yield strength of welds

The value of D_w/t_p is limited by

$$\frac{D_w}{t_p} > \frac{1.41F_y}{F_{EXX}}$$

This limit will ensure that the moment-shear interaction curve for the weld is greater than the interaction curve for the plate. Using F_y and F_{EXX} equal to 36 and 70 ksi, respectively,

$$D_w > 0.75t_p$$

The above limitation was derived for A36 steel and E70 electrodes. The general form of the above limit can be used even if material properties differ slightly. In treating single plates with standard holes, derivations similar to the above procedure were carried out and the resulting relationships were the same.

The preceding discussion suggests that in single-plate shear connections with standard or short slotted holes, two weld lines with a weld size equal to $0.75t_p$, one on each side of the plate, are necessary to ensure the desirable plate failure before weld failure. If this rule is satisfied, the design results in a matching weld where plate yielding occurs before widespread yielding of the weld.

Design of the beam web. Beam webs should be designed or checked for transfer of shear. Particular attention should be paid to coped beams.

6.3.3 Single-plate connection design

Design a shear tab that connects a girder to the flange of a column with the following properties:

Beam section: W24×117, $t_w = 0.550$ in (14 mm), A36 steel

Reaction: 50 kips (222 kN) service dead load and 40 kips (178 kN) service live load

Bolts: $\frac{7}{8}$ in (22 mm), A325-N, with 3-in (76-mm) spacing

Holes: standard round

Welds: E70XX fillet welds

Use Vol. II of the AISC LRFD Manual.[G87] From Table 8-11, the design shear strength of one bolt is $r_v = 21.6$ kips.

1. Calculate number of bolts

Shear reaction = $1.2D + 1.6L = 1.2 \times 50 + 1.6 \times 40 = 124$ kips

Assume $M = 0$; then

$$n_b = \frac{R}{r_v} = \frac{124}{21.6} = 5.74 \qquad \text{Try 6 bolts}$$

Check moment at the bolt line using Table 8-18. The supporting column flange can be considered a rigid support. Therefore, from Eq. (6.1),

$$e_b = n_b - 1 - a_{bw} = 6 - 1 - 3 = 2.0\ in = e_x$$

$$C = 5.45$$

$$r = C \times r_v = 5.45 \times 21.6 = 117.7\ kips < 124\ kips \qquad N.G.$$

where r is the design strength of a bolt group. Try seven bolts:

$$e_b = 7 - 1 - 3 = 3.0\ in \qquad thus\ C = 6.06$$

$$r = 6.06 \times 21.6 = 130.9\ kips > 124\ kips \qquad O.K.$$

Use seven bolts.

   2. Calculate plate thickness required to prevent shear fracture on the net section

$$l_p = 3n_b = 3 \times 7 = 21\ in$$

$$R_{ns} = \phi(0.6F_u)[l_p - n_b(d_b + 0.125)]t_p$$

hence

$$t_p \geq \frac{124}{0.75 \times 0.6 \times 58[21 - 7(0.875 + 0.125)]} = 0.34\ in$$

Try $\tfrac{3}{8}$-in plate. Check plate thickness limit:

$$t_p \leq 0.5\ d_b + g = 0.5 \times 0.875 + 0.0625 = 0.50\ in \qquad O.K.$$

$$t_p > \frac{l_p}{64} = \frac{21}{64} = 0.33\ in \qquad O.K.$$

Check yield capacity of gross section of the plate:

$$R_0 = \phi(0.6F_y)l_p t_p = 0.9 \times 0.6 \times 36 \times 21 \times 0.375 = 153.1\ kips > 124 \qquad O.K.$$

Check plate bearing capacity R_{br}:

$$R_{br} = C\phi(2.4F_u t_p d_b) = 6.06 \times 0.75 \times 2.4 \times 58 \times 0.375 \times 0.875$$

$$= 208\ kips > 124\ kips \qquad O.K.$$

Beam web is thicker than the plate, so there is no need to check bearing on the beam web.
Use $\tfrac{3}{8}$-in shear tab plate.

   3. Calculate fillet weld size D_w to develop strength of plate

Use $D_w = 0.75t_p = 0.75 \times 0.375 = 0.28$ in
Use weld size $\frac{5}{16}$ in.

   4. *Since beam is not coped, there is no need to check block shear failure of the beam web*

6.3.4 Tee connections

Tee connections listed in the LRFD AISC Manual[G87] are used in steel structures as simple connections. Published information on their behavior and design is limited, and none is available for structures with composite members. Typical applications of tee connections are shown in Fig. 6.8. The fasteners in tee connections can be either welds or bolts as illustrated in Fig. 6.9. Based on interviews with steel fabricators, it appears that type A is the most popular and efficient one with types C, D, and B following in the order of their popularity. This section is concerned with the design of tee connections of type A in which the tee section is bolted to the beam web and welded to the column support.[G56,G61]

   As for any shear connection, tee connections should satisfy the dual criteria of shear strength and rotational ductility. The connection should have enough shear strength to transfer the reaction of the beam. In addition, it should be flexible and ductile enough to permit end rotation and thus to prevent the

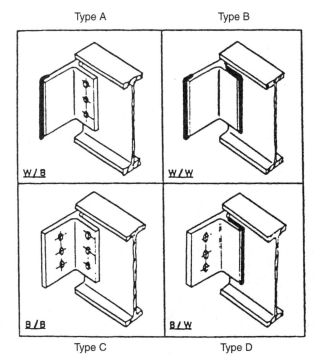

Figure 6.9   Types of tee connections.[G56]

development of any significant moment in the connection. Since relatively large rotations in the order of 0.03 radian are expected to develop at the ends of simply supported beams when a plastic hinge forms at midspan, the connections should have sufficient rotational ductility to accommodate the large rotations without fracture.

When the tee is welded to the support, adequate flexibility must be provided in the connection. As illustrated in Fig. 6.9, welds are placed along the toes of the tee flange with a return at the top as required by the LRFD specification.[D91] Welding across the entire top should be avoided, as it would inhibit flexibility and therefore the necessary end rotation of the connection.

Limit states.   The failure modes that have been observed in tests are listed below in the order of preference in design and are illustrated in Fig. 6.10. The most favorable limit states are (*a*) and (*e*), since they correspond to yielding of steel, which is ductile and reliable. Limit states (*c*) and (*d*) are the least desirable, since they are associated with fracture, which is generally brittle and less reliable than yielding. The order of decreasing preference is as follows:

Shear yielding of gross area of stem

Yielding of tee flange

Bearing yielding of beam web as well as tee stem

Shear fracture of net area of stem

Fracture of bolts connecting tee stem to beam web

Fracture of welds connecting tee flange to support

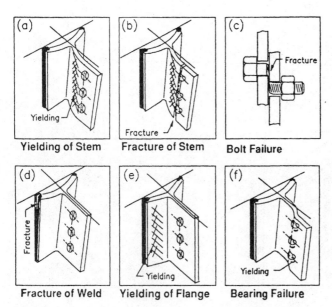

Figure 6.10   Typical failure modes of tee connections.[G56]

The tee connections for composite structures are designed and built in exactly the same way as for steel structures.

The design strength of bolts, welds, and connected elements must equal or exceed the required strength R_u:

$$\phi R_n \geq R_u$$

Design guidelines that assure that the particular limit state does not occur prematurely are given below for the six limit states.

Shear yielding of gross area of tee stem. The stem of the tee in tee connections is subjected to shear and a relatively small bending moment. In formulation of the proposed design equations only the shear force is considered and the effects of the bending moment are neglected. The tests reported in Ref. G61 have supported this assumption. The nominal strength defining this limit state is

$$R_n = 0.60 l_t t_{st} F_y$$

where l_t is the length of the tee and t_{st} is the thickness of the stem.

Yielding of tee flange. If the thickness of the tee flange is less than the thickness of the stem, the flange will experience considerable yielding. Particularly in built-up tees if the thickness of the flange is less than half the thickness of the stem, this limit state can be reached before the limit state of shear yielding of the tee stem. However, in tees produced by splitting hot-rolled wide-flange shapes this limit state is not likely to govern, since the flange is thicker than the stem.

This limit state is defined by

$$R_n = 1.2 l_t t_f F_y$$

where t_f is the thickness of the flange of the tee.

Bearing failure of tee stem or beam web. Research indicates that a limited amount of yielding in the bolt holes due to bolt bearing can be beneficial in reducing rotational stiffness of the connection. On the other hand, large bearing deformations can result in shear fracture of the net area of the connection.

To avoid exceeding this limit state, it is recommended to follow the established rule for horizontal and vertical edge distance of at least 1.5 times the bolt diameter. Bolt spacing should satisfy requirements of the AISC LRFD specification.[D91] In the absence of sufficient research data for other spacing, it is recommended to keep the bolt spacing at 3 in (76 mm).

Shear fracture of net area of tee stem. This limit state is reached when the critical net section of the tee stem fractures in shear. Research[G56,G61] clearly indicates that the critical net section in shear is located close to the edge of bolt holes rather than along their centerline. The effective net area in shear is more realistically calculated by averaging the net area along the bolt centerline and the gross area of the tee stem. The following equation defines this limit state based on the effective net area in shear:

$$R_n = 0.60A_nF_u$$

where

$$A_n = \{l_t - [0.5n_b(d_b + g)]\}t_{st}$$

n_b is the number of bolts, d_b is the diameter of the bolt, and g is equal to $\frac{1}{16}$ in. The numerical factor 0.5 in A_n reflects the averaging of net and gross areas of the stem to obtain the effective net area in shear as defined above.

The AISC LRFD specification[D91] requirements for standard bolt holes yield the following equation for calculating the net area in shear:

$$A_n = \{l_t - [n_b(d_b + g)]\}t_{st}$$

It results in a more conservative design, with fracture of the net area normally governing the strength of the connection.

If the beam is coped, block shear rupture of the beam web should also be considered in accordance with Tables 8-47 and 8-48 in the AISC LRFD Manual.[G87]

Shear failure of bolts. Bolts should be designed for a direct shear equal to the reaction of the beam. The eccentricity e_b for tee connections that have been studied is negligible, especially when the supporting member is a rigid element such as a nonrotating column flange or an embedded plate. In the absence of experimental data, it is suggested that for rotationally flexible supports a point of inflection is assumed at the weld line and the bolts are designed for direct shear and a bending moment equal to the shear force multiplied by distance a_{bw} between the bolt and weld lines. For rotationally rigid supports, the eccentricity e_b can be taken as

$$e_b = 0$$

and for rotationally flexible supports as

$$e_b = a_{bw}$$

By using Table 9-10 of the AISC LRFD Manual[G87] the bolts are designed for the combined effects of shear R_u and moment equal to $R_u e_b$.

Weld failure. The welds connecting the tee to the support must be designed for the combined effects of direct shear and the moment due to the eccentricity e_w of the reaction from the weld line. The eccentricity e_w is conservatively considered equal to the distance between bolt and weld lines:

$$e_w = a_{bw}$$

By using Table 8-38 of the AISC LRFD Manual,[G87] fillet welds are designed for the combined effects of shear R_u and moment equal to $R_u e_w$.

Design Procedure. The following design guidelines are suggested regarding the tees, bolts, and welds for tee connections. The procedure is applicable to standard and short slotted but not to oversized and long slotted bolt holes.

The material of the tee should be A36 steel. The ratio of l_t/a_{bw} of the tee stem should be more than 2. To ensure flexibility of the connection, the $b_f/2t_f$ ratio of the tee flange should be more than 6.5. The ratio of l_t/b_f of the tee should not exceed 3.5, and to ensure ductile behavior of the tee stem, the ratio $(t_{st}/d_b)/(t_f/t_{st})$ of about $\frac{1}{4}$ is preferred.

ASTM A325 or A490 bolts may be used. Fully tightened as well as snug-tight bolts are permitted, but snug-tight bolts are preferred. If for erection purposes some bolts need to be tightened, one or two bolts at the bottom of connection can be tightened and the rest left snug-tight. The bolts should be used in only one vertical row. Standard or short slotted punched or drilled holes are permitted. The number of bolts should not be more than nine or less than two. Vertical spacing between the bolts should be equal to 3 in (76 mm).

Welds should be fillet welds made with E70XX or E60XX electrodes. The top of the fillet welds should be returned a distance equal to 2 times the weld size. If the tee is welded to a column flange, it is recommended that the thickness t_f of the tee flange be smaller than thickness t_{fc} of the column flange.

The following steps result in an orderly design procedure for tee connections:

1. Select the type of bolts and calculate the number of bolts assuming no eccentricity

$$n_b = \frac{R_u}{A_b F_{uv}}$$

If the support is rotationally flexible, check the bolt group for combined effects of shear R_u and moment $R_u e_b$ using Table 9-10 of the AISC LRFD Manual,[G87] where e_b is taken as the distance from the bolt line to the weld line.

2. Calculate the required gross area of the tee stem

$$A_g = \frac{R_u}{0.60F_y}$$

3. Use A36 steel and select a tee to satisfy the following requirements

a. $b_f/2t_f$ of the tee ≥ 6.5
b. $d_b/t_{st} \geq 2.0$
c. l_h and $l_v \geq 1.50d_b$
d. Bolt spacings $= 3$ in (76 mm)
e. $l_t t_{st} \geq A_g$

f. $l_t/b_f \leq 3.5$

g. $t_{fc} > t_f$

h. $(t_{st}/d_b)/(t_f/t_{st}) \leq \frac{1}{4}$

4. *Calculate actual shear yield strength of the gross area of the stem*

$$R_0 = (l_t t_{st})(0.60F_y)$$

5. *Check the strength of the effective net area of the stem*

$$\left\{l_t - \left[\frac{n_b}{2}(d_b + g)\right]\right\}t_{st}0.60\phi F_u \geq R_0$$

or by using net area in shear as defined by AISC:

$$\{l_t - [n_b(d_b + g)]\}t_{st}0.60\phi F_u \geq R_0$$

6. *Check shear in the flange*

$$1.2l_t t_f F_y \geq R_u$$

7. *Design fillet welds* for the combined effects of shear and moment using Table 8-38. Shear is equal to R_0 and moment is equal to $R_0 a_{bw}$, where a_{bw} is the distance from the bolt line to the weld line.

8. *Check bearing strength* and satisfy the following equations for the tee stem

$$2.4n_b t_{st} d_b F_u \geq R_0$$

and for the beam web:

$$2.4n_b t_w d_b F_u \geq R_0$$

If the bolts are expected to resist a moment, as they normally would if the support is torsionally flexible, this calculation should reflect the reduced strength as determined from Table 9-10 of the AISC LRFD Manual.[G87]

9. *If the beam is coped, check block shear failure of the beam web*

6.3.5 Tee connection design

Design a tee connection to transfer the beam reaction to a supporting column.

Beam: W27×114, $t_w = 0.57$ in (14 mm)

Beam material: A36 steel

Support: flange of a W10×77 column

Reaction: 150 kips (factored load)

Bolts: ⅞-in-diameter (22-mm) A325-N (snug-tight)

Bolt spacing: 3 in (76 mm)

Welds: E70XX fillet welds

1. Calculate number of bolts

$$\text{Factored shear} = R_u = 150 \text{ kips}$$

$$\text{Assume } M = 0$$

Since the support is relatively rigid, the moment acting on the bolts can be neglected. From Table 8-11 in the AISC LRFD Manual[G87] the design strength of one $\frac{7}{8}$-in A325-N bolt is 21.6 kips. Thus the required number of bolts is

$$n_b = \frac{R_u}{\phi R_n} = \frac{150}{21.6} = 6.94$$

Try seven $\frac{7}{8}$-in-diameter A325-N bolts.

2. Calculate required gross areas of the tee stem

$$A_g = \frac{R_u}{0.60 F_y} = \frac{150}{0.60 \times 36} = 6.94 \text{ in}^2$$

3. Try a WT9×25 tee section to satisfy the following requirements

a. $b_f/2t_f$ of the tee ≥ 6.5
   $7.495/(2 \times 0.57) = 6.57 > 6.5$ O.K.

b. $d_b/t_{st} \geq 2.0$
   $0.875/0.355 = 2.46 > 2.0$ O.K.

c. l_h and $l_v \geq 1.50 d_b$
   l_h and $l_v = 1.50 d_b = 1.50 \times 0.875 = 1.32 \text{ in}$

Use $l_h = l_v = 1.5 \text{ in}$

d. Bolt spacings satisfy the AISC specification.

e. $l_t t_{st} \geq A_g$
   $l_t = 6 \times 3 + 2 \times 1.50 = 21.0 \text{ in}$
   $l_t t_{st} = 21 \times 0.355 = 7.46 > 6.94 \text{ in}^2$ O.K.

f. $l_t/b_f \leq 3.5$
   $21/7.495 = 2.8 < 3.5$ O.K.

g. $t_{fc} > t_f$
   $0.87 \text{ in} > 0.57 \text{ in}$ O.K.

h. $(t_{st}/d_b)/(t_f/t_{st}) = (0.355/0.875)/(0.57/0.355) = 0.25$ O.K.

4. Calculate actual shear yield capacity of the gross area of the stem

$$R_0 = 0.60 l_t t_{st} F_y = 0.60 \times 21 \times 0.355 \times 36 = 161.0 \text{ kips}$$

5. *Check capacity of effective net area of the stem*

$$R_{ne} = 0.60\left\{l_t - \left[\frac{n_b}{2}(d_b + g)\right]\right\}t_{st}\phi F_u \geq R_0$$

$$R_{ne} = 0.60\left\{21 - \left[\frac{7}{2}(\tfrac{7}{8} + \tfrac{1}{16})\right]\right\} \times 0.355 \times 0.75 \times 58$$

$$= 164.2 > 161 \text{ kips} \quad \text{O.K.}$$

or by using the net area in shear as defined by AISC:

$$R_{ns} = 0.60\{l_t - [n_b(d_b + g)]\}t_{st}\phi F_u \geq R_0$$

$$R_{ns} = 0.60\{21 - [7(\tfrac{7}{8} + \tfrac{1}{16})]\} \times 0.355 \times 0.75 \times 58$$

$$= 133.7 < 161 \text{ kips} \quad \text{N.G.}$$

If the AISC approach were used, a larger section would have to be selected and checked.

6. *Check shear in the flange*

$$1.2l_t t_f F_y \geq R_0$$

$$1.2 \times 21 \times 0.57 \times 36 = 517 > 161 \text{ kips} \quad \text{O.K.}$$

7. *Design fillet welds* for the combined effects of shear and moment using Table 8-38 in the AISC LRFD Manual.[G87] Shear is equal to R_0 and the moment is equal to $R_0 e$, where e is taken as the distance from the bolt line to the weld line:

$$R_0 = 161 \text{ kips}$$

$$M = 161 \times 3 = 483 \text{ in-kips}$$

Entering Table 8-38 with $k = 0$ and $a = e/l = 3/21 = 0.143$ yields $C = 2.75$. Using $C_1 = 1.0$, the required weld size in sixteenths of an inch is

$$D_{16} = \frac{R_0}{CC_1 l_p} = \frac{161}{2.75 \times 1.0 \times 21} = 2.79$$

or 2.79/16 = 0.17 in
Use ¼-in E70XX fillet welds.

8. *Check bearing capacity.* For tee stem:

$$R_n = 2.4d_b t_{st} F_u = 2.4 \times 0.875 \times 0.355 \times 58 = 43.2 \text{ kips}$$

with seven bolts, the design strength in bearing is

$$R_{br} = 7 \times 0.75 \times 43.2 = 226.8 > 161 \text{ kips} \quad \text{O.K.}$$

Since the beam web is thicker than the tee stem, bearing failure of the web will not govern.

9. Beam is not coped; therefore, there is no need for considering block shear rupture

6.4   Beam-to-Column Moment Connections

Three types of connections between columns and composite or steel beams are discussed in this section: those involving (1) encased composite or reinforced concrete columns, (2) filled composite columns, and (3) steel columns.[98,D59,D92]

6.4.1   Encased composite or concrete columns—general

The design of a moment-resisting connection between steel or composite beams and reinforced or composite columns in composite framed structures is presented in this section. Examples of this type of construction are found in moderate to high-rise buildings where the lateral-force-resisting system contains frames utilizing this type of rigid joint.

For economic reasons, it is often desirable in composite frames to minimize or altogether eliminate the steel columns embedded inside the concrete column. Such steel columns are usually designed for erection loads only. In such cases the steel section is generally small relative to the size of the beam. The connection is designed to transfer large forces between the steel beam and the concrete column, but the moment carried by the steel column is fairly small. For this reason, the steel columns are sometimes interrupted at the joint to allow the steel beam to be continuous through the joint. The beams are then spliced at midspan.

The design recommendations in this subsection are based principally on tests of interior planar beam-column joints subjected to forces associated with lateral deformation of the frame.[120] Where applicable, the recommendations draw on existing guidelines for steel and reinforced concrete joints, and on research on composite joints. The recommendations apply to interior and exterior configurations (Fig. 6.11a) where the steel beam extends through the full width of the concrete column. They do not apply to top-interior and top-corner connections (Fig. 6.11b) because for the latter connections supporting test data are not available and their basic force-transfer mechanism is considerably different. The major difference is the presence or absence of the concrete column both above and below the joint. Until test data become available for corner and top connections, it is suggested either to (1) use large steel column sections in the top story and detail the connections in structural steel or (2) design the connections as shear connections without moment resistance.

Limitations.   The recommendations apply for the transfer of shear forces and moments in beam-column joints meeting the following limitations (Fig. 6.12):

Joint aspect ratio: $0.75 \leq h/d \leq 2.0$, where h = depth of concrete column

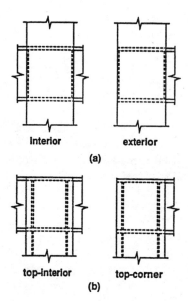

Interior   exterior

(a)

top-interior   top-corner

(b)

Figure 6.11   Joint configurations.[D92]

measured parallel to the beam and d = depth of steel beam measured parallel to the column

Materials: normal-weight concrete, where, for calculation purposes, $f_c' \leq 6$ ksi (41 MPa); $F_{yr} \leq 60$ ksi (413 MPa); $F_y \leq 50$ ksi (345 MPa)

Joint design forces: applicable for all cases of loading under dead, live, and wind forces; for earthquake loading, limited to regions of low to moderate seismic zones equivalent to seismic performance categories A, B, or C as defined in the 1994 NEHRP Recommended Provisions.[D96]

The limits on concrete strength and the type of aggregate are recommended owing to a lack of experimental data for composite joints with high-strength concrete and for composite joints with lightweight aggregates. Exceptions to the exclusion of high seismicity regions may be made where it can be demonstrated by tests or analysis that the joint behavior is acceptable under the anticipated inelastic response.

General detailing requirements.   The joint detailing considerations include requirements for attachments to the structural steel beam and for lateral and longitudinal reinforcing bars in the joint region. Attachments to the steel beam include face bearing plates (FBPs), extended face bearing plates, embedded steel columns, and vertical joint reinforcement (Fig. 6.12). As a minimum, face bearing plates should be provided within the beam depth on all beams which frame into the column and transfer significant moment through the joint. Their minimum width should be equal to the flange width.

The joint should be detailed to facilitate the anticipated construction sequence, including provisions for the erection of structural steel, fabrication

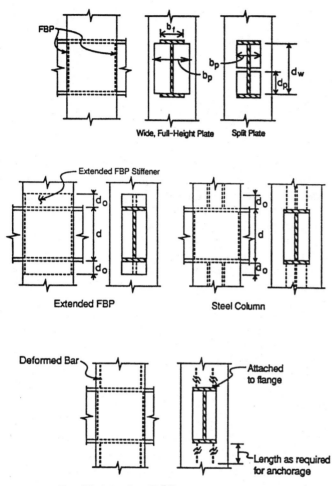

Wide, Full-Height Plate   Split Plate

Extended FBP   Steel Column

Figure 6.12 Possible joint details.[D92]

and erection of reinforcing bars, installation of formwork, and placement of concrete.

Design approach. The joint strength should be checked using the AISC LRFD.[D95] Factored loads should be determined using the ASCE recommendations[G88] or those required by the applicable code. The joint should be designed for the interaction of forces transferred to the joint by adjacent members, including bending, shear, and axial loads. These forces result from externally applied loads as well as from creep, shrinkage, temperature, and settlement. The forces on a typical joint are shown in Fig. 6.13. For connection design, these forces should reflect factored load combinations and must be in equilibrium. Note that, by definition, for an exterior joint $V_{b1} = M_{b1} = P_{b1} = 0$ (Fig. 6.14b).

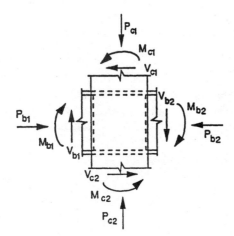

Figure 6.13 Member forces acting on a joint.[D92]

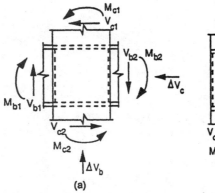
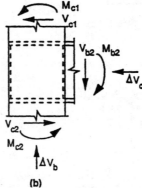

Figure 6.14 Joint design forces.[D92]

Only the forces shown in Fig. 6.14a and b are considered in calculating the strength of the joint. These forces can be related by the following moment equilibrium equation:

$$\Sigma M_c = \Sigma M_b + V_b h - V_c d \qquad (6.3)$$

where $\Sigma M_b = M_{b1} + M_{b2}$
  $V_b = (V_{b1} + V_{b2})/2$
  $V_c = (V_{c1} + V_{c2})/2$
  $\Sigma M_c = M_{c1} + M_{c2}$
  d = beam depth
  h = column width in the plane of bending

The net vertical beam shear transferred into the column and the net horizontal column shear transferred into the beam are

$$\Delta V_b = V_{b2} - V_{b1}$$

$$\Delta V_c = V_{c2} - V_{c1}$$

The design forces do not include the effects of the axial forces in the concrete column. Since axial forces in the beams are usually small, these are also neglected in the calculations. It is conservative to neglect the effects of axial compressive loads normally encountered in design. Tests have shown that compressive axial stresses tend to inhibit the opening of cracks in the joint. Test data are not available on the effects of axial tension in the column, but axial column tension could result in a decrease of shear strength as well as stiffness in the joint. Where net tension forces exist, it is recommended to neglect the contribution of concrete to the compression field shear strength.

Deformations of the joint should be considered in evaluating deflections under both service and factored loads. Many commercially available frame analysis programs used in practice do not have explicit functions to account for joint deformations. Nevertheless, joint distortions are usually considered in some fashion, either by neglecting entirely the finite size of the joint (e.g., calculating beam and column stiffness based on centerline dimensions) or by using a modified finite rigid joint dimension and/or modified member stiffness. The cracking and concentrated rotations that occur at the joint under service loads are similar in magnitude to those in reinforced concrete, and the concentrated rotations are also similar to those in fully welded structural steel joints.

Joint design strength is obtained by multiplying the nominal strength by a resistance factor ϕ. Phi for a joint should be taken equal to 0.70, a value that is conservative and approximately 20 percent below the value of 0.85 used for composite beams in the AISC LRFD specification. The lower value of ϕ reflects the philosophy of providing a greater reliability index for connections.

6.4.2 Encased composite or concrete columns—strength

The joint strength should be checked for two basic failure modes: panel shear failure and vertical bearing failure. The strength equations given here are based on these two failure modes and are dependent on satisfying the joint detailing provisions described in this procedure.

Joint behavior is characterized by the two modes of failure shown in Fig. 6.15. Panel shear failure is similar to that typically associated with structural steel or reinforced concrete joints; however, in composite joints both structural steel and reinforced concrete panel elements participate. Bearing failure occurs at locations of high compressive stresses associated with rigid body rotation of the steel beam within the concrete column. The vertical reinforcement shown in Fig. 6.15b is one source of strength against bearing failure of concrete.

Panel shear. The effective width of the joint (Fig. 6.16) within the column b_j is equal to the sum of the inner and outer panel widths b_i and b_o, given as

$$b_j = b_i + b_o \tag{6.4}$$

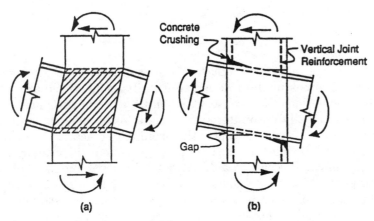

Figure 6.15   Joint-failure modes.[D92]

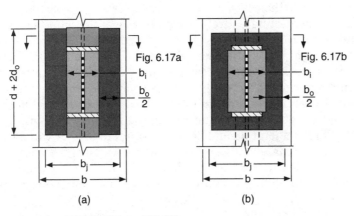

Figure 6.16   Effective joint width.[D92]

The inner width b_i should be taken equal to the greater of the face bearing plate width b_p and the beam flange width b_f. Where extended face bearing plates or steel columns are used, the outer panel width is calculated using the overall cross-section geometry according to the following:

$$b_o = C(b_m - b_i) < 2d_o \qquad (6.5)$$

where $b_m = (b_f + b)/2$ but not more than $b_f + h$ or more than $1.75b_f$
  b = column width measured perpendicular to beam
  $C = (x/h)(y/b_f)$
  d_c = steel column depth
  d_o = $0.25d$ (d = beam depth) when a steel column is present or the lesser of $0.25d$ or the height of the extended face bearing plates when these plates are present; where neither the steel column nor the extended face bearing plates are present, $b_o = d_o = 0$

h = column depth
y = greater of steel column or extended face bearing plate width
x = h where extended face bearing plates are present or $h/2 + d_c/2$
   when only the steel column is present

The joint shear strength is calculated based on an effective width of the concrete joint, which is the sum of the inner and outer panel widths, as shown in Fig. 6.16. The concrete in the inner panel is mobilized through bearing against the face bearing plates between the beam flanges. The participation of concrete outside of the beam flanges is dependent on mobilization of the horizontal compression struts that form through direct bearing of the extended face bearing plates or steel column on the concrete above and below the joint, as shown in Fig. 6.17a and b, respectively. The outward thrust at the end of the compression struts is resisted by horizontal ties above and below the beam. Referring to Fig. 6.17, the ties above and below the beam are required to resist tension forces both parallel and perpendicular to the beam. The forces perpendicular to the beam are self-equilibrating, and those parallel to the beam are transferred into the outer compression field. The effectiveness of the strut-and-tie mechanisms shown in Fig. 6.17 is based on the geometry and proportions of the concrete column and structural steel elements. The limits on d_o and Eqs. (6.4) and (6.5) are semiempirical and based on tests. The effective joint width is used to calculate the vertical bearing strength and also to calculate the joint shear strength.

Vertical bearing. The vertical bearing strength is considered adequate when the following equation is satisfied:

$$\Sigma M_c + 0.35h\Delta V_b \le \phi[0.7hC_{cn} + h_{vr}(T_{vn} + C_{vn})] \qquad (6.6)$$

where ΣM_c and ΔV_b are the applied forces and

$$C_{cn} = 0.6f'_c b_j h$$

In Eq. (6.6), T_{vn} and C_{vn} are the nominal strengths of the vertical joint reinforcement, in tension and compression, attached directly to the steel beam;

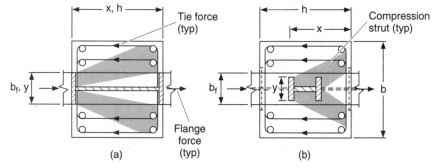

Figure 6.17 Horizontal force-transfer mechanism.[D92]

and h_{vr} is the distance between the bars. The following factors should be considered in the strength calculation for T_{vn} and C_{vn}: connection between the reinforcement and the steel beam, development of the reinforcement through bond or anchorage to concrete, and the material strength of the reinforcement. In addition, for use in Eq. (6.6) the contribution of the vertical reinforcement is limited as follows:

$$T_{vn} + C_{vn} \le 0.3f_c' b_j h \qquad (6.6a)$$

The vertical bearing forces on the joint (Fig. 6.18a) are due to the combined effects of moments and shears transferred between the beam and column. The moments and shears acting on the joint are shown in Fig. 6.18b. In Fig. 6.18c,

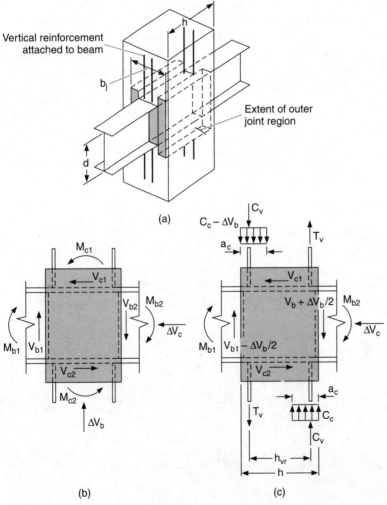

Figure 6.18   Equilibrium of joint design forces and internal force resultant.[D92]

the column moments M_{c1} and M_{c2} are replaced with the forces in the vertical reinforcement T_v and C_v and the vertical bearing forces C_c. The beam shears in Fig. 6.18b and c are related by Eq. (6.3). Equation (6.6) is derived from moment equilibrium of the forces acting on the joints in Fig. 6.18c and substituting the forces C_c, T_v, and C_v, with their respective nominal strength values. The lengths of the bearing zones a_c above and below the beam are assumed to be the same, and in Eq. (6.6) they are set equal to their maximum value of a_c = 0.3h. This limit is based on test data and is used in lieu of a limitation on the maximum concrete strain. The nominal concrete bearing strength C_{cn} is calculated using a bearing stress of $2f_c'$ over the bearing area with length a_c = 0.3h, and width b_j. The maximum bearing stress of $2f_c'$ reflects confinement of the concrete by the reinforcement and the surrounding concrete.

Vertical joint reinforcement may consist of reinforcing bars, rods, steel angles, or other elements attached directly to the steel beam to transfer vertical forces into the concrete column. Depending on the type of connection to the steel beam, the reinforcement may be considered to act in both tension and compression or in compression only (T_v = 0). Vertical stiffeners or other details may be required to transfer the forces from the vertical reinforcement into the web of the steel beam.

If the amount of vertical reinforcement is too high, there is a concern that the joint concrete between the top and bottom flanges of the steel beams may be subjected to excessive bearing stress. Equation (6.6a) is an upper limit for the contribution of vertical joint reinforcement to the joint bearing capacity.

Horizontal shear. The horizontal shear strength of the joint is the sum of the nominal shear resistance of: (1) the steel panel V_{sn}, (2) the inner concrete compression strut V_{cn}, and (3) the outer concrete compression field V_{fn}. The three joint shear mechanisms are shown in Fig. 6.19.

The values of V_{sn}, V_{cn}, and V_{fn} should be determined following the procedures described below. The horizontal shear strength is considered adequate if the following equation is satisfied:

$$\Sigma M_c - V_b jh \leq \phi[V_{sn}d_f + 0.75V_{cn}d_w + V_{fn}(d + d_o)] \tag{6.7}$$

where ΣM_c and V_b are as defined previously, d_f is the center-to-center distance between the beam flanges, d_w is the depth of steel web, d_o is as defined previously, and jh is given by the following:

$$jh = \frac{\Sigma M_c}{\phi[(T_{vn} + C_{vn} + C_c) - 0.5\Delta V_b]} \geq 0.7h \tag{6.7a}$$

where $C_c = 2f_c'b_jA_c$
$$a_c = 0.5h - \sqrt{0.25h^2 - K_p} \leq 0.3h$$
$$K_p = [\Sigma M_c + 0.5\Delta V_b h - \phi(T_{vn} - C_{vn})h_{vr}]/(\phi 2f_c'b_j)$$

Tests have shown that the contributions of the mechanisms are additive. The concrete contribution comes from the concrete compression strut which

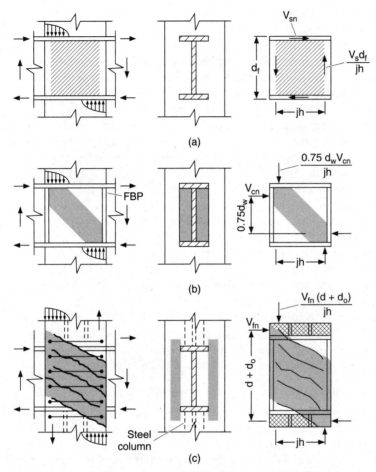

Figure 6.19 Joint shear mechanisms.[D92]

forms within the inner panel width b_i and the compression field which forms in the outer panel width b_o (Fig. 6.16). The concrete compression strut (Fig. 6.19b) is mobilized through bearing against the face bearing plates within the beam depth. The compression field (Fig. 6.19c) is mobilized through a horizontal strut-and-tie mechanism (Fig. 6.17) which forms through bearing against the steel column or the extended face bearing plates. For the case shown in Fig. 6.19c, the compression field is mobilized by the presence of the steel column above and below the beam.

Equation (6.7) is derived by equating the vertical shear through the joint, due to applied loads, to the total joint shear strength. The joint shear strength on the right side of Eq. (6.7) is expressed as the sum of the vertical shear components shown in Fig. 6.19. Referring to Fig. 6.18c, the applied shear through the joint is simply the sum of the beam shear and the internal column forces (C_c, C_v, T_v, ΔV_b) which are related to the column moments ΣM_c by Eq. (6.7a), where jh is equal to the horizontal distance between the resultant of the internal force couple. The left side of Eq. (6.7) is based on the applied joint shear expressed in terms of the total applied column moments ΣM_c and the beam shears V_b.

The joint shear strength increases as jh increases, so it is conservative to calculate the shear strength using the minimum value of $jh = 0.7h$. This is equivalent to the case for which there is no vertical joint reinforcement and $a_c = 0.3h$. A more accurate (larger) value of the shear strength will be obtained by solving for the actual values of C_c and a_c of Eq. (6.7a). The expressions for C_c and a_c are derived from equilibrium of forces in the joint using the maximum concrete bearing stress of $2f_c'$.

Steel panel. The nominal strength of the steel panel V_{sn} is calculated as

$$V_{sn} = 0.6F_{yp}t_{sp}jh \qquad (6.8a)$$

where F_{yp} and t_{sp} are the yield stress and thickness of the steel panel, respectively, and jh is given by Eq. (6.7a).

The nominal shear strength of the steel panel V_{sn} is calculated based on an average shear yield strength $0.6\,F_{yp}$ acting over an effective joint length jh.

Concrete encasement. The nominal strength of the concrete compression strut mechanism V_{cn} is calculated as the following:

$$V_{cn} = 0.63b_p h\sqrt{f_c'} \le 0.5f_c' b_p d_w \qquad (6.8b)$$

where f_c' and $\sqrt{f_c'}$ are in kips per square inch and the effective face bearing plate width b_p is limited by the following:

$$b_p \le (b_f + 5t_p) \qquad \text{and} \qquad b_p \le 0.2b_f \qquad (6.8c)$$

where t_p is the thickness of the face bearing plate.

The diagonal compression strut (Fig. 6.19b) is similar to that used to model shear in monolithic reinforced-concrete joints. V_{cn} is calculated based on an average limiting horizontal shear stress of $0.63\sqrt{f_c'}$ over the horizontal projection of the inner panel ($b_p h$) in Eq. (6.8b). The value of the average limiting horizontal shear stress is consistent with that used in reinforced concrete joints.[G46] To prevent bearing (crushing) failure at the ends of the strut, the horizontal shear in Eq. (6.8b) is limited by a bearing stress of $2f_c'$ over an area at the top and bottom of the face bearing plates (Fig. 6.19b) equal to $0.25b_p d_w$. The effective panel width is limited by Eq. (6.8c).

The nominal strength of the concrete compression field mechanism V_{fn} is calculated as

$$V_{fn} = V_c' + V_s' \le 0.63\, b_o h \sqrt{f_c'} \qquad (6.9)$$

where $\sqrt{f_c'}$ is in kips per square inch and V_c' and V_s' are calculated as shown below.

The equations for calculating the concrete compression field strength are similar to those used to calculate the nominal shear strength in reinforced concrete beams with an effective width of b_o and depth h. The upper limit on the nominal horizontal shear strength of the compression field V_{fn} is kept equal to the average shear stress of $0.63\sqrt{f_c'}$ over the horizontal projection of the outer panel $(b_o h)$. Where net axial tension is present in the column, the contribution of $V_c' = 0$.

6.4.3 Encased composite or concrete columns—detailing

Horizontal column ties at a joint, vertical bars, face bearing plates, and extended face bearing plates are discussed below.

Horizontal ties. Horizontal reinforcing bar ties should be provided in the column within the beam depth and above and below the beam to carry tension forces developed in the joint. The required ties within and adjacent to the joint should be calculated using the provisions contained in this section. Perimeter ties and cross ties may be developed either by 90° hooks which engage a longitudinal bar or by lap splicing the ties. Hook details and splice lengths should conform to the provisions of ACI 318-95.[D100]

Within the beam depth, horizontal ties carry tension forces associated with the compression field (Fig. 6.19c). Ties above and below the beam also participate in the horizontal strut-and-tie mechanism which transfers the shear outward to the compression field as shown in Fig. 6.17. Ties also provide confinement of the concrete in and adjacent to the joint (Fig. 6.20). Suggestions contained here are based largely on existing recommendations for reinforced concrete joints and elements[D100,G46] and on test data. Most of the tie requirements are related directly to the shear V_{fn} carried by the outer panel.

The maximum compression field strength V_{fn} is limited by the sum of forces resisted by the horizontal column ties and the concrete. For use in Eq. (6.9), the strength provided by the concrete is calculated as

$$V_c' = 0.16\, b_o h \sqrt{f_c'} \tag{6.10}$$

except where the column is in tension, in which case $V_c' = 0$. In Eq. (6.10), b_o is the outer panel width and h is the column width measured parallel to the beam. The term $\sqrt{f_c'}$ is in kips per square inch. The strength provided by the horizontal ties is calculated as

$$V_s' = \frac{A_{ct} F_{yh}\, 0.9h}{s_h} \tag{6.11}$$

A_{ct} is the cross-sectional area of reinforcing bars in each layer of ties spaced at s_h through the beam depth. A_{ct} is the area measured through a vertical plane perpendicular to the beam. In addition to the requirements of Eqs. (6.9) and (6.11), A_{ct} should not be less than the following:

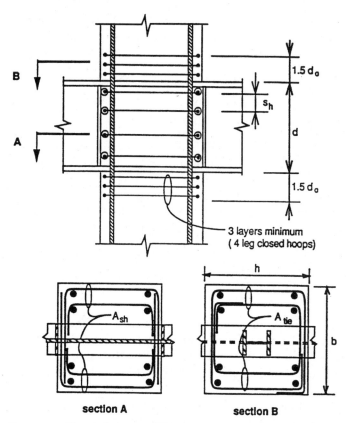

Figure 6.20 Tie reinforcement.[D92]

$$A_{ct} \geq 0.004bs_h \tag{6.11a}$$

Equations (6.9), (6.10), and (6.11) are similar to those used for calculating stirrup requirements for shear in reinforced concrete beams. Where the member is in tension, the horizontal ties must resist all of the shear present in the outer compression field (i.e., $V_c' = 0$). Usually, it is more economical to provide ties adequate to maximize V_{fn} [Eq. (6.9)] rather than to provide only minimum ties as calculated by Eq. (6.11a). The tie layout used in tests is shown in Fig. 6.20. Within the beam depth, one pair of cap ties in each layer should pass through holes in the beam web to provide continuous confinement around the joint. Tests have shown that the holes in the beam web do not reduce the web shear capacity, provided that (1) the holes are located within $0.15h$ of the column face, and (2) the net/gross area of the web measured through the holes is greater than 0.7. The face bearing plates provide confinement in the center of the column, enhancing the anchorage and development of the cap ties. The minimum reinforcement specified by Eq. (6.11a) is based on research and recommendations from the United States and Japan for reinforced concrete joints.

Additional tie requirements. As a minimum for all joints, three layers of ties should be provided above and below the beam, and the bars in each layer should be at least equivalent to the following:

For $b \le 20$ in (0.51 m), provide #3 bars with four legs in each layer.

For 20 in $< b \le 30$ in (0.76 m), provide #4 bars with four legs in each layer.

For $b > 30$ in, provide #5 bars with four legs in each layer.

These ties should be closed rectangular ties which can resist tension parallel and perpendicular to the beam. The three layers should be located within a distance of $0.4d$ above and below the beam.

Beyond this minimum requirement, where the outer compression field is used to resist joint shear, ties should be provided to transfer the force V_{fn} from the beam flanges into the outer concrete panel. The minimum total cross-sectional area based on this requirement can be expressed as

$$A_{ti} \ge \frac{V_{fn}}{F_{yh}} \tag{6.12}$$

where V_{fn} is the force carried by the outer compression field ($\le$ nominal V_{fn}) and F_{yh} is the yield strength of the transverse reinforcement. The calculated tie area A_{ti} is the total cross-sectional area of ties located within the vertical distance $0.4d$ of the beam. The tie area is measured through a plane perpendicular to the beam.

Ties above and below the beam serve two functions. First, the minimum required ties above and below the beam, as shown in Fig. 6.20, provide confinement in the highly stressed bearing region adjacent to the beam flange. Second, where the outer compression field is necessary to resist shear, the bars above and below the beam form the tie in the mechanism shown in Fig. 6.17. This mechanism is required to transfer the force V_{fn}, horizontally to the compression field. The force V_{fn} may be calculated using Eq. (6.7) by solving for the required strength V_{fn} in terms of ΣM_c, V_b, V_{sn}, and V_{cn}. In Eq. (6.12), the horizontal shear force is limited by the capacity of the ties parallel and transverse to the beam. If the tie area required by Eq. (6.12) is not satisfied, then the compression field strength V_{fn} should be reduced as indicated by Eqs. (6.7) and (6.9).

Vertical column bars. Except as outlined below, the size of vertical column bars passing through the joint should be limited as follows:

$$d_r < \frac{d + 2d_o}{20} \tag{6.13}$$

where for single bars d_r is the vertical bar diameter, and for bundled bars d_r is the diameter of a bar of equivalent area. Exceptions to Eq. (6.13) may be made where it can be shown that the change in force in vertical bars through the joint region ΔF_{vb} satisfies the following:

$$\Delta F_{vb} < 1.2(d + 2d_o)\sqrt{f_c'} \tag{6.14}$$

where $\sqrt{f_c'}$ carries the units of kips per inch.

The limit on bar size [Eq. (6.13)] is based on similar limits proposed for reinforced concrete joints to limit bar slip associated with possible large changes in bar forces due to the transfer of moments through the joint. The exception to Eq. (6.13) is provided for cases where large vertical bars are required to carry column axial forces and the restriction on bar size would be inappropriate. Referring to Fig. 6.21, the theoretical bar forces above and below the joint can be calculated based on the column forces ($P_{c1}, M_{c1}, P_{c2}, M_{c2}$) using common cracked section analysis for reinforced concrete. The bar anchorage requirement can then be calculated as the change in bar forces through the joint. The limit on ΔF_{vb} in Eq. (6.14) is based on developing a force/length of 1.2 to 1.5 times that used in ACI 318-95 for basic development lengths for deformed bars in tension. The more generous development value is permitted because (1) the actual development requirements in the joints are for a combination of tension and compression, and (2) as described in the ACI-ASCE Committee 352 report[G46] and on pp. 726–742 in Ref. G27, some slippage of vertical bars in reinforced concrete joints is generally permitted since standard development requirements would be prohibitive.

Face bearing plates. The face bearing plates within the beam depth should be detailed to resist the horizontal shear force in the concrete strut, $V_{cn} \leq$ nominal V_{cn}. Where split face bearing plates are used, the plate height d_p should not be less than $0.45\,d_w$. The face bearing plate thickness should meet the following conditions:

$$t_p \geq \frac{1}{0.6b_f F_{up}}(V_{cn} - b_f t_w F_{yw}) \tag{6.15a}$$

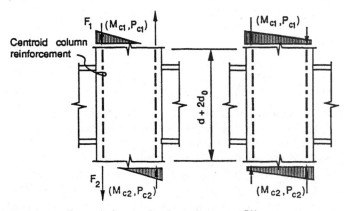

Figure 6.21 Forces in longitudinal reinforcement.[D92]

$$t_p = 0.20 \sqrt{\frac{V_{cn} b_p}{F_{yp} d_w}} \tag{6.15b}$$

$$t_p \geq \frac{V_{cn}}{1.2 b_f F_{up}} \tag{6.15c}$$

where F_{up} = tensile strength of bearing plate steel
$\quad\ F_{yp}$ = yield stress of bearing plate steel
$\quad\ F_{yw}$ = yield stress of beam web

Furthermore, the thickness t_p should be such that

$$t_p \geq \frac{b_p}{22}$$

and

$$t_p \geq \frac{b_p - b_f}{5}$$

The required thickness of the face bearing plate is a function of its geometry, support conditions, yield strength, and the distribution of concrete bearing force. Since the distribution of bearing force is nonuniform, traditional methods of analysis (e.g., yield line method) are not appropriate and usually result in overly conservative thicknesses. Equations (6.15) are semiempirical formulas derived from tests of joints. Equations (6.15a) and (6.15b) limit shear stresses in the face bearing plate, while Eq. (6.15c) limits flexural bending stresses. Welds connecting the plate to the beam should be proportioned for the full capacity of the plate in both shear and flexure. The force V_{cn} may be calculated using Eq. (6.7) and solving for the required strut capacity V_{cn} in terms of ΣM_c, V_b, V_{sn}, and $V_{fn} = 0$.

The vertical bearing force associated with joint shear in the steel panel causes bending of the steel beam flanges. The beam flanges can be assumed capable of resisting transverse bending if the thickness satisfies the following:

$$t_f \geq 0.30 \sqrt{\frac{b_f t_{sp} d F_{yp}}{h F_{yf}}} \tag{6.16}$$

where t_{sp} and F_{yp} are the thickness and yield stress of the steel panel, F_{yf} is the yield stress of the beam flanges, d the depth of the steel beam, and h the depth of the concrete column measured parallel to the beam.

Equation (6.16) is a semiempirical formula from joint tests for a bearing force equal to the shear strength of the steel panel. If the thickness of the beam flange does not satisfy Eq. (6.16), the flange should be reinforced to carry a bearing force equal to the vertical shear strength of the steel panel but not to exceed P_{eq}, where P_{eq} is the resultant of vertical forces acting on the inner panel. Force P_{eq} is resisted by concrete in bearing, by vertical joint reinforcement attached to the beam, and by shear friction provided by ties within the beam depth. Reinforcement could consist of additional vertical stiffeners or horizontal bearing plates welded to the flanges.

Extended face bearing plates. Where used, the extended face bearing plates and steel column should be designed to resist a force equal to the joint shear carried by the outer compression field V_{fn}. The average concrete bearing stress against these plate elements should be less than or equal to $2f_c'$ and should be considered to act over a maximum height above the beam flange equal to d_o. When these elements are not proportioned for the full required force, the value of V_{fn} in Eqs. (6.7) and (6.9) should be reduced accordingly.

The column flanges or the extended face bearing plates may be assumed capable of resisting transverse bending if their thicknesses satisfy Eq. (6.17):

$$t_f \geq 0.12 \sqrt{\frac{V_{fn} b_{pe}}{d_o F_y}} \tag{6.17}$$

where b_{pe} is the flange width of the steel column or the width of the extended face bearing plates and F_y is the specified yield strength of the plate. In addition to satisfying Eq. (6.17), the thickness of the extended face bearing plates should not be less than the thickness of the face bearing plates between the beam flanges.

The extended face bearing plates and/or the steel columns are required to bear against the horizontal compression struts, as shown in Fig. 6.17. The net bearing force parallel to the beam is equal to the shear force V_{fn}, where V_{fn} may be calculated as described previously. As shown in Fig. 6.17, when a steel column is used, most of the force is transferred through bearing to only one of the column flanges. The design of these elements is usually controlled by transverse bending in the plates or column flanges, shear strength of the support plate or the column web, and the connection to the steel beam. The maximum concrete bearing stress $2f_c'$ is the same as that permitted for bearing against the beam flanges. The maximum effective height of the bearing region $d_o \leq d/4$ (Fig. 6.12b) is chosen based on the limits of the available test data.

Traditional methods of analysis for the flexural bending of the extended face bearing plates (or column flanges) usually result in overly conservative thicknesses. Equation (6.17) is a semiempirical formula derived from joint tests and is based on the flexural bending considerations only. The extended face bearing plates or steel column flange should also be checked against shear fracture. Welds connecting these plates to the steel beam should be proportioned for the full capacity of these plates in both shear and flexure.

6.4.4 Beam-column joint design

The joint shown in Fig. 6.22 is subjected to the following factored forces:

$$V_{b1} = V_{b2} = 105 \text{ kips (467 kN)} \qquad V_{c1} = V_{c2} = 175 \text{ kips (778 kN)}$$

$$M_{b1} = M_{b2} = 919 \text{ ft-kips} = 11{,}028 \text{ in-kips } (1246 \text{ kN} \cdot \text{m})$$

$$M_{c1} = M_{c2} = 831 \text{ ft-kips} = 9972 \text{ in-kips } (1127 \text{ kN} \cdot \text{m})$$

Check the joint capacity and design the necessary details.

Known variables   (from Fig. 6.22)

$$A_{ct} = 0.8 \text{ in}^2$$

$$A_{ti} = 3.2 \text{ in}^2$$

$$b = 30 \text{ in}$$

$$b_f = 10.5 \text{ in} = b_i$$

$$b_p = 10.5 \text{ in}$$

$$b_{pe} = 7.96 \text{ in}$$

$$d = 29.8 \text{ in}$$

$$d_f = 29.1 \text{ in}$$

$$d_w = 28.3 \text{ in}$$

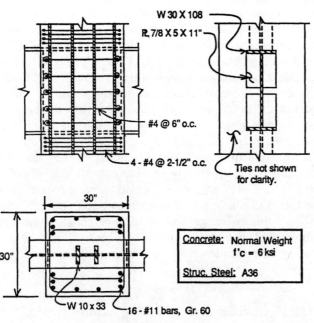

Figure 6.22   Design example—interior joint.[D92]

$$F_{up} = 58 \text{ ksi}$$

$$F_y = 36 \text{ ksi}$$

$$F_{yh} = 60 \text{ ksi}$$

$$F_{yp} = 36 \text{ ksi}$$

$$F_{yw} = 36 \text{ ksi}$$

$$f_c' = 6 \text{ ksi}$$

$$h = 30 \text{ in}$$

$$s_h = 6 \text{ in}$$

$$t_{sp} = 0.545 \text{ in}$$

$$T_{vn} = C_{vn} = 0$$

$$d_o = \frac{d}{4} = 7.45 \text{ in}$$

1. Joint design forces.   From Eq. (6.3):

$$V_b = \frac{V_{b1} + V_{b2}}{2} = 105 \text{ kips}$$

$$\Sigma M_c = M_{c1} + M_{c2} = 19{,}940 \text{ in-kips}$$

$$\Delta V_b = V_{b2} - V_{b1} = 0$$

2. Effective joint width.   From Eq. (6.5): $b_m = 0.5(b_f + b)$ but $\le (b_f + h)$ and also $\le 1.75b_f$

$b_m \le 0.5\,(10.5 + 30) = 20.25$, $b_f + h = 10.5 + 30 = 40.5$, and $1.75b_f = 1.75(10.5) = 18.4$. Therefore, $b_m = 18.4$ in.

$$C = \frac{x}{h} \frac{y}{b_f} = \frac{20}{30} \frac{8}{10.5} = 0.51$$

$$b_o = C(b_m - b_i) \le 2d_o$$

$$= 0.51(18.4 - 10.5) \le 2(0.25)(29.8)$$

$$= 4.0 \le 14.9$$

From Eq. (6.4):

$$b_j = b_i + b_o = 10.5 + 4.0 = 14.5 \text{ in}$$

3. Vertical bearing. From Eq. (6.6):

$$C_{cn} = 0.6f'_c b_j h$$

$$= 0.6(6)(14.5)(30) = 1566 \text{ kips}$$

$$\Sigma M_c + 0.35h\Delta V_b \leq \phi[0.7hC_{cn} + h_{vr}(T_{vn} + C_{vn})]$$

$$19,940 + 0 \leq 0.7[0.7(30)(1566) + 0]$$

$$19,940 \leq 23,020 \text{ in-kips}$$

Therefore, bearing does not control.

4. Joint shear. From Eq. (6.7):

$$\text{Check } \Sigma M_c - V_b jh \leq \phi[V_{sn}df + 0.75V_{cn}d_w + V_{fn}(d + d_o)]$$

From Eq. (6.7a):

$$K_p = \frac{1}{\phi 2f'_c b_j} [\Sigma M_c + 0.5\Delta V_b h - \phi(T_{vn} + C_{vn})h_{vr}]$$

$$= \frac{1}{0.7 \times 2 \times 6 \times 14.5} (19,944 - 0) = 163.7 \text{ in}^2$$

$$a_c = 0.5h - \sqrt{0.25h^2 - K_p} \leq 0.3h$$

$$= 15 - \sqrt{225 - 163.7} = 7.17 \text{ in} < 0.3(30) = 9 \text{ in}$$

$$C_c = 2f'_c b_j a_c = (2)(6)(14.5)(7.17) = 1248 \text{ kips}$$

$$jh = \frac{\Sigma M_c}{\phi(T_{vn} + C_{vn} + C_c - 0.5\Delta V_b)} \geq 0.7h$$

$$= \frac{19,940}{0.7(1248 - 0)} = 22.83 \geq 0.7 \times 30$$

$$= 22.83 \text{ in} \geq 21 \text{ in}$$

a. Steel panel. From Eq. (6.8a):

$$V_{sn} = 0.6F_{yp}t_{sp}jh = 0.6(36)(0.545)(22.83) = 269 \text{ kips}$$

b. Concrete compression strut. From Eq. (6.8b):

$$V_{cn} = 0.63b_p h \sqrt{f'_c} \leq 0.5f'_c b_p d_w$$

$$0.63(10.5)(30)\sqrt{6} \leq 0.5(6)(10.5)(28.3)$$

$$486 \leq 891$$

$$V_{cn} = 486 \text{ kips}$$

c. Concrete compression field. From Eq. (6.9):

$$V_{fn} = 0.63 b_o h \sqrt{f_c'} \text{ (assuming ties are adequate)}$$

$$= 0.63(4)(30)\sqrt{6} = 185 \text{ kips}$$

d. Resistance to joint shear failure. From Eq. (6.7):

$$\text{Check } \Sigma M_c - V_b jh \le \phi[V_{sn}d_f + 0.75V_{cn}d_w + V_{fn}(d + d_o)]$$

$$19{,}940 - 105(22.83) \le 0.7[269(29.1) + 0.75(486)(28.3) + 185(29.8 + 7.5)]$$

$$17{,}550 \approx 17{,}530 \qquad \text{O.K.}$$

5. Detailing provisions for joint shear
a. Ties within beam depth:
From Eq. (6.10):

$$V_c' = 0.16 b_o h \sqrt{f_c'} = 0.16(4)(30)\sqrt{6} = 47 \text{ kips}$$

From Eq. (6.7): Since shear is the limiting case,

$$V_{fn} = \text{nominal } V_{fn} = 185 \text{ kips}$$

From Eq. (6.9):

$$\text{Req'd } V_s' = V_{fn} - V_c' = 185 - 47 = 138 \text{ kips}$$

From Eq. (6.11):

$$\text{Req'd } \frac{A_{ct}}{s_h} = \frac{V_s'}{0.9hF_{yh}} = \frac{138}{0.9 \times 30 \times 60} = 0.085 \text{ in}^2/\text{in}$$

From Eq. (6.11a):

$$\text{Min}\left(\frac{A_{ct}}{s_h}\right) = 0.004b = 0.004 \times 30 = 0.120 \text{ in}^2/\text{in}$$

Provide 4#4 ties at 6 in o.c.

$$\frac{A_{ct}}{s_h} = \frac{4 \times 2 \times 0.196}{6} = 0.26 \text{ in}^2/\text{in} > 0.12 \text{ in}^2/\text{in} \qquad \text{O.K.}$$

b. Ties adjacent to joint:
From Eq. (6.12):

$$\text{Req'd } A_{ti} = \frac{V_{fn}}{F_{yh}} = \frac{185}{60} = 3.08 \text{ in}^2$$

Place within $0.4d = 11.25$ in of beam.
Provide four layers of 4#4 at $2\frac{1}{2}$ in o.c.

$$A_{ti} = 4 \times 4 \times 0.196 = 3.14 \text{ in}^2 > 3.08 \text{ in}^2 \qquad \text{O.K.}$$

6. Face bearing plate thickness.   From Eq. (6.7): Since shear is the limiting case,

$$V_{cn} = \text{nominal } V_{cn} = 486 \text{ kips}$$

From Eq. (6.15a):

$$\text{Req'd } t_p = \frac{V_{cn} - b_f t_w F_{yw}}{0.6 b_f F_{up}} = \frac{486 - (10.5)(0.545)(36)}{0.6 \times 10.5 \times 58} = 0.77 \text{ in}$$

From Eq. (6.15b):

$$\text{Req'd } t_p = 0.20 \sqrt{\frac{V_{cn} b_p}{F_y d_w}} = 0.20 \sqrt{\frac{486 \times 10.5}{36 \times 28.3}} = 0.45 \text{ in}$$

From Eq. (6.15c):

$$\text{Req'd } t_p = \frac{V_c}{1.2 b_f F_{up}} = \frac{486}{1.2 \times 10.5 \times 58} = 0.67 \text{ in}$$

$t_p = 0.77$ in controls; use ⅞-in-thick plate. Provide welds for full capacity all around.
From Eq. (6.15d):

$$\frac{b_p}{t_p} = \frac{10.5}{0.875} = 12 < 22 \qquad \text{O.K.}$$

7. Check flange thickness of beam for bearing.   From Eq. (6.16):

$$\text{Req'd } t_f = 0.30 \sqrt{\frac{b_f t_{sp} d F_{yp}}{h F_{yf}}} = 0.30 \sqrt{\frac{10.5 \times 0.545 \times 29.8 \times 36}{30 \times 36}} = 0.72 \text{ in}$$

$$\text{.Actual } t_f = 0.76 \text{ in} > 0.72 \text{ in} \qquad \text{O.K.}$$

8. Check flange thickness of steel column for bearing.   From Eq. (6.17):

$$\text{Req'd } t \geq 0.12 \sqrt{\frac{V_{fn} b_{pe}}{d_o F_y}} = 0.12 \sqrt{\frac{185 \times 7.96}{7.5 \times 36}} = 0.28 \text{ in}$$

$$\text{Column } t_{fc} = 0.435 \text{ in} > 0.28 \text{ in} \qquad \text{O.K.}$$

9. Additional considerations
   a. Check steel column nominal shear capacity for $V_{fn} = 185$ kips. If required, use doubler plates to enhance shear capacity of column. Design column-to-beam connection for full capacity.
   b. Check nominal shear strength in the flange of the steel columns and connecting welds under the bearing force $V_{fn} = 185$ kips.
   c. Check the size of the vertical reinforcing bars of the column and bond stress within the joint depth.

6.4.5 Filled composite columns

These are composite columns consisting of hollow steel tubes filled with high-strength concrete. Compressive strengths exceeding 10 ksi (69 MPa) are being used in high-rise buildings to carry the large vertical forces and for axial stiffness in resistance to lateral loads. Different methods of connecting steel beams to these columns at each floor level have been developed by designers. The relatively thin plate of the steel tube often prohibits connecting steel beams directly to the tube, especially in seismic areas.

Beam-column connections in concrete-filled steel tubes are currently constructed either by directly welding the steel beam to the tube or by using simple shear connections. In some buildings, a moment-resisting beam-column connection is required for structural economy and seismic and wind resistance of the structure. Past design practice for these connections has relied heavily on the judgment and experience of individual designers, with little research and testing information available.

The need for seismic resistance of such connections excludes the possibility of directly connecting the beam to the steel tube. An important consideration is the need to transmit beam forces to the column without overstressing the steel tube.

Possible connection details.   Column sizes currently used in practice are large. The relatively thin walls used in this type of column require extreme care in transferring beam forces to the column, particularly in high seismic areas where the connection may be subjected to force reversal. Welding of the steel beam or connecting element directly to the steel tube of the composite column should be avoided for the following reasons:

1. Transfer of tensile forces to the steel tube can result in separation of the tube from the concrete core, thereby overstressing the steel tube. In addition, the deformation of the steel tube increases connection rotation, decreasing its stiffness.

2. Welding of the thin steel tubes results in large residual stresses because of the restraint provided by other connection elements.

3. The steel tube is primarily designed to provide lateral confinement for the concrete, which could be compromised by the additional stresses due to the welded connection.

With these considerations in mind, attempts have been made to prevent direct transfer of beam forces to the steel tube. Two general types of connection details have been proposed, types A and B.

Type A connection detail, shown in Fig. 6.23, shows one alternative in which forces are transmitted to the core concrete via anchor bolts connecting the steel elements to the steel tube. In this alternative, all elements could be preconnected to the steel tube in the shop. The nut inside the steel tube is

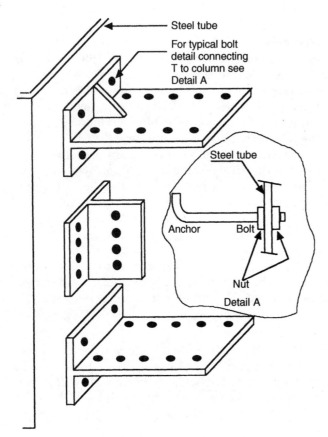

Figure 6.23   Type A connection with anchor bolt.[D83]

designed to accomplish this task. Alternatively, the anchor bolts can be attached by stud welding. The capacity of this type of connection would be limited to the pull-out capacity of the anchor bolts.

Another variation of the same idea is shown in Fig. 6.24, where connecting elements would be embedded in the core concrete via slots cut in the steel tube. In this variation slots must be welded to connection elements after beam assembly for concrete confinement. The ultimate capacity of this detail also would be limited to the pull-out capacity of the connection elements.

Type B connection detail is another option which passes the beam completely through the column (Fig. 6.25). This type of connection is believed to be the most suitable. In this option a slot in the form of an I shape must be made in the tube walls. After passing the beam through the column, the slot should be welded to the beam. This would be required to achieve confinement of the concrete.

In this detail a certain height of column tube, together with a short beam stub passing through the column and welded to the tube, could be shop-fabricated to form a tree column. The beam portion of the tree column could then be

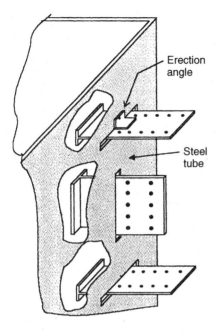

Figure 6.24 Type A connection with embedded elements.[D83]

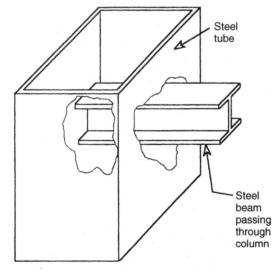

Figure 6.25 Type B connection—through connection detail.[D83]

bolted to girders in the field. An extensive nonlinear finite-element analysis of the through beam connection detail has been conducted to identify the force-transfer mechanism from beam to column. The findings of these analytical studies were then verified by experimental testing of a connection subassembly.

Figure 6.26 shows the force-transfer mechanism for the connection. It has been identified that for a square tube with the beam passing through the col-

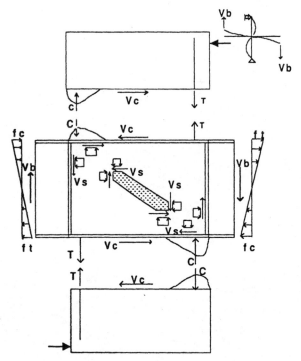

Figure 6.26 Through beam connection: force-transfer mechanism.[D83]

umn, the portion of the steel tube between the beam flanges acts as a stiffener, resulting in a concrete compression strut which assists the beam web within the joint in carrying shear. The effectiveness of the compression strut is maximized by increasing the thickness of the steel plate between the beam flanges. The width of the concrete compression strut on each side of the beam web in the direction normal to the beam web was approximately equal to half the beam flange width.

A compressive-force block is created when beam flanges are compressed against the upper and lower columns (Fig. 6.26). The width of this compression block is approximately equal to the width of the beam flange. In the upper and lower columns shown in Fig. 6.26 the compressive force C is shown to be balanced by the tensile force in the steel pipe. Embedded rods in the concrete and welded to the beam flanges can be provided to assist the steel tube in resisting the tensile forces and to minimize the tensile stresses in the steel tube.

Suggested design procedure.   A tentative design procedure for designing a through beam connection detail in conjunction with circular rather than square or rectangular column has been developed. The design procedure is in the form of equations relating the applied external forces to the connection details, such as thickness of steel pipe.

The design procedure follows the general guidelines of the AISC LRFD specification. In developing the design equations, the following assumptions are made:

1. Externally applied shear forces and moments at the joints are known.

2. At the ultimate condition the concrete stress distribution is linear and maximum concrete compressive stress is below its limiting value.

The joint forces implied in the first assumption can be obtained from analysis and require the knowledge of applied shear and moment at the joint at failure. These quantities are assumed to be related as follows:

$$V_c = \alpha V_b$$

$$M_b = l_1 V_b$$

$$M_c = l_2 V_c$$

where V_b and M_b are ultimate beam shear and moment, respectively, while V_c and M_c are ultimate column shear and moment, respectively.

The validity of the second assumption above can be justified by the following:

1. Column sizes for the type of construction considered here are generally much larger than the beam sizes.

2. The concrete type used in these columns is generally high-strength concrete with compressive strength well above 10 ksi (69 MPa). The uniaxial stress-strain characteristics of high-strength concrete exhibit a linear behavior up to maximum strength, followed by a sharp descending portion.

The type of joint is shown in Fig. 6.27. Figure 6.28 is a free-body diagram of the beam web within the joint and the upper column at ultimate load. With reference to Fig. 6.28, the following additional assumptions are made in deriving the design equations:

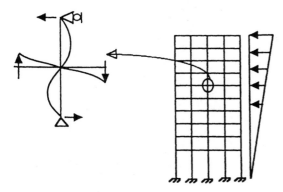

Figure 6.27 Assumed forces on an interior joint.[D83]

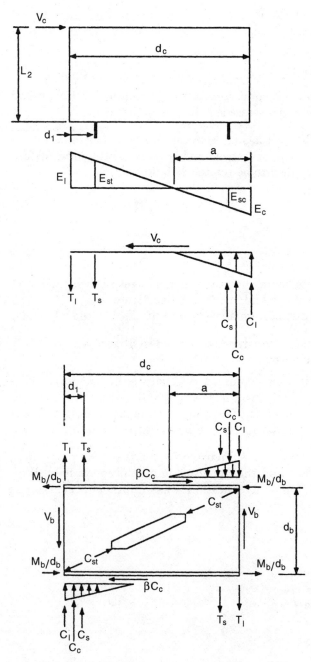

Figure 6.28 Free-body diagram for a joint web.[D83]

1. The concrete stress distribution is assumed to be linear. The width of the concrete stress block is assumed to equal the beam flange width b_f.

2. As shown in Fig. 6.28, strain distribution over the upper column is assumed to be linear.

3. The steel pipe and concrete act compositely.

4. The portion of the upper column shear V_c transferred to the steel beam is assumed to be $ßC_c$, where C_c is the resultant concrete compressive force bearing against the beam flange and ß is the coefficient of friction.

5. Applied beam moments are resolved into couples concentrated at beam flanges.

6. The resultant of concrete compression strut is along a diagonal as shown in Fig. 6.28.

Considering the above assumptions and the strain distribution shown for the upper column in Fig. 6.28, maximum strain in concrete ϵ_c can be related to ϵ_t, steel pipe strain in tension:

$$\epsilon_c = \frac{a}{d_c - a}\epsilon_t \tag{6.18}$$

Next, maximum stress in concrete and stresses in the steel pipe are calculated as follows:

$$f_c = E_c\epsilon_c \tag{6.19}$$

$$f_{tc} = E_s\epsilon_c \tag{6.20}$$

$$f_{tt} = E_s\epsilon_t \tag{6.21}$$

where f_c, f_{tc}, and f_{tt} are maximum concrete compressive stress, stress in steel pipe in compression, and stress in steel pipe in tension, respectively.

Substituting Eq. (6.18) into Eqs. (6.19) through (6.21) and multiplying Eqs. (6.19) through (6.21) by the corresponding area, the resultant forces for different connection elements are calculated as follows:

$$C_c = \frac{0.5}{n}\, b_f \frac{a^2}{d_c - a}\, \xi F_{yt} \tag{6.22}$$

$$C_1 = \gamma b_f t_t \frac{a}{d_c - a}\, \xi F_{yt} \tag{6.23}$$

$$T_1 = \gamma b_f t_t \xi F_{yt} \tag{6.24}$$

where d_c = diameter of steel pipe
a = depth of neutral axis
n = ratio of modulus of elasticity for steel to modulus of elasticity of concrete

t_t = thickness of steel pipe

γ = factor reflecting portion of steel pipe effective in carrying tensile forces; experimental data for square tubes indicate that this factor can be assumed equal to 2; the same value is assumed for pipe columns

ξF_{yt} = stress level in steel pipe at ultimate ($\xi = 0.75$)

b_f = beam flange width

F_{yt} = yield stress of pipe steel

Using the free-body diagram of the upper column shown in Fig. 6.28, Eqs. (6.22) through (6.24), and satisfying vertical force equilibrium, the following equation is obtained:

$$t_t = \frac{a^2}{d_c - 2a} \frac{1}{2\gamma n} \tag{6.25}$$

Next, considering the moment equilibrium of the free-body diagram of the upper column shown in Fig. 6.28, the following expression can be derived:

$$\frac{1}{d_c - a}\left[\frac{a^3 d_c}{d_c - 2a} + a^2\left(d_c - \frac{a}{3}\right)\right] = \frac{2n}{\xi F_{yt}} \frac{al_2}{b_f} V_b \tag{6.26}$$

where F_{yt} is the yield stress of the steel pipe, α is the ratio of column shear V_c to beam shear V_b, and l_2 is the ratio of M_c over V_c.

In Eq. (6.26), ξF_{yt} is the stress level the steel pipe is allowed to approach at ultimate condition. Based on experimental data and until further research is conducted, it is suggested that a value of 0.75 be used for ξ.

Equations (6.25) and (6.26) relate the externally applied force V_b directly and the externally applied forces V_c and M_b indirectly (through the coefficients α and l_2) to different connection parameters.

Design approach. Before proceeding with the steps necessary in designing the through beam connection detail, additional equations are derived to relate the shear stress in the beam web within the joint to the compressive force in the concrete compression strut and externally applied forces.

Considering the free-body diagram of a portion of the beam web within the joint area as shown in Fig. 6.29 and satisfying the horizontal force equilibrium, the following equation is derived:

$$V_w + C_{st}\cos(\theta) + \beta C_c - \frac{2M_b}{d} = 0 \tag{6.27}$$

where C_{st} = resultant of compression strut shown in Fig. 6.28

V_w = shear force in beam web at ultimate condition

θ = arctan (d/d_c)

d = beam depth

Equations (6.25), (6.26), and (6.27) can be used to proportion the through beam connection detail.

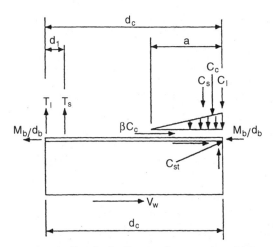

Figure 6.29 Free-body diagram for a portion of joint web.[D83]

The following steps are suggested for designing the through beam connection detail in the LRFD format:

1. From analysis, obtain factored joint forces.
2. Select the following quantities: b_f, d_c, F_{yt}.
3. Solving Eq. (6.26), obtain the depth of the neutral axis a.
4. Solving Eq. (6.25), obtain the required thickness t_t of the pipe steel wall.
5. Check stress in different connection elements.
6. From vertical equilibrium requirement of the free-body diagram shown in Fig. 6.29:

$$C_{st} = \frac{C_c}{\sin(\theta)} \qquad (6.28)$$

Using Eq. (6.22), calculate C_c and then using Eq. (6.28) calculate C_{st}.

7. Using Eq. (6.27), calculate V_w, the shear force in the beam at ultimate, and compare it to V_{wy}, the shear yield capacity of the beam web given by the following equation:

$$V_{wy} = 0.6 \, F_{yw} t_w d_c \qquad (6.29)$$

where F_{yw} = beam web yield stress
     t_w = thickness of beam web

If necessary, increase the thickness of the web within the joint region. In this design procedure the assumption is that at the factored load level, the web starts to yield.

8. Check shear stress in concrete in the joint area. Taking the limiting shear force V_u as that suggested by the ACI-ASCE Committee 352,[G46]

$$V_u = \phi R A_o \sqrt{f_c'} \tag{6.30}$$

where $\phi = 0.85$

$R = 632, 474$, and 379 for interior, exterior, and corner joints, respectively

A_o = product of effective joint width, taken as $2b_f$, and column diameter d_c

f_c' = concrete compressive strength, ksi

It is suggested that the value of f_c' in the expression $\sqrt{f_c'}$ be limited to 10 ksi (69 MPa). The units of V_u in Eq. (6.30) are kips.

The procedure described above should be viewed as a general guideline until further research is carried out. It should be noted that the effect of axial load in the column on performance of the connection was not considered but is believed to be conservative since compressive axial stresses tend to inhibit opening of cracks in the joint.

6.4.6   Filled composite column joint design

Design a through beam connection detail with the following geometry and properties:

$$b_f = 5.5 \text{ in (139.7 mm)}$$

$$d_b = 14.5 \text{ in (368.3 mm)}$$

$$d_c = 15.98 \text{ in (406 mm)}$$

$$F_{yt} = 36 \text{ ksi (248.2 MPa)}$$

$$F_{yw} = 36 \text{ ksi (248.2 MPa)}$$

$$t_w = 0.25 \text{ in (6.35 mm)}$$

$$\alpha = 0.85$$

$$l_2 = 32.0 \text{ in (813 mm)}$$

$$V_b = 79.0 \text{ kips (351.4 kN)}$$

$$M_b = 138.3 \text{ ft-kips (187.5 kN-m)}$$

$$\beta = 0.5$$

$$\xi = 0.75$$

$$n = 4.3$$

$$f_c' = 14 \text{ ksi (96.5 MPa)}$$

$$E_s = 29,000 \text{ ksi (200 GPa)}$$

$$E_c = 6,700 \text{ ksi (46 GPa)}$$

The very high strength concrete, $f'_c = 14$ ksi, was chosen in the original design to provide high stiffness. However, $f'_c = 10$ ksi was used in strength calculations.

Calculate a, the depth of the neutral axis. Equation (6.26) yields a fourth-degree polynomial which can be shown to have only one positive, real root. For this example Eq. (6.26) yields

$$a = 5.9 \text{ in}$$

Calculate the required thickness of the steel pipe using Eq. (6.25):

$$t_t = \frac{5.9^2}{15.98 - (2 \times 5.9)} \; \frac{1}{2 \times 2 \times 4.3} = 0.48 \text{ in}$$

Use $t_t = \frac{1}{2}$ in.

Check stresses in different connection elements against their limit values. First calculate tensile strain in the steel tube.

$$\epsilon_t = \frac{\xi F_{yt}}{E_s} = \frac{0.75 \times 36}{29,000} = 0.000931$$

Calculate f_c using Eqs. (6.18) and (6.19)

$$\epsilon_c = \frac{a}{d_c - a} \epsilon_t = \frac{5.9}{15.98 - 5.9} \times 0.000931 = 0.000545$$

$$f_c = 0.000545 \times 6700 = 3.65 \text{ ksi} < f'_c = 10.0 \text{ ksi} \qquad \text{O.K.}$$

Calculate stresses in other connection elements using Eqs. (6.20) and (6.21). This yields

$$f_{tc} = \frac{29,000 \times 3.65}{6700} = 15.8 \text{ ksi} < \phi_c F_y = 0.85 \times 36 = 30.6 \text{ ksi} \qquad \text{O.K.}$$

$$f_{tt} = 29,000 \times 0.000931 = 27.0 \text{ ksi} < \phi_t F_y = 0.9 \times 36 = 32.4 \text{ ksi} \qquad \text{O.K.}$$

Calculate compressive force in concrete compression strut using Eqs. (6.22) and (6.28):

$$\theta = \arctan\left(\frac{14.5}{15.98}\right) = 42.2°$$

$$C_c = \left(\frac{0.5}{\eta}\right) b_f \frac{a^2}{d_c - a} \xi F_{yt}$$

$$= 0.5 \times 0.23 \times 5.5 \times \frac{5.9^2}{15.98 - 5.9} \times 0.75 \times 36$$

$$= 59.0 \text{ kips}$$

$$C_{st} = \frac{C_c}{\sin \theta} = \frac{59.0}{\sin 42.2} = 87.8 \text{ kips}$$

Calculate V_w using Eq. (6.27):

$$V_w + C_{st} \cos \theta + \beta C_c - \frac{2M_b}{d_b} = 0$$

$$V_w + (87.8 \cos 42.2) + (0.5 \times 59.0) - \frac{2 \times 138.3 \times 12}{14.5} = 0$$

$$V_w = 134.4 \text{ kips}$$

From Eq. (6.29) the shear yield capacity of the beam is

$$V_{wy} = 0.6 \times 36 \times 0.25 \times 15.98 = 86.3 \text{ kips} < 134.4 \text{ kips}$$

Since the shear yield capacity V_{wy} of the web within the joint is not sufficient, increase the web thickness to

$$t_w = \frac{134.4}{0.6 \times 36 \times 15.98} = 0.389 \text{ in}$$

Using $t_w = \frac{3}{8}$ in would result in less than 4 percent overstress; if 4 percent is not acceptable, a web plate thicker than $\frac{3}{8}$ in must be used. The shear force carried by concrete within the joint between the beam flanges is assumed to be the horizontal component C_{st}.

$$V_c = C_{st} \cos \theta$$

$$= 87.8 \cos 42.2 = 65.0 \text{ kips}$$

For the interior joint the shear capacity [Eq. (6.30)] is

$$V_u = \phi \times 632 \times 2b_f \times d_c \times \sqrt{f_c'}$$

$$V_u = 0.85 \times \frac{632}{1000} \times 2 \times 5.5 \times 15.98 \times \sqrt{10} = 298.6 \text{ kips} > 65.0 \text{ kips} \qquad \text{O.K.}$$

Composite columns of the type described above have been found to be economical in practical tall building designs.

6.4.7   Connection to steel columns

Perhaps the most common type of moment connection between a steel or composite beam and a wide-flange column is shown in Fig. 6.30.[G41]

Figure 6.30a shows a connection with the beam flanges welded to the column flange with full-penetration groove welds. The typical weld joint of this type for a rolled beam can be expected to shrink about $\frac{1}{16}$-in in the length of the joint preparation when it cools and contracts. Thicker welds, as for welded plate girder flanges, will shrink even more—up to $\frac{1}{8}$ or $\frac{3}{16}$ in.

This amount of shrinkage can cause problems in erection, on continuous

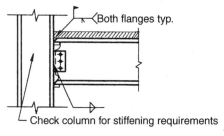

Check column for stiffening requirements

(a) Column flange support

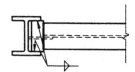

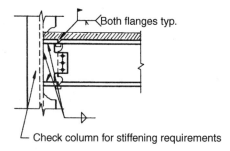

Check column for stiffening requirements

(b) Column web support

Figure 6.30 Composite beam to steel column moment connection.[G79]

runs, in maintaining correct centerline dimensions and in plumbing the columns. This shrinkage can be controlled best by having the beams fabricated longer than required by the amount of expected shrinkage. An optional method, increasing the weld joint opening, requires additional welding and usually is not cost-effective.

The beam web is provided with a circular access hole to permit down-hand welding to backing bars located at the bottom of the bottom flange and the underside of the top flange. The extension bars normally are not removed at a column connection unless they create an interference or if the joint is subject to dynamic loading. This practice in currently under scrutiny in light of the failures observed in the 1995 Northridge earthquake. The access hole should be left open, i.e., not welded up.

It has been shown in full-scale laboratory tests that a beam's plastic moment capacity M_p can be fully developed when its flanges are fully welded to the column flange and the beam web is either bolted or welded to a single-plate type of splice plate designed for the beam shear.

The apparent increase in beam capacity above the flexure theory occurs because of strain hardening of the flanges, which provides full transfer of the beam plastic moment to the support. The shear forces are carried by the beam web and the web connection.

Connections of beams to the column webs are preferably made outside of the column outstanding flanges in order to provide adequate clearances for welding and bolting (Fig. 6.30b). The design of this connection is fairly simple and routine and is covered in AISC publications.[D95]

The details shown in Fig. 6.30 are adequate for connections subjected to wind loads where shears are not expected in the inelastic range. However, for severe cyclic stress excursions into the inelastic range, as might be expected in high seismic zones, this detail is highly suspect, as shown by the problems experienced in the 1994 Northridge earthquake in California. The brittle nature of this welded connection in large beam-column joints as shown by performance during this earthquake has prompted a reexamination and new testing for this type of connection when used in high seismic zones.[G91]

Sometimes the engineer may desire to increase the negative moment capacity of the connection using reinforcing steel cast into the composite slab. This could occur, for instance, if beam depth were restricted or additional moment capacity was required without wanting to increase beam size and tonnage.

The AISC specification states that the negative moment flexural strength $\phi_b M_n$ shall be determined for the steel section alone or alternatively, the negative moment flexural strength $\phi_b M_n$ may be computed with $\phi_b = 0.85$ and M_n determined from the plastic stress distribution in the composite section, provided that:

1. The steel beam is an adequately braced compact section.

2. Shear connectors connect the slab to the steel beam in the negative-moment region.

3. Slab reinforcement parallel to the steel beam, within the effective width of the slab, is properly developed.

The flexural strength in the negative-moment region is the strength of the steel beam alone or the plastic strength of the composite section made up of the longitudinal slab reinforcement and the steel section.

When an adequately braced compact steel section and adequately developed longitudinal reinforcing bars act compositely in the negative-moment region, the nominal flexural strength is determined from the plastic stress distributions shown in Fig. 3.19. The tensile force T in the reinforcing bars is the smaller of

$$T = A_r F_{yr}$$

$$T = \Sigma Q_n$$

where A_r = area of properly developed slab reinforcement parallel to the steel beam and within the effective width of the slab, in^2
F_{yr} = specified yield stress of slab reinforcement, ksi

ΣQ_n = sum of the nominal strengths of shear connectors between points
of maximum negative moment and zero moment to either side,
kips

A third theoretical limit on T is the product of the area and yield stress of the
steel section. However, this limit is redundant in view of practical limitations
on slab reinforcement and shear connectors.

The longitudinal slab steel should be kept within a column strip of six column flange widths and should extend at least 12 in (0.3 m) past the theoretical point of inflection. The bar size should be kept small (less than a #7), and
at least three bars on either side of the column should be used. Steel should
be provided (#3 at 12 in) in the perpendicular direction and extended at least
12 in past the negative reinforcing steel bars.

6.5   Semirigid Connections[97,121,125]

6.5.1   Concept of semirigid connections

Traditionally, beam-column connections have been categorized as being either
simple connections where ideal hinge behavior is assumed and the connection
is proportioned for shear only, or fully rigid moment connections where ideal
rigid behavior is assumed and the connection is proportioned for both shear
and moment. The design of these connections was discussed in the previous
sections. The concepts of simple and fully rigid connections are ideal simplifications of true behavior made to simplify the analysis in the design process.

Recently, the concept of semirigid composite connections has been developed. The additional strength and stiffness provided by the floor slab is activated by adding shear studs and slab reinforcement in the negative-moment
region of the slab adjacent to the columns, while at the same time using a
seat angle and double-angle shear connection to the web. This connection, fitting into the category of type PR construction, as defined by the AISC LRFD
specification, is a very economical solution and simple extension of a practical
connection in common practice (Fig. 2.6). Several advantages can be cited for
this connection type:

1. Reduction in short- and long-term deflections, cracking, and vibrations
inherent in many modern composite floors proportioned by limit states methods using high-strength steels.

2. Reduction in effective length of columns as a result of connection
restraint.

3. PR composite connections can provide the required lateral stiffness for
unbraced frames up to 10 stories for design governed by wind or moderate
seismic action.

4. They can be detailed to limit their strength, so that problems with local
buckling of beam flanges near connections, shear yielding of the column panel
zone, and formation of weak column–strong beam mechanisms can be avoided.

5. Reduction in overall structural steel costs because of lighter beams and columns. Connection restraint can be added at very low added cost derived from a small increase in the size of framing angles, an increase in the number of shear studs, and a small number of reinforcing bars in the slab over the connections.

6.5.2 Design of floor framing for gravity loads

As an illustration of the principles discussed in the previous section, the design and analysis method for composite semirigid connections proposed by Leon and Ammerman[125] will be presented in detail, with reference to a non-sway braced composite frame. The method is based on the following assumptions:

The composite joint form is that shown in Fig. 2.6, consisting of web angles to transmit shear, and one seat angle and slab reinforcing steel to transmit bending. The same joint is used at both ends of the beam.

For this type of joint, design to two strength levels is discussed. A joint is here considered strong if capable of transmitting a bending moment equal to the plastic capacity of the steel beam alone at a rotation less than 5 milliradians. An intermediate joint will allow about one-half of the beam plastic moment capacity to be transmitted at a rotation less than 10 milliradians.

Unshored construction is assumed. This means that the joints behave as pinned before the concrete hardens, and that the basic dead load is applied at this stage.

The joints frame into the strong axis of the column. The column satisfies shear yielding criteria without requiring stiffeners.

A very important preliminary step in the design procedure is the arbitrary selection of the degree of fixity desired at the columns. For optimum semi-rigid design, in fact, the moments at the support and at the centerline should be the same ($Pl_b/6$ or $w_d l_b^2/16$), if the section is symmetrical and homogeneous. Composite beam cross section is neither symmetrical nor homogeneous. Therefore, upper and lower bounds and suggested values for some common loading cases of composite beams are listed in Table 6.1.

The design, to some extent, is controlled by the number of bolts that can be attached to the bottom flange of the beam. It will be assumed that for practical reasons that limit is six bolts (three on each side of the web). The joint should be expected to be slip-critical at service loads.

The slab is considered as effective in tension, in that it can mobilize the tensile resistance of longitudinal reinforcing bars, for a breadth equal to seven column flange widths.

The exterior column joint in the frame is designed and detailed as a simple joint. Thus the exterior spans are pinned at one end and partially restrained at the other.

TABLE 6.1   Range of End Moments for Different Loadings[125]

Load case	Rigid joints			Pinned joints			Semirigid joints
	$M_{fe,e}$	$M_{fe,c}$	δ_{fe}	M_{ss}	θ_{ss}	δ_{ss}	$M_{sr,e}$
↓↓↓↓↓↓↓↓↓↓↓ w	$\dfrac{wL_b^2}{12}$	$\dfrac{wL_b^2}{24}$	$\dfrac{wL_b^4}{384EI_c}$	$\dfrac{wL_b^2}{8}$	$\dfrac{wL_b^3}{24EI_c}$	$\dfrac{5wL_b^4}{384EI_c}$	$\dfrac{wL_b^2}{14}$ to $\dfrac{wL_b^2}{24}$
↓P	$\dfrac{PL_b}{8}$	$\dfrac{PL_b}{8}$	$\dfrac{PL_b^3}{192EI_c}$	$\dfrac{PL_b}{4}$	$\dfrac{PL_b^2}{16EI_c}$	$\dfrac{PL_b^3}{48EI_c}$	$\dfrac{PL_b}{10}$ to $\dfrac{PL_b}{16}$
↓P ↓P	$\dfrac{2PL_b}{9}$	$\dfrac{PL_b}{9}$	$\dfrac{5PL_b^3}{648EI_c}$	$\dfrac{PL_b}{3}$	$\dfrac{PL_b^2}{9EI_c}$	$\dfrac{23PL_b^3}{648EI_c}$	$\dfrac{PL_b}{6}$ to $\dfrac{PL_b}{9}$
↓P ↓P ↓P	$\dfrac{5PL_b}{16}$	$\dfrac{3PL_b}{16}$	$\dfrac{PL_b^3}{96EI_c}$	$\dfrac{PL_b}{2}$	$\dfrac{5PL_b^2}{32EI_c}$	$\dfrac{19PL_b^3}{384EI_c}$	$\dfrac{PL_b}{4}$ to $\dfrac{PL_b}{8}$
↓P ↓P ↓P ↓P	$\dfrac{2PL_b}{5}$	$\dfrac{PL_b}{5}$	$\dfrac{13PL_b^3}{1000EI_c}$	$\dfrac{3PL_b}{5}$	$\dfrac{PL_b^2}{5EI_c}$	$\dfrac{63PL_b^3}{1000EI_c}$	$\dfrac{7PL_b}{20}$ to $\dfrac{PL_b}{10}$

M = moment
δ = midspan deflection
θ = end rotation
L_b = beam length
E = modulus of elasticity of steel
I_c = moment of inertia of composite section
Subscripts: fe = fixed ends, ss = simple supports, sr = semirigid joints, e = at end of span, c = at center of span.

The following steps are required for design:

1. Calculate design moments M_{cf} due to factored construction loads, and the design dead-load moments M_D assuming simple supports. The self-weight of the girder and floor beams is assumed to be included in the overall dead loads. Appropriate resistance factors should be selected for the steel beams as well as for the composite beams; in the framework of AISC LRFD specifications,[D91] the values 0.90 and 0.85, respectively, are suggested for the resistance factor ϕ.

2. Select the degree of restraint desired by assuming the amount of the factored live-load moment M_{ue}, desired at the supports (Table 6.1). Once M_{ue} has been chosen the factored moment at the center M_{uc} can be computed as the difference between the ultimate simply supported factored moment M_{us} and M_{ue}. For exterior bays M_{uc} is the difference between M_{us} and $M_{ue}/2$.

3. Select a composite beam to carry M_{uc}, based on a steel beam capable of carrying M_{cf} without reaching its plastic capacity and M_D without yielding.

4. Choose a seat angle based on the area of the angle leg A_a being capable of transmitting the total required horizontal force H_a on the bottom angle determined as

$$H_a = \frac{M_{ue}}{d_s + Y_2} \tag{6.31}$$

i.e., assuming a lever arm equal to the steel beam depth d_s plus the distance Y_2 from the top of the beam to the center of the slab force, which may be different for positive and negative moment. Thus,

$$A_a = 1.33 \frac{H_a}{F_{ya}} \tag{6.32}$$

where F_{ya} is the yield stress of the seat angle and the 1.33 factor is adopted in order to ensure that the slab reinforcing steel, which is also designed on the basis of the horizontal force H_a, yields first.

For connection purposes the angle needs to be at least as wide as the beam flange; therefore, select an angle width l_a at least equal to the beam flange width b_f and determine the angle thickness t_a as

$$t_a = \frac{A_a}{l_a} \tag{6.33}$$

5. Compute the amount of slab reinforcement A_r based on the force H_a and the reinforcing steel yield strength F_{yr}:

$$A_r = \frac{H_a}{F_{yr}} \tag{6.34}$$

The longitudinal slab steel should be kept within a column strip less than or equal to six column flange widths and should extend at least 12 in (0.3 m) past the point of inflection. The bar size should be kept small (less than a #7), and at least three bars on either side of the column should be used. Transverse steel should be provided at each column line and should extend at least 12 in outside the column strip.

6. Determine the moment capacity for the joint designed above at service and ultimate by using the formulas proposed by Leon and Forcier[136] for negative moments.

For service loads the moment capacity M_s is given by

$$M_s = 0.17(4A_r F_{yr} + A_a F_{ya})(d_s + Y_2) \tag{6.35}$$

while for ultimate the moment capacity M_u is given by

$$M_u = 0.245(4A_r F_{yr} + A_a F_{ya})(d_s + Y_2) \tag{6.36}$$

Equations (6.35) and (6.36) represent nominal moments. To obtain design moments, they should be multiplied by the appropriate resistance factor. Resistance factor $\phi = 0.85$ is recommended when the AISC LRFD specification[D91] is used.

The complete moment-rotation curve is given by

$$M(\theta) = C_1(1 - e^{-A\theta}) + C_3\theta \tag{6.37}$$

where $C_1 = A_r F_{yr}(d_s + Y_2)$
$A = C_2 = 32.9(A_a/A_r)^{0.15}(d_s + Y_2)$
$C_3 = 24 F_{ya} A_a (d_s + Y_2)$
θ = rotation, radians

7. To check the compatibility condition, several techniques are used. The two simplest are discussed here:

   a. Assume that the serviceability condition will be reached at a rotation of 2.5 milliradians, and the ultimate at 10 milliradians. For these values of θ compute the moments from Eq. (6.37). If the moments obtained exceed those required, the connection is satisfactory.

   b. Develop a beam line for the beam (Fig. 6.31) with the given loading conditions by calculating the fixed-end moment M_f and simply supported rotation θ_s for both service and factored live loads. For exterior spans with the exterior connection pinned, the moment at the end of a propped cantilever should be used in place of the fixed-end moment to achieve compatibility at the interior connection. An estimate of I_c can be obtained by using a weighted average of moments of inertia in the positive-moment region and negative-moment region, e.g., from the tables of I_{LB} given on pages 5-9 and 5-50 to 5-65 in the LRFD Manual.[D91] Approximately 60 percent of the span is subjected to positive moment in interior spans. Therefore, it is suggested to use Eq. (5.1).

   Find the rotations (θ_{rs} or θ_{rf}) at the intersection of the beam line with the moment-rotation curve for service and factored loads. This can be done graphically or analytically. The latter involves solving the equations

$$M(\theta_{rs}) = M_{fs}\left(1 - \frac{\theta_{rs}}{\theta_{ss}}\right)$$ (6.38)

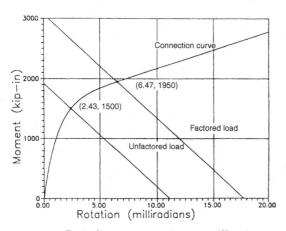

Figure 6.31 Beam line vs. connection curve.[125]

$$M(\theta_{rf}) = M_{ff}\left(1 - \frac{\theta_{rf}}{\theta_{sf}}\right) \tag{6.39}$$

8. Check the stresses in the composite section due to unfactored loads. Under the arbitrary point in time concept the expected live load is half of the full live load. Therefore, a reasonable stress check rather than full live plus dead load is

$$1.2\sigma_D + 0.5\sigma_L < 0.9F_y \tag{6.40}$$

This check ensures that yielding does not occur under service loads.

9. Design the web angles for maximum factored shear as a bearing-type connection. Select the size of the bolts in the web connections to match those in the beam flange to avoid confusion during erection.

10. Calculate dead-load deflection for cambering, and service load deflections.

11. To ensure complete composite action, supply the required number of shear connectors in the beam. This procedure should also work with partially composite sections, which would allow a reduction in the number of studs, but no experimental data have been gathered on the effect of partial shear connection on the connection moment–rotation characteristics.

This design method was developed for typical floor framing of buildings and has several limits of applicability. Most of these limits come from uncertainty of the connection moment–rotation behavior. The method should not be used for spans longer than about 50 ft (15 m), for beams deeper than W27, and for beams with flange thicknesses greater than 0.8 in (20 mm). The last limitation is based on the presumption that for beams with very thick flanges it would be difficult to develop the force in the bottom flange with a seat angle bolted to the flange.

6.5.3 Semirigid connection design for gravity loads

The design procedure described in Sec. 6.5.2 is illustrated with a numerical example for a braced frame with semirigid composite connections.

The general layout of the structure is given by Fig. 6.32. The typical girder to be designed is located along column line B and is limited in depth to 18 in (0.46 m). The span is 30 ft (9 m) and the beams are spaced at 10 ft (3 m). The materials are A572 steel with yield stress of F_y = 50 ksi (345 MPa) for the girder, A36 steel with F_y = 36 ksi (248 MPa) for the connection angles, grade 60 steel with F_y = 60 ksi (413 MPa) for the reinforcing bars, and a lightweight concrete with a compressive strength f_c' = 3.5 ksi (24 MPa). The beams have a tributary area of 240 ft^2 (22 m^2), and the loading for the girders is simulated by point loads at the third points.

Design a typical interior bay using the following data:

$$S_D = \text{service dead load} = 60 \text{ lb/ft}^2$$

$$F_D = \text{factored dead load} = 1.2 \times 60 = 72 \text{ lb/ft}^2$$

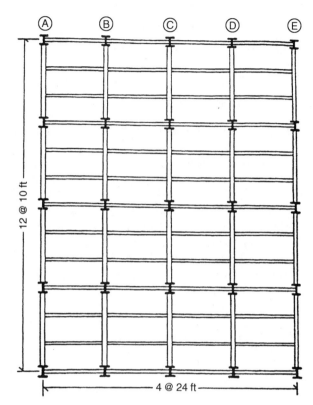

Figure 6.32 Typical floor layout for design example.[125]

$$S_L = \text{service live load} = 100 \text{ lb/ft}^2$$

$$F_L = \text{factored live load} = 1.6 \times 100 = 160 \text{ lb/ft}^2$$

$$P_D = \text{point load on girder due to service dead load} = 14.40 \text{ kips}$$

$$P_L = \text{point load on girder due to service live load} = 24.00 \text{ kips}$$

$$P_{Df} = \text{factored } P_D = 24 \times 10 \times 72 = 17.28 \text{ kips}$$

$$P_{Lf} = \text{factored } P_L = 24 \times 10 \times 160 = 38.40 \text{ kips}$$

$$P_f = \text{factored point load on girder} = 17.3 + 38.4 = 55.7 \text{ kips}$$

The floor slab is made with lightweight concrete of 110 lb/ft³ and is 5 in thick, including 2-in formed steel deck. Thus the weight of wet concrete is about 40 lb/ft², and the construction loads are:

$$S_{cD} = \text{construction dead load} = 60 \text{ lb/ft}^2$$

$$F_{cD} = \text{factored construction dead load} = 1.2 \times S_{cD} = 72 \text{ lb/ft}^2$$

S_{cL} = construction live load = 20 lb/ft²

F_{cL} = factored construction live load = 20 × 1.6 = 32 lb/ft²

F_{cT} = factored construction loads = $F_{cD} + F_{cL}$ = 104 lb/ft²

P_{cf} = factored construction point load on girder = 24.96 kips

The maximum moment M_{cf} during construction is 249.6 ft-kips (resisted by the steel section alone), and the maximum centerline moment at ultimate M_{uc} is 556.8 ft-kips (resisted by the composite section). The W18×46 is the lightest W18 shape that can resist these moments. For this section with full composite action ϕM_{pc} = 611 ft-kips, so partial composite action could be used with ΣQ_n = 492 kips and ϕM_{pc} = 569 ft-kips. With this choice of partial composite action the required number of ¾-in shear studs is 50 for the entire span. The service-load deflection for this beam is 0.82 in, or about $l/441$.

The design of braced steel frame utilizing semirigid composite connections entails the following steps described in Sec. 6.5.2.

Step 1.   Calculate design moments M_{cf} and M_D:

$$M_{cf} = \frac{P_{cf}l}{3} = \frac{24.96 \times 30 \times 12}{3} = 2995 \text{ in-kips}$$

$$M_D = \frac{P_{Df}l}{3} = \frac{17.28 \times 30 \times 12}{3} = 2074 \text{ in-kips}$$

Step 2.   Calculate the factored live-load moment M_{ue} desired at the supports and the factored moments M_{us} and M_{uc} for a simply supported beam (see Table 6.1):

$$M_{ue} = \frac{P_{Lf}l}{9} = \frac{38.4 \times 30 \times 12}{9} = 1536 \text{ in-kips}$$

$$M_{us} = \frac{P_f l}{3} = \frac{55.7 \times 30 \times 12}{3} = 6684 \text{ in-kips}$$

$$M_{uc} = M_{us} - M_{ue} = 6684 - 1536 = 5148 \text{ in-kips}$$

Step 3.   Assuming A572 steel (F_y = 50 ksi; 345 MPa), the required elastic section modulus S_s and plastic section modulus Z_s for the steel beam are

$$S_s = \frac{M_D}{F_y} = \frac{2074}{50} = 41.5 \text{ in}^3$$

$$Z_s = \frac{M_{cf}}{\phi_b F_y} = \frac{2995}{0.9 \times 50} = 66.6 \text{ in}^3$$

The lightest W18 which meets these criteria is a W18 × 35, with S_s = 57.6 in³, Z_s = 66.5 in³, and ϕM_{pc} = 5628 in-kips.

As for most cases of unshored construction, the construction loads are going to determine the beam size. Although reasonable values of construction loads were assumed in this example, the composite section is still much stronger than needed.

An alternate method for design is to find the steel section required for the construction loads and provide sufficient end restraint so the composite section with this steel shape is sufficient for the full loads. This can be expressed as

$$M_{ue} = \frac{P_f l}{3} = \phi M_{pc}$$

This equation is subject to the limit $M_{ue} < 1.2M_p$. If this limit is exceeded, a larger beam section is required, and construction loads do not control the design. This is the case when the ratio of full load to construction load is greater than the ratio of $\phi M_{pc}/\phi_b M_p$.

Step 4. From Eq. (6.31), taking Y_2 as 4.1 in,

$$H_a = \frac{M_{ue}}{d_s + Y_2} = \frac{1536}{17.7 + 4.1} = 70.5 \text{ kips}$$

The limit on H_a imposed by the friction force capable of being transmitted by bolts to the angles is 158 kips. Thus 70.5 kips governs. From Eq. (6.32) using yield stress F_{ya} of the seat angle:

$$A_a = \frac{1.33H_a}{F_{ya}} = \frac{1.33 \times 70.5}{36} = 2.61 \text{ in}^2$$

The connection is slip-critical for the unfactored live-load moment. Using six bolts and observing that the live-load factor is 1.6, the required shear strength of each bolt at service load is

$$V_b = \frac{H_a}{1.6 \times 6} = \frac{70.5}{1.6 \times 6} = 7.34 \text{ kips}$$

From AISC LRFD Manual[D95] Table 8-16 the design resistance to shear at service loads of one $3/4$-in-diameter A325 bolt is 7.51 kips. Use six $3/4$-in A325 bolts.

Since six bolts are required for the connection, the angle leg along the beam should be about 9 in long. For connection purposes the angle needs to be at least as wide as the beam flange (W18 $\times$ 35, $b_f = 6.0$ in); therefore, select an angle width l_a of 6.0 in. The required thickness of the angle, based on the minimum width of 6 in, is calculated from Eq. (6.33):

$$t_a = \frac{A_a}{l_a} = \frac{2.61}{6.0} = 0.435 \approx 7/16 \text{ in}$$

The smallest thickness available in a 9-in angle is $1/2$ in; therefore, the seat angle is a 6.0-in-long L9 $\times$ 4 $\times$ $1/2$ connected with six $3/4$-in A325 fully tightened bolts. Alternately, one can use a 6.0-in-long L6 $\times$ 4 $\times$ $7/16$ with four $7/8$-in A490 bolts.

Step 5. Calculate A_r from Eq. (6.34) for slab steel yield strength F_{yr} = 60 ksi:

$$A_r = \frac{H_a}{F_{yr}} = \frac{70.5}{60} = 1.18 \text{ in}^2$$

This requires 6#4 bars (1.20 in²) or 4#5 bars (1.24 in²). Because the intent is to yield the slab steel first, care must be taken not to provide an excess amount of slab steel. The 6#4 bars will be selected here. The total area is 1.20 in². For best efficiency these should be grouped within a strip equal to 7 times the column flange width, or 84 in if a W12 column is assumed.

Step 6. Calculate the moment capacity of the connection at service and ultimate loads. Using Eq. (6.35) with ϕ = 0.85, A_r = 1.2 in², and A_a = 0.5 × 6.0 = 3 in², the service design moment is

$$\phi M_s = 0.85 \times 0.17(4A_r F_{yr} + A_a F_{ya})(d_s + Y_2)$$

$$= 0.85 \times 0.17 \times [(4 \times 1.2 \times 60) + (3 \times 36)](17.7 + 4.1)$$

$$= 1247 \text{ in-kips} > \frac{M_{ue}}{1.6} = \frac{1536}{1.6} = 960 \text{ in-kips}$$

The ultimate moment capacity M_u is given by Eq. (6.36). As the only difference between Eqs. (6.35) and (6.36) is their numerical coefficient, the ultimate moment capacity may be computed as

$$\phi M_u = \phi M_s \frac{0.245}{0.17} = 1247 \frac{0.245}{0.17} = 1797 \text{ in-kips} > M_{ue} = 1536 \text{ in-kips}$$

Since both the service- and ultimate-load capacities exceed the required moments, the design is adequate. If the required moments were not satisfied, then it would be necessary to either go back to step 2 and assume a smaller value for M_{ue} or increase the strength of the connection in steps 4 and 5.

Step 7. Two simple techniques are illustrated below for checking the compatibility.

1. Calculate the moment from Eq. (6.37) assuming that the serviceability condition is reached at the rotation θ of 2.5 milliradians and the ultimate at 10 milliradians:

$$C_1 = A_r F_{yr}(d_s + Y_2) = 1.20 \times 60(17.7 + 4.1) = 1570 \text{ in-kips}$$

$$A = 32.9\left(\frac{A_a}{A_r}\right)^{0.15}(d_s + Y_2)$$

$$= 32.9\left(\frac{0.5 \times 6.0}{1.20}\right)^{0.15}(21.8) = 823$$

$$C_3 = 24F_{ya}A_a(d + Y_2) = 24 \times 36 \times 3 \times 21.8 = 56{,}500 \text{ in-kips}$$

For $\theta = 0.0025$

$$1 - e^{-A\theta} = 1 - e^{-(823 \times 0.0025)} = 0.873$$

$$\phi M_{2.5} = 0.85(0.873C_1 + C_3\theta)$$

$$= 0.85[(0.873 \times 1570) + (56{,}500 \times 0.0025)]$$

$$= 1285 \text{ in-kips} > 956 \text{ in-kips}$$

and for $\theta = 0.01$

$$1 - e^{-A\theta} = 1 - e^{-(823 \times 0.01)} = 1.0$$

$$\phi M_{10} = 0.85[(1.0 \times 1570) + (56{,}500 \times 0.01)]$$

$$= 1815 \text{ in-kips} > 1536 \text{ in-kips}$$

Since the moments obtained from Eq. (6.37) exceed those required, the connection is satisfactory.

2. Calculate the fixed-end moment M_f and the simply supported rotation θ_s for both service and factored live loads. For two factored concentrated loads placed at the third points of the span, the moment at the fixed end of a propped cantilever is

$$M_{ff} = \frac{2P_{Lf}l}{9} = \frac{2 \times 38.4 \times 30 \times 12}{9} = 3072 \text{ in-kips}$$

Compute I_c from Eq. (6.38) using AISC LRFD Manual,[D95] p. 5-60. Assuming that the plastic neutral axis is in the top flange, the lower-bound moment of inertia for W18 × 35 and $Y_2 = 4$ in is 1360 in⁴ for the bottom flange in the positive-moment region. For the steel section alone in the negative-moment region the moment of inertia is 510 in⁴. Assuming a moderate allowance for slab reinforcement, the lower-bound moment of inertia in the negative-moment regions is estimated at 655 in⁴. Using Eq. (5.1),

$$I_c = 0.6 \times 1360 + 0.4 \times 655 = 1078 \text{ in}^4$$

The simly supported end rotations and the service-load fixed-end moment are

$$\theta_{sf} = \frac{P_{Lf}l^2}{9EI_c} = \frac{38.4 \times 30^2 \times 144}{9 \times 29{,}000 \times 1078} = 17.7 \times 10^{-3} \text{ radian}$$

$$M_{fs} = \frac{2P_L l}{9} = \frac{2 \times 24 \times 30 \times 12}{9} = 1920 \text{ in-kips}$$

$$\theta_{ss} = \frac{P_L l^2}{9EI_c} = \frac{24}{38.4} \, 17.7 \times 10^{-3} = 11.1 \times 10^{-3} \text{ radian}$$

The rotations (θ_{rs} or θ_{rf}) at the intersection of the beam line with the connection moment-rotation curve for service and factored loads are found by solving Eqs. (6.38) and (6.39). From the graph in Fig. 6.31, $\theta_{rs} = 0.0024$ radian and $\theta_{rf} = 0.0065$ radian. Find the service and factored live-load moments as

$$M_{sl} = M_{fs} - \frac{M_{fs}\theta_{rs}}{\theta_{ss}} = 1920\left(1 - \frac{0.0024}{0.0111}\right) = 1505 \text{ in-kips}$$

$$M_{fl} = M_{ff} - \frac{M_{ff}\theta_{rf}}{\theta_{sf}} = 3072\left(1 - \frac{0.0065}{0.0177}\right) = 1944 \text{ in-kips}$$

and recalculate the factored moment at centerline:

$$M_{uc} = \frac{P_f l}{3 - M_{fl}} = \frac{55.7 \times 30 \times 12}{3} - 1944 = 4740 \text{ in-kips}$$

This is less than the 5630 in-kips that the W18 × 35 with a 5-in slab can carry as a composite section, and thus the section is satisfactory.

Step 8. Check the stresses in the section due to unfactored loads:

$$\sigma_D = \frac{P_D l}{3S_s} = \frac{14.4 \times 30 \times 12}{3 \times 57.6} = 30.0 \text{ ksi}$$

$$\sigma_L = \frac{(P_L l/3) - M_{sl}}{S_{tr}}$$

S_{tr} can be approximated from the table of I_{LB} in the LRFD Manual[D95] for full composite action by the equation

$$S_{tr} = \frac{I_{LB}}{0.75d + 0.5Y_2} = \frac{1360}{0.75 \times 17.7 + 4.1 \times 0.5} = 88.7 \text{ in}^3$$

$$\sigma_L = \frac{[(24 \times 30 \times 12)/3] - 1505}{88.7} = 15.5 \text{ ksi}$$

This gives a total stress under unfactored loads of 45.5 ksi, which is less than the nominal yield stress of 50 ksi. The live-load stresses given are for the full live load. Under the arbitrary point in time concept the expected live load is half of the full live load. Therefore, a reasonable stress check, rather than full live plus dead load, is

$$1.2\sigma_D + 0.5\sigma_L = (1.2 \times 30) + (0.5 \times 15.5) = 43.8 \text{ ksi} < 0.9F_y = 45 \text{ ksi}$$

Thus the W18 × 35 is satisfactory for this case.

Step 9. Design connection web angles using ¾-in A325 bolts with threads in the shear plane. The maximum shear is

$$V_u = \frac{P_f}{\phi_v} = \frac{55.7}{0.75} = 74.3 \text{ kips}$$

Checking for bearing and shear on the beam web, the number of bolts is found as

$$n_b = \frac{V_u}{2.4F_u dt} = \frac{74.3}{2.4 \times 65 \times 0.75 \times 0.3} = 2.12$$

$$n_b = \frac{\phi V_u}{31.0 \text{ (kips/bolt)}} = \frac{0.75 \times 74.3}{31} = 1.80$$

Therefore, three bolts are required. Checking bearing on the angles, we can find the angle thickness t_a:

$$2t_a = \frac{V_u}{2.4F_u n_b d} = \frac{74.3}{2.4 \times 58 \times 3 \times 0.75} = 0.237 \text{ in}$$

Therefore, a $\frac{1}{4}$-in angle is sufficient. Based on clearance and minimum distances, select a pair of $4 \times 4 \times \frac{1}{4}$ angles 8.5 in long for the web.

The tests on which this method is based all had a minimum of three bolts for the connection of the web angles to the beam; therefore, it is not recommended to use a lower number of bolts.

Step 10. Calculate dead-load and service live-load deflections:

$$\delta_d = \frac{23P_D l^3}{648EI_s}$$

$$= \frac{23 \times 14.4 \times 30^3 \times 1728}{648 \times 29,000 \times 510} = 1.61 \text{ in}$$

$$\delta_l = \frac{5P_L l^3}{648EI_c} + \frac{l\,\theta_{rs}}{4} = \frac{5 \times 24 \times 30^3 \times 1728}{648 \times 29,000 \times 1078}$$

$$+ (0.25 \times 30 \times 12 \times 0.0024) = 0.49 \text{ in}$$

This live-load deflection is equal to $l/731$, much lower than the largest acceptable $l/360$. This is as expected for beams with semirigid composite connections. The small service-load deflection suggests that vibration problems are likely to be minimized.

Step 11. The negative moment at the support is 1949 in-kip and the positive moment under the point loads is 4740 in-kip. This implies that the inflection point will be 35 in from the end. From the AISC LRFD Manual p. 5-44, $\Sigma Q_n = 515$ kips in the positive-moment region, which will require fifty-two $\frac{3}{4}$-in diameter studs over the center 290 in. In the negative-moment region,

$$\Sigma Q_n = A_r F_{yr} = 1.2 \times 60 = 72 \text{ kips}$$

which will require four studs in the end 35 in. One stud every 6 in over the entire span will be sufficient. NOTE: Discount the value of the stud by 25 percent because of the single stud per row.

For this example the use of semirigid composite connections resulted in a beam selection of W18 × 35 with sixty ¾-in shear studs, as opposed to the W18 × 46 with fifty ¾-in shear studs required if the beam were designed as simply supported. The savings of 24 percent in weight is offset by 20 percent increase in the number of shear studs and the addition of 1.20 in² of reinforcing at each end of the span. This small amount of reinforcing may have been provided also in the simply supported beam design in order to reduce the amount of cracking in the concrete slab at the columns. The major difference is in the service-load deflections, for which the semirigid composite beam gives $l/731$ versus $l/441$ for the simply supported one.

6.5.4   Unbraced frames with semirigid connections

The connection described in the previous section can also be used for unbraced frames up to about 10 stories. In frames in which the lateral loading is large when compared to the gravity loading, the connections will experience moment reversal and be loaded under positive moment. In this case it is desirable to detail the connection so it has stiffness in the positive-moment region similar to that in the negative-moment region. This requires increasing the area (and especially the thickness) of the seat angle and increasing the area of the web angles. It is recommended to provide a seat angle area of 1.5 times that required for negative moments and increase the size of the web angles by 50 percent from that required for shear. These increases are needed because the connection angles have different behavior when loaded in tension from that when loaded in compression.

Semirigid composite frames have much better behavior than other semirigid frames when subjected to combined gravity and lateral loads. Generally semirigid connections are very nonlinear, but semirigid composite connections have nearly linear behavior in the service region, and the complete moment rotation curve can be modeled quite accurately with a trilinear curve approximating Eq. (6.37).

The calculation of drift for serviceability requires a second-order analysis because of the semirigid nature of the connections. Usually for frames less than 10 stories the P-Δ moments are small, and many designers do not perform second-order analysis for these structures. When the connections are semirigid, however, the drifts associated with even these low-rise structures can be substantial and the P-Δ moments can become significant. For this reason it is recommended that a second-order analysis be used for all structures with semirigid connections.

A check should be made for the adequacy of the connections. If any connection rotation is greater than 0.020 radian, the connection should be stiffened. It is very unlikely a frame which meets all serviceability criteria could have connection rotations this large. If the moment at any connection is greater than the assumed moment, that connection must be strengthened. If the frame is adequate, the final design of the connections can be done. The number of bolts required can be determined from the largest moment at the connection, as the stiffness of the connection, prior to slip, is not affected by the number of bolts.

If the preliminary frame design proves to be too flexible or fails due to stability, the frame must be stiffened. This can be done in several ways. The least expensive way is to increase the stiffness of the connections by increasing the size of the connection angles and the amount of reinforcing which is continuous across the slab. If the connections have reached their maximum size and drift is still too large, then the framing members must be strengthened. If the depth of the beam is increased, this will also increase the strength and stiffness of the connections, or else the stiffness of the columns can be increased, either by using deeper columns of the same nominal weight or by using heavier columns of the same depth.

6.5.5 Stub-girder column connections

The stub-girder system was developed in 1970 as an integrated structural and mechanical floor framing system for office buildings.[D28,D41] An elevation of a typical stub girder is shown in Fig. 6.33. The stub girder usually consists of W14 bottom chord utilizing A572-50 steel and shop-attached stub pieces which vary in length from approximately 3 to 6 ft (0.9 to 1.8 m). The girder frames between building columns and is shored during construction. Floor beams span transversely between girders and are spaced between 8 and 15 ft (2.4 and 4.6 m) on centers. Corrugated steel deck $1\frac{1}{2}$ to 3 in (38 to 76 mm) deep spans between the floor beams, and the assembly is completed by the placement of shear studs, reinforcement, and a concrete slab. More information on the stub-girder system can be found in Chap. 3.

Structurally, the behavior of the stub girder is similar to that of a

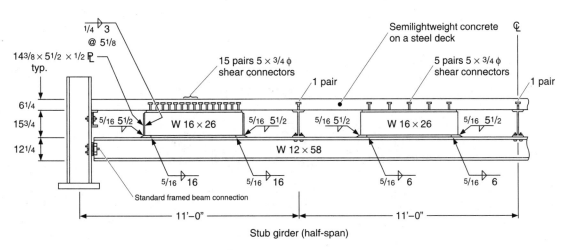

Figure 6.33 Elevation of full-size stub girder.[D41]

Vierendeel girder with a concrete slab as compression top chord, a high-strength steel bottom tension chord, and steel stubs as verticals. Hence the utilization of concrete and steel to their optimum material strengths results in savings in cost. This section concentrates on the end connection of the stub girder to its supporting column. Consideration is given to the simple shear connection for carrying gravity loads only, as is most often the case, and also the special case where the stub girder is connected to the column with a moment connection to provide continuity for carrying superimposed floor loads or to carry lateral frame loads.

Typically a stub girder is connected to its supporting column to carry only gravity loads in pure shear (Fig. 6.33). The bottom chord of the girder is provided with a standard double-angle framed beam web connection proportioned for direct shear only. The connection may be either welded or bolted and is designed according to standard AISC practices. The top slab is usually provided with an angle or channel seat support to the column. Often the slab is doweled. These connections are consistent with the usual Vierendeel analysis of the stub girder. The bottom chord and top slab is assumed to be pinned to the column.

An alternative connection to the column has been proposed as shown in Fig. 6.34. This configuration has several advantages, including a deeper space for the end connection to the column, more room available for studs on the end stub, and more direct space available at the girder end, permitting better integration of building services.

In wind-resisting systems, the design of the girder column connections is one of the critical aspects of the design. The fundamental problem is the moment transfer at the column-girder interface. For relatively large moments, the solution is to extend the first stub piece to the column face as shown in Fig. 6.35. The top flange of the stub piece and the bottom flange of the W14 girder are welded to the column, as in a typical moment connection.

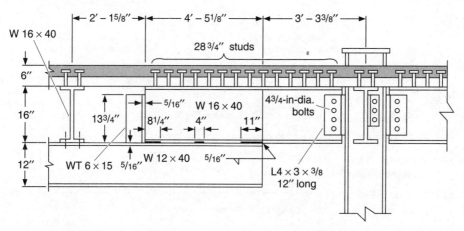

Figure 6.34 Modified end connection.

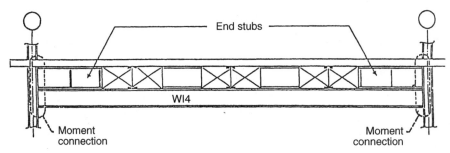

Figure 6.35 Moment-resisting stub girder.[C58]

The design of the connection, therefore, is identical to that of any other beam-to-column moment connection. Care should be exercised that the girder system is checked along its full length for the critical combination of gravity- and wind-load forces. Depending upon the magnitude of reversal of stresses due to wind load, the bracing of the bottom chord may be necessary. The model used for the analysis is a simulated Vierendeel beam where the concrete slab and the bottom steel piece are simulated as linear elements and each stub piece is subdivided into several vertical elements. The gravity- and wind-load exterior forces and moments are then introduced as load cases, and the combined axial forces and moments in each section of the stub girder are obtained. All parts of the girder are then checked for combined axial forces, shear, and moments by the AISC and ACI codes. The controlling section for the slab is generally at the end of the first stub piece farthest from the column.

In the case where the wind moments are small, an alternate detail shown in Fig. 6.36 is possible. In this case, the moment transfer at the column takes place through the concrete slab and the W14 steel section. The slab needs to be attached to the column either by long deformed shear studs or by reinforcing bars welded to the column. If the deformed studs are used, reinforcing bars are generally placed alongside the studs to transfer the forces past the end of the stubs. In the case of extremely low wind moments, it is also possible to design the frame utilizing the girder with different moments of inertia at its two ends.

At the end where the concrete slab is in compression, the full depth of section is used (the slab width is reduced to the width of the column face), whereas at the other end, the moment of inertia of the W14 bottom steel section is considered alone.

6.6 Beam-to-Wall Connections

In mid- and high-rise buildings, concrete shear walls are often used to provide resistance to lateral wind and seismic loads. Frequently, the architectural layout is such that corridors or lobby access to the central core of the building require walls to be separated or interrupted by large openings (Fig. 6.37). From a structural standpoint, the overall performance of the lateral-load-

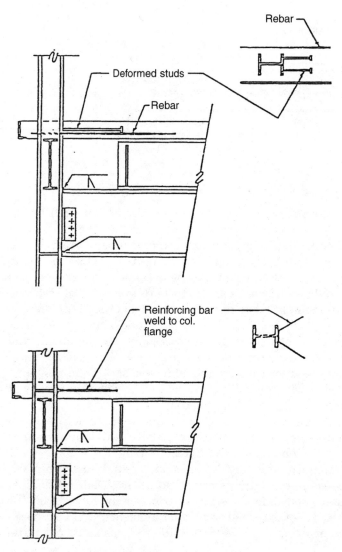

Figure 6.36 Wind-resisting stub-girder frame.[C58]

resisting system can be dramatically improved if these walls are "coupled" rather than act independently. This coupling, while improving the lateral stiffness, puts a large shear demand on the coupling element, whether steel or reinforced concrete.

Properly designed coupled walls have many desirable earthquake-resistant design features. Large lateral stiffness and strength can be achieved. The energy dissipation can be controlled to occur over the height of the building in the coupling beams rather than concentrating it predominantly at the foundation level. Postearthquake repair costs can be reduced, as damage in the coupling beams may be kept within tolerable limits. Considering these

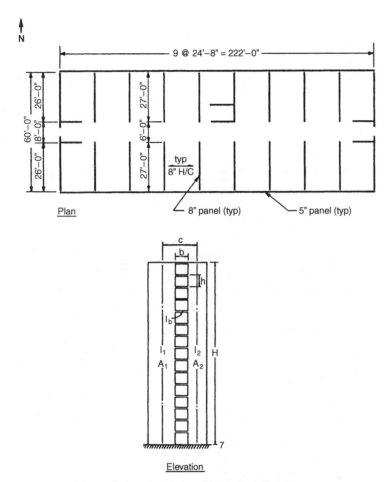

Figure 6.37 Plan and elevation of a multistory building.[141]

advantages, seismic design of structural walls coupled by reinforced concrete beams has been studied extensively in the past. Well-established design guidelines are now available.

During major earthquakes, large seismic forces are transferred between individual wall piers through the coupling beams. The coupling beams are expected to undergo large inelastic load reversals without a significant loss of strength, stiffness, and energy-dissipation capability. That is, the coupling beams should be adequately stiff and strong and should possess stable hysteresis response. Such requirements on conventional reinforced concrete coupling beams will demand special detailing, adequate anchorage of the reinforcement in the wall piers, and closely spaced confinement around the main reinforcement to prevent buckling. As a result, reinforced concrete coupling beams are typically deep, making them unsuitable for structures with low-story heights. For such cases, structural steel beams embedded in door lintels are commonly used as coupling beams (Fig. 6.38). The transfer of forces

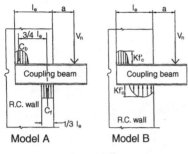

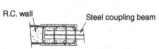

Figure 6.38 Coupling beam detail and modeling.[141,D88]

between the steel coupling beams and reinforced concrete wall piers has not been completely understood until the completion of recent research.

Recent research was conducted at the University of Cincinnati[141] and at McGill University in Montreal.[134] On the basis of his studies at Cincinnati, Shahrooz concluded the following regarding the performance of steel beam coupled shear walls:

1. The steel coupling beams have stable hysteresis curves with little loss of strength. The theoretical plastic moment capacities can be reached and exceeded when the connection region is under compressive stresses. When the boundary element is subjected to large tensile stresses, the resulting cracks reduce the stiffness. Hence the moment that can be developed in the beam becomes smaller. The addition of vertical bars to the beam flanges helps to develop equal moments for cycles producing tensile and compressive stresses on the connection region.

2. A significant portion of energy is dissipated through "plastic hinges" in the exposed portion of the coupling beams. The contributions of flexural and shear deformations are significant.

3. The stiffness of the coupling beam is found to be different depending on whether the overturning moment and axial load would cause compressive or tensile stresses in the boundary element around the connection region. For details with auxiliary bars attached to the beam flanges, the stiffness is more symmetrical and larger.

4. The rate of stiffness degradation, although small, is also different for cycles resulting in tensile and compressive stresses in the connection region. Addition of auxiliary vertical bars to the beam flanges slightly helps to maintain the overall stiffness.

5. The initial stiffness of the coupling beams is smaller than the value computed assuming full fixity at the face of the wall. The beams are effectively fixed at a point inside the boundary elements. However, it should be noted that a similar lack of rigidity at the support face is also possible for reinforced concrete coupling beams.

6. If the additional flexibility of the coupling beam is considered, the

demands in the walls and the overall lateral deflections obviously become larger than those obtained if the beams are assumed to be fully fixed at the face of the walls.

7. If the connection between steel beams and concrete walls does not have special details to improve the stiffness, models that simulate fixity of coupling beams inside the wall piers should be used. The "effective fixed point" of the coupling beam can be taken at approximately one-third of the embedment length from the face of the wall.

6.6.1 Embedment length of coupling beams

The required embedment length of the steel coupling beams in the walls can be evaluated based on two methods that are variations of the Prestressed Concrete Institute guidelines for design of steel beams used as brackets.[G77] In each model (Fig. 6.38), the concrete strain is assumed to vary linearly, with the maximum concrete strain taken as 0.003 at the face of the wall. The first model, model A, is that proposed by Mattock and Gaafar.[81] Using the distribution of bearing stresses shown in Fig. 6.38, the required embedment length l_e can be computed from

$$V_u = 0.9 f_b \beta_1 b_f l_e \frac{0.58 - 0.22\beta_1}{0.88 + a_u/l_e} \tag{6.41}$$

where f_b = bearing strength, ksi = $1.71(t_w/b_f)^{0.66}\sqrt{f_c'}$
  t_w = width of wall (a boundary element)
  b_f = beam flange width
  f_c' = concrete compressive strength, ksi
  β_1 = ratio of the average concrete compressive stress to the maximum stress as defined in the ACI building code,[100] Sec. 10.2.7.3
  l_e = embedment length
  $a_u = M_u/V_u$
  M_u = ultimate beam moment
  V_u = ultimate shear

The required embedment length to develop a vertical shear at the distance a from the face of the wall is computed from this equation. In the second method, model B, the concrete stress distribution is modified to reflect larger strength and stiffness due to the confinement provided by large amounts of transverse reinforcement in typical boundary elements. The modified Kent-Park model[G38] can be used to represent the concrete stress-strain relationship, and the assumed stress distribution is changed as shown in model B of Fig. 6.38. Similar to the derivation of the model proposed by Gaafar and Mattock, the effective bearing width is taken as $b_f(t_w/b_f)^{0.66}$. A closed-form expression for computing the required embedment length l_e cannot be derived. The necessary length l_e for developing the computed shear and moment of the coupling beam at any floor can be calculated for a number of different levels of confinement expressed in terms of the ratio of the compressive strength of confined concrete f'_{cc} to the nominal compressive strength of concrete f'_c.

6.6.2   Computer modeling of coupled shear walls

The observed lack of fixity of the steel coupling beam at the face of the wall during tests raises concerns about the level of coupling that can be developed between individual reinforced concrete shear walls. A simple model that is easy to apply in practice is to assume that the beam is effectively fixed at some distance inside the wall as shown in Fig. 6.39. This "effective fixed point" of the coupling beam can be taken as approximately one-third of the embedment length from the face of the wall. The actual design of the shear wall system should account for this fixity of the coupling beams.

6.6.3   Detailing considerations

The longitudinal bars in the boundary elements should be so arranged that the coupling beams can fit within the boundary element. This constraint usually results in bars that are placed on opposite faces of the boundary element with a clear distance at least equal to the width of the coupling beam. Large

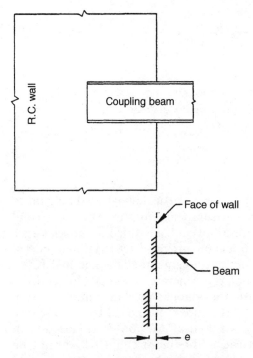

Figure 6.39 Effective fixed point of a coupling beam.[141,D88]

axial loads can develop in coupling beams as compression and tensile loads from flexural, axial, and shear stiffness characteristics of wall piers. Adequate headed studs should be welded to the beam over the embedment length. A majority of the studs should be distributed over the top and bottom flanges. These studs have the added benefit of transferring bearing stresses into the surrounding concrete and helping to increase the stiffness. Standard design methods can be used to compute the size and number of the studs. Small holes may be punched in the web to facilitate compaction of concrete. The effects of these holes on the shear capacity of the web should be checked.

6.6.4 Coupled shear wall design

Typical design and detailing procedures are illustrated in this example using the structure shown in Fig. 6.40. The reinforced concrete walls are coupled by steel beams embedded in the door lintels. The lateral loads are assumed to be resisted entirely by the coupled walls. The contribution of reinforced concrete door lintels, which are usually reinforced lightly, to the strength and stiffness of the coupling beams is neglected. Seismic design forces may be determined according to the requirements of the Uniform Building Code (UBC). The reinforced concrete walls are proportioned and detailed in accordance with the UBC and seismic provisions of the ACI Building Code.

Design of steel coupling beams and the design of the connection between steel coupling beams and reinforced concrete walls are illustrated with reference to a typical floor. Similar calculations can be carried out at other locations.

Design of steel coupling beams. Ultimate required moment M_u and shear V_u are

$$M_u = 558 \text{ ft-kips (757 kN-m)}$$

$$V_u = 323.7 \text{ kips (1440 kN)}$$

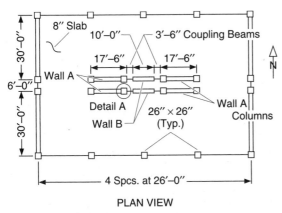

PLAN VIEW

Figure 6.40 Floor plan with coupled shear walls.[141,D88]

Design web thickness:

$$V_u \leq 0.6 F_y d t_w$$

$F_y = 36$ ksi (A36 steel) and $d = 18$ in (depth of beam)
Solve for t_w (web thickness) from

$$323.7 \leq 0.6 \times 36 \times 18 t_w$$

$$t_w \geq 0.833 \text{ in}$$

Use $t_w = \frac{7}{8}$ in.
Design beam flanges:

$$M_u \leq F_y Z$$

where $Z = [(b_f t_f)(d - t_f)] + \left[\dfrac{t_w}{4}(d - 2t_f)^2 \right]$

b_f = flange width = 8 in
t_f = flange thickness

$$Z = \frac{M_u}{F_y} \geq \frac{558 \times 12}{36} = 186 \text{ in}^3$$

$$186 \leq [8t_f(18 - t_f)] + \left[\frac{0.875}{4}(18 - 2t_f)^2 \right]$$

Solve for $t_f \geq 0.948$ in
   Use $t_f = 1.0$ in.
Check local buckling requirements:
Flange:

$$\frac{b_f}{2t_f} \leq \frac{52}{\sqrt{F_y}} = 8.67$$

$$\frac{b_f}{2t_f} = \frac{8}{2 \times 1.0} = 4.0 \qquad \text{O.K.}$$

Web:

$$\frac{d}{t_w} \leq \frac{412}{\sqrt{F_y}} = 68.7$$

$$\frac{d}{t_w} = \frac{18}{0.875} = 20.6 \qquad \text{O.K.}$$

Design of connection between coupling beam and wall.   The required embedment
length is computed using the method proposed by Mattock and Gaafar.[81]

Substitute the following values into Eq. (6.41):

$$a_u = \frac{M_u}{V_u} = \frac{558}{323.7} = 1.72 \text{ ft} = 20.7 \text{ in}$$

$$f'_c = 4 \text{ ksi}$$

$$\beta_1 = 0.85 \text{ (for 4-ksi concrete)}$$

$$t_w = \text{thickness of boundary element} = 20 \text{ in}$$

$$b_f = \text{flange width of coupling beam} = 8 \text{ in}$$

$$f_b = 1.71\left(\frac{t_w}{b_f}\right)^{0.66}\sqrt{f'_c}$$

$$= 1.71\left(\frac{20}{8}\right)^{0.66}\sqrt{4} = 6.26 \text{ ksi}$$

Then

$$323.7 = 0.9 \times 6.26 \times 0.85 \times 8 \times l_e \frac{0.58 - (0.22 \times 0.85)}{0.88 + (20.7/l_e)}$$

Solve for l_e. The required embedment length l_e is 33 in.

6.7 Miscellaneous Connections

6.7.1 Transition composite column

In multistory buildings a portion of the height is frequently constructed using one structural system while another portion is constructed using a different structural system. For example, structural steel is used in the upper levels because of speed and ease of erection, and reinforced concrete is used in the lower levels for parking. If a large steel base plate is required on top of the concrete, the joint between the two columns can be architecturally and structurally cumbersome.

It is advantageous to use a transition composite column between the steel and concrete columns as an effective means to transmit the axial forces between the two structural systems (Fig. 6.41). The transition column is made composite and the axial forces are transmitted along the length of the column using headed stud shear connectors or other shear-transmitting device. In this way, a nominal base plate, totally confined within the nominal steel column cross section, can be used that does not project outside the footprint of the concrete column and does not pose an architectural problem. This detail also permits the column concrete to stop below the floor construction (Fig. 6.41), thus making the forming easier. Usually the reinforcing steel cage from the concrete column below is used in the composite transition col-

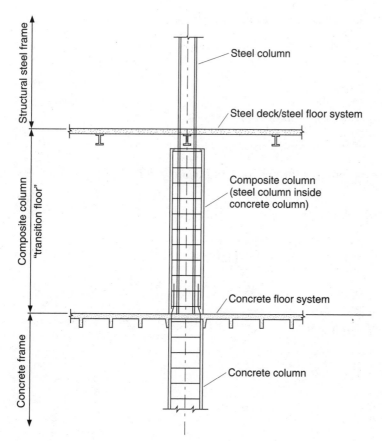

Figure 6.41 Transition composite column.

umn. The vertical column bars project up past the nominal steel column base plate.

6.7.2 Steel brace to composite columns

Braced composite megasystems such as that used in the 72-story Bank of China building[C80,C90,M21] in Hong Kong rely on the transfer of large axial forces between steel or composite braces and reinforced concrete columns. To describe the behavior and design of connections for such structures, a hypothetical composite braced building system shown in Fig. 6.42 is considered. This hypothetical building includes many of the design features used in the Bank of China building, but to simplify the discussion the structure has a more regular geometry.

The building shown in Fig. 6.42 is 48 stories tall and its geometry is based on four braced modules which measure 157 ft (48 m) by 157 ft (48 m) for a total height of 624 ft (190 m). Each module includes 12 stories with a floor-to-floor height of 13 ft (4 m). The primary structural system consists of the

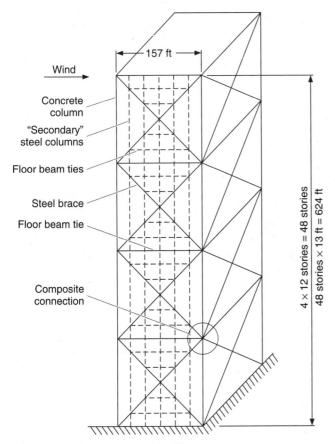

Figure 6.42 Composite braced building system.

perimeter braced frame made up of four large concrete columns at the corners connected by diagonal steel braces and horizontal steel floor beam ties. In the overall structural concept, this perimeter frame resists all lateral loads and carries approximately one-half of the total gravity load. The remainder of the gravity load is carried by interior columns located in the building's service core. The members shown dashed in Fig. 6.42 are steel columns and floor beam ties which transfer gravity loads to the main diagonals. In turn, the diagonals carry the loads to the corner columns. The dashed steel columns and ties create a secondary bracing system that provides lateral stability to the floors between the panel points of the main composite bracing system. The main system provides rigid brace points at every sixth floor, and the secondary system provides brace points at every other floor.

Two main advantages of the composite nature of the braced megasystem are related to the economy of the concrete columns and the simplicity of the corner connection details. First, the system is designed to carry much of the gravity load and all of the column overturning wind forces in the four reinforced concrete columns. This improves the economy of the system, since reinforced concrete is a more cost-effective compression material than structural steel and the maximum overturning forces and tendency for tension in the columns are minimized. The second main advantage is that the connections between the bracing and the four corner columns are greatly simplified by the composite connection detail. For an all-steel system, the corner connection would require complicated weldments to connect to the diagonals framing into the joint in three dimensions. In the composite system, all steel elements and connections are planar, and the forces in the third direction are transferred through shear stresses in the concrete encasement.

The following discussion is focused on the design of the braced corner connection at the 12th floor shown in the circled detail in Fig. 6.42. Forces in the diagonals, horizontal ties, and columns framing into this joint are shown schematically in Fig. 6.43. The dead- and live-load forces in the diagonals result from loads transferred into the diagonals by the secondary members shown dashed in Fig. 6.42. The wind loads are for the case of wind coming from the left. The wind is resisted by forces in the bracing members in the front and back elevations. The forces shown in Fig. 6.43 are from simple hand calculations which neglect any forces in the diagonals on the windward and leeward elevations caused by axial shortening and elongation of the corner columns due to the wind.

A plan and elevation view of the corner connection are shown in Figs. 6.44 and 6.45. As indicated, the steel diagonals consist of W14 (W360) shapes oriented with their flanges in the plane of the bracing. At the 12th floor, the

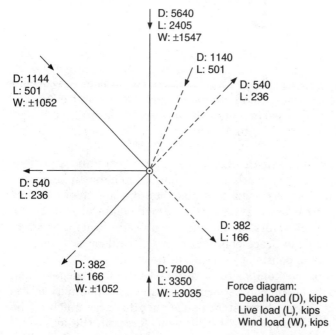

D: 5640
L: 2405
W: ±1547

D: 1140
L: 501

D: 540
L: 236

D: 1144
L: 501
W: ±1052

D: 540
L: 236

D: 382
L: 166

D: 382
L: 166
W: ±1052

D: 7800
L: 3350
W: ±3035

Force diagram:
Dead load (D), kips
Live load (L), kips
Wind load (W), kips

Figure 6.43 Forces at composite corner connection at 12th floor.

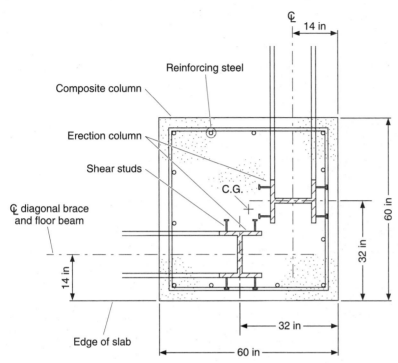

Figure 6.44 Section at corner column at 12th floor.

reinforced concrete column measures 60×60 in (1.5×1.5 m) and encases two steel sections designed to resist the concentrated vertical reaction of the diagonal braces in the two orthogonal planes. The encased steel columns also serve as erection members during the construction of the building. While the centerline locations of the encased steel columns remain fixed through the height of the building, the centroid of the reinforced concrete column moves as the column size changes based on the total axial load in the column. The column size is changed while maintaining the outer two edges of the floor slabs and varying the locations of the inner faces of the corner columns. The minimum column size at the top of the building is constrained by the locations and sizes of the encased steel columns. The locations of the encased steel columns are fixed in the direction parallel to the facade based on the 48-m module for the bracing (Fig. 6.42) and are set back from the edge of the slab the minimum amount required to allow for fireproofing and for fabrication and erection tolerances.

Referring to Fig. 6.45, the basic idea in the composite connection is to transfer the force from the flanges of the W-shaped braces and encased columns through large steel connection plates. The inside surfaces of the connection plates are aligned to match the inside flange-to-flange dimension of the W14 (W360) brace and column members; the web plates carry little load and serve primarily to hold the flanges in place. Horizontal forces are trans-

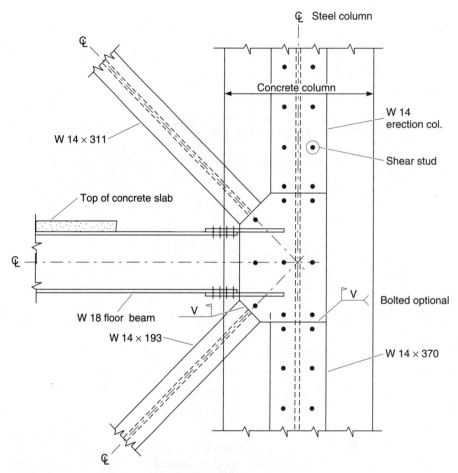

Figure 6.45 Elevation of brace detail at 12th floor.

ferred into the floor beam ties through top and bottom flange plates welded to the inside of the connection plates, and field bolted to the W18 (W460) ties. The net design forces for the upper diagonal and the steel columns above and below the connection are primarily compression, so forces can be transferred to the connection plate through bearing with only nominal tension connections made by partial-penetration groove welds or bolted splices. Since the lower diagonal is governed by tension design force, it will require full-penetration welding of its flanges to the connection plate. It is generally advantageous to make the full-penetration welds in the shop while using partial-penetration welding and bolting in the field.

The steel-to-steel connections shown in Fig. 6.45 are similar to those for ordinary structural steel construction and are relatively straightforward. The primary purpose of the composite aspect of the connection is the transfer of the resultant vertical force between the encased steel column and the reinforced

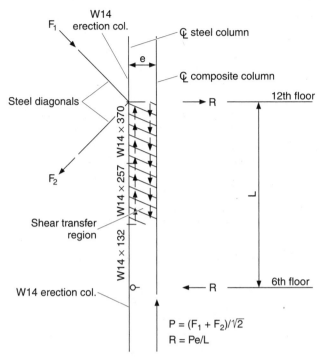

Figure 6.46 Schematic diagram of force transfer.

concrete column. A schematic diagram of this force transfer is shown in Fig. 6.46, where it is assumed that the vertical axial load applied to the steel column at the 12th floor is transferred into the reinforced concrete column gradually over the six floors below the 12th floor. This is the reason why the steel column below the 12th floor is a relatively large member while the member above the 12th floor is the minimum size required for erection. As shown in Fig. 6.46, the encased steel column decreases in size going downward from the 12th to the 6th floor, and this pattern repeats itself below the corner bracing connections at the 12th, 24th, 36th, and 48th floors. As the steel column sizes decrease, the force in the concrete portion of the column is increasing, and therefore the concrete dimensions or the reinforcing bar area is increasing.

Referring to Fig. 6.46, the total force P transferred from the steel to the concrete column is equal to the resultant of the vertical force in the two main diagonals:

$$P = \frac{F_1 + F_2}{\sqrt{2}}$$

Assuming that this force is transferred uniformly over the development length l_d, there is no moment induced in either the steel or reinforced concrete column, provided that a means is provided to resist the resultant horizontal forces R, as shown in Fig. 6.46. Comparing Figs. 6.46 and 6.44, these horizontal forces are applied in the direction of the eccentricity which, in general, is out of the plane of the bracing framing into the steel column. As shown below, the resultant force can usually be resisted by the typical floor beams and their connections which frame into the steel or reinforced concrete column at each floor level.

For the loading shown in Fig. 6.43, the total vertical forces transferred from the steel column to the concrete are P_D = 1079 kips (4.8 MN), P_L = 472 kips (2.1 MN), and P_W = 1488 kips (6.6 MN). Using the ASCE 7-95 load combination of $1.2D + 0.5L + 1.3W$, this results in a factored transfer force P_u = 3467 kips (15.4 MN). The question then arises as to what means are available for transferring this force out of the structural steel column and into the surrounding concrete. Mechanisms which are at work include (1) adhesion and friction between the steel and concrete, (2) transfer through shear studs attached to the steel column, and (3) local bearing beneath the floor beams and connection plates framing into the steel column at each floor. Since the strength of the bond (1) and bearing (3) are difficult to quantify, a conservative and reasonable assumption is to include only the strength of the shear studs for transferring the force. Using the strength design provisions of the AISC LRFD specification[D91] and assuming normal-weight concrete with a strength of at least f_c' = 4 ksi (27.6 MPa), the nominal shear strength of a ¾-in (20-mm) stud is 26.1 kips (116 kN). Since the required stud capacity is being calculated based on the applied factored load, a resistance factor of ϕ = 0.85 should be applied which gives a design stud strength of 22.2 kips (99 kN). Using this value, 156 studs are required to transfer the factored load of 3467 kips (15.4 MN). Attaching four studs to the flanges as shown in Fig. 6.44, the required studs can be provided with a minimum vertical stud spacing of 24 in (0.6 m) on the encased columns over the transfer length between the 6th and 12th floors. In spite of the fact that the design approach of neglecting both bond and bearing is very conservative, the resulting minimum stud spacing is fairly modest and on the order of what one would use as a minimum to maintain integrity of the column.

The eccentricity e shown in Fig. 6.46 between the steel and reinforced concrete column centerlines can be determined by referring to the column section drawing in Fig. 6.44. For the instance shown where the outer column dimensions are 60×60 in (1500×1500 mm), the eccentricity

$$e = \sqrt{16^2 + 2^2} = 16.1 \text{ in (0.41 m)}$$

Using the transfer force of P_u = 3467 kips (15.4 MN) and the transfer length of 80 ft (24 m), the eccentricity of 16 in (0.41 m) results in a required lateral bracing force R_b = 58 kips (260 kN). This force could easily be carried by the two orthogonal floor beams framing into each of the two encased steel columns. For example, assuming the floor beams were connected to the columns with ⅞-in-diameter (22-mm) A490 bolts, the 58-kips (260-kN) brace force would require an addition of at most two bolts. Another way to consider the relative significance of the 58-kip force is to compare it to a nominal required column bracing equal to 0.5 percent of the total axial load in the column. In this case, the total factored load $(1.2\,D + 1.6\,L)$ just below the 12th story is 14,720 kips (65.5 MN), 0.5 percent of which is 74 kips (330 kN). Thus the force R arising from the eccentricity is on the order of the standard bracing force considered in design. As in any tall building where column forces are large, the floor beams and their connections to the columns should be checked to assure adequate strength and stiffness to resist out-of-plane bracing requirements.

There are several additional aspects to the design of the composite connection and the column which are not addressed in this example or the referenced figures but should be considered. These include the following items:

1. For clarity, lateral reinforcing bar ties are not included in the column cross section shown in Fig. 6.44. Such ties should be provided according to the ACI-318 provisions to (*a*) reduce shrinkage cracking, (*b*) facilitate erection and prevent buckling of the longitudinal reinforcement, and (*c*) provide modest confinement to the concrete.

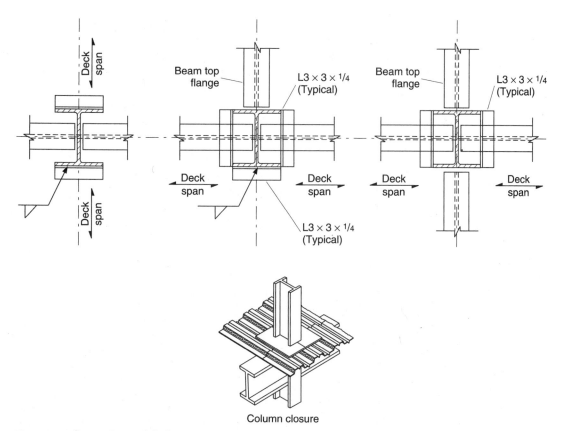

Column closure

Figure 6.47 Composite steel deck support at a column.

2. Since the steel frame is usually erected in advance of the concrete encasement, erection connections and temporary bracing must be provided to stabilize the steel frame during construction.

3. Detailing of both longitudinal and transverse reinforcement in the column needs to be carefully coordinated with the structural steel and the variation in column sizes up the height of the building.

6.7.3   Connections to composite floor slabs

In most building structures, the floor slabs function as horizontal diaphragms for the purpose of delivering the in-plane shear forces from lateral loads to the vertical-load-resisting elements. It is important that a clear load path is provided, particularly in cases where there is an abrupt change in the configuration or stiffness of the vertical elements resisting lateral loads. In such cases (Fig. 6.47) and also in situations where the diaphragm is interrupted or contains large openings, these in-plane shear forces can be very large, warranting special supplemental reinforcement in the way of reinforcing bars in the concrete slab or even horizontal steel bracing. This condition is discussed more fully in Chap. 5.

The floor slab is often called upon to brace the columns in situations where there is no floor beam framing to the column in one or both directions. In such cases the connection of the slab to the column must provide 0.5 percent times the column load as a bracing force to stabilize the column.

Finally, the composite floor slab around the column must be adequately supported to transmit the dead and live floor loads. This can be accomplished by using a light-gage steel deck closure furnished by the deck manufacturers and custom-fitted around the column as shown in the bottom portion of Fig. 6.47. Alternatively, supplemental angle or channel framing can be provided by the steel fabricator to support the floor slab as shown in the top part of Fig. 6.47. In both cases, reinforcing edge bars are often placed in the slab to help transmit the floor loads around the column opening.

Chapter

7

Literature

7.1 Guide to References

References throughout this book refer to equally designated items in Secs. 7.2 through 7.6. References to literature dealing with composite construction are listed in Secs. 7.2 through 7.5, while those dealing with topics other than composite construction are given in Sec. 7.6, General. The entries within each section are listed by years in ascending order.

References dealing with composite construction are subdivided according to their principal characteristics: Sec. 7.2, Research; Sec. 7.3, Design; and Sec. 7.4, Construction. Section 7.4 covers the building process as well as descriptions of completed structures. All other references on the topic of composite construction, either cutting across two or all three principal categories or not fitting into any one of them, are listed in Sec. 7.5, Miscellaneous Composite. Research references are identified by numbers. All other references are identified by a letter and a number starting with D for design, C for construction, M for miscellaneous, and G for general. A few references were added after the manuscript was essentially completed. Their designation includes capital letter A following the number.

7.2 Research

1. W. H. Burr, "Composite Columns of Concrete and Steel," *Proceedings,* The Institution of Civil Engineers (ICE), vol. 188, 1912, pp. 114–126.
2. A. N. Talbot and A. R. Lord, "Tests of Columns: An Investigation of the Value of Concrete as Reinforcement for Structural Steel Columns," *Bulletin* 56, Univ. Ill. Eng. Exp. Sta., 1912.
3. H. M. MacKay, P. Gillespie, and C. Leluau, "Report on the Strength of Steel I-Beams Haunched with Concrete," *Engineering Journal,* Engineering Institute of Canada, vol. 6, no. 2, 1923, pp. 365–369.
4. "Load Tests," Truscon Steel Co., Youngstown, Ohio, 1923.

5. "Impact Tests on Highway Bridges," Progress Report of Cooperative Research Conducted at Ames, Iowa, *Public Roads,* vol. 5, September 1924, pp. 10–13.
6. W. B. Scott, "The Strength of Steel Joists Embedded in Concrete," *The Structural Engineer,* June 1925, pp. 201–209, 228.
7. H. M. MacKay, "Steel I-Beams Haunched with Concrete," *Engineering and Contracting* (Chicago), vol. 66, no. 2, 1927, pp. 53–57.
8. S. G. Martin, "Tests of Steel Floor Framing Encased in Concrete—Part I," *Journal,* Western Society of Engineers (WSE), vol. 35, June 1930, pp. 157–171.
9. C. C. Whittier, "Tests of Steel Floor Framing Encased in Concrete—Part II," *Journal,* WSE, vol. 35, June 1930, pp. 171–199.
10. F. A. Randall, "Tests of Steel Floor Framing Encased in Concrete—Part III," *Journal,* WSE, vol. 35, June 1930, pp. 199–225.
11. M. Roš, "Les constructions acier-béton, système Alpha," *L'Ossature Métallique* (Bruxelles), vol. 3, 1934, pp. 105–208.
12. A. Voellmy, "Strength of Alpha Composite Sections under Static and Dynamic Stresses," Swiss Federal Materials Testing Laboratory, Zürich, 1936.
13. "Tests Made on Four Floor Panels Designed According to the Alpha System," Porete Manufacturing Company, North Arlington, N.J., 1937.
14. C. Batho, S. D. Lash, and R. H. H. Kirkham, "The Properties of Composite Beams, Consisting of Steel Joists Encased in Concrete, under Direct and Sustained Loading," *Journal,* ICE, vol. 11, no. 4, 1939, pp. 61–104.
15. H. Maier-Leibnitz, "Versuche über das Zusammenwirken von I-Trägern mit Eisenbetondecken," *Die Bautechnik* (Berlin), vol. 19, 1941, pp. 265–270.
16. R. M. Mains, "Report of Tests on Composite Steel-Concrete Beams," Fritz Engineering Laboratory, Lehigh University, May 1943.
17. "Report of Tests of Composite Steel and Concrete Blocks," Fritz Engineering Laboratory, Lehigh University, 1943.
18. M. Roš, "Träger in Verbundbauweise," Report 149, Swiss Federal Institute for Testing Materials, Zürich, 1944.
19. A. Voellmy, "Shrinkage Tests on Two Composite Beams," Porete Manufacturing Co., North Arlington, N.J., 1945.
20. A. Voellmy, "Tests to Investigate the Influence of Initial Bending Stresses on the Carrying Capacity of Composite Beams," Porete Manufacturing Co., North Arlington, N.J., 1945.
21. D. Fuchs, "Versuche mit Spannbeton-Verbundträgern," *Der Bauingenieur* (Berlin), vol. 25, 1950, pp. 289–294.
22. O. Graf, "Versuche über den Verschiebewiderstand von Dübeln für Verbundträgern," *Der Bauingenieur,* vol. 25, 1950, pp. 297–303.
23. E. W. Blumenschein, "Can Reliance Be Placed on Natural Bond between Concrete and Steel?" *Civil Engineering,* American Society of Civil Engineers (ASCE), vol. 21, no. 7, 1951, pp. 42–43.
24. H. A. Fuller, "Skunk River Bridge Exhibits Composite Action After Twenty-Eight Years of Service," *Civil Engineering,* ASCE, vol. 21, no. 7, 1951, pp. 40–42.
25. O. Graf, "Über Versuche mit Verbundträgern," *Abhandlungen aus dem Stahlbau,* Stahl-Tagung Karlsruhe, 1951, pp. 74–90.
26. N. M. Newmark, C. P. Siess, and I. M. Viest, "Tests and Analysis of Composite Beams with Incomplete Interaction," *Proceedings,* Society for Experimental Stress Analysis, vol. 9, 1951, pp. 75–92.
27. C. P. Siess, I. M. Viest, and N. M. Newmark, "Studies of Slab and Beam Highway Bridges, Part III—Small Scale Tests of Shear Connectors and Composite T-beams," Bulletin 396, Univ. Ill. Eng. Exp. Sta., 1952.
28. I. M. Viest, C. P. Siess, J. H. Appleton, and N. M. Newmark, "Studies of Slab and Beam Highway Bridges, Part IV—Full Scale Tests of Channel Shear Connectors and Composite T-beams," Bulletin 405, Univ. Ill. Eng. Exp. Sta., 1952.
29. V. Lapsins, "A Comparative Study of Composite Action in Structural Steel and Concrete Beams," M.S. thesis, Department of Civil Engineering, State University of Iowa, 1953.
29A. I. M. Viest and C. P. Siess, "Composite Construction for I-Beam Bridges," *Proceedings,* Highway Research Board (HRB), 1953, pp. 161–179.
30. I. M. Viest, "Tests of Spiral Shear Connectors," Nelson Stud Welding, Lorain, Ohio, 1955; see also *Engineering Test Data,* Nelson Stud Welding, Lorain, Ohio, 1956.
31. G. M. Sinclair, "Fatigue Strength of 3/4 inch Welded Stud Shear Connectors," *Engineering*

Test Data, Nelson Stud Welding, Lorain, Ohio, 1956; see also *ACI Journal,* American Concrete Institute, vol. 27, 1956, pp. 1442–1445.

32. I. M. Viest, "Investigation of Stud Shear Connectors for Composite Concrete and Steel T-Beams," *ACI Journal,* vol. 27, 1956, pp. 875–891.

33. I. M. Viest, "Tests of Stud Shear Connectors, Parts I, II and III," *Engineering Test Data,* Nelson Stud Welding, Lorain, Ohio, 1956.

34. J. Cassillas G. de L., N. Khachaturian, and C. P. Siess, "Studies of Reinforced Concrete Beams and Slabs Reinforced with Steel Plates," *Civil Engineering Studies,* Structural Research Series 134, University of Illinois, 1957.

35. I. M. Viest, "Tests of Stud Shear Connectors, Part IV," Nelson Stud Welding, Lorain, Ohio, 1957.

36. B. Thürlimann, "Composite Beams with Stud Shear Connectors," Bulletin 174, HRB, Washington, D.C., 1958, pp. 18–38.

36A. I. M. Viest, R. S. Fountain, and C. P. Siess, "Development of the New AASHO Specifications for Composite Steel and Concrete Bridges," Bulletin 174, HRB, Washington, D.C., 1958, pp. 1–17.

37. B. Thürlimann, "Fatigue and Static Strength of Stud Shear Connectors," *Journal,* ACI, vol. 30, 1959, pp. 1287–1302.

38. J. C. Chapman, discussion of Ref. 38, *Journal of the Structural Division,* ASCE, December 1960, pp. 127–128.

39. I. M. Viest, "Review of Research on Composite Steel-Concrete Beams," *Journal of the Structural Division,* ASCE, June 1960, pp. 1–21.

40. S. Balakrishnan, "The Behavior of Composite Steel and Concrete Beams with Welded Shear Connectors," Ph.D. thesis, London University, 1962.

41. D. E. Branson, "Time-Dependent Effects in Composite Concrete Beams," *ACI Journal,* vol. 61, 1964, pp. 212–229.

42. J. C. Chapman, "Composite Construction in Steel and Concrete—The Behavior of Composite Beams," *The Structural Engineer,* vol. 42, April 1964, pp. 115–125.

43. J. C. Chapman and S. Balakrishnan, "Experiments on Composite Beams," *The Structural Engineer,* vol. 32, November 1964, pp. 369–383.

43A. J. W. Baldwin, J. R. Henry, and G. M. Sweeney, "Study of Composite Bridge Stringers, Phase II," University of Missouri, May 1965.

44. J. Chin, "Pushout Tests on Lightweight Composite Slabs," *AISC Engineering Journal,* vol. 2, American Institute of Steel Construction (AISC), October 1965, pp. 129–134.

45. R. G. Slutter and G. C. Driscoll, "Flexural Strength of Steel-Concrete Composite Beams," *Journal of the Structural Division,* ASCE, vol. 91, 1965, pp. 71–99.

46. A. A. Toprac, "Fatigue Strength of 3/4-in. Stud Shear Connectors," *Highway Research Record* 103, HRB, 1965, pp. 53–57.

47. J. Giriyappa, "Behavior of Composite Castellated Hybrid Beams," M.S. thesis, University of Missouri, 1966.

48. R. G. Slutter and J. W. Fisher, "Fatigue Strength of Shear Connectors," *Highway Research Record* 104, HRB, 1966, pp. 65–88.

49. J. H. Daniels and J. W. Fisher, "Static Behavior of Continuous Composite Beams," Lehigh University, *Fritz Engineering Laboratory Report* 324.2, March 1967.

50. R. W. Furlong, "Strength of Steel-Encased Concrete Beam Columns," *Journal of the Structural Division,* ASCE, October 1967, pp. 113–124.

51. R. P. Johnson, K. Van Dalen, and A. R. Kemp, "Ultimate Strength of Continuous Composite Beams," *Proceedings,* Conference on Structural Steelwork, London 1966, British Constructional Steelwork Association, 1967, pp. 27–35.

52. R. J. Mainstone and J. B. Menzies, "Shear Connectors in Steel-Concrete Composite Beams for Bridges, Part 1: Static and Fatigue Tests of Push-Out Specimens," *Concrete,* London, vol. 1, September 1967, pp. 291–302.

53. H. Robinson, "Tests on Composite Beams with Cellular Decks," *Journal of the Structural Division,* ASCE, vol. 93, August 1967, pp. 139–164.

54. J. W. Roderick, N. M. Hawkins, and L. C. Lim, "Behavior of Composite Steel and Concrete Lightweight Beams," *Civil Engineering Transactions,* Institution of Civil Engineers, Australia, vol. CE9, October 1967, pp. 265–275.

55. P. C. Wang and D. J. Kaley, "Composite Action of Concrete Slab and Open Web Joist (without the Use of Shear Connectors)," *AISC Engineering Journal,* January 1967, pp. 10–16.

56. A. O. Adekola, "Effective Width of Composite Beams of Steel and Concrete," *The Structural Engineer,* vol. 9, September 1968, pp. 285–289.

57. A. O. Adekola, "Partial Interaction between Elastically Connected Elements of a Composite Beam," *International Journal of Solids and Structures,* vol. 4, 1968, pp. 1125–1135.
58. G. G. Goble, "Shear Strength of Thin Flange Composite Specimens," *AISC Engineering Journal,* vol. 5, April 1968, pp. 62–65.
59. A. H. Mattock and S. B. Johnston, "Behavior under Load of Composite Box-Girder Bridges," *Journal of the Structural Division,* ASCE, vol. 94, October 1968, pp. 2351–2370.
59A. L. C. P. Yam and J. C. Chapman, "Inelastic Behaviour of Simply Supported Composite Beams of Steel and Concrete," *Proceedings,* ICE, 1968, pp. 651–683.
60. H. Robinson, "Composite Beam Incorporating Cellular Steel Decking," *Journal of the Structural Division,* ASCE, vol. 95, March 1969, pp. 355–380.
60A. P. K. Dai, T. R. Thiruvengadam, and C. P. Siess, "Inelastic Analysis of Composite Beams," *Proceedings,* ASCE Specialty Conference, University of Missouri, May 1965.
61. R. P. Johnson, "Longitudinal Shear Strength of Composite Beams," *Journal,* ACI, vol. 67, June 1970, pp. 464–466.
62. R. P. Johnson, "Research on Composite Steel-Concrete Beams, 1960–1968," *Journal of the Structural Division,* ASCE, vol. 96, March 1970, pp. 445–459.
63. R. H. R. Tide and T. V. Galambos, "Composite Open-Web Joists," *AISC Engineering Journal,* vol. 7, January 1970, pp. 27–36.
64. J. G. Ollgaard, R. G. Slutter, and J. W. Fisher, "Shear Strength of Stud Connectors in Lightweight and Normal-Weight Concrete," *AISC Engineering Journal,* vol. 8, April 1971, pp. 55–64.
64A. Y. C. Wu, R. G. Slutter, and J. W. Fisher, "Analysis of Continuous Composite Beams," Fritz Engineering Laboratory *Report* 359.5, Lehigh University, 1971.
65. M. H. Azmi, "Composite Open-Web Trusses with Metal Cellular Floor," M.E. thesis, McMaster University, April 1972.
66. J. A. Cran, "Design and Testing Composite Open Web Steel Joists," Technical Bulletin 11, The Steel Company of Canada, Ltd., January 1972.
67. J. H. Daniels, G. D. Kroll, and J. W. Fisher, "Behavior of Composite-Beam to Column Joints," *Journal of the Structural Division,* ASCE, vol. 96, May 1972, pp. 671–685.
68. A. Dobruszkes, J. Janss, and C. Massonnet, "Experimental Researches on Steel Concrete Frame Connections," Publication 29-11, International Association for Bridge and Structural Engineering (IABSE), 1972, pp. 67–100.
69. R. P. Johnson and M. Hope-McGill, "Semi-Rigid Joints in Composite Frames," *Preliminary Report,* Ninth Congress, IABSE, 1972, pp. 133–144.
70. R. P. Johnson and R. T. Willmington, "Vertical Shear in Continuous Composite Beams," *Proceedings,* ICE, vol. 53, September 1972, pp. 189–205.
71. Y. Maeda and Y. Kajikawa, "Fatigue Strength of Steel Plates with Stud Shear Connectors for Application to Continuous Composite Beams," *Preliminary Report,* Ninth Congress, IABSE, Amsterdam, 1972, pp. 145–156.
72. J. W. Roderick, "Further Studies of Composite Steel and Concrete Structures," *Preliminary Report,* Ninth Congress, IABSE, 1972, pp. 165–172.
73. C. P. Heins and H. M. Fan, "Effective Composite Beam Width at Ultimate Load," *Journal of the Structural Division,* ASCE, vol. 102, November 1976, pp. 2163–2179.
74. W. D. Henderson, "Effects of Stud Height on Shear Connector Strength in Composite Beams with Lightweight Concrete in Three-Inch Metal Deck," M. S. thesis, The University of Texas, Austin, 1976.
75. M. L. Porter and C. E. Ekberg, Jr., "Behavior of Steel-Deck Reinforced Slabs," *Journal of the Structural Division,* ASCE, vol. 102, November 1976, pp. 663–667.
76. P. Burkhardt, "Le Comportement Elastique et Plastique des Poutres Mixtes," Thesis 264, Department of Civil Engineering, Ecole Polytechnique Federal de Lausanne, Switzerland, 1977.
77. J. A. Grant, J. W. Fisher, and R. G. Slutter, "Composite Beams with Formed Steel Deck," *AISC Engineering Journal,* 1st Quarter 1977, pp. 24–43.
78. R. Bjorhovde, "Full Scale Test of a Composite Truss," *Structural Engineering Report* 97, Department of Civil Engineering, University of Alberta, 1980.
79. W. C. Clawson and D. Darwin, "Strength of Composite Beams with Web Openings," *Journal of the Structural Division,* ASCE, vol. 108, 1982, pp. 623–641.
80. W. C. Clawson and D. Darwin, "Tests of Composite Beams with Web Openings," *Journal of the Structural Division,* ASCE, vol. 108, 1982, pp. 145–162.
81. A. H. Mattock and G. H. Gaafar, "Strength of Embedded Steel Sections as Brackets," *ACI Journal,* March-April 1982, pp. 83–98.

82. T. C. Griffis, "Stiffness Criteria for Stub Girder Floor Systems," M. S. thesis, University of Arizona, Tucson, Ariz., 1983.

83. R. G. Redwood and G. Poumbouras, "Tests of Composite Beams with Web Holes," *Canadian Journal of Civil Engineering,* vol. 10, 1983, pp. 713–721.

84. R. G. Redwood and G. Poumbouras, "Analysis of Composite Beams with Web Openings," *Journal of Structural Engineering,* ASCE, vol. 110, 1984, pp. 1949–1958.

85. C. Roeder, "Shear Transfer from Pushout Tests of Composite Columns," Second U.S.–Japan Joint Seminar on Composite and Mixed Construction, Seattle, 1984.

86. L. A. Zeitoun, "Development of Resistance Factors for Stud Shear Connectors," M. S. thesis, University of Arizona, Tucson, Ariz., 1984.

87. R. Bjorhovde, "Behavior and Strength of Stub Girder Floor Systems," *Proceedings,* U.S.–Japan Joint Seminar on Composite and Mixed Construction, ASCE, 1985, pp. 13–27.

88. R. Furlong, "Binding and Bonding Concrete to Composite Columns," *Proceedings,* U.S.–Japan Joint Seminar on Composite and Mixed Construction, ASCE, 1985, pp. 330–336.

89. B. Kato and J. Tagami, "Beam-to-Column Connection of a Composite Structure," *Proceedings,* U.S.–Japan Joint Seminar on Composite and Mixed Construction, ASCE, 1985, pp. 205–214.

90. K. Minami, "Beam to Column Stress Transfer in Composite Structures," *Proceedings,* U.S.–Japan Joint Seminar on Composite and Mixed Construction, ASCE, 1985, pp. 215–226.

91. P. C. Perdikaris and R. N. White, "Shear Modulus of Pre-Cracked R/C Panels," *Journal of Structural Engineering,* ASCE, February 1985, pp. 270–289.

92. C. W. Roeder, "Bond Stress of Embedded Steel Shapes in Concrete," *Proceedings,* U.S.–Japan Joint Seminar on Composite and Mixed Construction, ASCE, 1985, pp. 227–240.

93. A. W. Taylor, "A Study of the Behavior of Simply-Supported Composite Beams," M.S. thesis, Department of Civil Engineering, University of Washington, Seattle, 1985.

94. A. Brattland and D. J. L. Kennedy, "Shrinkage and Flexural Tests of Two Full-Scale Composite Trusses," *Structural Engineering Report* 143, The University of Alberta, Edmonton, Alberta, 1986.

95. D. J. Oehlers and C. G. Coughlan, "The Shear Stiffness of Stud Shear Connections in Composite Beams," *Journal of Constructional Steel Research,* vol. 2, no. 6, 1986.

96. R. T. Leon and J. H. Curry, "Behavior of Long-Composite Joists," *Building Structures,* ASCE, 1987, pp. 390–403.

97. R. T. Leon, L. Jihshya, and R. McCauley, "Semi-Rigid Composite Steel Frames," *Engineering Journal,* AISC, 4th Quarter 1987, pp. 147–155.

98. T. M. Sheikh, J. A. Yura, and J. O. Jirsa, "Moment Connections between Steel Beams and Concrete Columns," Phil M. Ferguson Structural Engineering Laboratory, University of Texas at Austin, Report 87-4, 1987.

99. I. Alsamsam, "An Investigation into the Behavior of Composite Open Web Steel Joists," M.S. thesis, Department of Civil and Mineral Engineering, University of Minnesota, April 1988.

100. R. Q. Bridge, "The Long-Term Behavior of Composite Columns," *Proceedings,* Engineering Foundation Conference on Composite Construction, ASCE, 1988, pp. 460–471.

101. M. Crisinel, "New System of Connection with Non-Welded Shear Connectors," *Proceedings,* Engineering Foundation Conference on Composite Construction, ASCE, 1988, pp. 636–645.

102. J. H. Curry, "Full-Scale Tests on Two Long-Span Composite Open Web Steel Joists," M.S. thesis, Department of Civil and Mineral Engineering, University of Minnesota, September 1988.

103. B. Daniels and M. Crisinel, "Composite Slabs with Profiled Sheeting," *Proceedings,* Engineering Foundation Conference on Composite Construction, ASCE, 1988, pp. 656–662.

104. R. C. Donahey and D. Darwin, "Web Openings in Composite Beams with Ribbed Slabs," *Journal of Structural Engineering,* ASCE, vol. 114, 1988, pp. 518–534.

105. B. S. Jayas and M. U. Hosain, "Behavior of Headed Studs in Composite Beams: Push-out Tests," *Canadian Journal of Civil Engineering,* vol. 15, 1988, pp. 240–253.

106. B. S. Jayas and M. U. Hosain, "Composite Beams with Perpendicular Ribbed Metal Deck," *Proceedings,* Engineering Foundation Conference on Composite Construction, ASCE, 1988, pp. 511–526.

107. D. C. Klyce, "Shear Connector Spacing in Composite Members with Formed Steel Deck," M. S. thesis, Lehigh University, Bethlehem, Pa., 1988.

108. R. Leon, "Semi-Rigid Composite Construction," *Proceedings,* Engineering Foundation Conference on Composite Construction, ASCE, 1988, pp. 585–597.

109. S. Morino, Y. Uchida, and M. Ozaki, "Experimental Study of the Behavior of SRC Beam-Columns Subjected to Biaxial Bending," *Proceedings,* Engineering Foundation Conference on Composite Construction, ASCE, 1988, pp. 753–77.

110. Y. Orito, T. Sato, N. Tanaka, and Y. Watanabe, "Study of Unbonded Steel Tube Concrete Structure," *Proceedings,* Engineering Foundation Conference on Composite Construction, ASCE, 1988, pp. 786–804.

111. M. Patrick and R. Q. Bridge, "Behavior of Australian Composite Slabs," *Proceedings,* Engineering Foundation Conference on Composite Construction, ASCE, 1988, pp. 663–679.

112. H. Robinson, "Multiple Stud Shear Connections in Deep Ribbed Metal Deck," *Canadian Journal of Civil Engineering,* vol. 15, 1988, pp. 553–569.

113. H. Robinson and K. S. Naraine, "Slip and Uplift Effects in Composite Beams," *Proceedings,* Engineering Foundation Conference on Composite Construction, ASCE, 1988, pp. 487–497.

114. Shao-Huai Cai, "Ultimate Strength of Concrete-Filled Tube Columns," *Proceedings,* Engineering Foundation Conference on Composite Construction, ASCE, 1988, pp. 702–727.

115. M. Wakabayashi, "A Historical Study of Research on Composite Construction in Japan," *Proceedings,* Engineering Foundation Conference on Composite Construction, ASCE, 1988, pp. 400–427.

116. G. G. Deierlein, T. M. Sheikh, J. A. Yura, and J. O. Jirsa, "Beam-Column Moment Connections for Composite Frames, Part 2," *Journal of Structural Engineering,* ASCE, November 1989, pp. 2877–2896.

117. B. S. Jayas and M. U. Hosain, "Behavior of Headed Studs in Composite Beams: Full-Size Tests," *Canadian Journal of Civil Engineering,* vol. 16, 1989, pp. 712–724.

118. S.-J. Lee and Le-Wu Lu, "Cyclic Tests of Full-Scale Composite Joint Subassemblages," *Journal of Structural Engineering,* ASCE, vol. 115, August 1989, pp. 1977–1998.

119. J. M. Ricles and E. P. Popov, "Composite Action in Eccentrically Braced Frames," *Journal of Structural Engineering,* ASCE, vol. 115, August 1989, pp. 2046–2066.

120. T. M. Sheikh, G. G. Deierlein, J. Yura, and J. O. Jirsa, "Beam-Column Moment Connections for Composite Frames, Part 1," *Journal of Structural Engineering,* ASCE, November 1989, pp. 2858–2876.

121. D. J. Ammerman and R. T. Leon, "Unbraced Frames with Semi-Rigid Connections," *AISC Engineering Journal,* April 1990, pp. 12–21.

122. R. Bjorhovde, "Construction Stability of Composite Frames," *Proceedings,* IABSE Symposium at Brussels, IABSE Report, vol. 60, Zurich 1990, pp. 293–298.

123. D. J. L. Kennedy, "Tests of Two Full-Scale Composite Trusses," *Proceedings,* AISC Engineering Conference, AISC, Chicago, 1990, pp. 14.1–14.27.

124. R. T. Leon, "Semirigid Composite Construction," *Journal of Constructional Steel Research,* vol. 15, no. 2, Elsevier, 1990, pp. 99–120.

125. R. T. Leon and D. J. Ammerman, "Semi-rigid Composite Connections for Gravity Loads," *AISC Engineering Journal,* 1st Quarter 1990, pp. 1–10.

126. R. M. Lloyd and H. D. Wright, "Shear Connection between Composite Slabs and Steel Beams," *Journal of Constructional Steel Research,* vol. 15, 1990, pp. 255–285.

127. W. K. Lucas and D. Darwin, "Steel and Composite Beams with Web Openings," SM *Report* 23, Center for Research, University of Kansas, Lawrence, 1990.

128. I. Alsamsam and R. T. Leon, "Experimental Investigation of Composite Beam Deflections," *Proceedings,* Third International Conference on Steel-Concrete Composite Structures, Sept. 26–29, 1991, Fukuoka, Japan, pp. 401–407.

129. R. P. Johnson and N. Molenstra, "Partial Shear Connection in Composite Beams for Buildings," *Proceedings,* Institution of Civil Engineers, vol. 91, part 2, December 1991, pp. 679–704.

130. S. A. Mirza and B. W. Skrabek, "Reliability of Short Composite Beam-Column Strength Interaction," *Journal of Structural Engineering,* ASCE, 1991, no. 8, pp. 2320–2339.

131. M. Aschheim, A. Astaneh, and J. Moehle, "Experimental Studies of Short Composite Columns," *Proceedings,* Structures Congress 92, ASCE, 1992, pp. 910–913.

132. A. Azizinamini, B. Prakash, and D. Salmon, "Force Transfer Mechanism for Steel Connections to Tubes Filled with Concrete," Pacific Structural Steel Conference, Tokyo, 1992.

133. A. Brattland and D. J. L. Kennedy, "Flexural Tests of Two Full-Scale Composite Trusses," *Canadian Journal of Civil Engineering,* vol. 19, no. 2, 1992, pp. 279–295.

134. K. A. Harries, "Seismic Response of Steel Beams Coupling Concrete Walls," Department of Civil Engineering and Engineering Mechanics, McGill University, Montreal, 1992.

135. R. Kanz, B. Schneider, and J. G. Bouwkamp, "Results and Correlative Analysis of a Composite Two Storey Eccentric Braced Frame Test," *Proceedings* of the Tenth World Conference on Earthquake Engineering, A. Balkema, Rotterdam, vol. 6, 1992, pp. 3441–3446.

136. R. T. Leon and G. P. Forcier, "Parametric Study of Composite Frames," *Proceedings,* Second International Workshop on Connections in Steel Structures, AISC, Chicago, 1992, pp. 152–159.

137. K. Morita, M. Teraoka, and T. Suzuki, "Experimental Study on Connections between Concrete Filled Square Tubular High-Strength (780 N/mm^2) Steel Column and H-Beam," Pacific Structural Conference, Tokyo, 1992.

138. N. M. Nader and A. Astaneh-Asl, "Seismic Behavior of Semi-Rigid Steel Frames," Earthquake Engineering Research Center, Report UCB/EERC-92/06, University of California, Berkeley, 1992.

139. J. M. Ricles and S. H. Paboojian, "Behavior of Composite Columns under Seismic Loading," *Proceedings,* Tenth World Conference on Earthquake Engineering, vol. 6, Balkema, 1992, pp. 3431–3436.

140. J. M. Ricles and S. Paboojian, "Seismic Performance of Composite Beam-Columns," ATLSS Research Report 93-01, Lehigh University, Bethlehem, Pa., 1992.

141. B. M. Shahrooz, F. Qin, and M. E. Remmetter, "Seismic Resistance of Composite Coupled Walls," Cincinnati Infrastructure Institute, Report 92/01, University of Cincinnati, 1992.

142. C. Amadio and M. Fragiacomo, "A Finite Element Model for the Study of Creep and Shrinkage Effects in Composite Beams with Deformable Shear Connectors," Construzione Metalliche, April 1993, pp. 213–228.

143. E. Cosenza and S. Mazzolani, "Analisi in campo lineare di travi composte con conessioni deformabili: formule esatte e resoluzioni alla differenze," *Proceedings,* First Italian Workshop on Composite Structures, University of Trento, June 1993, pp. 1–21.

144. W. S. Easterling, D. R. Gibbings, and T. M. Murray, "Strength of Shear Studs in Steel Deck on Composite Beams and Joists," *AISC Engineering Journal,* vol. 30, 1993, pp. 44–55.

145. R. Kanno, "Cyclic Behavior and Seismic Design of Connections between Steel Beams and Reinforced Concrete Columns," Ph.D. thesis, School of Civil and Environmental Engineering, Cornell University, Ithaca, N.Y., 1993.

146. R. T. Leon and I. Alsamsam, "Performance and Serviceability of Composite Floors," *Structural Engineering in Natural Hazard Mitigation,* ASCE, New York, 1993, pp. 1479–1484.

147. T. Sato and K. Suzuki, "Theory on Column Lateral Deformation Based on Axial Deformation under Seismic Loads," *Proceedings,* Engineering Foundation Conference Composite Construction II, ASCE, 1993, pp. 710–725.

148. B. M. Shahrooz, M. E. Remmetter, and F. Qin, "Seismic Response of Composite Coupled Walls," *Proceedings,* Engineering Foundation Conference Composite Construction II, ASCE, 1993, pp. 429–441.

149. C. O. Rex and W. S. Easterling, "Semi-Rigid Composite Beam-to-Girder Connections," *Proceedings,* National Steel Construction Conference, AISC 1994, pp. 6-1 to 6-20.

150. M. B. Maurer and D. J. L. Kennedy, "Shrinkage and Flexural Tests of a Full-Scale Composite Truss," Structural Engineering Report 206, Department of Civil Engineering, University of Alberta, Edmonton, Alberta, 1994.

151. J. M. Ricles and S. D. Paboojian, "Structural Performance of Steel Encased Composite Columns," *Journal of Structural Engineering,* ASCE, August 1994, pp. 2474–2494.

152. B. F. Woldegiorgis and D. J. L. Kennedy, "Some Behavioural Aspects of Composite Trusses," Structural Engineering Report 195, Department of Civil Engineering, University of Alberta, Edmonton, Alberta, 1994.

153. D. J. Oehlers and M. A. Bradford, "Composite Steel and Concrete Structural Members, Fundamental Behavior," Pergamon, 1995.

154. N. Gattesco and E. Giuriani, "Behavior of Steel and Concrete Composite Beams Subjected to Repeated Loads," *Proceedings,* First Italian Workshop on Composite Structures, University of Trento, June 1993, pp. 65–84.

7.3   Design

D1. U.S. Patent 743,086, Serial 155,677, "Composite Structural Member," issued to Julius Khan of Detroit, Mich., on Nov. 3, 1903.

D2. "Progress Report of the Special Committee on Concrete and Reinforced Concrete," *Transactions,* ASCE, vol. 66, 1910, pp. 431–493.

D3. E. S. Andrews, *Elementary Principles of Reinforced Concrete Construction,* Scott, Greenwood and Sons (England), 1912.

D4. "Progress Report of the Special Committee on Concrete and Reinforced Concrete," *Transactions,* ASCE, vol. 77, 1914, pp. 385–437.

D5. "Final Report of the Joint Committee on Concrete and Reinforced Concrete," *Transactions,* ASCE, vol. 81, 1917, pp. 1101–1206.

D6. U.S. Patent 1,597,278, Serial 465,352, "Composite Beam Construction," issued to Julius Khan of Youngstown, Ohio, on Aug. 24, 1926.

D7. R. R. Zipprodt, "A Review of Tests to Determine Effect of Concrete Floors and Fireproofing on Stresses in Structural Steel," *Journal,* WSE, vol. 34, 1929, pp. 286–299.

D8. "The Steel and Iron Amendment to New York City's Building Code," *Engineering News-Record,* Apr. 10, 1930, pp. 622–624.

D9. "Joint Standard Building Code," ACI, Detroit, 1932.

D10. U.S. Patent 2,016,616, "Spiral Shear Connectors," issued to Otto Schaub on Oct. 8, 1935.

D11. "Specification for the Design, Fabrication and Erection of Structural Steel for Buildings," AISC, 1936.

D12. C. P. Cueni, "Composite Steel and Reinforced Concrete Construction for Highway Bridges," *Roads and Streets,* December 1939, pp. 48–49.

D13. *Alpha Composite Construction Engineering Handbook,* Porete Manufacturing Co., 1940. Expanded editions published in 1949 and 1953.

D13A. I. M. Viest and C. P. Siess, "Design of Channel Shear Connectors for Composite I-Beam Bridges," *Public Roads,* Apr. 1954, pp. 9–16.

D14. "Standard Specifications for Highway Bridges," American Association of State Highway Officials (AASHO), Washington, D.C., 1957.

D15. I. M. Viest, R. S. Fountain, and R. C. Singleton, *Composite Construction in Steel and Concrete for Bridges and Buildings,* McGraw-Hill, New York, 1958.

D16. Joint ASCE-ACI Committee on Composite Construction, "Tentative Recommendations for the Design and Construction of Composite Beams and Girders for Buildings," *Journal of the Structural Division,* ASCE, vol. 86, December 1960, pp. 73–92; see also *Journal,* ACI, December 1960, pp. 609–628.

D17. "Specification for the Design, Fabrication and Erection of Structural Steel for Buildings," AISC, 1961.

D18. "Specification for the Design, Fabrication and Erection of Structural Steel for Buildings," AISC, 1963.

D19. R. S. Delameter, "Experimental Design for Short-Span Bridges," *Engineering News-Record,* vol. 172, Mar. 26, 1964, pp. 22–23.

D20. R. W. Furlong, "Design of Steel Encased Concrete Beam-Columns," *Journal of the Structural Division,* ASCE, January 1968, pp. 267–281.

D21. "Interim Specifications 1966–1967," AASHO Committee on Bridges and Structures, Washington, D.C., 1968.

D22. G. S. Vincent, "Tentative Criteria for Load Factor Design of Steel Highway Bridges," Bulletin 15, American Iron and Steel Institute, March 1969.

D23. "Specification for the Design, Fabrication and Erection of Structural Steel for Buildings," AISC, 1969.

D24. J. W. Fisher, "Design of Composite Beams with Formed Metal Deck," *AISC Engineering Journal,* July 1970, pp. 88–96.

D25. E. E. Dellaire, "Cellular Steel Floors Mature," *Civil Engineering,* ASCE, vol. 41, July 1971, pp. 70–74.

D26. W. C. Hansell and I. M. Viest, "Load Factor Design for Steel Highway Bridges," *AISC Engineering Journal,* October 1971, pp. 113–123.

D27. "Interim Specification, 1971," AASHO Committee on Bridges and Structures, Washington, D.C., 1971.

D28. J. P. Colaco, "A Stub-Girder System for High-Rise Buildings," *Engineering Journal,* AISC, vol. 9, 2d Quarter, 1972, pp. 89–95.

D29. R. P. Johnson, "Design of Composite Beams with Deep Haunches," *Proceedings,* ICE, vol. 51, January 1972, pp. 83–90.

D30. A. G. Tarics, "Concrete-Filled Steel Columns for Multistory Construction," *Modern Steel Construction,* vol. 12, AISC 1972, pp. 12–15.

D31. P. Weidlinger, "Shear Field Panel Bracing," ASCE Annual and National Environmental Meeting, October 1972, Houston, Tex.

D32. J. P. Colaco, "Partial Tube Concept for Mid-Rise Structures," *Engineering Journal,* AISC, vol. 11, 4th Quarter, 1974, pp. 81–85.

D33. C. Davies, *Steel-Concrete Composite Beams for Buildings,* George Goodwin Limited, London, 1975.

D34. R. P. Johnson and I. M. May, "Partial Interaction Design of Composite Beams," *The Structural Engineer,* vol. 53, no. 8, August 1975, pp. 305–311.

D35. R. W. Furlong, "AISC Column Logic Makes Sense for Composite Columns, Too," *AISC Engineering Journal,* 1st Quarter 1976, pp. 1–7.

D36. "Building Code Requirements for Reinforced Concrete (ACI 318-77)," ACI, Detroit, 1977.

D37. W. C. Hansell, T. V. Galambos, M. K. Ravindra, and I. M. Viest, "Composite Beam Criteria in LRFD," *Journal of the Structural Division,* ASCE, vol. 104, September 1978, pp. 1409–1426.

D38. H. Robinson, E. H. Fahmy, and M. H. Asmi, "Composite Open-Web Joists with Deformed Metal Floor," *Canadian Journal of Civil Engineering,* March 1978, pp. 1–10.

D39. "Specification for the Design, Fabrication and Erection of Structural Steel for Buildings," AISC, 1978.

D40. SSRC Task Group 20, "A Specification for the Design of Steel-Concrete Composite Columns," *AISC Engineering Journal,* 4th Quarter, 1979, pp. 101–115.

D41. R. Bjorhovde and T. J. Zimmerman, "Some Aspects of Stub Girder Design," *AISC Engineering Journal,* vol. 17, 3d Quarter, 1980, pp. 54–69.

D42. T. V. Galambos and J. Chapuis, "Criteria for Composite Columns and Beam Columns," Washington University, St. Louis, Mo., 1980.

D43. T. J. Zimmerman and R. Bjorhovde, "Analysis and Design of Stub Girders," *Structural Engineering Report* 90, University of Alberta, Edmonton, Canada, March 1981.

D44. E. Martinez-Romero, "Continuous Stub Girder Structural System for Floor Decks," *Technical Report,* EMRSA, Mexico City, Mexico, 1983.

D45. R. Bjorhovde, "Effects of End Restraint on Column Strength—Practical Applications," *AISC Engineering Journal,* 1984, pp. 1–13.

D46. H. Bode, "Einige Bemerkungen zur Verwendung von Profilblechen im Stahlverbundbau," *Festschrift Roik,* Institut für konstruktiven Ingenieurbau, Ruhr-Universität Bochum, September 1984, pp. 399–411.

D47. E. Y. L. Chien and J. K. Ritchie, *Composite Floor Systems,* Canadian Institute of Steel Construction, Willowdale, Ontario, Canada, 1984.

D48. N. M. Hawkins and D. Mitchell, "Seismic Response of Composite Shear Connections," *Journal of Structural Engineering,* ASCE, vol. 110, 1984, pp. 2120–2136.

D49. "Rectangular, Concentric, and Eccentric Unreinforced Web Penetrations in Composite Beams—A Design Aid," U.S. Steel Corp., Pittsburgh, 1984.

D50. "Specifications and Commentaries for Composite Steel Floor Deck," Steel Deck Institute, 1984.

D51. "Specifications for the Design and Construction of Composite Slabs and Commentary on Specifications for the Design and Construction of Composite Slabs," ASCE, 1984.

D52. C. Vallenilla and R. Bjorhovde, "Effective Width Criteria for Composite Beams," *AISC Engineering Journal,* vol. 22, 1985, pp. 169–175.

D53. L. G. Griffis, "Some Design Considerations for Composite Frame Structures," *AISC Engineering Journal,* 2d Quarter, 1986, pp. 59–64.

D54. M. Wakabayashi, *Design of Earthquake Resistant Buildings,* McGraw-Hill, New York, 1986.

D55. "Load & Resistance Factor Design," *Manual of Steel Construction,* AISC, 1986.

D56. "Load and Resistance Factor Design Specification for Structural Steel Buildings," AISC, Chicago, Ill., 1986.

D57. "Structural Calculations of Steel Reinforced Concrete Structures," Architectural Institute of Japan, 1987.

D58. D. Darwin and R. C. Donahey, "LRFD for Composite Beams with Unreinforced Web Openings," *Journal of Structural Engineering,* ASCE, vol. 114, 1988, pp. 535–552.

D59. G. G. Deierlein, J. A. Yura, and J. O. Jirsa, "Design of Moment Connections for Composite

Framed Structures," Phil M. Ferguson Structural Engineering Laboratory, University of Texas at Austin, Report 88-1, 1988.

D60. C. M. Donoghue, "Composite Beams with Web Openings: Design," *Journal of Structural Engineering,* ASCE, vol. 114, no. 3, 1988, pp. 518–534.

D61. R. W. Furlong, "Steel-Concrete Composite Columns—II," in *Steel-Concrete Composite Structures,* edited by R. Narayanan, Elsevier Applied Sciences, 1988, pp. 195–220.

D62. W. Zellner, "Recent Design of Composite Bridges and a New Type of Shear Connectors," *Proceedings,* Engineering Foundation Conference on Composite Construction, ASCE 1988, pp. 240–252.

D63. "Vibration of Steel-Concrete Slab Floors," Technical Digest 5, Steel Joist Institute, Myrtle Beach, S.C., 1988.

D64. R. B. Heagler, "LRFD Design Manual for Composite Beams and Girders with Steel Deck," Steel Deck Institute, Inc., Canton, Ohio, 1989.

D65. M. Patrick and D. Tse, "Composite Beam Web Penetration Design Methods—Putting Theory into Practice," *Steel Construction* (Australia), vol. 23, no. 3, 1989, pp. 11–28.

D66. "Building Code Requirements for Reinforced Concrete and Commentary, ACI 318-89 & ACI 318R-89," ACI, Detroit, 1989.

D67. "Specification for Structural Steel Buildings, Allowable Stress Design and Plastic Design," AISC, Chicago, 1989.

D68. D. Darwin, "Design of Steel and Composite Beams with Web Openings," Steel Design Guide Series 2, AISC, Chicago, 1990.

D69. D. Darwin and W. C. Lucas, "LRFD for Steel and Composite Beams with Web Openings," *Journal of Structural Engineering,* ASCE, vol. 116, 1990, pp. 1579–1593.

D70. J.-P. Lebet, "Composite Bridges," *Short Course,* IABSE, Brussels 1990, pp. 147–164.

D71. R. T. Leon, "Serviceability Criteria for LRFD Composite Floors," *Proceedings,* National Steel Conference, AISC, Chicago, 1990, pp. 18.1–18.23.

D72. R. T. Leon, "Serviceability Criteria for Composite Beams," *Tall Buildings: 2000 and Beyond,* Lehigh University, Bethlehem, Pa., 1990, pp. 947–962.

D73. I. Alsamsam, "Serviceability Criteria for Composite Floor Systems," Ph.D. thesis, The University of Minnesota, August 1991.

D74. L. G. Griffis, "Load and Resistance Factor Design of W-Shapes Encased in Concrete," Steel Design Guide Series 6, AISC, Chicago, 1992.

D75. A. M. Price and D. Anderson, "Composite Beams," *Constructional Steel Design,* Elsevier Science Publishers, New York, 1992, pp. 421–442.

D76. K. Roik and R. Bergmann, "Composite Columns," *Constructional Steel Design,* Elsevier Science Publishers, New York, 1992, pp. 443–470.

D77. R. Zandonini and R. T. Leon, "Composite Connections," *Constructional Steel Design,* Elsevier Science Publishers, 1992, pp. 501–522.

D78. ASCE Task Committee on Design Criteria for Composite Structures in Steel and Concrete, "Commentary on Proposed Specification for Structural Steel Beams with Web Openings," *Journal of Structural Engineering,* vol. 118, December 1992, pp. 3325–3349.

D79. ASCE Task Committee on Design Criteria for Composite Structures in Steel and Concrete, "Proposed Specification for Structural Steel Beams with Web Openings," *Journal of Structural Engineering,* vol. 118, December 1992, pp. 3315–3324.

D80. "Building Code Requirements for Reinforced Concrete ACI 318-89(92) and Commentary ACI 318R-89(92)," ACI, Detroit, 1992.

D81. *LRFD Design Manual for Composite Beams and Girders with Steel Deck,* Steel Deck Institute, Canton, Ohio, 1992.

D82. D. E. Allen and T. M. Murray, "Vibration of Composite Floors," *Proceedings,* Structures Congress, ASCE, 1993, pp. 1491–1496.

D83. A. Azizinamini and B. Prakash, "A Tentative Design Guideline for New Steel Beam Connection Detail to Composite Tube Columns," *AISC Engineering Journal,* 3d Quarter 1993, pp. 108–115.

D84. R. B. Heagler, L. D. Luttrell, and W. S. Easterling, *Composite Deck Design Handbook,* Steel Deck Institute, Canton, Ohio, 1993.

D85. R. P. Johnson and D. Anderson, *Designers' Handbook to Eurocode 4; Part 1.1: Design of Composite Steel and Concrete Structures,* Thomas Telford, London, 1993.

D86. R. M. Lawson, "Shear Connection in Composite Beams," *Proceedings,* Conference Composite Construction in Steel and Concrete II, ASCE, 1993, pp. 81–97.

D87. M. L. Porter, "Highlights of the New ASCE Standards on Composite Deck Floor Slabs,"

Proceedings, Engineering Foundation Conference on Composite Construction II, ASCE 1993, pp. 114–124.

D88. B. M. Shahrooz, M. E. Remmetter, and F. Qin, "Seismic Design and Performance of Composite Coupled Walls," *Journal of Structural Engineering,* ASCE, vol. 119, November 1993, pp. 3291–3309.

D89. A. Staeger and R. T. Leon, "Design of Semi-Rigid Composite Frames," *Design Guide* 10, AISC, Chicago, 1993.

D90. N. Wexler, "Composite Girders with Partial Restraints: A New Approach," *AISC Engineering Journal,* 2d Quarter 1993, pp. 68–75.

D91. "Load and Resistance Factor Design Specification for Structural Steel Buildings," AISC, Chicago, 1993.

D92. ASCE Task Committee on Design Criteria for Composite Structures in Steel and Concrete, "Guidelines for Design of Joints between Steel Beams and Reinforced Concrete Columns," *Journal of Structural Engineering,* ASCE, August 1994, pp. 2330–2357.

D93. "Composite Steel and Concrete Structure Design Requirements," chap. 7, NEHRP Recommended Provisions for Seismic Regulations for New Buildings, Building Seismic Safety Council, 1994.

D94. "Eurocode no. 4—Design of Composite Steel and Concrete Structures," Commission of the European Communities, British Steel Institute, London, 1994.

D95. "Load & Resistance Factor Design," *Manual of Steel Construction,* AISC, 1994.

D96. "NEHRP Recommended Provisions for Seismic Regulations for New Buildings," Building Seismic Safety Council, 1994 Edition, Washington, D.C., 1994. (Issued by Federal Emergency Management Agency as documents FEMA 222A and 223A, May 1995.)

D97. "Proposed Revisions to Building Code Requirements for Reinforced Concrete (ACI 318-89)(Revised 1992), and Commentary—ACI 318R-89 (Revised 1992)," *Concrete International,* ACI, December 1994, pp. 76–128.

D98. "Standard Specification for Highway Bridges—LRFD Approach," American Association of State Highway and Transportation Officials (AASHTO), Washington, D.C., 1994.

D99. "Structural Welding Code—Steel, ANSI/AWS D1.1-94," chap. 7—Stud Welding, American Welding Society, 1994.

D100. "Building Code Requirements for Structural Concrete (ACI 318-95) and Commentary (ACI 318R-95)," ACI, Farmington Hills, Mich., 1995.

D101. ASCE Task Committee on Design Criteria for Composite Structures in Steel and Concrete, "Proposed Specification and Commentary for Composite Joists and Composite Trusses," *Journal of Structural Engineering,* ASCE, vol. 122, 1996, pp. 350–358.

7.4   Construction

C1. "A Remarkable House in Port Chester, N.Y.," *The American Architect and Building News,* Aug. 18, 1877; see also *ACI Journal,* March 1975, pp. 105–110.

C2. W. E. Ward, "Beton in Combination with Iron as a Building Material," *Transactions,* American Society of Mechanical Engineers, vol. 4, part II, June 1883, pp. 388–400.

C3. S. E. Loring, "Building Materials and Their Use in Fire-Proof Construction," *Buildings* (New York City), December 1887 et seq.

C4. "Lindsay's Steel Flooring," *Engineering News,* November 1887, p. 379.

C5. "A New Fire-Proof Floor," *Engineering News,* vol. 23, Apr. 19, 1890, pp. 367–369.

C6. J. J. Webster, "Fire-Proof Construction," *Proceedings,* ICE, vol. 105, 1891, pp. 249–288.

C7. "Effects of Fire on a Chicago Building of Fire-Proof Construction," *Engineering News,* Dec. 1, 1892, pp. 511–512.

C8. W. W. Sabin, "Fire Proof Construction," *Journal,* Association of Engineering Societies, vol. 12, March 1893, pp. 132–153.

C9. "The Temple Court Fire, New York City," *Engineering News,* Apr. 13, 1893, p. 356.

C10. C. Gayler, discussion of Ref. C12, *Transactions,* ASCE, vol. 31, 1894, pp. 467–469.

C11. C. T. Purdy, discussion of Ref. C12, *Transactions,* ASCE, vol. 31, 1894, pp. 458–459.

C12. Fr. von Emperger, "The Development and Recent Improvement of Concrete-Iron Highway Bridges," *Transactions,* ASCE, vol. 31, April 1894, pp. 438–457.

C13. J. M. Wilson, discussion of Ref. C12, *Transactions,* ASCE, vol. 31, 1894, pp. 459–460.

C14. "A Melan Arch Railway Bridge," *Engineering Record,* Sept. 28, 1895, p. 309.

C15. "Concrete Arch Bridge," *Engineering News,* Nov. 7, 1895, p. 306.

C16. "Melan Arch Bridge," *Engineering News,* Oct. 3, 1895, p. 649.

C17. "The Roebling Wire and Concrete Construction for Floors and Walls," *Engineering News,* July 18, 1895, pp. 44–46.

C18. "Melan Concrete and Steel Arch Bridge, Topeka, Kan.," *Engineering News,* Apr. 2, 1896.

C19. F. B. Abbott, "Fireproofing of Warehouses," *Journal,* WSE, April 1898.

C20. G. Hill, "Steel-Concrete Construction," *Transactions,* ASCE, vol. 39, June 1898, pp. 617–635.

C21. C. T. Purdy, "Can Buildings Be Made Fireproof?" *Transactions,* ASCE, vol. 39, 1898, pp. 121–146.

C22. "Concrete and Expanded Metal Highway Bridge Construction in Allegheny County, Pa." *Engineering News,* 1898, p.50.

C23. "Construction of the Topeka Melan Bridge," *Engineering Record,* Apr. 16, 1898.

C24. "Two Recent Melan Arch Bridges," *Engineering News,* Nov. 10, 1898.

C25. J. K. Freitag, *The Fireproofing of Steel Buildings,* Wiley, New York, 1899, pp. 31–40, 58–75, 222–223.

C26. "Three-Span Melan Arch Bridge across Passaic River, Paterson, N.J.," *Engineering News,* Mar. 16, 1899.

C27. J. S. Sewell, "Columns for Buildings," *Engineering News,* vol. 48, Oct. 23, 1902, pp. 334–335.

C28. "Fourth Street Bridge, Waterloo, Iowa," *Engineering Record,* February 13, 1904.

C29. "Short-Span Bridges on the Baltimore and Ohio Railroad," *Engineering Record,* June 16, 1906.

C30. W. H. Burr, "The Reinforced Concrete Work of the McGraw Building," *Transactions,* ASCE, vol. 60, 1908, pp. 443–457.

C31. J. A. Jamieson, discussion of Ref. C30, *Transactions,* ASCE, vol. 60, 1908, pp. 464–466.

C32. J. Melan, *Plain and Reinforced Concrete Arches,* translated by D. B. Steinman, New York, 1917.

C33. H. G. Balcom, "New York's Tallest Skyscraper," *Civil Engineering,* ASCE, vol. 1, March 1931, pp. 467–471.

C34. E. W. Bowden, "Roadways on Bridges," *Engineering News-Record,* Mar. 17, 1938, pp. 395–399.

C35. E. W. Bowden, "Roadways on Bridges," part II, *Engineering News-Record,* Mar. 24, 1938, pp. 442–444.

C36. A. B. Cohen, "Major Bridge Replacement under Traffic," *Engineering News-Record,* vol. 128, September 1942, pp. 926–929.

C37. F. Leonhardt, "Gedanken zur baulichen Durchbildung von Durchlaufträgern in Verbund-Bauweise," *Der Bauingenieur* (Berlin), vol. 25, 1950, pp. 305–306.

C38. C. M. Noble, "Standardized Design and Careful Scheduling Speed Construction," *Civil Engineering,* ASCE, vol. 22, January 1952, pp. 46–47.

C39. G. D. Fish, "Composite Construction Makes Sense," *Consulting Engineer,* vol. 7, May 1956, pp. 51–55.

C40. K. R. Scurr, "Welded-Stud Shear Connectors for South Dakota Bridge," *Civil Engineering,* ASCE, vol. 26, June 1956, pp. 38–40.

C41. A. W. Coutris, "Europe's Longest Suspension Bridge," *Engineering News-Record,* May 14, 1959, pp. 41–46.

C42. "Tancarville Suspension Bridge," *The Engineer,* Aug. 14, 1959, pp. 82–86.

C43. I. Hooper and J. G. Hotchkiss, "Record for Composite Construction," *Engineering News-Record,* vol. 164, Mar. 24, 1960, pp. 84–85.

C44. "Detroit's Convention Arena and Cobo Hall," *Civil Engineering,* ASCE, vol. 31, February 1961, pp. 33–37.

C45. P. P. Page, Jr., "Composite Design for Buildings," *Proceedings,* ASCE Conference on Steel and Concrete for Buildings and Bridges, Pittsburgh, Pa., March 27–28, 1962, pp. 1–10.

C46. "World Trade Center, an Innovation in Steel Construction," *Modern Steel Construction,* AISC, 1st Quarter 1964, pp. 3–5.

C47. L. S. Feld, "Superstructure for 1,350-ft World Trade Center," *Civil Engineering,* ASCE, June 1971, pp. 66–70.

C48. "Building Design Reduces Steel with Concrete-Tube Wind Bracing," *Engineering News-Record,* June 3, 1971, pp. 18–19.

C49. "Core's Shape, Plastic Design Join for High-Rise Economy," *Engineering News-Record,* Nov. 4, 1971, pp. 26–27.

C50. D. Belford, "Composite Steel-Concrete Building Frame," *Civil Engineering,* ASCE, July 1972, pp. 61–65.

C51.   H. S. Iyengar. "Bundled Tube Structure for Sears Tower," *Civil Engineering,* ASCE, vol. 42, November 1972, pp. 71–75.

C52.   "Stubs Atop Girder Flange Cut Building Cost 60 Cents per Sq Ft," *Engineering News-Record,* Aug. 31, 1972, p. 31.

C53.   G. De Kalbermatten and R. Ryser, "Bridge over the Chandelard," *Bulletin Technique de la Suisse Romande,* vol. 99, April 1973, pp. 138–140.

C54.   S. H. Iyengar and J. J. Zils, "Composite Floor System for Sears Tower," *AISC Engineering Journal,* 3d Quarter, 1973, pp. 74–81.

C55.   J. P. Colaco and P. V. Banavalkar, "Pennzoil Place—A New Slant in Structural Systems," ASCE-IABSE Regional Conference on Tall Buildings, Bangkok, Thailand, 1974.

C56.   "Topical Buildings," information compiled by Leslie E. Robertson Assoc. for the Council on Tall Buildings & Urban Habitat; about 1975.

C57.   J. P. Cook, "Composite Construction Methods," Wiley, New York, 1977.

C58.   J. P. Colaco and P. V. Banavalkar, "Recent Uses of the Stub Girder System," presented at the AISC National Engineering Conference held in Pittsburgh, Pa., 1979.

C59.   A. F. Wong, "Conventional and Unconventional Composite Floor Systems," M.E. thesis, University of Alberta, Edmonton, Alberta, Canada, 1979.

C60.   I. M. Viest, "Truss Bridges for Medium Spans," *Final Report,* Eleventh Congress, IABSE, 1980, pp. 803–806.

C60A. "Pumped Concrete Climbs 75 Flights," *Engineering News-Record,* Mar. 5, 1981, pp. 28–29.

C61.   P. V. Banavalkar, "Texas Commerce Tower, Houston (Texas, USA)," *IABSE Periodica,* January 1982, pp. 16–17.

C62.   W. J. LeMessurier, "Toward the Ultimate in Composite Frames," *Building Design & Construction,* November 1982, pp. 18–21.

C63.   "John Hancock Centre, Chicago, Illinois (USA)," *IABSE Periodica,* 4/1982, pp. 74–75.

C64.   "Sears Tower, Chicago, Illinois (USA)," *IABSE Periodica,* 4/1982, pp. 76–77.

C65.   D. C. Brown, "Composite Tower, Steel Base," *Building Design & Construction,* June 1983, pp. 110–113.

C66.   "Tower Touches Few Bases," *Engineering News-Record,* June 16, 1983, pp. 24–25.

C67.   P. V. Banavalkar, "Texas Commerce Tower, Houston (Texas USA)," *Proceedings,* International Conference on Tall Buildings, Singapore, October 1984.

C68.   W. J. LeMessurier, "Structural Design of Dallas Main Center," Canadian Structural Engineering Conference, 1984.

C69.   J. P. Colaco, "75-Story Texas Commerce Plaza, Houston—the Use of High-Strength Concrete," *Special Publication* SP-87-1, ACI, 1985, pp. 1–8.

C70.   K. Roik and R. Bergmann, "Composite Columns—Design and Examples for Construction," *Proceedings,* U.S.–Japan Joint Seminar on Composite and Mixed Construction, ASCE 1985, pp. 267–278.

C71.   "Fine Tuning an Exceptional Frame," *Engineering News-Record,* July 4, 1985, pp. 36–39.

C72.   "William J. LeMessurier's Super-Tall Structures: Architecture/Engineering," *Architectural Record,* February 1985, pp. 149–157.

C73.   "William J. LeMessurier's Super-Tall Structures: A Search for the Ideal," *Architectural Record,* January 1985, pp. 145–151.

C74.   D. A. Platten, "Postmodern Engineering," *Civil Engineering,* ASCE, June 1986, pp. 84–86.

C75.   "Classical Arts, Structural Mix Blend in Tower," *Engineering News-Record,* Nov. 13, 1986, pp. 30–34.

C76.   C. J. Bauer, "New Standards for Innovative Composite Construction," *The Construction Specifier,* April 1988, pp. 84–89.

C77.   H. S. Iyengar, "Composite & Mixed Lateral Load Systems," *Civil Engineering Practice,* spring 1988, pp. 31, 33.

C78.   D. A. Platten, "Momentum Place, Steel Solves Complex Geometries," *Modern Steel Construction,* no. 2, 1988, pp. 9–15.

C79.   K. Roik and J. Haensel, "Composite Bridges for High Speed Trains," *Proceedings,* Engineering Foundation Conference on Composite Construction, ASCE 1988, pp. 207–213.

C80.   J. L. Tuchman and R. Gibb, "Architect's Vision, Banks Visibility," *Engineering News-Record,* Oct. 13, 1988, pp. 36–46.

C81.   "Put That in Your Pipe and Cure It," *Engineering News-Record,* Feb. 16, 1989, pp. 44–53.

C82.   "Concrete and Steel Unite," *Engineering News-Record,* July 19, 1990, pp. 30–32.

C83.   W. H. Jordy, "Bank of China Tower," *Architecture and Urbanism,* no. 249, June 1991, (42)-124.

C84. M. R. Smith, "Super Columns Speed C&S Plaza Building," *Atlanta Business Chronicle,* Oct. 7, 1991.

C85. "Composite Design Creates Slender Structure," *Modern Steel Construction,* AISC, August 1991, pp. 32–35.

C86. "Configuration Poses Challenges," *Engineering News-Record,* July 29, 1991, pp. 24–25.

C87. "Spire Tops Off 1,027-ft Tower," *Engineering News-Record,* Nov. 18, 1991, p. 24.

C88. J. P. Colaco, P. V. Banavalkar, J. Malik, and A. Wahidi, "Criss-Cross Composite Super-Column Frames for 57-Story Nations Bank Plaza, Atlanta," *Proceedings,* Third Pacific Structural Steel Conference, Oct. 26–28, 1992, Tokyo, Japan.

C89. R. A. Henige, Presentation of the design of the 73-story Interfirst Plaza Building in Dallas, Tex., Engineering Foundation Conference Composite Construction II, Potosi, Mo., 1992.

C90. L. Griffis and Y. Maeda, "Summary Report, Case Histories Session," *Proceedings,* Second Engineering Foundation Conference on Composite Construction, ASCE, 1993, pp. 574–576.

7.5 Miscellaneous Composite

M1. R. A. Caughey, "Composite Beams of Concrete and Structural Steel," *Proceedings,* 41st Annual Meeting, Iowa Engineering Society, 1929, pp. 96–104.

M2. R. A. Caughey, *Reinforced Concrete,* Van Nostrand, New York, 1936.

M3. K. Sattler, "Some Remarks on Problems Relating to Composite Structures (Elevated Roadways)," *Preliminary Publication,* IABSE, Seventh Congress, 1964, pp. 657–667.

M4. H. T. Yan, *Composite Construction in Steel and Concrete,* Orient Longmans, Calcutta, 1965.

M5. Subcommittee on the State-of-the-Art Survey, "Composite Steel-Concrete Construction," *Journal of the Structural Division,* ASCE, vol. 100, May 1974, pp. 1085–1139.

M6. R. P. Johnson, *Composite Structures of Steel and Concrete,* vol. 1: *Beams, Columns, Frames and Applications in Buildings,* Crosby Lockwood Staples, London, 1975.

M7. H. S. Iyengar, "Composite or Mixed Steel-Concrete Construction for Buildings," ASCE, 1977.

M8. *Handbook of Composite Construction Engineering,* edited by G. M. Sabnis, Van Nostrand, New York, 1979.

M9. Committee A41, "Mixed Construction," *Structural Design of Tall Steel Buildings,* chap. SB-9, ASCE, 1979, pp. 619–804.

M10. H. Bode, "Developments in Concrete Filled Tubular Columns," *Proceedings,* U.S.–Japan Seminar on Composite and Mixed Structural System, Gihodo Shuppan Co., Ltd., Tokyo, 1980, pp. 260–269.

M11. L. Yam, *Design of Composite Steel-Concrete Structures,* Surrey University Press, London, 1981.

M12. "Developments in Composite and Mixed Construction," *Proceedings,* U.S.–Japan Seminar on Composite Structures and Mixed Structural Systems, edited by B. Kato and Le-Wu Lu, Gihodo Shuppan Co., Ltd., Tokyo, 1980.

M13. H. Iyengar, "Recent Developments in Mixed Steel-Concrete Systems," Composite and Mixed Construction, ASCE, 1984, pp. 173–184.

M14. "Composite and Mixed Construction," *Proceedings,* U.S.–Japan Joint Seminar, edited by C. W. Roeder, ASCE, 1985.

M15. E. P. Johnson and R. J. Buckey, *Composite Structures of Steel and Concrete,* vol. 2: *Bridges,* Collins, London, 1986.

M16. J. B. Schleich, "Computer Assisted Analysis of the Fire Resistance of Steel and Composite Concrete-Steel Structures," *Final Report* EUR, Luxembourg, 1987.

M17. "Composite Steel Concrete Structures," *Proceedings,* International Symposium, Czechoslovak Scientific Technical Society, Bratislava, 1987.

M18. "Composite Construction in Steel and Concrete," *Proceedings,* Engineering Foundation Conference, edited by C. D. Buckner and I. M. Viest, ASCE, 1988.

M19. "Mixed Structures Including New Materials," *Symposium,* IABSE, Brussels, 1990.

M20. *Proceedings,* 3d International Conference on Steel-Concrete Composite Structures, Association for International Cooperation and Research in Steel-Concrete Composite Structures, Fukuoka, Japan, September 1991.

M21. L. G. Griffis, "Composite Frame Construction," *Constructional Steel Design,* Elsevier Applied Science, New York, 1992, pp. 523–554.

M22. "Composite and Hybrid Structures," *Proceedings,* U.S.–Japan Workshop, edited by S. Goel and H. Yamanouchi, University of Michigan, 1992.

M23. "Composite Construction in Steel and Concrete II," *Proceedings,* Engineering Foundation Conference, edited by W. S. Easterling and W. M. K. Roddis, ASCE, 1993.

M24. T. T. Lie and V. K. R. Kodur, "Fire Resistance of Steel Columns Filled with Bar-Reinforced Concrete," *Journal of Structural Engineering,* ASCE, January 1996, pp. 30–36.

7.6 General

G1. G. Hill, "Tests of Fireproof Flooring Material," *Transactions,* ASCE, vol. 34, December 1895, pp. 542–568.

G2. F. H. Lewis, "The Cement Industry," *Engineering Record,* New York, 1900, pp. 20–22, 34.

G3. C. C. Schneider, "The Evolution of the Practice of American Bridge Building," *Transactions,* ASCE, vol. 54, June 1905, p. 233.

G4. E. Duryea, Jr., C. D. Marx, F. Riffle, A. L. Adams, and W. W. Harts, "The Effects of the San Francisco Earthquake of April 18th, 1906, on Engineering Construction," *Transactions,* ASCE, vol. 59, 1907, pp. 208–329.

G5. H. P. Boardman, "The Substructure of Glasgow Bridge over the Missouri River," *Transactions,* ASCE, vol. 65, 1909, pp. 104–119, 130–131.

G6. W. Sooy Smith, discussion of Ref. 7, *Transactions,* ASCE, vol. 65, 1909, pp. 119–130.

G7. J. A. L. Waddell, *Bridge Engineering,* 1st ed., vol. 1, Wiley, New York, 1916, pp. 27–28, 56.

G8. D. B. Steinman and S. R. Watson, *Bridges and Their Builders,* Putnam, New York, 1941, pp. 197–200.

G9. *Steel Construction,* A Manual for Architects, Engineers and Fabricators of Buildings and Other Steel Structures, 5th ed., AISC, New York, 1946.

G10. F. R. Shanley, "Inelastic Column Theory," *Journal of Aeronautical Science,* May 1947.

G11. J. S. Young, *A Brief Outline of the History of Cement,* Lehigh Portland Cement Company, Allentown, Pa., 1955, p. 18.

G12. B. Bresler, "Design Criteria for Reinforced Concrete Columns under Axial Load and Biaxial Bending," *ACI Journal,* 1960, pp. 481–490.

G13. C. W. Condit, *American Building Art, The Nineteenth Century,* Oxford University Press, New York, 1960, pp. 52–53, 249–250.

G14. G. M. Sturm, S. P. Shah, and G. Winter, "Microcracking and Inelastic Behavior of Concrete," *Proceedings,* International Symposium on Flexural Mechanics of Reinforced Concrete, ASCE, Miami, 1964, pp. 473–499.

G15. O. W. Blodgett, *Design of Welded Structures,* The James F. Lincoln Welding Foundation, Cleveland, 1966.

G16. C. W. Condit, *American Building, Materials, and Techniques from the First Colonial Settlements to the Present,* The University of Chicago Press, Chicago, Ill., 1968, pp. 156–157.

G17. M. Fintel and F. R. Khan, "Effects of Column Creep and Shrinkage in Tall Structures—Prediction of Inelastic Shortening," *ACI Journal,* December 1969, p. 957.

G18. F. R. Khan, "Recent Structural Systems in Steel for High-Rise Buildings," Conference on Steel in Architecture, November 1969.

G19. R. G. Redwood, "The Strength of Steel Beams with Unreinforced Web Holes," *Civil Engineering and Public Works Review* (London), vol. 64, 1969, pp. 559–562.

G20. F. L. Brannigan, "Building Construction for the Fire Service," National Fire Protection Association, Boston, Mass., 1971, p. 9.

G21. W. T. Hogan, *Economic History of the Iron and Steel Industry in the United States,* vol. 1, Lexington Books, D. C. Heath, Lexington, Mass., 1971, p. 1.

G22. F. L. Porter and G. H. Powell, "Static and Dynamic Analysis of Inelastic Frame Structures," Report EERC 71-3 Earthquake Engineering Research Center, University of California, Berkeley, 1971.

G23. Z. P. Bažant, "Prediction of Concrete Creep Effects by the Age-Adjusted Modulus Method," *ACI Journal,* vol. 69, no. 4, April 1972, pp. 212–217.

G24. J. W. Fisher and J. H. A. Struik, *Guide to Design Criteria for Bolted and Riveted Connections,* Wiley, New York, 1973.

G25. J. F. Wiss and R. A. Parmelee, "Human Perception of Transient Vibrations," *Journal of the Structural Division,* ASCE, April 1974, pp. 773–787.

G25A. A. J. Gouwens, "Biaxial Bending Simplified," *Reinforced Concrete Columns,* ACI SP50, 1975, pp. 233–261.

G26. T. M. Murray, "Design to Prevent Floor Vibrations," *AISC Engineering Journal,* vol. 12, 1975, pp. 82–87.

G27. R. Park and T. Paulay, "Reinforced Concrete Structures," Wiley, New York, 1975.

G28. D. E. Allen and H. Ranier, "Vibration Criteria for Long-Span Steel Floors," *Canadian Journal of Civil Engineering,* vol. 3, no. 2, 1976.

G29. K. J. Bathe, "Static and Dynamic Geometric and Material Nonlinear Analysis Using ADINA," *Report* 82448-2, Acoustic and Vibration Labs, Mechanical Engineering Department, Massachusetts Institute of Technology, Cambridge, Mass., 1976.

G30. R. L. Koosman and P. B. Cooper, "Design Example for Beams with Web Openings," *AISC Engineering Journal,* vol. 13, no. 2, 1976, pp. 48–56.

G31. M. K. Ravindra and T. V. Galambos, "Load and Resistance Factor Design for Steel," *Journal of the Structural Division,* ASCE, vol. 104, September 1978, pp. 1337–1353.

G31A. *AISI Metric Practice Guide,* 3d ed., American Iron and Steel Institute, Washington, D.C., 1978.

G32. R. W. Furlong, "Concrete Columns under Biaxially Eccentric Thrust," *ACI Journal,* 1979, pp. 1093–1118.

G33. W. H. Hawes, "Plastic Design of Steel Floor Beams," *AISC Engineering Journal,* 4th Quarter, 1979, pp. 127–135.

G34. R. G. Redwood and M. Uenoya, "Critical Loads for Webs with Holes," *Journal of the Structural Division,* ASCE, vol. 105, 1979, pp. 2053–2076.

G35. R. G. Redwood and S. C. Shrivastava, "Design Recommendations for Steel Beams with Web Holes," *Canadian Journal of Civil Engineering,* 1980, pp. 642–650.

G36. *Rectangular, Concentric, and Eccentric Unreinforced Web Penetrations in Steel Beams—A Design Aid,* U.S. Steel Corp., Pittsburgh, 1981.

G37. L. D. Martin and W. J. Korkosz, "Connections for Precast Prestressed Concrete Buildings," Technical Report 2, Prestressed Concrete Institute, 1982.

G38. R. Park, M. J. N. Priestly, and W. D. Grill, "Ductility of Square Confined Concrete Columns," *Journal of Structural Engineering,* ASCE, April 1982, pp. 929–950.

G39. ACI Committee 209, "Creep and Shrinkage in Concrete Structures," SP 76, ACI, Detroit, 1982.

G40. "Design of Concrete Structures: New Zealand Standard 3101," Standards Association of New Zealand, Wellington, New Zealand, 1982.

G41. "Engineering for Steel Construction," AISC, 1982.

G42. "Structural Fire Protection," ASCE Manual 78, ASCE, 1982.

G43. M. Fintel and S. K. Ghosh, "Accounting for Column Length Changes," *Civil Engineering,* April 1984, pp. 55–60.

G44. *CRSI Handbook,* Concrete Reinforcing Steel Institute, Schaumberg, Ill., 1984.

G44A. "ISO Standard 6897," International Organization of Standardization, 1984.

G45. *Rectangular, Concentric, and Eccentric Unreinforced Web Penetrations in Steel Beams—A Design Aid,* U.S. Steel Corp., Pittsburgh, 1984.

G46. ACI-ASCE Committee 352, "Recommendations for Design of Beam Column Joints in Monolithic Reinforced Concrete Structures," *ACI Journal,* March 1985, pp. 266–283.

G47. R. M. Korol, A. Ruthenberg, and D. Bagnariol, "On Primary and Secondary Stresses in Triangulated Trusses," *Journal of Constructional Steel Research,* vol. 6, 1986, pp. 123–142.

G48. P. K. Mehta, *Concrete: Structures, Properties, and Materials,* Prentice-Hall, New York, 1986.

G49. *Rectangular, Concentric, and Eccentric Reinforced Web Penetrations in Steel Beams—A Design Aid,* U.S. Steel Corp., Pittsburgh, 1986.

G50. M. Fintel, S. K. Ghosh, and H. Iyengar, "Column Shortening in Tall Structures—Prediction and Compensation," Portland Cement Association, Chicago, 1987.

G51. X. Tang and S. C. Goel, "Seismic Analysis and Design Considerations of Braced Steel Structures," Department of Civil Engineering, University of Michigan, *Research Report* UMCE 87-4, April 1987.

G52. *Steel Deck Institute Diaphragm Design Manual,* Steel Deck Institute, 1987.

G53. T. V. Galambos, *Guide to Stability Design Criteria for Metal Structures,* 4th ed., Wiley, New York, 1988.

G54. "Uniform Building Code," International Conference of Building Officials, Whittier, Calif., 1988.

G55.   A. Astaneh, S. M. Call, and K. M. McMullin, "Design of Single Plate Shear Connections," *AISC Engineering Journal,* 1st Quarter 1989, pp. 21–32.

G56.   A. Astaneh and M. N. Nader, "Design of Tee Framing Shear Connections," *AISC Engineering Journal,* 1st Quarter 1989, pp. 9–20.

G57.   S. H. Hsieh, G. G. Deierlein, W. McGuire, and J. F. Abel, "Technical Manual for CU-STAND," *Structural Engineering Report* 89-12, School of Civil & Environmental Engineering, Cornell University, Ithaca, N.Y., 1989.

G58.   G. S. Miazga and D. J. L. Kennedy, "Behavior of Fillet Welds as a Function of the Angle of Loading," *Canadian Journal of Civil Engineering,* vol. 16, no. 4, 1989, pp. 583–599.

G58A. F. Naeim and R. Boppana, "Seismic Design of Floor Diaphragms," chap. 7 in *The Seismic Design Handbook,* Van Nostrand, New York, 1989.

G59.   B. J. Wallace and H. Krawinkler, "Small-Scale Model Tests of Structural Steel Assemblies," *Journal of Structural Engineering,* ASCE, vol. 115, August 1989, pp. 1999–2015.

G60.   CSA, *CAN3-S16.1-M84—Steel Structures for Buildings (Limit States Design),* 4th ed., Canadian Standards Association, Rexdale, Ontario, 1989.

G60A. *Reinforced Concrete Personal Computer Design Helper,* Prince, Davidson and Wilson Co., Austin, Tex., 1989.

G61.   A. Astaneh and M. N. Nader, "Experimental Studies and Design of Steel Tee Shear Connections," *Journal of Structural Engineering,* ASCE, October 1990, pp. 2882–2902.

G62.   D. F. Lesik and D. J. L. Kennedy, "Ultimate Strength of Fillet Welded Connections Loaded in Plane," *Canadian Journal of Civil Engineering,* vol. 17, no. 1, 1990, pp. 55–67.

G63.   L. E. Robertson, "On the Design of Leaning High-Rise Buildings," *Journal of Constructional Steel Research,* Elsevier Science Publishers, New York, 1990, pp. 163–191.

G64.   *Minimum Design Loads for Buildings and Other Structures (ASCE 7-88),* ASCE, 1990.

G64A. "National Building Code of Canada," Canadian Commission on Building and Fire Codes, National Research Council of Canada, Ottawa, 1990.

G65.   "Prediction of Creep, Shrinkage, and Temperature Effects in Concrete Structures," ACI Committee 209 *Report, ACI Manual of Concrete Practice,* part 1, ACI, Detroit, Mich., 1990.

G66.   T. M. Murray, "Building Floor Vibrations," *AISC Engineering Journal,* 3d Quarter, 1991, pp. 102–109.

G67.   A. F. Shaker and D. J. L. Kennedy, "The Effective Modulus of Elasticity on Concrete in Tension," *Structural Engineering Report* 172, Department of Civil Engineering, The University of Alberta, Edmonton, 1991.

G68.   "CEB-FIP Model Code 1990," CEB *Bulletins* 203–205, Comite Euro-International du Beton, Lausanne, 1991, 637 pp.

G69.   *Design Handbook,* vol. 2, *Columns,* ACI 340.2R-90, ACI, Detroit, 1990.

G70.   "Europe Starts Building High-Speed Train Tracks to Link Major Cities," *Engineering News-Record,* Apr. 15, 1991, pp. 22–24.

G70A. *Stability of Metal Structures—A World View,* 2d ed., Lehigh University, Bethlehem, Pa., 1991, pp. 701–702.

G71.   "Uniform Building Code," International Conference of Building Officials, Whittier, Calif., 1991.

G72.   J. G. MacGregor, *Reinforced Concrete: Design and Mechanics,* 2d ed., Prentice-Hall, New York, 1992.

G73.   J. O. Malley, "Slip in Torqued Bearing Connections at Service Loads," *Proceedings,* Tenth Structures Congress, ASCE, New York, 1992, pp. 31–34.

G74.   W. McGuire, "Computer-Aided Analysis," *Constructional Steel Design,* edited by P. J. Dowling, J. E. Harding, and R. Bjorhovde, Elsevier Applied Science, New York, 1992, pp. 915–932.

G75.   K. C. Wang and C. G. Salmon, *Reinforced Concrete Design,* 5th ed., HarperCollins, New York, 1992.

G76.   R. D. Ziemian, W. McGuire, and G. G. Deierlein, "Inelastic Limit States Design: Part 1—Planar Frame Studies," *Journal of Structural Engineering,* ASCE, 1992, pp. 2532–2549.

G77.   PCI Design Handbook, *Precast and Prestressed Concrete,* chap. 6, Design of Connections, Precast/Prestressed Institute, 1992.

G78.   *Seismic Provisions for Steel Buildings,* AISC, Chicago, 1992.

G79.   "Volume II, Connections, ASD/LRFD," *Manual of Steel Construction,* AISC, 1992.

G80.   M. P. Collins, D. Mitchell, and J. G. MacGregor, "Structural Design Considerations for High Strength Concrete," *Concrete International: Design and Construction,* ACI, May 1993, pp. 27–34.

G81. K. M. McMullin, A. Astaneh-Asl, G. L. Fenves, and E. Fukuzawa, *Innovative Semi-Rigid Steel Frames for Control of the Seismic Response of Buildings,* Department of Civil Engineering, University of California, Berkeley, 1993.

G82. *Eurocode No. 3—Design of Steel Structures—Part 1: General Rules and Rules for Buildings,* Commission of the European Communities, British Steel Institute, London, 1993.

G83. *Annual Book of ASTM Standards,* vol. 01.04: "Steel Structural, Reinforcing, Pressure Vessel, Railway," American Society for Testing and Materials, Philadelphia, 1993.

G83A. "Metric Guide for Federal Construction," 4th printing, National Institute of Building Sciences, Washington, D.C., 1993.

G84. ACI Committee 209, "Prediction of Creep, Shrinkage, and Temperature Effects in Concrete Structures (ACI 209-R92)," *Manual of Concrete Practice,* vol. 1, American Concrete Institute, Detroit, 1994.

G85. ASTM E119-83, "Fire Testing of Building Construction and Materials," American Society for Testing and Materials, Philadelphia, 1994.

G86. CSA, "CAN3-S16.1-M94—Limit States Design of Steel Structures," Canadian Standards Association, Rexdale, Ontario, 1994.

G87. "Load and Resistance Factor Design, vol. II—Connections," *Manual of Steel Construction,* AISC, Chicago, 1994.

G88. *Minimum Design Loads for Buildings and Other Structures,* ASCE, New York, 1994.

G89. "Standard Specification for Steel Bars, Carbon, Cold-Finished, Standard Quality, ASTM 108," American Society for Testing and Materials, Philadelphia, 1994.

G90. C. Wandmacher and A. I. Johnson, *Metric Units in Engineering—Going SI,* rev. ed., ASCE, New York, 1995.

G91. SAC Joint Venture, "Interim Guidelines: Evaluation, Repair, Modification and Design of Steel Moment Frames," FEMA 267, Federal Emergency Management Agency, August 1995.

Analysis of Steel-Concrete Interaction

This appendix contains a derivation of the governing equations for the case of a composite beam in which the concrete slab and the steel beam are connected by linear elastic springs. First a few remarks are made with respect to the load-slip characteristics of stud shear connectors and their influence on both the analysis and the design. Then a rigorous derivation of the differential equations, describing the behavior of this system, is presented following the work of Robinson and Naraine.[113] Appendix A is concluded with comments concerning uplift and the effects of combined stresses on the shear strength of stud shear connectors.

A.1 Load-Slip Characteristics

All types of shear connectors utilized in practice share some similarities in their shear-slip behavior. Figure A.1 shows a typical shear-slip relationship for a headed shear stud obtained from a push-out test discussed in Secs. 3.3.2 and 3.3.3. It represents a refinement of Fig. 3.10. Three quantities can be used to characterize the stiffness, strength, and ductility of shear studs for design purposes. The most important characteristic of a typical shear-slip curve is that it is nonlinear from the beginning of loading, and therefore its stiffness is not constant. However, at typical service levels, it is possible to utilize a linear elastic approximation to the stiffness k_s without significant loss of accuracy. As the slip exceeds service load level, the response becomes highly nonlinear and the assumption of linear behavior cannot be made.

To properly compute deflections, the flexibility of the shear studs needs to be included. This has led to the development of simplified approaches which eliminate the need for lengthy calculations and provide reasonably accurate

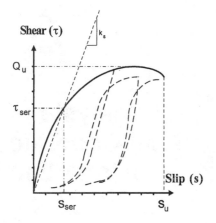

Figure A.1   Shear-slip behavior of stud shear connectors.

results. The lower-bound moment of inertia tabulated in the AISC Manual[D95] falls into this category. Another important phenomenon that cannot be addressed by a formulation that assumes a linear elastic k_s, such as that used in Sec. A.3, is the loss of stiffness and strength due to permanent changes in concrete. The stiffness represented by k_s (expressed per unit length) is a combination of the stiffness of the stud base, the stud itself, and the concrete against which the stud bears. The stress-strain curve for the concrete is nonlinear, and substantial compaction or crushing and tensile cracking can occur locally. These phenomena are important under cyclic loads, since the concrete next to the stud can be compacted, crushed, and cracked rapidly, which leads to progressively increasing slips for the same shear load.

The ultimate strength of the connector Q_u is important, since it governs the design of the shear connection, i.e., the number and distribution of the studs. It should be remembered that current American specifications do not use a ϕ factor for studs and thus the value of Q_u is an average value and not a lower bound. The use of an average rather than a lower-bound value has important implications for behavior. In most cases the desired governing case is yielding of the steel beam which is calculated based on a lower-bound yield strength (95 percent exclusion rule). This value of a force, generally A_sF_y, is then used to compute the number of studs needed based on the capacity of one stud given by Q_u. Since the real value of F_y is often substantially higher than the nominal one assumed in the design, a composite beam designed in accord with Chap. 3, if tested in the laboratory, may well respond to loading in a manner different from that intended in formulating the recommended design procedures. Generally, initial yielding of the steel cross section would be followed by significant deformations at the interface as the demands on the studs increase. The beam may fail by shearing of the studs or by formation of a longitudinal crack over the studs before full plastification of the steel section. Because the strength of the studs would begin to govern the behavior as the loads exceed the design level, the deformations or ductility would come not from the plastification and consequent softening of the beam but from the nonlinear behavior of the shear connection. The failure would occur at a strength greater than the design one because of both the actual higher yield strength and the inclusion of a ϕ factor in the flexural-strength calculations. Thus from the standpoint of ultimate-strength design this behavior does not present a problem. However, it means that the system may not be as ductile as one would expect based on a full plastification of the cross section.

The ultimate slip s_u is important because current specifications, particularly for the case of partial shear connection, assume that there is enough ductility in the connection to allow for large deformation before the system fails. American specifications do not have any requirements for ductility of shear studs since most tests indicate that they can undergo slips as large as 0.2 in (5 mm) without fracturing. This is considered more than sufficient to ensure a ductile failure of the system. Designers should remember, however, that the demands on the shear studs are a function of the degree of interaction desired. Thus typically the studs in a fully composite beam are stressed less at the design flexural strength of the beam than the studs in a beam with 50 percent interaction. This is because the shear-slip curve is nonlinear and the plastic design of composite beams does not take deformation compatibility into account.

For the case of cyclic loading, the behavior is highly dependent on the load history. If unloading occurs at low loads, the behavior is essentially linear and the system shakes down with a stiffness very close to k_s. If unloading occurs after the stud enters the grossly nonlinear range, the unloading occurs initially at k_s. However, because the concrete in front of the connector has undergone permanent deformations, the unloading is not perfectly elastic and large residual displacements occur (Fig. A.1). If the load is reapplied, large slips take place with little increase of the load because of the void that formed in the concrete behind the stud at higher loads. Upon continued reloading the stud may not reach the monotonic envelope, and a decrease in strength and stiffness may be observed.[154]

In modeling the behavior of shear studs it is usually assumed that only the horizontal displacement is important and that the vertical displacement between the slab and beam is zero. This implies that constant curvature exists in the cross section, considerably simplifying the analysis. In fact it should be recognized that there is the possibility of vertical displacement since the systems possess some large but finite vertical stiffness k_v. If vertical displacements take place between the top of the beam and the bottom of the slab, the assumption of constant curvature cannot be made and the analysis becomes more complicated. Experimental and analytical studies have shown that the influence of the vertical displacements is very small if the connectors are provided with some means of transferring vertical forces. Thus most connectors used today provide a "head" to transfer these vertical forces. As is discussed in Secs. A.3 and A.4, for most practical purposes the effects of uplift can be ignored in design.

In Sec. A.3 a complete derivation is given of the equations relating slip, shear, and curvature for the case of a linearly elastic connection between a beam and a slab. The derivations are taken directly from the work of Robinson and Naraine.[113] Some compact solutions from recent work by Cosenza and Mazzolani[143] are also shown. These derivations are included here with only minor editorial changes because they are not readily accessible to American engineers. Section A.2 contains a complete set of notation used in the derivations.

The equations as derived here are general. The case of linearly elastic connection provides great insight into the behavior of the system. However, it should be understood that because of the nonlinear characteristics of both k_s and k_t an elastoplastic relationship such as that shown in Fig. 3.10 is only an approximation. Step-by-step solutions based on nonlinear material properties are also available[43A,59A,60A,64A] but are tedious.

A.2   Notation (see Fig. 3.14)

A = a parameter defined by Eq. (A.16)

B = a parameter defined by Eq. (A.17)

D = a parameter defined by Eq. (A.32)

d = half depth of the steel beam (Fig. 3.14)

E = modulus of elasticity

$(EA)_B$ = axial stiffness of the beam

$(EA)_T$ = axial stiffness of the slab

EA_{eq} = a parameter defined by Eq. (A.42)

$(EI)_B$ = flexural stiffness of the beam

$(EI)_T$ = flexural stiffness of the slab

EI_{abs} = a parameter defined by Eq. (A.43)

EI_{full} = a parameter defined by Eq. (A.44)

F = longitudinal force at the centroids of the slab and the beam (Fig. 3.14)

G = a parameter defined by Eq. (A.33)

H = a parameter defined by Eq. (A.34)

h = distance between centroids of the beam and slab elements

I = moment of inertia

I_{abs} = moment of inertia for no interaction defined by Eq. (A.43)

I_{eff} = equivalent moment of inertia defined by Eq. (A.50)

I_{full} = moment of inertia for full interaction defined by Eq. (A.44)

k_s = shear stiffness of a shear connector per unit length (lb/in^2)

k_t = axial stiffness of a shear connector

l = span length

M = moment

M_B = moment resisted by the steel beam

M_T = moment resisted by the concrete slab

q = uniformly distributed load

R_1, R_2 = constant coefficients in Eq. (A.39)

$s(x)$ = slip along the beam

T = vertical tensile force at the beam-slab interface (Fig. 3.14)
t = half slab thickness (Fig. 3.14)
V_B = vertical shear resisted by the steel beam (Fig. 3.14)
V_T = vertical shear resisted by the slab (Fig. 3.14)
v = slip defined by Eq. (A.23)
x = distance along the beam (Fig. 3.14)
y_B = beam vertical deflection (Fig. 3.14)
y_T = slab vertical deflection (Fig. 3.14)
α = a parameter defined by Eq. (A.45)
γ = a parameter defined by Eqs. (A.47), (A.48), and (A.49)
ϵ_B = beam strain at the beam-slab interface
ϵ_T = slab strain at the beam-slab interface
μ = coefficient of friction
σ_t = tension in a shear connector
τ = shear stress
$\chi(x)$ = curvature along the beam

A.3 Theory of Incomplete Interaction

The force transfer in a composite beam with partial shear connection can be visualized by separating the problem into its constituents, the beam and the slab, and drawing their free-body diagrams (Fig. 3.14). For each of these constituents we can write the following equations of equilibrium:[57,113]
  For the concrete slab:

$$\partial V_T = - T \, \partial x \tag{A.1}$$

$$\partial F = \tau \, \partial x \tag{A.2}$$

$$\partial M_T = V_T - t \, \partial F \tag{A.3}$$

For the steel beam:

$$\partial V_B = T \, \partial x \tag{A.4}$$

$$\partial F = \tau \, \partial x \tag{A.5}$$

$$\partial M_B = V_B - d \, \partial F \tag{A.6}$$

The moment at any cross section is given by

$$M = M_T + M_B + hF \tag{A.7}$$

Differentiating Eqs. (A.3) and (A.6) twice with respect to x yields

$$\frac{d^2 M_T}{dx^2} = \frac{dV_T}{dx} - t \frac{d^2 F}{dx^2} \tag{A.8}$$

$$\frac{d^2 M_B}{dx^2} = \frac{dV_B}{dx} - d\,\frac{d^2 F}{dx^2} \tag{A.9}$$

Recalling that

$$M = -EI\,\frac{d^2 y}{dx^2} \tag{A.10}$$

Eqs. (A.8) and (A.9) can now be rewritten as

$$-(EI)_T\,\frac{d^4 y_T}{dx^4} = T - t\,\frac{d^2 F}{dx^2} \tag{A.11}$$

$$-(EI)_B\,\frac{d^4 y_B}{dx^4} = T - d\,\frac{d^2 F}{dx^2} \tag{A.12}$$

The tension force T is

$$T = k_t(y_B - y_T) \tag{A.13}$$

Differentiating Eq. (A.13) four times with respect to x yields

$$\frac{d^4 T}{dx^4} = k_t\left(\frac{d^4 y_B}{dx^4} - \frac{d^4 y_T}{dx^4}\right) \tag{A.14}$$

Substituting Eqs. (A.11) and (A.12) into Eq. (A.13) gives

$$\frac{d^4 T}{dx^4} + k_t\left[\frac{1}{(EI)_B} + \frac{1}{(EI)_T}\right]T - k_t\left[\frac{d}{(EI)_B} - \frac{t}{(EI)_T}\right]\frac{d^2 F}{dx^2} = 0 \tag{A.15}$$

Defining:

$$A = k_t\left[\frac{1}{(EI)_B} + \frac{1}{(EI)_T}\right] \tag{A.16}$$

$$B = k_t\left[\frac{d}{(EI)_B} - \frac{t}{(EI)_T}\right] \tag{A.17}$$

Eq. (A.15) can then be written as

$$\frac{d^4 T}{dx^4} + AT - B\,\frac{d^2 F}{dx^2} = 0 \tag{A.18}$$

Differentiating Eq. (A.13) twice with respect to x yields

$$\frac{d^2 T}{dx^2} = k_t\left(\frac{d^2 y_B}{dx^2} - \frac{d^2 y_T}{dx^2}\right) \tag{A.19}$$

Substituting the curvatures from Eq. (A.10) into Eq. (A.19) and rearranging gives

$$-\frac{M_B}{(EI)_B} + \frac{M_T}{(EI)_T} = \frac{1}{k_t}\,\frac{d^2 T}{dx^2} \tag{A.20}$$

From Eqs. (A.7) and (A.20) the moments in the upper and lower elements are

$$\frac{M_T}{(EI)_T} = \left[\frac{M - Fh}{(EI)_B} + \frac{1}{k_t}\frac{d^2T}{dx^2}\right]\frac{(EI)_B}{(EI)_T + (EI)_B} \tag{A.21}$$

$$\frac{M_B}{(EI)_B} = \left[\frac{M - Fh}{(EI)_T} + \frac{1}{k_t}\frac{d^2T}{dx^2}\right]\frac{(EI)_T}{(EI)_T + (EI)_B} \tag{A.22}$$

The rate of change of slip (dv/dx) at the common interface at any point is equal to the differential strain at that point:

$$\frac{dv}{dx} = \epsilon_B - \epsilon_T \tag{A.23}$$

$$\epsilon_B = \frac{F}{(EA)_B} - \frac{M_B d}{(EI)_B} \tag{A.24}$$

$$\epsilon_T = \frac{F}{(EA)_T} - \frac{M_T t}{(EI)_T} \tag{A.25}$$

Utilizing Eqs. (A.20) through (A.22) and Eqs. (A.24) and (A.25), Eq. (A.23) can be written as

$$\frac{dv}{dx} = \left[\frac{1}{(EA)_T} + \frac{1}{(EA)_B} + \frac{h^2}{(EI)_T + (EI)_B}\right]M + \frac{d(EI)_T - t(EI)_B}{k_t[(EI)_T + (EI)_B]}\frac{d^2T}{dx^2} \tag{A.26}$$

The axial force F transferred from the lower element to the upper element by means of the elastic shear connection is given by either:

$$F = \int k_s v\, dx \quad \text{for regions of positive uplift} \tag{A.27}$$

$$F = \int k_s v\, dx + \int \mu T\, dx \quad \text{for regions of negative uplift} \tag{A.28}$$

where μ is the coefficient of friction. The second term in Eq. (A.28) represents the contribution of friction and is proportional to the uplift force per unit length of beam (T). From this:

$$\frac{d^2F}{dx^2} = k_s\frac{dv}{dx} \tag{A.29}$$

$$\frac{d^2F}{dx^2} = k_s\frac{dv}{dx} + \mu\frac{dT}{dx} \tag{A.30}$$

depending on whether the uplift is positive or negative.

Substituting for dv/dx from Eqs. (A.29) and (A.30) into Eq. (A.26) and rearranging gives

$$\frac{d^2F}{dx^2} - k_s \left[\frac{1}{(EA)_T} + \frac{1}{(EA)_B} + \frac{h^2}{(EI)_T + (EI)_B} \right] F$$

$$- \frac{k_s}{k_t} \frac{d(EI)_T - t(EI)_B}{(EI)_T + (EI)_B} \frac{d^2T}{dx^2} - \mu \frac{dT}{dx} = - \frac{k_s h}{(EI)_T + (EI)_B} M \quad \text{(A.31)}$$

The last term on the left-hand side will appear only for cases of uplift. Defining:

$$D = k_s \left[\frac{1}{(EA)_T} + \frac{1}{(EA)_B} + \frac{h^2}{(EI)_T + (EI)_B} \right] \quad \text{(A.32)}$$

$$G = \frac{k_s}{k_t} \frac{d(EI)_T - t(EI)_B}{(EI)_T + (EI)_B} \quad \text{(A.33)}$$

$$H = \frac{k_s h}{(EI)_T + (EI)_B} \quad \text{(A.34)}$$

Ignoring the contribution of friction, Eq. (A.31) can be rewritten as

$$\frac{d^2F}{dx^2} - DF - G \frac{d^2T}{dx^2} = -HM \quad \text{(A.35)}$$

Equations (A.18) and (A.35) give the complete solutions for axial and uplift forces from which slip, differential deflections, and stresses can be determined. These equations are not useful for design but help in visualizing what the interaction forces are. It should also be pointed out that comparatively little is known of the relationship between k_s and k_t and therefore about the values of the variable G [Eq. (A.33)]. From one of the few studies that have looked at this ratio experimentally, Balakrishnan[40] reported a ratio of 1000/446 tons/in (175/78 kN/m) for k_s/k_t for tests on pairs of ¾-in (19-mm) studs spaced at 8.5 in (0.22 m).

Ignoring uplift, i.e., taking k_t as infinite, the third term on the left side of Eq. (A.35) vanishes, leaving the well-known Newmark-Siess-Viest equation:[26,27]

$$\frac{d^2F}{dx^2} - DF = - HM \quad \text{(A.36)}$$

Equation (A.36), of course, cannot predict the uplift forces. They are obtained as follows.

Rewriting Eq. (A.35) as

$$- G \frac{d^2T}{dx^2} = - HM(x) + DF - \frac{d^2F}{dx^2} \quad \text{(A.37)}$$

and differentiating Eq. (A.37) twice leads to

$$\frac{d^4T}{dx^4} = \frac{H}{G}\frac{d^2}{dx^2}M(x) - \frac{D}{G}\frac{d^2F}{dx^2} + \frac{1}{G}\frac{d^4F}{dx^4} \tag{A.38}$$

Integrating Eq. (A.38) twice and dividing by G leads to

$$T = \frac{H}{G}\int\int M(x)dx - \frac{D}{G}\int\int F\,dx + \frac{1}{G}F + R_1 x + R_2 \tag{A.39}$$

Substituting Eqs. (A.38) and (A.39) into Eq. (A.18) yields

$$\frac{H}{G}\frac{d^2}{dx^2}M(x) - \frac{D}{G}\frac{d^2F}{dx^2} + \frac{1}{G}\frac{d^4F}{dx^4} + \frac{AH}{G}\int\int M(x)\,dx - \frac{AD}{G}\int\int F\,dx$$

$$+ \frac{A}{G}FL(x) + AR_1 x + AR_2 - B\frac{d^2F}{dx^2} = 0 \tag{A.40}$$

Differentiating Eq. (A.40) twice to remove the integrals gives

$$\frac{d^6F}{dx^6} - (D + GB)\frac{d^4F}{dx^4} + A\frac{d^2F}{dx^2} - ADF(x) + AHM(x) = 0 \tag{A.41}$$

The solution of this equation requires six boundary conditions. In general the approach is to write the moments along the beam as a function of x, and enforce the known conditions that the force F is zero at the ends and that the force F, shear, slip, and uplift are continuous. Since M can seldom be written as a function of x for the entire beam, the process generally requires that Eq. (A.41) be written for separate segments of the beam and compatibility enforced at the boundaries of these segments. The solution for Eq. (A.35) is somewhat simpler, since only the force F and shear need to be continuous.

For convenience, the solutions recently provided by Cosenza and Mazzolani[143] for Eq. (A.35) are reproduced below, but the intermediate steps are not shown. Defining

$$EA_{eq} = \frac{(EA)_T (EA)_B}{(EA)_T + (EA)_B} \tag{A.42}$$

$$EI_{abs} = (EI)_T + (EI)_B \tag{A.43}$$

$$EI_{full} = EI_{abs} + EA_{eq}h^2 \tag{A.44}$$

$$\alpha^2 = \frac{k_s}{EA_{eq}}\frac{EI_{full}}{EI_{abs}} \tag{A.45}$$

the curvatures are given by

$$\chi(x) = -\frac{M}{EI_{abs}}\gamma_1 - \frac{M}{EI_{full}}(1 - \gamma_1) \tag{A.46}$$

The functions M and γ_1 in Eq. (A.46) depend on type of loading. Solutions for three common cases are listed below.

1. Distributed load:

$$\gamma_1 = 2 \, \frac{\cosh(\alpha l)\sinh(\alpha x) - \cosh(\alpha x)\sinh(\alpha l) + \sinh(\alpha l) - \sinh(\alpha x)}{\alpha x\,(\alpha l - \alpha x)\sinh(\alpha l)} \qquad (A.47)$$

2. Point load at midspan:

$$\gamma_1 = \frac{\sinh(\alpha x)}{(\alpha l)\cosh(\alpha l/2)} \qquad (A.48)$$

3. Constant moment:

$$\gamma_1 = \frac{\sinh(\alpha x) - \cosh(\alpha l)\sinh(\alpha x) + \cosh(\alpha x)\sinh(\alpha l)}{\sinh(\alpha l)} \qquad (A.49)$$

An interesting side result is that the effective inertia for the composite beam can then be expressed as

$$EI_{\text{eff}} = \frac{EI_{\text{abs}}\,EI_{\text{full}}}{\gamma_1 EI_{\text{full}} + (1 - \gamma_1)EI_{\text{abs}}} \qquad (A.50)$$

The force along the beam is given by

$$F(x) = \frac{M(x)}{h}\left(1 - \frac{EI_{\text{abs}}}{EI_{\text{full}}}\right)(1 - \gamma_1) \qquad (A.51)$$

The slip, for the case of a uniformly distributed load q, is given by

$$s(x) = \frac{qh}{EI_{\text{abs}}\alpha^3}\left[\frac{1 - \cosh(\alpha l)}{\sinh(\alpha l)}\cosh(\alpha x) + \sinh(\alpha x) + \frac{\alpha l}{2} - \alpha x\right] \qquad (A.52)$$

The slip to the left of a point load, for the case of a point load P applied at a distance U from the left end of the beam, is given by[154]

$$s(x) = \frac{EA_{\text{eq}}hP}{k_s EI_{\text{full}}}\left\{\left(1 - \frac{U}{l}\right) - \frac{\sinh\{\alpha l[1 - (U/l)]\}}{\sinh \alpha l}\cosh \alpha l\left(\frac{x}{l}\right)\right\} \qquad (A.53)$$

The slip, for the case of a constant moment M, is given by[154]

$$s(x) = \frac{Mh}{EI_{\text{abs}}\alpha}\left(\sinh \alpha x + \frac{1 - \cosh \alpha l}{\sinh \alpha l}\cosh \alpha x\right) \qquad (A.54)$$

A.4   Characteristics of Structural Response

Utilizing Eq. (A.41), Robinson[113] studied the distribution of slip and uplift. For the case of a point load acting on the top slab there is close agreement between the elastic solution given by Eq. (A.41) and that given by Eq. (A.36) (the Newmark-Siess-Viest equation[26,27]) for the horizontal slip. This indicates that for practical cases the effect of uplift is small.

The results also indicate that for the case of a point load acting on the slab, in addition to uplift at the supports, there is also a high degree of uplift beneath the load point. In addition, immediately adjacent to these uplift regions there are smaller regions of negative uplift. For the case of a point load pulling down on the steel beam, uplift again occurs at the supports, with corresponding regions of small positive uplift adjacent to the regions of negative uplift. However, with this loading condition maximum positive uplift occurs at the load point. Robinson also showed that for the case of a point load on the slab, the slab itself carried more than 75 percent of the shear in the area near the load.

The important point to recognize from this discussion and Eq. (A.41) is that studs are loaded at least in a combination of shear and tension. The magnitude of the tensile forces can be large, but they are highly localized. For a typical connector in a critical location, if a tensile force equal to 50 percent of yield is present, the available shear capacity decreases by only about 10 to 12 percent according to current shear-tension interaction formulas for connectors. However, this small reduction is predicated on the assumption that the stud is loaded only in shear and tension. In fact the shear stud transfers the force by bearing against the concrete (Fig. 3.11), and thus significant bending can be present. The distribution of forces along the height of the stud is not completely understood. It is important in the case of ribbed deck because the force transfer would seem to take place higher in the stud than in a solid slab, resulting in larger bending stresses near the bottom of the stud. It is not clear what effect the interaction of shear, bending, and tension has on the strength of the stud, but in any case it probably lowers the shear capacity. On the positive side, the reduction factor given by Eq. (3.3), based on numerous tests of composite beams,[77] results frequently in sizable reductions of the design strength of studs located in the ribs of a steel deck.

B

Analyses of Composite Columns

B.1 Slenderness Ratio and Axial Compression Strength

The construction of graphs for concentric compression strength $\phi_c P_n$ as a function of the slenderness ratio Kl/r is illustrated in the examples that follow. The cross sections of two composite columns, one encased and the other filled, are included. The calculation procedure is based on the AISC LRFD specification.[D91] Given the geometric properties of the section components, the procedure consists of the following four steps:

1. Determine the modified properties F_{my}, E_m, and r_m of the composite cross section as described in Sec. 4.4.5.

2. Calculate buckling parameter $A = \lambda_c^2$ for several values of Kl using Eq. (4.10c).

3. Determine critical stresses F_{cr} from Eq. (4.10a) or (4.10b) as applicable.

4. Compute the design strength $\phi_c P_n$ for each value of Kl using Eq. (4.9).

Encased composite column. The encased composite column shown in Fig. B.1 consists of a W8×40 section of A36 steel ($F_y = 36$ ksi = 248 MPa) in a 16 × 16-in (406 × 406-mm) reinforced concrete encasement with 8#6 ($A_b = 0.44$ in^2 = 284 mm^2) longitudinal grade 60 ($F_{yr} = 60$ ksi = 414 MPa) reinforcing bars. The strength of concrete is $f_c' = 3.5$ ksi (24 MPa). Note that F_y and F_{yr} are limited to a maximum of 60 ksi (414 MPa).

Section geometric properties:

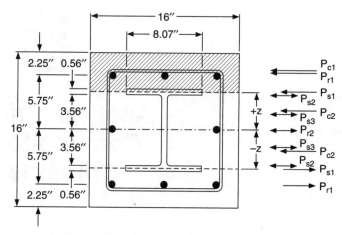

Figure B.1   Cross section of an encased composite column.

$$h = b = 16 \text{ in} \qquad r = 0.3h = 0.3 \times 16 = 4.80 \text{ in}$$
$$A_s = 11.7 \text{ in}^2 \qquad r_x = 3.53 \text{ in}$$
$$A_r = 8A_b = 8 \times 0.44 = 3.52 \text{ in}^2$$
$$A_c = h \times b - A_s - A_r = 16^2 - 11.7 - 3.52 = 240.8 \text{ in}^2$$
$$Z_x = 39.8 \text{ in}^3$$

1. *Modified material properties.*   From Table 4.1, for concrete-encased shapes $c_1 = 0.7$, $c_2 = 0.6$, and $c_3 = 0.2$. The modified yield stress [Eq. (4.11a)] is

$$F_{my} = F_y + c_1 F_{yr} \frac{A_r}{A_s} + c_2 f_c' \frac{A_c}{A_s}$$

$$= 36 + 0.7(60)\frac{3.52}{11.7} + 0.6(3.5)\frac{240.8}{11.7} = 91.9 \text{ ksi}$$

For normal-weight concrete, w is taken as 145 lb/ft³. The modulus of elasticity of concrete [Eq. (4.1)] is

$$E_c = w^{1.5}\sqrt{f_c'} = 145^{1.5}\sqrt{3.5} = 3270 \text{ ksi}$$

and the modified modulus of elasticity [Eq. (4.11b)] is

$$E_m = E_s + \frac{c_3 E_c A_c}{A_s} = 29{,}000 + 0.2(3270)\frac{240.8}{11.7} = 42{,}500 \text{ ksi}$$

The radius of gyration of the composite column cross section is the greater of r and r_x. Thus $r_m = 4.8$ in.

2. *Buckling parameter $A = \lambda_c^2$.*   Using Eq. (4.10c) for λ,

$$A = \lambda_c^2 = \left(\frac{Kl}{\pi r}\right)^2 \frac{F_{my}}{E_m} = \left(\frac{Kl}{4.8\pi}\right)^2 \frac{91.9}{42,500} = \frac{(Kl)^2}{105,200}$$

3. *Critical stress* F_{cr}. For $A \le 2.25$, the critical stress is given by Eq. (4.10a):

$$F_{cr} = F_{my}(0.658^A) = 91.9 \times 0.685^A$$

and for $A > 2.25$, the critical stress is given by Eq. (4.10b):

$$F_{cr} = F_{my} \frac{0.877}{A} = \frac{80.6}{A}$$

4. *Design strength* $\phi_c P_n$. With the capacity reduction factor $\phi_c = 0.85$, the design strength of the column is computed from Eq. (4.9) as

$$\phi_c P_n = \phi_c A_s F_{cr} = 0.85 \times 11.7 F_{cr} = 9.95 F_{cr}$$

Values of A and $\phi_c P_n$, computed for nine selected values of Kl, are listed in Table B.1, and the effect of slenderness on the strength of the encased composite column is shown in Fig. 4.9 by the upper curve.

Filled composite column. The filled composite column shown in Fig. B.2 is a $10 \times 10 \times \frac{1}{4}$-in ($254 \times 254 \times 6.4$-mm) steel tube filled with concrete. The steel tube has a yield stress $F_y = 46$ ksi (317 MPa) and the concrete strength is $f_c' = 8$ ksi (55 MPa).
Section geometric properties:

$$h = b = 10 \text{ in} \qquad\qquad r = 0.3 \times 10 = 3 \text{ in}$$

$$A_s = (10^2 - 9.5^2) = 9.75 \text{ in}^2 \qquad r_s = \sqrt{\frac{I_s}{A_s}}$$

$$I_s = \frac{10^4 - 9.5^4}{12} = 155 \text{ in}^4 \qquad = \sqrt{\frac{155}{9.75}} = 3.99 \text{ in}$$

TABLE B.1 Encased Composite Column Slenderness vs. Strength

Kl, in	$A < 2.25$	$\phi_c P_n$, kips	Kl, in	$A > 2.25$	$\phi_c P_n$, kips
60	0.034	902	500	2.376	337
120	0.137	868	600	3.422	234
180	0.308	813			
240	0.548	743			
300	0.856	661			
360	1.232	573			
420	1.677	485			

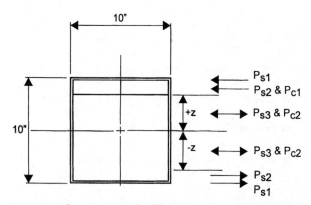

Figure B.2   Cross section of a filled composite column.

$$A_c = 10^2 - 9.75 = 90.25 \text{ in}^2$$

General equations used for evaluating the strength of filled composite columns are the same as those given above for encased columns. They are not repeated below.

1. *Modified material properties.*   From Table 4.1, for concrete-filled tube c_1 = 1.0, c_2 = 0.85, and c_3 = 0.4. Thus

$$F_{my} = 46 + 1.0(0) + \frac{0.85 \times 8.0 \times 90.25}{9.75} = 108.9 \text{ ksi}$$

$$E_c = (145)^{1.5} \sqrt{8.0} = 4940 \text{ ksi}$$

$$E_m = 29{,}000 + \frac{0.4 \times 4940 \times 90.25}{9.75} = 47{,}300 \text{ ksi}$$

$$r_m = 3.99 \text{ in}$$

2. *Buckling parameter $A = \lambda_c^2$*

$$A = \left(\frac{Kl}{3.99\pi}\right)^2 \frac{108.9}{47{,}300} = \frac{(Kl)^2}{68{,}200}$$

3. *Critical stress F_{cr}.*   When $A \le 2.25$

$$F_{cr} = 108.9 \times 0.658^A$$

and when $A > 2.25$

$$F_{cr} = \frac{108.9 \times 0.877}{A} = \frac{95.5}{A}$$

TABLE B.2 Filled Composite Column Slenderness vs. Strength

Kl, in	$A < 2.25$	$\phi_c P_n$, kips	Kl, in	$A > 2.25$	$\phi_c P_n$, kips
60	0.053	883	420	2.587	306
120	0.211	826	500	3.666	216
180	0.475	740	600	5.279	150
240	0.845	634			
300	1.320	519			
360	1.900	407			

4. *Design strength $\phi_c P_n$*

$$\phi_c P_n = 0.85 \times 9.75 \times F_{cr} = 8.29 F_{cr}$$

Values of A and $\phi_c P_n$, computed for nine values of Kl, are listed in Table B.2, and the effect of slenderness on the strength of the filled composite column is shown in Fig. 4.9 by the lower curve.

B.2 Plastic Analysis of Cross-Section Strength

The combined axial load and bending strength of composite cross sections of normal proportions can be determined accurately from an analysis that assumes plastic stress conditions at the limit state of strength. Four sets of coordinates for P and M are computed, one for zero axial force, one for zero bending moment, and two for forces associated with two convenient locations of the neutral axis.

Plastic stress on steel is taken as equal to the compression yield on the compression side and to the tension yield on the tension side of the neutral axis. The magnitude of plastic stress in compressed concrete is taken as 75 percent of the cylinder strength f'_c. Concrete is assumed to resist no tensile stress. The limit of $F_y \leq 60$ ksi is observed.

Encased composite column. Cross-section dimensions and components of limit forces for the encased column section of Sec. B.1 are shown in Fig. B.1. The force components are defined as:

P_{c1} = force on concrete above the distance $+z$ from middepth

P_{c2} = force on concrete from $\pm z$ to middepth

P_{r1} = force on reinforcement at top or bottom of section

P_{r2} = force on reinforcement at middepth

P_{s1} = force on steel flange outside z from middepth

P_{s2} = force on steel flange inside z from middepth

P_{s3} = force on half of steel web

When there is no bending moment, i.e., when $\phi_b M_n = 0$, the strength of the column is computed from Eq. (4.5):

$$P_o = A_s F_y + A_r f_{yr} + 0.85 A_c f_c'$$

$$= 11.7 \times 36 + 8 \times 0.44 \times 60 + 0.85 \times 240.8 \times 3.5 = 1349 \text{ kips}$$

$$\phi_c P_o = 0.85 \times 1349 = 1147 \text{ kips}$$

When there is no axial force, the sum of compression forces must equal the sum of tension forces on the section. Generally, tension forces on the bottom flange steel and the bottom reinforcement are the same as compression forces on the top flange and the top reinforcement. If the neutral axis is located in the web at a distance z above middepth, the forces in the web outside the z distance are in equilibrium, and the position of the neutral axis is determined as follows:

$$0.75 f_c' \, b(0.5h - z) = P_{r2} + 2F_y t_w z$$

where t_w = web thickness. Thus,

$$0.75(3.5)16(0.5 \times 16 - z) = 2(0.44)60 + 2(36)0.36z$$

which yields $z = 4.17$ in, placing the neutral axis above the top flange of the steel shape rather than in the web as assumed.

Assuming next that the neutral axis is located in the top flange, the distance z is determined as follows:

$$0.75 f_c' \, b(0.5h - z) = P_{r2} + 2P_{s3} + 2F_y b_s (z - 0.5h_s)$$

where b_s and h_s are the flange width and web height of the steel shape. Therefore,

$$0.75(3.5)16(0.5 \times 16 - z) =$$

$$2(0.44)60 + 2(36)0.36[0.5(8.25 - 2 \times 0.56)] + (2)36(8.07)(z - 0.5 \times 7.12)$$

which yields $z = 3.63$ in. The neutral axis is in the top flange of the steel shape as assumed.

With the known position of the neutral axis, the force components acting on the composite section are calculated below:

$$P_{r1} = 3(0.44)60 = 79.2 \text{ kips}$$

$$P_{r2} = 2(0.44)60 = 52.8 \text{ kips}$$

$$P_{s1} = 36(8.07)(3.56 + 0.56 - 3.63) = 142.4 \text{ kips}$$

$$P_{s2} = 36(8.07)(3.63 - 3.56) = 20.3 \text{ kips}$$

TABLE B.3 Interaction Diagram Data Encased Composite Section

Force	Distance to mid-height, in	z = 3.63 in		z = 0		z = −3.63 in	
		Force, kips	Moment, in-kips	Force, kips	Moment, in-kips	Force, kips	Moment, in kips
P_{c1}	5.815	183.5	1067	183.5	1067	183.5	1067
P_{r1}	5.75	79.2	455	79.2	455	79.2	455
P_{s1}	3.875	142.4	552	142.4	552	142.4	552
P_{s2}	3.665	−20.3	−74	20.3	74	20.3	74
P_{c2}	1.815			152.5	277	152.5	277
P_{s3}	1.78	−46.1	−82	46.1	82	46.1	82
P_{r2}	0.0	−52.8	0	0	0	52.8	0
P_{s3}	−1.78	−46.1	82	−46.1	82	46.1	−82
P_{c2}	−1.815					152.5	277
P_{s2}	−3.665	−20.3	74	−20.3	74	20.3	−74
P_{s1}	−3.875	−142.4	552	−142.4	552	−142.4	552
P_{r1}	−5.75	−79.2	455	−79.2	455	−79.2	455
Sum,		−2.1	3081	336.0	3670	674.1	3081
ft-kips			257		306		257

$$P_{s3} = 36(3.56)0.36 = 46.1 \text{ kips}$$

$$P_{c1} = 0.75(3.5)16(0.5 \times 16 - 3.63) = 183.5 \text{ kips}$$

$$P_{c2} = 0.75(3.5)16(3.63) = 152.5 \text{ kips}$$

The distances from the middepth to each force component, the force components, and the corresponding moments are listed in Table B.3 for the neutral axis at $z = 3.63$, 0, and −3.63 in. The resulting interaction curve is shown as the solid line in Fig. B.3.

Filled composite column. Cross-section dimensions and components of limit forces for the filled composite column section of Sec. B.1 are shown in Fig. B.2. The force components are defined as

P_{c1} = force on concrete above the distance + z from middepth

P_{c2} = force on concrete from ± z to middepth

P_{s1} = force on the top wall of the steel tube

P_{s2} = force on sidewalls outside the distance z from middepth

P_{s3} = force on sidewalls inside the distance $_z$ from middepth

When there is no moment, i.e., when $\phi M_n = 0$, the strength of the column is computed from Eq. (4.5):

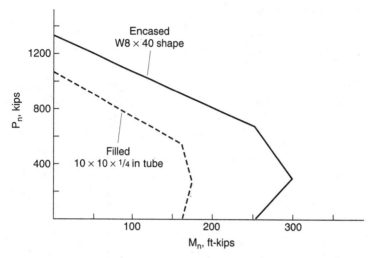

Figure B.3 Interaction diagrams for composite beam columns.

$$P_o = A_s F_y + A_r F_{yr} + 0.85 f'_c A_c$$

$$= 9.75(46) + 0 + 0.85(8.0)90.25 = 1062 \text{ kips}$$

$$\phi_c P_n = (0.85)1062 = 903 \text{ kips}$$

When there is no axial force, the sum of compression forces must equal the sum of tension forces on the section. The compression forces on the top wall and the top portion of each sidewall of the steel tube are equal and opposite the tension forces on the bottom wall and the bottom portion of each sidewall. The tension forces on the portion of each sidewall within distance z from the middepth are in equilibrium with the compression force resisted by concrete. The position of the neutral axis is determined as

$$0.75 f'_c (h_2 - 2t)(0.5h_1 - t - z) = 2z2tF_y$$

where h_2 is the width, h_1 the depth, and t the wall thickness of the steel tube. Then,

$$0.75(8.0)(10 - 2 \times 0.25)(0.5 \times 10 - 0.25 - z) = 4z(0.25)46$$

which yields $z = 2.63$ in.

With the known position of the neutral axis, the force components acting on the composite section are calculated below:

$$P_{c1} = 0.75(8.0)9.5(4.75 - 2.63) = 120.8 \text{ kips}$$

$$P_{c2} = 0.75(8.0)9.5(2.63) = 149.9 \text{ kips}$$

TABLE B.4 Interaction Diagram Data Filled Composite Section

Force	Distance to mid-height, in	z = 2.63 in Force, kips	Moment, in-kips	z = 0 Force, kips	Moment, in-kips	z = −2.63 in Force, kips	Moment, in kips
P_{s1}	4.875	115.0	561	115.0	561	115.0	561
P_{s2}	3.69	48.8	180	48.8	180	48.8	180
P_{c1}	3.69	120.8	446	120.8	446	120.8	446
P_{s3}	1.315	−60.5	−80	60.5	80	60.5	80
P_{c2}	1.315			149.9	0	149.9	197
P_{s3}	−1.315	−60.5	80	−60.5	80	60.5	−80
P_{c2}	−1.315					149.9	−197
P_{s2}	−3.69	−48.8	180	−48.8	180	−48.8	180
P_{s1}	−4.875	−115.0	561	−115.0	561	−115.0	561
Sum,		−0.2	1928	270.7	2088	541.6	1928
ft-kips			161		174		161

$$P_{s1} = 10(0.25)46 = 115.0 \text{ kips}$$

$$P_{s2} = 2(4.75 - 2.63)0.25(46) = 48.8 \text{ kips}$$

$$P_{s3} = 2(2.63)0.25(46) = 60.5 \text{ kips}$$

The distances from the middepth to each force component, the force components, and the corresponding moments are listed in Table B.4 for the neutral axis at $z = 2.63$, 0, and -2.63 in. The resulting interaction curve is shown as the dashed line in Fig. B.3.

Index

ABOUT THE EDITORS

Ivan M. Viest (Bethlehem, Pa.) is president of IMV Consulting. **Joseph P. Colaco** (Houston, Tex.) is president of CBM Engineers, Inc. **Richard W. Furlong** (Austin, Tex.) is E. C. H. Bantel Professor of Engineering Practice at the University of Texas at Austin. **Lawrence G. Griffis** (Houston, Tex.) is senior vice president and director of structural engineering at Walter P. Moore & Associates, Inc. **Roberto T. Leon** (Atlanta, Ga.) is professor of civil engineering at the Georgia Institute of Technology. **Loring A. Wyllie, Jr.** (San Francisco, Calif.) is senior principal and chairman of Degenkolb Engineers.